# CLIFFORD SIFTON

# CLIFFORD SIFTON

Volume One

THE YOUNG NAPOLEON

1861–1900

D. J. HALL

UNIVERSITY OF BRITISH COLUMBIA PRESS
VANCOUVER AND LONDON

CLIFFORD SIFTON

*Volume 1, The Young Napoleon, 1861–1900*

Canadian Cataloguing in Publication Data

Hall, D.J. (David John), 1943–
    Clifford Sifton

    Includes index.
    Contents: v. 1. The young Napoleon, 1861–1900.
    ISBN 0-7748-0135-2 (v. 1)

    1. Sifton, Clifford, Sir, 1861–1929.
    2. Statesmen—Canada—Biography. 3. Canada—Politics and
    government—1867–1896.* 4. Canada—Politics and government—
    1896–1911.* I. Title.
    FC551.S53H3          971.05′6′0924          C81–091153–1
    F1033.S53H3

*32,778*

INTERNATIONAL STANDARD BOOK NUMBER 0-7748-0135-2

*Printed in Canada*

For Ann

*This book has been published with the help of a gift to scholarly publishing made in honour of Dr. Harold S. Foley for his distinguished services to the University of British Columbia*

*a gift in memory of Walter H. Gage*

*and a grant from the Social Science Federation of Canada, using funds provided by the Social Sciences and Humanities Research Council of Canada*

# Contents

# Photographic Credits

Plates 1, 2, 3, 4, 5, 6, 7, 9, 10, 11, 20, and 21 are reproduced with the permission of the Public Archives of Manitoba; Plate 22 is from the Foote Collection of the PAM; Plates 8(C74461), 12(PA27942), 13(PA30907), 14(C1860), 18(PA16874), 19(C14474), and 23(C681) are from the National Photography Collection, Public Archives of Canada. The *Winnipeg Free Press* has kindly contributed Plates 15 and 16.

# Illustrations

# Preface

Few Canadian politicians have been at once so respected and so feared, if not hated, as Clifford Sifton. He was a brilliant political strategist who revelled in partisan conflict and public combat. Undoubtedly he enjoyed the exercise of political power, though his opponents considered him both unprincipled and unscrupulous. For Sifton, however, the political game was a means to an end. Political power was essential to the implementation of the policies of development that he considered vital for Canada. This book is therefore about Sifton's efforts to achieve and maintain political power, as well as about the problems he faced in its exercise. The great issues in which he became embroiled—the Manitoba school question, immigration and settlement, the Yukon gold rush, tariff and railway policy—were certainly inherently controversial; but Sifton's combative style often tended to aggravate rather than conciliate.

Clifford Sifton's life is also fascinating because his vision of Canada and of the role of government frequently varied from that of Sir Wilfrid Laurier, whose views commonly dominate histories of the era. He would never have accepted the theory that Confederation entailed a bicultural compact; and he earnestly believed in the need for a government dynamically involved in shaping Canadian development. During the period to 1900 there was a high degree of co-operation between Sifton and Laurier, but the roots of future friction may readily be discerned.

The present work is, of necessity, a political biography. Sifton was an intensely private man, and the tradition still carries on in the family. When the voluminous Sifton Papers (see Note on Sources) were deposited in the Public Archives of Canada, they had been stripped of all personal and most business correspondence. The political papers are, nevertheless, astonishingly complete. The passage of nearly a half century since the appearance of John W. Dafoe's semi-official biography now permits a much more frank and detailed assessment of Sifton and his public life and times.

For their co-operation and patience during the research of this volume, I should like to thank the staffs of the Public Archives of Canada, the National Library, the Library of Parliament, the Manitoba Provincial Archives and Library, the Winnipeg Free Press Library, the Elizabeth Dafoe Library of the University of Manitoba, Les Archives de l'Archevêché de St. Boniface, the Public Archives of Saskatchewan, the Public Archives of Ontario, the University of Toronto Library, the Victoria College Archives, the Douglas

Library of Queen's University, the Library and Archives of the University of Western Ontario, the Public Archives of Nova Scotia, the Rutherford Library of the University of Alberta, and the Library of the Alberta Legislature.

It is impossible to mention all of the colleagues, friends and other individuals whose advice, encouragement, and co-operation have contributed to this project. There are, however, a few whose particular assistance must be noted.

Professor R. Craig Brown gave unstintingly of his time and editorial talent, first as supervisor of my doctoral dissertation and later in reading and commenting upon the first ten chapters of this manuscript. The result is immeasurably better for his suggestions. I should like also to remember the late Professor D.G. Creighton, who volunteered to read part of the manuscript despite failing health and whose enthusiasm for the project and comments on style were immensely encouraging to a young scholar. I shall always be grateful for the privilege of his friendship.

Professor Gerald Friesen was kind enough to agree to read and comment upon the first five chapters, sharing his special knowledge of the early political history of Manitoba. The late Col. Clifford Sifton consented to an interview, as did Professor F.W. Gibson, R.S. Malone, and the late Douglas Murray.

Among other colleagues, friends and relatives whose co-operation and advice merit special mention are John Bovey, Barry Hyman, Gilbert Comeault, Lionel Dorge, John Eagle, John Foster, Stuart Mackinnon, Rod Macleod, Lewis H. Thomas, Lewis H. Green, John Tobias, Ken Tyler, Roland Wright, the late Mr. Justice James McLennan, and Stuart Forbes, Q.C. Mrs. Olive Baird and Mrs. Dorothy Robinson cheerfully and patiently typed and retyped the manuscript.

The Canada Council supported me in this project when I was a graduate student and also with a Leave Fellowship. Finally, a special word of thanks to my wife, Ann, whose help and unfailing support has often roused me from discouragement and aided in bringing this project to fruition.

# Prologue

.

For the emigrants awaiting their ship near Cork, Ireland had never appeared more enchanting, her hills more verdant, her familiar roads and cottages more alluring. Anguished thoughts of the land and, more poignantly, of family and friends shortly to be left forever behind aroused apprehension in their hearts. Almost overwhelming was the fear stirred by the prospect of the dangers and hardships of the Atlantic crossing and of the unknown land which lay beyond. Yet so strong was the intention to leave the familiar and risk the unknown, so irrevocable the decision, that none of the party changed their minds despite three long weeks of delay between the time they assembled near Cork harbour and the arrival of their vessel.

They knew Ireland to be a deceptively harsh and demanding mistress. The bitter feuds of Protestant and Roman Catholic, of English and Irish, and the grinding, unremitting toil required to eke out a living exacted an appalling toll. These endemic problems were intensified by the contracting economy and social insecurity at the end of the Napoleonic Wars in 1815. This impetus sent tens of thousands of people to seek a fresh beginning in the New World.

One man determined to take this step was Richard Talbot, a squire of Tipperary, who for years had sacrificed and sought to develop useful connections to obtain commissions in the British army for his sons as a step toward the higher rungs on the ladder of social preferment. Peace in Europe not only put an end to these hopes but also resulted in ruinous instability in the market for agricultural produce. Abruptly the life hitherto dedicated to slowly climbing the ladder of success became a struggle to maintain his position. If he was to preserve his own station and prevent his "children from retrograding in the scale of society," Talbot concluded that he must leave Ireland and start again in Upper Canada.[1]

He had chosen undeveloped Canada over the United States because, as he later put it, it was unthinkable that a loyal subject of the Crown should ever sever those ties and dwell under republican institutions. Besides, he had some expectation of assistance in emigrating to Upper Canada and of there securing a large estate befitting one of his position, education, and influence.

The British government, however, had decided to reconsider its policies of assistance to emigrants. Individual settlers could expect no assistance, Talbot was informed, beyond the promise of twenty-five acres of free land. But the government would provide transportation for those organizing parties of at least ten settlers and their families. Each settler would receive one hundred acres of land in the colony, the organizer somewhat more. To discourage the settlers from failing to fulfil their obligations, each was required to deposit £10 with the government, redeemable when he actually took up residence on his land.

Talbot promptly set out to organize his party and began to advertise locally. He was astounded at the response. Almost before he knew it fifty-four intending emigrants had made their deposits; with their families, they constituted a party of nearly two hundred. Their eagerness simply reflected the desire of thousands to leave their present circumstances if someone provided a lead and the means. Among those joining the party were four brothers, small farmers near Clonmel, Tipperary: Bamlet, Charles, John, and Joseph Sifton.[2]

The Talbot expedition sailed from Cork harbour on 13 June 1818, bound for Québec. The government had provided them with an excellent ship, the *Brunswick*, 541 tons, with a capacity of over 250 passengers. She had taken on a cargo of 150 tons as well as three months' provisions for the settlers, so conditions were crowded and miserable. The Talbots, of course, went "cabin class," sharing these superior accommodations with "three other families of respectability." The rest, including the Siftons, went in steerage, sleeping six adults to a berth. It was a hard crossing. An initial two weeks of stormy seas and continuous nausea left the stench of sickness and death for the rest of the journey. Most of the passengers heartily regretted their decision as unrelenting adverse winds beset their ship. After a month at sea they sighted Newfoundland, but they found little comfort in the cold, rocky, densely forested coasts and islands that followed. Finally, on 27 July, after a voyage of forty-three days, they anchored at Québec. They had already paid a terrible price to reach their new land: no less than twenty-four children had been buried at sea or on the coasts and islands of North America.[3]

The difficulties had just begun. From Québec the expedition sailed to Montreal, where it began to break up. A few were enticed to take up land in Lower Canada. Thirty-one settlers and their families elected to go to Perth, accessible via the Ottawa River, rather than undertake the rigours and expense of the journey to western Upper Canada.[4] The Talbots, however, were determined to press on, partly because they considered Lower Canada to have inferior soil and a severe climate, and also "in consequence of its being almost wholly in the occupation of a people with whose customs, language and religion, we were very imperfectly acquainted."[5] The Siftons went with them. From Montreal they travelled by Durham boats to Prescott, poling the boats, sometimes drawing them in water up to their armpits. By night they camped without canvas wherever they happened to land on shore, often going long stretches without seeing any settlements. From Prescott they were able to sail to Kingston and York, where they encountered Richard Talbot's eccentric namesake, Colonel Thomas Talbot.

The colonel had arrived with a British regiment in the late eighteenth century. He had been so attracted by the Canadian wilderness that he sold his commission and obtained from the British government a 100,000-acre tract of land on the condition that he should settle one family on every two hundred acres. While some settlement had taken place, his curious habits and hermit-like existence did not suggest deep dedication to rapid development. "He not only lives a life of cheerless celibacy," wrote Richard's son, E.A. Talbot, "but enjoys no human society whatever."[6]

Colonel Talbot suggested that the party settle in London township, which they finally reached by the end of October 1818. Although the area had been surveyed some years previously, only one or two white settlers preceded the Talbot expedition into the virgin forest. By early December makeshift dwellings were prepared for the coming winter. Still ahead lay the backbreaking task of clearing the land and living for years at a subsistence level before the modest security and prosperity to which the settlers aspired would be realized.

So it was that the Siftons came to Canada, the family, it is believed, from which sprang all those of that name in North America.[7] Their story was not unusual. Simple farmers with a simple faith, they believed deeply in the sustaining powers of devotion to God and plain hard work. But they looked forward to a better life and more varied opportunities for their children. Their dreams would be amply fulfilled.

From this background emerged Sir Clifford Sifton. Rooted in this experience were the beliefs that conditioned the man, his family, and his generation of Canadians. The man who would shape Canadian immigration policy at the turn of the century had before him the story of his own ancestors. It was, he believed, in the pioneer's struggle and determination to survive, in the farmer's ceaseless toil and devotion to his faith, that the character of the nation was both determined and regenerated. Beneath the complexity, the inconsistency, the paradox of this great politician and powerful businessman, these themes run steadily and recurrently. National greatness, he believed, was founded on those who thought imaginatively, acted boldly and aggressively, burst beyond the constraints of their circumstances, and determined to create a better future for themselves and their country.

# 1

# Father and Sons
# (1861–82)

The Siftons had never set down deep roots in Ireland. One hundred and twenty-five years could not make them truly Irish, although the Island was their only home. They knew, and were constantly reminded by the local population and their own increasingly tenuous circumstances, that they were aliens in a strange and inhospitable land. Etched into the conscious memory of every member of the family were tales of murderous battles with the Roman Catholic peasantry, of the deaths of beloved relatives and friends.[1] Small wonder, then, that the first generation of Canadian Siftons would emphasize that their "ancestors on both sides" were English, even suggesting that they had come to Canada simply via Tipperary.[2]

Almost certainly the name is a variation of the northern English Sefton. The earliest known Sifton served as a sergeant in the forces invading Ireland under William of Orange in 1690. His reward was a small estate near Clonmel, part of a broad programme to establish a permanent loyal and Protestant population in the rebellious island. Succeeding generations lived as minor gentry and small farmers, but with generally declining fortunes. Thus, while there was a natural hesitation to leave, for the Siftons of the early nineteeth century the decision to emigrate was perhaps made fairly readily.

After the first Siftons reached London, they were joined in 1819 by Charles Sifton, the family patriarch, and by another of his sons, Robert. All appear to have become farmers. The most determined, able, and ambitious of the first Canadian-born generation was John Wright Sifton. Born in London township on 10 August 1833, the youngest son of Bamlet and Mary Sifton, he sustained a series of blows during his life that would have discouraged lesser men. Restless and resourceful, he repeatedly saw the prizes for which he grasped turn to dust in his hands, the security for which he strove torn from him. Time and again his Christian faith restored his optimism and renewed his drive for success.

Raised on his father's farm, he received such formal education as was available in the public and grammar schools of the fledgling city of London. He then began farming on his own and apparently tried his hand at some minor business enterprises with indifferent success. At twenty years of age he married, on 1 October 1853, Kate Watkins, daughter of Anglo-Irish immigrants from King's County, Ireland. A devoted, God-fearing Victorian wife, her personality appears to have been completely submerged in the lives of her dominant husband and sons. John and Kate Sifton had five children, of whom a son and a daughter died in infancy. Their eldest surviving child was a daughter, Sophia, who was thoroughly overshadowed by her illustrious brothers, both born in the family farmhouse near Arva in Middlesex County: Arthur Lewis, 26 October 1858, and Clifford, 10 March 1861. They would be devoted and loyal sons, owing much of their success to their father's influence, profiting from his efforts, and learning from his experience.

Despite his family responsibilities, J.W. Sifton impatiently waited for a chance to break out of the restraints of life in a rural community. He was frustrated by the lack of opportunity to farm on a larger and more profitable scale and by the difficulty of rapid advancement in the by now well-established patterns of finance and services in the London area. Then, in 1859, the first commercial oil well in North America was put down at Oil Springs in Lambton county. Sifton promptly caught the "oil madness." By early 1860, when he was twenty-seven, he was engaged in producing and refining oil as founder and manager of the St. Clair Oil Company. The name was impressive, but he was just one of more than a dozen independent producers trying to supply a limited market from a very small petroleum field. Business boomed for a short time, but cooled rapidly in 1863 and 1864. The pioneer economy had few uses for petroleum, and soon a larger discovery and more efficient management at nearby Petrolia overshadowed the Oil Springs development. Sifton hung on, hoping that the collapse in the market was temporary. He became reeve of Oil Springs and a member of the Lambton county council from 1867 to 1869. He also served as chairman of the school board.[3] But Oil Springs was beginning to resemble a ghost town, and finally in 1870 J.W. Sifton forlornly concluded a decade of endeavour, sold out to an American company, and removed to Paris, Ontario. It was, remarked his grandson many years later, the first in a series of unsuccessful investments in oil made by the Sifton family.[4]

Located on the Grand River in Brant county, Paris was a quiet rural town of perhaps three thousand people. After two years of minor financing and small-scale contracting, John Sifton had an important break. He successfully tendered for a contract to construct some forty miles of the Canada Southern Railway.[5] The venture was reasonably profitable, and he moved back to London in 1873 where he engaged in private banking and had an interest in a company of coal and wood dealers, all the while seeking out associates and backers for further large-scale enterprises.[6]

John Sifton also had a private reason for returning to London. For the first time in several years his family was united. After primary education in various public schools, the children had been sent to private schools, Sophia to the Hamilton Female College, and Arthur and Clifford to a boys' school at Dundas. They all returned to London, where the boys attended high school. The children had been raised in an atmosphere of devotion to their family and to the Wesleyan Methodist church and were powerfully influenced by their father. Wherever he lived, John Sifton was one of the most active and devout laymen of his denomination, dedicated particularly to Sunday School teaching and to the cause of temperance. In 1852, at the age of nineteen he had joined the Order of the Sons of Temperance, and he maintained a passion for prohibition throughout his life.

This Methodist passion to redeem society also extended to politics. John Sifton had a natural affinity for the moralistic, crusading politics of George Brown and Alexander Mackenzie. His children were nurtured on the principles of representation by population, free trade, and western expansion. Familiar to them were the cries of "no Popery" and "French domination." John Sifton held minor political offices, and he worked tirelessly in the Reform cause, particularly in Lambton, represented by Mackenzie. In his household there was a constant traffic of churchmen, politicians, lawyers, and businessmen. It was a stimulating crossroads, producing dozens of valuable contacts for both father and sons. Little wonder that the boys shared their father's enthusiasms and ambitions.

The boys were, nevertheless, of contrasting temperaments. A popular and engaging personality, Arthur seemed to inherit his father's restlessness, impulsiveness and—at least in his youth—talent for near-success. He was the sort who gaily skipped classes at college, confident of his own ability to pass, preferring to broaden his mind in other ways. He won a prize from his fellow students for being "intellectually, morally, physically and erratically preeminent in virtue and otherwise, especially otherwise."[7] Such frivolity was beyond Clifford. Though far from unpopular, he seemed for some years to play the sober second fiddle. He was a serious student, faithful in attendance, and steadily won academic awards. At the age of fifteen in 1876, he graduated from high school at the same time as his eighteen-year-old brother.

Perhaps the most important factor in shaping Clifford's character was his partial deafness. A boyhood attack of scarlet fever had left him with what was diagnosed as "chronic catarrh of the middle ear," a condition not curable then or in his lifetime despite the best possible treatment.[8] As a result, he had an intermittent loss of hearing, fortunately not serious enough to hinder his education or curtail drastically other normal activities. However, it was a steadily worsening condition. With him always was the desperate fear of total deafness. He was humiliated when he suddenly could not hear conversation or understand questions. Yet Clifford gave way to neither insecurity nor introspection. He developed a rigorously disciplined mind, capable of prodigious concentration and incisive analysis. He read widely and carefully in newspapers, periodicals, and books. He constantly dissected and evaluated his own experiences and those of others. A remarkable iron will asserted itself, a fierce determination to overcome the handicap and to prove himself.

When his sons were attending high school, fortune again smiled on John Sifton. The fall of the Conservative government of Sir John A. Macdonald in the wake of the Pacific Scandal of 1873 had brought Alexander Mackenzie to power as the first Liberal prime minister. The new government immediately faced an irritating dilemma. The Liberals had strongly opposed the rash actions of the Tories in 1870, but the stubborn fact remained that the government of Canada had then undertaken an obligation to British Columbia to build a transcontinental railway. Once in power, nevertheless, Mackenzie sought to change the terms. To attempt to build the line as one grand project, and to do so by 1881 as required in the agreement with B.C. argued the Liberals, would ruin the country. The government must build the line only as the country could afford it and in sections over which the government could retain some control of expenditure. Unhappily, idealism and honesty could not compensate for inexperience on the part of the government or some of its contractors. But the day of reckoning still lay in the future. The new government lost little time in rewarding its faithful supporters such as J.W. Sifton with available contracts.

Through companies which he either controlled or shortly bought out, Sifton successfully tendered for three contracts. All entailed construction west of the Great Lakes. The first, known as Canadian Pacific Railway contract number 1, awarded 17 October 1874; involved construction of a telegraph line northwest from Fort Garry to Fort Pelly. It required the clearing of a strip of land 132 feet wide where the line ran through forests, "formation of a trail for pack animals," and maintenance and operation of the line for five years after completion. In April 1875, two more contracts, numbers 13 and 14, were awarded Sifton for the grading and bridging, but not the track-laying and ballasting, of two sections of the Canadian Pacific main line. The former was 32.5 miles west from Fort William to Sunshine Creek; the latter was 76 miles east from the Red River at Selkirk to Cross Lake.[9]

J.W. Sifton's future seemed assured. He was in on the ground floor of the greatest construction project ever undertaken in Canada. The overwhelming Liberal victory in the election of 1874 seemed bound to ensure many years of favour under Liberal governments. He had before him projects which would likely propel him to prominence in Canadian contracting and financial circles and which would satisfy his adventurous spirit. With characteristic energy, he was in Winnipeg in early 1874, making arrangements to push the telegraph construction throughout the winter.[10] Having two railway contracts in hand the following spring, he decided to settle his family in Manitoba. Kate and Sophia joined him on a farm near the headquarters of his operations at Selkirk, while Arthur and Clifford completed high school at Wesley College, a Methodist institution in Winnipeg.[11]

To settle in Manitoba in 1874 was a not inconsiderable act of faith. Even to reach the tiny isolated community required an arduous journey. It was possible to travel via St. Paul to the banks of the Red River in the United States by rail. From there the journey was completed by steamer down river in the summer and by stage, sleigh, or Red River cart during the rest of the year. Although the buffalo had virtually disappeared, travellers still could see vast tracts of uncultivated prairie along the Red River and far into the limitless western horizon.

The social milieu was unsettled. The uneasy balance between French and English, mixed blood and white, Roman Catholic and Protestant, which had prevailed in 1870 at the birth of the province was already collapsing. A settlement frontier was being superimposed on a small but long-settled community. The Siftons were in the vanguard of those who would generate changes and they were typical of the Ontarians who would soon be a majority wanting to establish familiar forms and institutions. Many were, like the Siftons, followers of the Reformers who in 1870 had denounced, as likely to be productive of trouble, the guarantees made in the Manitoba Act to the French and Catholic population.[12] They came, not with an active dislike for local customs, but with a simple disregard for them, a sense that they were backward and irrelevant.

If John Wright Sifton represented anything to Manitobans, it was progress. As a contractor for the railway, that one necessity which westerners implicitly believed would cause their waiting Garden of Eden to bloom, he received flattering attention. The railway was a major boost to the local economy. Both as a contractor and as an employer John Sifton had a reputation for being tough and demanding, but fair. Reflecting his personal views, one of his advertisements for labourers observed that "Men wanting but little work and considerable whiskey had better not go."[13]

His reputation was enhanced by his endeavours to establish his roots in the province as a farmer. He risked a large part of his capital on large-scale progressive farming. Despite the export of a few hundred bushels of grain by Red River steamer in 1876,[14] Manitoba growers were still essentially restricted to the local market. Sifton nevertheless sowed two hundred acres to oats in 1876 and averaged fifty bushels an acre, a large enough crop to excite public interest.[15] He increased his acreage in 1877, but neither the techniques of prairie farming nor the system of transportation had progressed adequately to sustain a large-scale farming enterprise over any length of time. Yet Sifton had an unflagging faith that large-scale farming was the way of the future in the West.

Few activities earned Sifton more attention, however, than his perpetual prohibitionist zeal. In his capacity as a justice of the peace, it was once noted, "everybody knows he has his face set as a flint against drunkenness and all violations of the law in connection with the liquor business." He himself once declared that he had expended half a million dollars in Manitoba in connection with railway contracts and he calculated that nearly half that amount had "gone to drink."[16] In March 1877, he became Grand Worthy President of the provincial lodge of the United Temperance Association. He was one of the driving forces behind the building of the Temperance Hall in Winnipeg, for use by the Sons of Temperance, the Independent Order of Good Templars, and the United Temperance Association. And again he was the central figure in pressing these organizations to co-operate in 1879 to form the Manitoba branch of the Dominion Alliance for the Total Suppression of the Liquor Traffic, of which he became president for seven successive years.[17]

He spoke on temperance wherever he could find an audience, establishing local associations across the province. He had seen the ravages of alcohol in the railway camps and had tried to discourage the traffic. With other reformers of his day, he singled out alcohol as the principal cause of poverty, disease, crime, and "premature death." Alcohol "was ruining thousands and sending many to a drunkard's grave." The government must be pressed for legislation, for "if good prohibitory laws were made and enforced, drinking alcoholic liquors would become a thing of the past."[18]

Perhaps the height of John Sifton's prestige in Manitoba occurred during the tour of the province in 1877 by Governor General Lord Dufferin. Sifton was in charge of arrangements for His Excellency's visit to Selkirk, personally underwriting much of the expense. Aboard the freshly painted steamer *Keewatin*, Dufferin and his entourage arrived on 17 August to be greeted by triumphal arches, an enthusiastic though makeshift band, and hundreds of excited townsfolk, farmers, labourers, and Indians. A procession formed up, "a motley cortege nearly a mile long and including fifty or sixty vehicles of various descriptions." Invariably gracious, Dufferin always managed appropriate remarks, even in face of a central arch which "supported the various tools used in railway construction, tastefully grouped." Such artistic items as plows, scrapers, picks, shovels, crowbars, and wheelbarrows were displayed, with the superscriptions "Shortest Route—Atlantic to Pacific" and "Speed the railway!" It was perhaps symbolic of Sifton's career that, during the ceremonies in which he presented the governor general with an address of welcome, part of the platform collapsed. Fortunately no one was injured.[19]

While John Sifton was making his mark in Manitoba, Arthur and Clifford were attending Victoria College at Cobourg, Ontario. It was a small Methodist institution, comprising in 1876 a single three-story, neo-classical structure and a student body of less than one hundred. The cost of tuition, board, and incidentals was less than $150, but even this fee placed a college education beyond all but a small elite group of Canadians. The curriculum was still rigorously classical: philosophy, church history, Greek, Latin, algebra, trigonometry, chemistry, and English. It was made to order for the studious Clifford; he compiled an outstanding record and took prizes in each year, graduating in 1880 as the gold medallist of his class.[20]

However, the winds of educational change were beginning to blow in Cobourg as elsewhere, and the Siftons—particularly Clifford— reaped the benefits. The college was moving beyond the preparation of ministers and the provision of a general arts programme for men. The first women were admitted to undergraduate lectures in 1877; shortly, a respected medical faculty would be established. But it was the completion of Faraday Hall, a modern science building, in 1877 and the institution of a science programme under the energetic direction of the Silesian Eugene Haanel that seized Clifford's attention. The decision to implement a serious science programme had been taken in 1873; Haanel had agreed to come from Europe only if a major commitment to proper facilities was made. He was a superb, enthusiastic teacher, possessed of a severely disciplined, analytical mind. Such qualities strongly appealed to Clifford, and throughout his later career he often had recourse to Haanel's judgment. He became an active member of the Science Association, being in charge of experiments in his junior year and president in his senior year, when he delivered an "inaugural address" on the subject of glaciers. In 1880, following his graduation, he remained to take a graduate course in science, apparently one of the first students to do so.[21] For the rest of his life he placed a much higher premium on science and such "practical" studies than on what he conceived to be the much less useful humanities.

Clifford was also one of the founders of the college newspaper, the *Acta Victoriana,* established in 1878. It was a modest enterprise, intended to serve both students and alumni, to facilitate inter-college communication, to publish the literary efforts of students, and, of course, to provide local news and light commentaries. Sifton was the first business manager of the paper, and in his senior year was associate editor. It was the beginning of a lifelong association with newspapers.[22]

The summers of those college years were amongst the happiest and most relaxed of their lives for Arthur and Clifford. For the three months between July and September their family was reunited. It had been slightly expanded when in 1878 Sophia married A.N. Molesworth, a civil engineer employed on her father's construction projects.[23] The boys helped on their father's farm, accompanied him on inspections of the railway and telegraph lines, and joined in the social life of Selkirk. They were active in founding a local literary club which put on public entertainments every two or three weeks with debates, recitations, and musical numbers. And there were sports, particularly lacrosse. Once both Arthur and Clifford were part of a Selkirk lacrosse team which rashly challenged a Winnipeg team and was soundly defeated. The games were vigorous and rough and decidedly amateur. "There was room for a great deal of improvement in the playing of both clubs," noted one observer, "The great desideratum apparently being to achieve individual glory by making spasmodic runs with the ball, rather than to act in concert, and thus save a considerable unnecessary expenditure of wind and labour."[24] Both young men joined in their father's church and temperance activities, and in 1879 they were elected to the executive of the Selkirk branch of the Independent Order of Good Templars.[25]

With his standing in the community as a contractor, farmer, churchman, and temperance worker and given his ambitions and past experience, it was scarcely surprising when John Sifton entered politics. He could hardly have chosen a more inauspicious occasion than the 1878 dominion elections. The Liberals had done precisely nothing to provide effective organization, even after the Conservatives established a provincial organization in March to fight the federal election.[26] Not until 21 August did Sifton chair a meeting to organize the Reform party in Lisgar constituency, in which Selkirk was located; and not until 30 August was he nominated as Reform candidate, scarcely three weeks before the election.[27] The sitting Conservative member was the redoubtable Dr. John Christian Schultz, a man who had become notorious during the Riel rebellion in 1869–70 and who now was a substantial property owner and land speculator in Selkirk. Sifton attacked the National Policy protective tariff proposals of the Tories, promised policies to promote the rapid development of Manitoba, "the Garden of the Dominion," and committed himself to try to enable farmers to sell products in "the dearest markets" and to purchase supplies "in the cheapest."[28]

He never had the opportunity to test Schultz at the polls. The Manitoba contests were to be held a week after those in the rest of the country, and the doleful news of the crushing defeat suffered by the Liberal government decided the issue. Sifton hurriedly met with his supporters and meekly withdrew. There had been no development of partisan loyalties in the constituency, and the contest had been fought on the basis of the personalities of Schultz and Sifton and with the slogan on Sifton's side, "Don't go agin' the Government." Given Mackenzie's defeat, Sifton later said, it was in the interest of the people of Lisgar "to return a supporter of whatever Government might be in power." Only a Liberal victory could have ensured his success. For Arthur and Clifford, both in Manitoba during the campaign, it was a discouraging but useful introduction to the vagaries of political fortunes.

More than political defeat, however, was on John Sifton's mind. He realized that the return of his political enemies would have more blighting personal effects. The real reason for his withdrawal, in fact, was privately reported to have been that he "had an account to settle with the Government and by persisting in running [he] would perhaps strongly prejudice his case." He particularly feared future trouble with respect to the telegraph line. Soon it was apparent that his fears were well founded.[29]

There remained, however, provincial politics, where non-partisanship still received more than lip service. Avoiding partisan divisions in local politics, it was widely believed, would enable the provincial government to remain on good terms with Ottawa, whichever party was in power. As the federal government grant constituted the largest portion of the provincial budget, and since Ottawa controlled the purse strings for railway development and the sale of public lands, a friendly relationship was vital. The task for a provincial government was to promote local interests and balance the concerns of French and English, old residents and newcomers.

A belief that the provincial government had been ineffective in recognizing the changing balance of power in the province had caused the formation of a loose opposition organization between 1875 and 1878. When Premier R.A. Davis resigned in October 1878 for personal reasons, the government was reconstituted under John Norquay, an able representative of the so-called "country-born," or English-speaking mixed-blood community. Somewhat greater recognition by Norquay of the English-speaking majority only partially defused the opposition, which continued in manifest hostility to any accommodation with the French-speaking element.[30] John Sifton decided to run as an independent supporter of Norquay in St. Clement's riding, on a platform calling for introduction of the secret ballot in provincial elections, building a railway west from the Red River, and representation by population. He was elected by 87 votes, to a combined total of 67 for his two opponents.[31]

When the legislature met in 1879, J.W. Sifton was elected speaker. He presided over what started out as an unexciting session. Norquay adjourned the session in the spring while he and Public Works Minister Joseph Royal travelled to Ottawa in search of "better terms." In return for giving the federal government control of railway policy and agreeing to charter no new railways without Ottawa's approval, the province was promised federal support for construction of public buildings, the interest on capital accumulated from the sale of school lands, federal responsibility for the care of lunatics, and an increase of one-sixth over two years in the provincial subsidy.[32]

Such terms required careful discussion, as the future would show. But the day after they were announced, Norquay was faced with a serious political crisis which precluded such debate. His French cabinet colleagues, led by Royal, resigned in an attempt to force the premier to accept the principle of double majority, the necessity of maintaining majority support from both French and English-speaking members. Probably Royal was seeking to outmanoeuvre Norquay and seize the premiership.[33]

Whatever their designs, the French members had in fact overreached themselves. Their actions were an understandable, if unrealistic, reaction to a developing garrison mentality in the Franco-Manitoban community. Gradually their position of equality and power was being eroded as more and more English-speaking settlers arrived. Changes in the system of allotment of school monies and abolition of the provincial legislative council had already taken place. On all sides there were demands for the abolition of the use of French in the government, the secularization of the school system, and the redistribution of seats in the legislature on the basis of population rather than race or group. As Royal made clear, the French people believed that they had an inherent right to the same proportion of seats in the legislature and places in the cabinet as they had had hitherto. They contended that such was the basis of the "compact" of 1870.

Many of the English members, by contrast, believed that the privileges gained by the French in 1870 had been wrongfully extorted by rebellion and were bad in principle. In a prompt reaction to the move by Royal, Norquay secured the support of every English-speaking member, including J.W. Sifton, for a memorandum which called for abolition of the publication of government documents in French as an economy measure; redistribution of all seats according to population; more expenditure on roads; more care in the proportional expenditure of school grants; and expansion of the boundaries of the province.[34] Bills were then passed adding several English constituencies, though not wholly according to population, and abolishing the use of French in the government. Thus, in direct confrontation, the English people of the province had shown that they could stand united. Although he did not immediately attempt to realize all the terms of the memorandum, Norquay had proven that he could secure the backing of the English members for such measures, which would force the French members to be more cautious. Ottawa did disallow the language bill, but the redistribution bill stood. The premier was then able to convince the French members to return to the cabinet on his terms.

Unfortunately for John Sifton, Norquay decided to call an election on the basis of the redistribution. His government was sustained in the December elections with seventeen supporters against two independents and one in outright opposition. Sifton ran again as a supporter of Norquay and came at the bottom of the poll, won by the Independent E.H.G.G. Hay. Wrote one of his supporters, "Sifton has been badly beat. From the shape the new redistribution bill left the constituencies it was a foregone conclusion that he was out a seat. Nearly the whole Canadian vote supported him, but he was far behind with the half breeds."[35]

The defeat, then, was the result of local issues and the lack of effective organization, which Sifton never seems to have established. But possibly it was also caused by increasing harrassment by the Conservatives over his telegraph and railway contracts and repeated enquiries into how he had obtained and executed them. The attacks had begun during the 1878 general election campaign, when the Conservatives were determined to embarrass both John Sifton and his partner in the telegraph venture, David Glass, who was running as a Liberal in East Middlesex.[36] Once in office, the vengeful Tories commenced a campaign to prove that the party of purity and efficiency had been as besmirched by corruption, bungling, and incompetence in railway administration as had the Tories themselves during the Pacific Scandal.

At the first session of the new Parliament in 1879, the railway contracts were carefully investigated by the Public Accounts Committee. When questioning Sifton, the committee members were especially interested in why his costs had risen by as much as 80 per cent over his tender price. Unable to find any evidence of corruption, the committee concluded that the contracts had been let "without sufficient information as to the character and quantities of the work" and with inadequate and inconsistent methods of calling for tenders. Contracts 13 and 14 had been let with undue haste, upon "what we call a preliminary survey, not on a thoroughly located line."[37] Simply, the problem had been that the volume of earth and rock to be moved had proven in actual excavation greatly to exceed the estimates of the surveyors; and most of the contract had been calculated on a certain amount per cubic yard of material to be moved. Despite evidence of government engineers corroborating Sifton's calculations about the work done, the government was not satisfied. A new crew was sent out to remeasure the work done on contract 14, in the belief that it had been overestimated.[38] No evidence was found to support this contention. The government had come up with little of substance with which Sifton could be attacked; but his reputation unquestionably suffered from the adverse publicity.

His pocketbook was also suffering. The very projects which he had hoped would make his fortune now caused an endless succession of headaches. The greatest loss was on the telegraph line located along the route originally surveyed for the railway, running northwest close to Lake Manitoba. Sifton had counted on making his profits out of the heavy use of the line as the railway was built; the endless delays and eventual choice of a more southerly route west from Winnipeg destroyed that prospect. More seriously, the route had evidently been surveyed in dry years, and successive years of flooding after construction raised the cost of maintaining the line to exorbitant levels. In 1880, with still a year of maintenance required in his contract, Sifton estimated that his firm had spent about $15,000 in excess of receipts in repairing and operating the line.[39] His pleas for reconsideration of the terms of the contracts now fell on unsympathetic ears.

Macdonald's Tories were far from through in their endeavours to discredit the Mackenzie government. In 1880 the government established a royal commission on the Canadian Pacific Railway, a highly partisan affair whose consideration of the evidence, certainly as far as it concerned Sifton, was biased and unsympathetic.[40] In its conclusions it appears to have considered mainly the dubious, and possibly false and malicious, evidence of a man fired from the telegraph contract and implied that Sifton was practically incompetent. No weight seems to have been given to sworn affidavits countering this evidence, nor was any attempt made to seek out those who might have had a more balanced perspective.[41] Serious enough charges remained, nevertheless. Sifton had obtained the telegraph contract under questionable circumstances and built it as cheaply as permissible, thus adding to the costs of maintenance. Once again, however, the investigators were forced to conclude that he had fulfilled his obligations satisfactorily with respect to the railway contracts; difficulties and cost overruns were directly attributable to incompetent or incomplete surveying and undue haste in calling for tenders.[42]

There was meagre consolation for John Sifton in the commission's findings. Little immediate prospect of future contracts remained, and the farm had been less than successful. Discouraged and rejected by his constituents, he left Selkirk for Winnipeg in 1879. He had recently turned to dealing in real estate,[43] but he lost money even in that occupation. In the spring of 1879 real estate values in Selkirk had jumped by 50 per cent in the wake of a government announcement that the main line of the CPR would indeed cross the Red River there. Within a few months they fell again as Winnipeg emerged the clear victor in the struggle for the main line, hurting those like Sifton who had speculated in Selkirk.

Winnipeg at least provided the advantage that John and Kate would again be near their sons. Through college at last, they now began to article with Winnipeg law firms, Arthur with A. Monkman and Clifford with S.C. Biggs, a prominent Reform politician and temperance advocate. Both sons, especially Arthur, were now caught up in their father's temperance activities as well. John Sifton and the Dominion Alliance were in the midst of a campaign to have plebiscites held in the electoral districts of Lisgar and Marquette in order to bring into effect the local option provisions of the Canada Temperance Act, or Scott Act, of 1878.[44] Since dominion-wide prohibition seemed out of the question for the time being, the Scott Act was intended to permit a majority of local voters to keep their district dry. The Manitoba prohibitionists worked with a will. During the campaign in Marquette, for example, the "Cold Water Brigade," as it was styled by the *Manitoba Free Press,* circulated five thousand copies of a prohibition pamphlet, ran articles in the Winnipeg *Times* and *Free*

*Press,* and conducted an exhaustive series of meetings, Arthur addressing at least sixteen, and J.W. Sifton eight.[45]

The campaigns were a great success. Lisgar and Marquette both voted for prohibition by substantial majorities, and John Sifton was able to claim that more than half of Manitoba was about to become "dry." Just as plans were being made to dry up the rest of the province, the victory crumbled. It was found that "these districts not being counties within the meaning of the Act, the voting was of no effect."[46] The battle would be joined again, and apparently won, but the law was partially nullified through lax enforcement. Prohibitionists were beginning to find that demonstrating the will of the majority and actually implementing it were often two very different things.

What had John Sifton to show in 1880 for five years' endeavour in Manitoba? Certainly his hopes and expectations were far from realized. Apparently he had come about as far as fortune and his own competence could take him. He was, of course, not impoverished; and with the inner resources of the devout, he demonstrated resilience, a renewed conviction that his day would yet come.

His hopes were stimulated by the resurgence of prosperity which swept the province during the railway boom of 1881–82. The CPR was taking shape, property values soared, and it was anticipated that a flood of land-hungry immigrants would secure the province's destiny. Everywhere optimism prevailed, speculation was rampant, and paper fortunes were made. Winnipeg was largely in the hands of established capitalists and land dealers, but there were booming new districts anticipating the arrival of the railroad. Hurriedly John Sifton left the capital in order to get in on the ground floor in Brandon, a burgeoning town near the western edge of territory recently added to the province. Arthur cheerfully abandoned his law books and joined his father in the mad rush of profiteering from the spiralling prices of prairie lots.

Of the family, only Clifford seemed unmoved. Scrambling for money, or for anything else, would never be his way. He was careful and systematic, preferring to build a firm foundation. When he at last joined his father and brother in Brandon the boom was over. But the boom-and-bust cycle of 1881–82 typified the careers of John and Arthur in the next few years. The lesser known but singleminded Clifford would carry the family name to provincial and national prominence within the next decade.

# 2

# Brandon
# (1882–88)

Brandon was substantially a product of the Canadian Pacific Railway.[1] A scattered vanguard of settlers had begun drifting into the Brandon Hills in the late 1870's. The incorporation of the district into Manitoba in 1881, accompanied by the decision of the CPR to run its line on a more southerly course than originally planned, decisively ended its isolation. The surveyors were pressing westward, crossing the serpentine Assiniboine River in late April. Here, as avaricious land speculators and real estate dealers knew, would be an important divisional point and the likely site of the town which would serve most of southwestern Manitoba. Overnight bald prairie lots on the plains rising behind the south bank of the river began to trade for thousands of dollars. A tent city sprang up in early June, and frenzied construction of frame dwellings commenced. In little more than a year Brandon was incorporated as a city, and the first civic elections were held on 30 June 1882.[2]

By the spring of 1882, however, the city's bubble of prosperity had already burst. For months a stunned populace tried to digest the situation. Some clung to the undiminished stream of settlers as evidence that the economy was simply in a temporary decline. Others angrily tried to strike back at what they already perceived as domination from Winnipeg, or Ottawa, or by the CPR itself. Yet others hoped to restore prosperity by promoting colonization railways centred on Brandon. Nothing worked; in 1883 recession gave way to depression. So Brandon became a principal centre of political protest and a focal point for the expression of agrarian discontent.

In the 1880's the city and its hinterland had a practically homogeneous population racially. A tiny scattering of French Canadians and Europeans was lost in the flood of settlers of British stock. And of the total, 60 to 65 per cent were Ontario-born.[3] They shared certain assumptions about the nature of their society which they were prepared to unite to defend. On most public questions, however, homogeneity of race or religion was no guarantee of unanimity of outlook. Nor did the fact that all were newcomers to the district from a variety of backgrounds lend any noticeable breadth of perspective to their concerns. Nevertheless, uprooted and parochial as they were, out of their experiences and difficulties was forged a sense of identity as westerners, a potent force for politicians to exploit.[4] Frequently this sentiment was at variance with that of ambitious urban Winnipeg or with the traditions of the older settled regions which by the end of the decade would be engulfed by the society springing to life in the new districts.

Clifford Sifton had lived in Winnipeg for two remarkably turbulent years, during an even more dramatic boom-and-bust cycle than that of Brandon. Yet in two years of legal apprenticeship—which was what articling amounted to— he appeared to have concentrated on little but the law and, as always, had acquitted himself well. Apart from the practical training in a law office, there were four series of examinations on assigned legal texts administered by the benchers of the Law Society of Manitoba. Early in November 1882 Clifford completed his examinations for what was then termed barrister and attorney and was called to the Manitoba bar. He perhaps considered practising in the provincial capital with his fellow graduate and good friend Isaac Campbell; but he elected to settle in Brandon near his parents and open a practice with his brother.[5]

Neither Clifford nor Arthur appears to have regarded the law as anything but a stepping stone to a political career. And Arthur was already off to a flying start. Officially he had been running a Brandon law office for Monkman of Winnipeg. But he was not yet qualified for independent practice, a matter of little moment to him because he had been engaged in speculation in real estate, was active in the temperance movement and involved in organizing a loan company, and had been elected as an alderman to Brandon's first city council. He also had found time to marry, on 20 September 1882, Mary H. Deering of Cobourg. When Clifford arrived in Brandon, he found his brother in the midst of what would be a successful campaign for a second term on council.[6]

Even Arthur could not match his father's energetic activity, however. John Sifton had plunged into provincial politics again when the Norquay government called by-elections to send representatives to Winnipeg from the new western areas of the province. Facing a multitude of ill-organized opponents, he was elected for Brandon on 2 November 1881. He had served only one session when Premier Norquay called a general election for 23 January 1883. Clifford had hardly stepped off the train when he was recruited into his father's campaign. The help he could provide was badly needed, for John Sifton had been dissipating his energies in diverse activities: he was prominent in the Independent Order of Good Templars and was still president of the Manitoba branch of the Dominion Alliance; he supported the provincial Sunday School Association, which he had been instrumental in founding five years previously; he was the leading layman in the Brandon Methodist Church; he was engaged in both newspaper and railway ventures; and he was operating a farm of over a thousand acres near the city. He also had been one of the leaders in seeking a school for Brandon and was a driving force in a campaign for funds to establish a local hospital.

Despite his energy, John Sifton was in political trouble. Elected as an independent supporter of Norquay, within a few months he had become a harsh critic of the government and prominent in a burgeoning provincial rights movement. The principal causes of disaffection were railway policy and the federal power of disallowance. Responding to popular demand, in 1881 Norquay had allowed several railway bills to pass through the legislature, some of which were in violation of the agreement of 1879. This agreement had been confirmed in 1880 and formed part of the basis on which the CPR had been given its "monopoly"—a clause in its charter guaranteeing freedom for twenty years from effective competition in western Canada. Prime Minister Macdonald promptly disallowed the offending bills, otherwise within provincial powers, as a matter of national policy. Since almost 70 per cent of the provincial budget was still supplied by the federal subsidy and federally controlled funds, Premier Norquay had little alternative but meek acquiescence.[7]

At the 1882 session of the legislature John Sifton joined a vociferous opposition of six or eight members, led by Thomas Greenway of Crystal City. They demanded a vigorous provincial response to Ottawa's action and defiance if necessary. Manitoba, they contended, should have the same rights and be put on as independent a footing as all the other provinces. Instead she had been treated as a second-class province, her people as slaves, her resources as plunder for the rest of the Dominion. Deprived, by federal control, of her legitimate revenues from her public lands and prevented from building needed railways, the impoverished province could not meet the meagre basic requirements of her people.[8]

With their rhetoric Greenway and Sifton touched a responsive chord in the population. Provincial rights agitation spread like a prairie fire. Angered by Norquay's open association with Tories despite his professed non-partisanship, Liberals believed that the provincial rights movement could become the vehicle to counter the already strong Conservative organization in the province. Frustrated railway promoters, farmers in need of railway facilities, discontented speculators, and other losers in the collapse of the railway boom hastened to join the protest. It was a motley organization, but, as the premier knew, it was dangerously effective.

Ever resourceful and devious, Norquay realized that he had to seize the initiative. In October, a Conservative convention was held which created a platform designed to outdo the provincial righters. It took vigorous stands on provincial control of public and school lands, further extension of the provincial boundaries, and restriction of the federal power of disallowance. Railways were to be supported as long as they did not conflict with the CPR monopoly.[9] The campaign quickly boiled down to a contest about which party could better protect provincial rights.

The fight in Brandon was a vicious one, which neither the Tories nor the CPR intended to lose. All pretence of non-partisanship was abandoned. Conservatives and Liberals, for example, had joined in establishing the *Brandon Sun* in January 1882. It had dutifully remained fairly neutral on provincial rights issues, even attacking both Norquay and Greenway for their "partyism."[10] Then the Conservatives decided that they needed a partisan paper, withdrew their support from the *Sun,* and announced that they would shortly establish the *Mail,* probably with the indirect aid of the CPR.[11] Liberals rushed to rescue the *Sun,* which promptly swung round to denounce both the dominion government and the "imbeciles" in Winnipeg on the disallowance issue.[12]

At the same time the Tories established a constituency organization with Mayor Thomas Mayne Daly as president and selected J.E. Woodworth to run as a straight supporter of Norquay and Macdonald. A wealthy Mason, hotel owner, land dealer, and brickmaker, Woodworth was able to claim to be the best candidate to defend provincial rights as a friend of both governments.[13] Only months earlier Woodworth had been supported by John Sifton against Daly in the mayoralty contest.[14] Now he harshly accused Sifton of treasonably abandoning his 1881 promise to support Norquay. And the *Mail* wasted no time in reminding its readers of all the public investigations into Sifton's contracts, condemning him by inference rather than with specific allegations of wrongdoing.[15]

John Sifton faced opponents who were well organized, well financed, and not chary of near-libellous accusations. The provincial rights men worked with a will, but they had a weak organization and were probably over-confident. Certainly some, like young Clifford Sifton, were inexperienced. He spoke on behalf of his father at several public meetings, which were essentially platform debates and harangues between opposing sides. That he had yet to master the techniques of swaying audiences was immediately obvious. Even the *Sun* admitted that a meeting at Carberry had been a Tory victory, while the gleeful *Mail* ridiculed young Sifton's "lame and impotent" attempts "to bamboozle and bulldoze the intelligent electors."[16] The twenty-one-year-old lawyer, as the press made clear, had not made the transition from debates in the literary clubs and among law students at which he excelled. But he was an apt pupil; never again would the Tories be able to dismiss him so sneeringly.

Even so, the potency of the provincial rights cry still could partially compensate for other weaknesses. The Conservative organizers admitted difficulty in countering "the insane ideas Sifton Greenway et al thro their organs have been trying to instil into the people."[17] But they succeeded. The Norquay ministry was returned on 23 January with about twenty supporters, including some independents, and a popular vote of nearly 53 per cent, to around ten seats for Liberals and provincial righters.[18]

In Brandon John Sifton suffered a convincing defeat. The Liberals admitted to having been "out-generalled." They made the usual losers' claims of manipulated voting lists, impersonation and perjury at the polls, and a turnout of rural voters too small to offset CPR machinations in Brandon city. Indeed, the CPR was perceived as the principal cause of the Liberal defeat in Brandon and throughout the province as it struggled to keep the opponents of monopoly from the citadels of power. Conservative organizers allegedly were able to drive men "in droves" to the polls from the railway offices and yards, "men whom no one knew but those in charge of them, and who were never suspected of being voters until they presented themselves at the polling places." This was but the first example of the enormous power "the Syndicate can and will exercise in the Government of this province." These potentates of the CPR, gloomily predicted the *Brandon Sun,* would cling to their monopoly and "squeeze the cities and towns along the line into complete subjection. This province is not only to be at their mercy commercially but politically."[19]

It had been but the first flexing of the CPR's political muscle. The railway company was an enemy, acting in concert with its political supporters at Winnipeg and Ottawa to subvert the will of the people. Or so thought many Liberals. Some, like Clifford Sifton, calmly filed the experience away. In the meantime, there were some consolations for the defeated. The Norquay government's veneer of non-partisan politics had been ripped asunder and its essential Toryism exposed. An issue had arisen which had begun to polarize provincial politics on altogether new lines. And Norquay had been forced to champion a version of provincial rights in order to offset the anti-disallowance agitation. It remained to be seen what part of his platform he would—or could—deliver.


By the time of the election Manitoba was slipping steadily into a depression. Business for a young lawyer hoping to establish a practice was annoyingly slow; indeed, for long periods there was no work at all. Clifford Sifton once reminisced that his earnings that year were but $428, "and I lived on it too."[20] His spare time he gave over to assorted political interests and voracious reading in British, American, and Canadian history, law, and politics.

The staple diet of most western lawyers was land and homestead law. Sifton recalled some years later that he had begun to practise law "as little more than a boy ... in a town where the whole country surrounding was filled with homesteads newly taken up. The various difficulties and questions in connection with the homestead law and the trials and troubles of the settlers were matters of everyday talk, and discussion, by the legal men of the town."[21] Gradually Clifford and Arthur developed reputations for solid competence, and their clientele expanded accordingly.

Clifford also found time to court Elizabeth Armanella Burrows, whom he married in a small family ceremony in Winnipeg on 13 August 1884. She was the granddaughter of John Burrows, an English civil engineer who had served on the staff of Colonel By during construction of the Rideau Canal and who had been one of the first settlers in Ottawa.[22] Her brother, Theodore Arthur Burrows, had for some years been engaged in the lumber business at Selkirk and had probably met Clifford through the temperance organization in which they were both active. Arma, as she was known to the family, was charming and lively. Her engaging and outgoing personality was in marked contrast to the severe and often forbidding character of her husband. If she did not fully share his intellectual gifts, she was sensitive to his needs and a strong bond of affection grew between them.

Although a faithful member of his church, Clifford never sought prominence in it. An irreverent wag once suggested that, in light of Clifford's later wealth, it was appropriate that he and Arthur should have started out by taking up the collection. Actually, Clifford took his religion very seriously and daily family worship was part of the routine of his private life.[23] He also served from time to time as a lay preacher. In this capacity he would not have offered passionate evangelical calls to repentance and salvation. The function of the church, in his opinion, was to instil in society a common set of moral values, which he and many of his fellow Methodists believed to be the very underpinning of British and American civilization. Beyond his church, Clifford was active in few organizations, including temperance societies, which were not political in nature.

His financial resources cannot have been as restricted as his first year's income from his law practice suggests. In April 1883, he purchased a 480-acre farm for $6,000, probably as a speculation.[24] He was certainly involved in other land dealings and advertised that he had money available to lend for school debentures and mortgages. Either he had obtained money from his father or brother, or he too had managed to profit during the railway boom.

He also invested $1,000 in stock of the Brandon Sun Printing and Publishing Company in the spring of 1883. His father held $2,000 of the stock; and other Liberal shareholders included A.C. Fraser, A.M. Peterson, James A. Smart, and *Sun* editor W.J. White.[25] Clifford's interest was more than financial: the *Mail* once claimed that he wrote half the editorial columns of the *Sun*, and A.M. Peterson the other half.[26] Even allowing for natural exaggeration, Sifton did make significant contributions, and for some years the paper was widely regarded as his organ.

Arthur, in the meantime, was growing restless again. He had managed to settle down and pass his barrister's examinations, though not those for attorney, in the spring of 1883. In June he became a full-fledged partner in his younger brother's firm,[27] and in August his first child, a daughter, was born. He continued to serve in civic politics, on the school board, and in the Reform Association, as well as in the Brandon Agricultural Society and the Literary Society. In 1884 he even considered running for mayor of Brandon, but he did not have the requisite backing. A year later, for unexplained reasons, he resolved to move to Prince Albert, dissolving the partnership of Sifton & Sifton.

John Sifton continued his labours in the cause of temperance, which had fallen on hard days. From the beginning of the railway boom, it had been widely acknowledged that drunkenness was a serious social problem in Brandon and the surrounding area.[28] If, as he stated at a temperance rally, many people had moved to Brandon and western Manitoba "to get away from liquor," such conditions must have been demoralizing. The Brandon lodge of the Independent Order of Good Templars, John Sifton informed the brethren in Winnipeg, required encouragement and prayer. It was defensive in character and frankly needed an injection of the aggressiveness of the Winnipeggers.[29] Yet even in the provincial capital the movement's zeal was flagging; Sifton had to postpone a meeting of the Dominion Alliance owing to lack of interest. He was now trying to trim the sails of the movement to permit co-operation with moderates to obtain sufficient support to curb the worst abuses of alcohol.[30] To provide an alternative for social drinkers, he also sought to establish a coffee-house movement.[31]

J.W. Sifton was a leader among those seeking structural changes in the Methodist church. He first pushed for a separate Manitoba and North-West Conference of the Wesleyan Methodists. The Toronto Conference, which then included the West, was not thought to be sufficiently responsive to the region's changing needs. This step was accomplished in 1882.[32] Next he gave strong support to the movement for union of the five branches of the Methodist church in Canada, finally realized in 1884.[33] As a lay delegate to most of the regional and national Methodist conventions in the early 1880's he constantly reminded his co-religionists of the golden promise of the West and of the vast field open for missionary endeavour.

His vision of the great future of the West was voiced with conviction. He believed particularly in the possibilities of the rich prairie lands. He threw his energies wholeheartedly into his farm and committed most of his savings to make it a great success. Under his supervision some 600 acres were put in crop in 1883, 350 in wheat, and the rest in oats, barley, flax, and assorted field and root crops. He had built a large stable and granary, had another under construction, and anticipated employing ten men and eight teams of horses. His farm was to be as highly mechanized as was then possible, with a large array of binders, plows, breakers, seeders, mowers, and harrows. In 1884, with over 700 acres in crop, he was regarded as "the largest agricultural 'operator' in Western Manitoba."[34] If dedication, optimism, and substantial amounts of capital could make a success of farming, John Sifton intended to do it.

A severe frost on 20 September 1883 precipitated the next political crisis. Feeling amongst the farmers was already running high in face of the unrealistically high freight rates announced in January by the CPR. By the end of the summer, it was clear that the crop would be disappointingly small. The frost was the final blow, ruining thousands and driving them from their farms and throwing thousands of others even more deeply into debt.

The simmering discontent in the province was made to order for aspiring Liberal politicians. The issues raised in the provincial rights and anti-disallowance agitation had not vanished. Following the January election, Premier Norquay had abandoned his belligerent attitude toward Ottawa and began to tread lightly as he sought financial concessions from the Macdonald government. Unfortunately, his gamble that a policy of moderation could succeed had been undermined by events beyond his control. In a fighting mood the farmers of western Manitoba gathered at Brandon on 20 November to form the Manitoba and North West Farmers' Union. The Tories complained, with some justice, that the meeting had been called by "political wire-pullers"—the Liberals—but the Union became the first effective farmers' organization in the West.[35]

The litany of grievances had a familiar ring. The farmers denounced the protective tariff; they sought the right to charter provincial railways freely and provincial ownership of public lands. They believed that competition would bring lower freight rates; they denounced the elevator monopoly and demanded a railway to Hudson Bay. Most of the delegates were "relatively successful farmers," who hoped that the Union would be the means to secure and improve their positions.[36]

They were not, however, generally successful politicians. At Brandon, and at a provincial convention at Winnipeg on 19 December, it became apparent that Liberal politicians, rather than farmers, had manoeuvered themselves into positions of power, which resulted in the eventual resignations of some Conservatives who had helped to give the movement an initial bi-partisan flavour.[37] Among the Liberal manipulators were John, Arthur, and Clifford Sifton. John Sifton, of course, was a leading farmer. Arthur, also engaged in farming, had been a principal organizer, and was elected to the Union council. Early in December Clifford attracted attention when he addressed a farmers' protest meeting in Brandon. He charged the CPR with setting extortionate freight rates and declared that competition would reduce rates by eight cents per bushel, or 25 to 30 per cent. The western United States was progressing much more quickly than the Canadian prairies, had lower freight rates, and there the railways followed rather than preceded settlement. By comparison, in Canada—as the farmers well knew—the CPR was rushing to complete its main line in unsettled regions while the needs of established districts were being overlooked. He contended that "if this country had been thrown open to the Americans a few years ago, we would have had more railways."[38] Evidently his continentalist sentiments pleased his audience, for he was promptly elected as a delegate to the Winnipeg convention.

The Union appeared likely to be short-lived. Liberal efforts to use the movement for partisan purposes led to enervating internal conflicts on secondary issues. Then at Winnipeg in March 1884 the passage of a resolution opposing continuing encouragement of immigration under existing conditions in the West further shredded the fragile fabric of unity and left the Union open to charges of near treason. And in his chameleon response to political pressures, Norquay again seized the initiative. He told John A. Macdonald that the agitation was so serious that a request might arise for secession from Confederation.[39] To counter it, he rushed a provincial bill of rights through the legislature, demanding many of the points in the farmers' platform.[40]

At the same time, however, another organization, the Manitoba and North-West Farmers' Co-operative and Protective Union, was gathering strength. It was more oriented toward the needs of the farming community and to action rather than agitation. It advocated such radical measures as the co-operative marketing of grain. The success of a small marketing endeavour late in 1883 lent it some credibility. In June 1884 it merged with the weakening Farmers' Union, and Clifford Sifton became a director of the new organization. Many structural difficulties would contribute to the ultimate failure of both the co-operative schemes and the new Union.[41] There was a substantial internal struggle going on because many of the farm leaders saw their salvation in co-operative marketing and purchasing and in collective measures against the monopoly interests, while Sifton and several of his associates believed that the Union should remain "an organ for the agitation of political and social questions." The farmers, he thought, had no idea of how to carry out large-scale business ventures, and the Union was incapable as constituted of maintaining the kind of permanent staff required. "The grain buying idea," he argued, "was initiated and carried out by a few [in the executive], and was not entertained by the Union [membership] at large."[42] Nevertheless, the Union went its own way, failed in its co-operative efforts in 1884 and 1885, even found some of its own agents making highly suspect deals with the CPR, and was virtually defunct by 1886.

During Sifton's tenure as a director an episode occurred whose importance became apparent only some years later. The executive decided to approach A.M. Burgess, deputy minister of the interior, who was touring the West in July 1884. They wished to outline the farmers' grievances, particularly with respect to the administration of public lands. In a written submission they decried the frequent changes in the law, "conflicting constructions of the same by different officials, and the apparently arbitrary exercise of discretionary authority," and suggested a number of reforms. Sifton and Dr. Alexander Fleming, president of the Union and a Brandon druggist, physician, and farmer, were granted an audience with Burgess on 15 July. From 9:15 A.M. until 4:00 P.M. they were kept cooling their heels. When at last they were ushered in, they found Burgess surrounded by local Tory officials and lackeys, evidently well briefed on the political sins of his supplicants and decidedly irritated at this intrusion upon his time. Burgess grumpily suggested that Sifton and Fleming were acting for speculators, not genuine settlers, and that they were probably troubling him for their own personal and political ends. He informed them "in language forcible, if not courteous, that he knew twice as much about the country and the effect of the law as they did."

Compounding the insult, in his annual report Burgess gave a distorted account of the meeting and dismissed Sifton and Fleming's submission as of little significance. Outraged, the young lawyer lost no time in setting the record straight in a lengthy effusion to the editor of the *Brandon Sun*. Their memorial, he asserted, was a "just true and correct" representation of the situation. "Many of us knew only too well the disastrous effect which the Government policy had upon the country. No one has escaped its paralysing influence." Yet there was a measure of triumph in his observation that "notwithstanding the alleged impropriety of our remarks, the department has profited by our recommendations and to some extent has adopted the course which we directed."[43]

Sifton would have his revenge. Unhappily for Burgess, the man whom he had chosen to dismiss with contempt would one day be his political superior. And twelve years scarcely softened the memory of their first meeting.

By early 1885 Manitoba Liberals recognized that continued identification with the Farmers' Union would lead to a dead end. It had served its purpose.

Leading Liberals, particularly Thomas Greenway, had become household names in rural Manitoba through their advocacy of the farmers' cause. If the agitation had not made all the farmers good Liberals, it had severely shaken the traditional support of Macdonald and Norquay. A viable alternative party would receive a sympathetic hearing.

In February the Liberals in Winnipeg created a permanent organization with two prominent lawyers, James Fisher and F.C. Wade, as president and secretary. A month later the Brandon Liberals created a Reform Association with Mayor James Smart as president and Clifford Sifton as first vice-president. At that meeting there was some support for avoiding "the eastern name" and creating a decisively "Manitoba first" party. While Sifton and Smart successfully fought for the name "Liberal," it was an early indication of westerners' suspicion of the traditional parties as a solution to their problems.[44]

Local organizations having been established, a provincial convention was called to meet at Winnipeg on 31 March and 1 April. Unhappily, the rout of the North-West Mounted Police by the métis at Duck Lake on 26 March upstaged the Liberals' carefully planned publicity campaign. "War news" of the second Riel rebellion filled the newspapers, and the Liberal meetings were relegated to a few columns on the back pages. The delegates established "The Association of Manitoba Liberals" along the lines of Liberal organization in Ontario. Thomas Greenway was elected party leader, and a provincial executive, all from Winnipeg, was established, with James Fisher as president, W.F. Luxton and Captain D.H. McMillan as vice-presidents, J.D. Cameron as secretary, and A.A. McArthur as treasurer. In addition, the presidents of local branches, members and ex-members of the legislature and House of Commons were vice-presidents of the association. The executive committee consisted of all the above, and the first vice-presidents and secretaries of the local associations.[45] This, of course, meant that both John and Clifford Sifton would be members of the executive committee.

The Siftons' role at the convention was minor. Clifford moved a resolution endorsing the provincial bill of rights adopted a year earlier. And John moved a resolution denouncing the latest terms—a so-called final settlement—dictated to Premier Norquay by the Macdonald government. In return for a substantial increase in the subsidy and compensation for crown lands, the premier had agreed to abandon both the claim to provincial ownership of the lands and any challenge to the CPR monopoly.[46] This, the Liberals believed, gave them a major election issue.

Strenuous efforts were made to create local Liberal organizations across the province, and early in June 1886 another convention was held in Winnipeg as the great send-off to an anticipated election campaign. The platform adopted stated categorically in its first plank, "It is of the very essence of Confederation to give to the people of each Province, through their own

Legislature, full control of their own affairs." Once again the Liberals adopted a provincial rights platform, but with several important additions. They advocated representation by population and manhood suffrage; an improved form of municipal government; a land drainage scheme; effective promotion of immigration and colonization; economy in government and application of provincial revenues to reduce local school, municipal, and other property taxes; and, of course, they denounced the National Policy tariff. A meeting of Young Liberals had anticipated much of the platform, but in addition it called for better legislation to ensure the proper payment of working men and discontinuance of the use of the French language in printing government documents.[47]

Patched over in public, but ominous for the future, was a division in the party between the Winnipeg-based executive and the party leader, and, more broadly, between the aspirations of urban Winnipeg and rural Manitoba. Few Winnipeggers seemed to have any inherent sympathy for the plight of the farmer; if they demanded the provincial power to charter railways freely, it was often because there were among them several disappointed would-be promoters or because they assumed that more railways centred on Winnipeg would enhance the power of the metropolis. Fairly or otherwise, many farmers and citizens of smaller centres were convinced that Winnipeg could become as much an enemy of their interests as Ottawa or the CPR.

Evidence of these conflicts had been mounting for some time. In the summer of 1885 the CPR and the St. Paul, Minneapolis and Manitoba Railway concluded a pooling arrangement to prevent competition and maintain high freight rates. The CPR then responded to the pressure of Winnipeg merchants and structured its rates to centralize all western traffic in Winnipeg. The federal government decided to give the Winnipeg Board of Trade the right to determine grain standards for all western wheat, thus ensuring Winnipeg's dominance. Winnipeg businessmen had strenuously opposed attempts by the Farmers' Union to purchase goods such as binder twine co-operatively, to sell grain co-operatively, and to break the Ogilvie elevator monopoly. Finally, there were justifiable suspicions that the Winnipeg press was stacked against a fair expression of the concerns of rural Manitoba. Naturally Winnipeg papers would push the interests of the capital. But several had also been apologists of the Macdonald and Norquay governments and of the CPR. Even the *Manitoba Free Press,* that supposed pillar of Liberalism and the most important of Winnipeg papers, may have been to some extent under the influence of the CPR from the inception of the syndicate; certainly it often treated the CPR with extraordinary caution.[48] Only the feeble Winnipeg *Sun* unreservedly supported the Liberal cause and rural concerns.

It was hardly surprising, then, that the rural delegates to the convention put up a strong fight to retain Greenway as leader despite a carefully planned coup by the Winnipeg executive to replace him with Fisher. The Winnipeg clique had to concede or they would have destroyed even the semblance of unity. Greenway was not a strong leader, but he was a farmer from southern Manitoba, and his victory was more than symbolic. One of the leaders in shaping the anti-Winnipeg sentiment had been Clifford Sifton, who months before the convention had been calling the attention of the people of Brandon to the fact that all railway construction then going on in the province was centred on the capital. Why, he demanded, should Brandon not be getting a piece of the action?[49]

By the time Premier Norquay called the election he had very nearly lost control of the province. It was no longer possible to pretend that his government could outbid the Liberals on provincial rights. His final settlement with Ottawa in 1885 was branded a sellout, and his pleas that there had been little alternative hardly satisfied the militants. The premier was also guilty in the eyes of prohibitionists for not rigorously enforcing existing legislation.

No quarter was asked as the battling campaigners crisscrossed the snow and windswept landscape in late November and early December in open buggies and sleighs, cajoling, pleading with, and sometimes bribing settlers and labourers. Disallowance naturally dominated the battle, but an old and dangerous issue was also revived. Once again the official status of the French language came under attack, led by one of Greenway's most volatile lieutenants, Joseph Martin of Portage la Prairie. And whispers began about French domination in the Norquay cabinet. It took little to goad A.A.C. LaRivière, Norquay's French lieutenant, into angrily calling upon French voters to unite behind the premier, who was said to sympathize with their position. In turn, this further stimulated anti-French sentiment among the Liberals.[50]

The prospects for the Liberals in Brandon appeared very good. The constitutency of 1883 had now been divided in two: Brandon East, which included the city; and Brandon West, which comprised four rural municipalities. The Brandon Tories were divided, and the *Mail* had taken to attacking Norquay while continuing to support Macdonald in Ottawa. To counter this desertion, the friends of the Manitoba government established the Brandon *Times*. In Brandon East the Liberals nominated the popular mayor, James Smart, a prominent hardware merchant and Baptist layman. In Brandon West "the old war horse" John W. Sifton was nominated, after Clifford had been nominated and had withdrawn.[51] Opposing J.W. Sifton in Brandon West was J.N. Kirchhoffer, an immigrant English farmer and entrepreneur from Plum Creek, who drew the ire of the Liberals when he observed that he expected to receive the vote of the "old country gentlemen, all of whom are Conservatives: only navvies and laborers are Grits."[52]

The Tories again pulled out all the stops. Prime Minister Macdonald gave what amounted to a series of election speeches for Norquay as he crossed the province during his transcontinental tour of the summer. And as a pointed answer to charges of CPR neglect of the district, W.C. Van Horne arrived, associated himself ostentatiously with Kirchhoffer, and announced immediate plans to build branch lines.[53]

Clifford Sifton was rapidly growing in stature as a political performer. After a summer of serious illness, he threw himself into both his father's and Smart's campaigns. He denounced the Norquay régime for giving up the provincial right to build railways which would be competitive with the CPR and for centralizing railways in Winnipeg to Brandon's detriment. And he earned rousing cheers when his seasoned opponent, T.M. Daly, had the temerity to claim at a meeting that John Sifton had been elected in 1881 only by importing thirty votes from Winnipeg. Where was Daly's proof, roared Clifford Sifton as he leapt to his feet, eyes blazing. Produce it, or retract the statement! Flushed and astonished at the vehemence of the counterattack, Daly retreated.[54]

The elections of 9 December, the first in Manitoba to use the secret ballot, narrowly returned the Norquay government, with 18 seats and 49.7 per cent of the popular vote. The Liberals took 15 seats and 48.5 per cent of the vote; and two independents were returned. But once again John Sifton went down to disappointing defeat, with 484 votes to 498 for Kirchhoffer.[55] It proved to be his last political battle. He had had only two victories in one federal and five provincial campaigns in Manitoba, and even so he had served but two sessions in the legislature. He now had neither the means, nor strength, nor perhaps the will to battle again.

Clifford Sifton had little time for despondency, for on 7 November he and Arma had become the parents of a son, christened John Wright, junior. The new year, 1887, would be the most peaceful he would know for many years, punctuated mainly by the baby's cries.

For John Wright, senior, however, it was a time of difficult decision. As if to compound his electoral defeat, he and Kate were struck down with typhoid fever early in the new year. During the slow recovery he contemplated the decline of his political and personal fortunes. The farm had not been a success. The bad spring and early frost of 1883 had been followed by low prices for grain in 1884, another early frost in 1885, and drought and another fall in prices in 1886. He certainly had lost a good deal of his capital, and he was forced to leave his farm to his creditors. Hoping to recoup his fortunes and his health, John Sifton obtained a railway contract in Missouri, where he went in the late spring; later, he and Kate moved to Pasadena and Riverside, California. Twelve years of endeavour in Manitoba had produced so little, and so much had slipped through his grasp.[56]

As fate would have it, John Sifton left the province as Liberal fortunes were again on the rise. Disaster, aided by an unsympathetic Conservative government in Ottawa, was rapidly overtaking the hapless Norquay ministry. Lurching from crisis to crisis, the premier was being quickly boxed in by popular demand for railway competition, on the one hand, and by the intransigence of the prime minister and the CPR, on the other. The premier had to dissociate himself irrevocably from the Macdonald government and pose a direct challenge to Ottawa's disallowance policy if he was to salvage his position. So Norquay, hitherto one of the perpetual beggars in the dominion soup kitchen, attended the premiers' conference called by Premier Mercier of Québec, which roundly denounced the centralizing policies of the prime minister. He also decided to attempt to build a railway to the American border which, it was hoped, would provide competition despite any legal or constitutional roadblocks which Ottawa might choose to erect.

Begun in the summer, the Red River Valley Railway was intended to provide an immediate link between Winnipeg and the United States. It was to be government-built and open to the traffic of any railway that wished to use it. The province was by now a unit on the subject of disallowance, and even the Conservative members of Parliament from Manitoba had been obliged to take the anti-disallowance pledge. But Macdonald, furious at Norquay's reneging on his promises and his inability to keep his province "in line," vowed that both the premier and the railway must be destroyed. He and the CPR used every available means to prevent the province from borrowing the necessary capital in foreign markets, and Macdonald was even accused of perjuring himself concerning agreements made with Manitoba officials.

In one of his objects he was successful: Norquay was hounded out of office, broken and bitter, by the end of 1887. His successor, Dr. D.H. Harrison, attempted to form a new Conservative administration, but resigned when he lost two ministerial by-elections in January 1888. The lieutenant-governor had no alternative but to call on Thomas Greenway to form a Liberal administration. Macdonald's manoeuverings had simply helped to bring to power a party which made a virtue of attacking the dominion government and gloried in the prospect of a battle on disallowance.

The new government was as determined as its predecessor to complete the RRVR. In the spring of 1888 the CPR and the federal Conservatives concluded they could not win by direct challenge and agreed not to oppose the new line. A triumphant Premier Greenway with Attorney General and Railway Commissioner Joseph Martin returned from Ottawa to Winnipeg and prepared for an election.[57] Some of their party promises were introduced —manhood suffrage, redistribution of seats, and financial reforms—and the election was called for 11 July.

The jubilant Liberals of Brandon were off and running early. They now had three seats to prepare for: Brandon City, in which James Smart, now minister of public works, was to run; and Brandon North and Brandon South, both essentially rural. On 7 May the Young Liberals and the Liberal Association of Brandon were amalgamated, Clifford Sifton becoming president of the new organization. And on 17 May he was nominated for Brandon North. By then his organization had already canvassed every township in the constituency. Sifton "is a young man," noted the *Brandon Sun,* "but there is no one in the province better posted upon its political affairs. He is a fine speaker...and will be a credit to his position."[58]

By the end of May, still without an announced Conservative opponent, Sifton published a rather curious electoral address. It roundly denounced the Norquay government; but it offered cool support to Greenway's, approving its accomplishments since coming to office, yet claiming to be opposed to "partyism in Local affairs." Governments, he believed, should be assessed "from a business standpoint" and whether their policies made for "material, moral and social prosperity."[59] Evidently Sifton laid stress on his independence because there was still a strong non-partisan sentiment. But he must have assumed a remarkable credulity in the rural electorate, most of whom ought to have been aware of his public commitment to the Liberal cause since 1882.

The youthful campaigner found that he revelled in political combat. His own vigorous efforts and confidence greatly encouraged his organization. He was fortunate too in his opponent, W.A. Macdonald, also a popular young Brandon lawyer. Macdonald's considerable ability prevented the Liberals from being overconfident, and his frank dissociation from the Norquay government forced Sifton to dwell on more than the iniquities of that régime. On the stump the two lawyers were fairly evenly matched, and their slashing debates proved to be great public entertainment.

But the Liberals were riding the crest of the wave of popularity. They took 57.8 per cent of the popular vote and 31 of the 38 seats in the legislature, including the three Brandons. In Brandon North Sifton's victory margin of 335 to 293 was very close to what he had predicted in May. An exultant torchlight victory parade for the triumphant Liberals was organized on election night. Sifton was in brilliant form as he addressed the crowd to repeated ovations.

As he spoke, however, he might have remembered his absent father and considered how John Sifton would have savoured that moment. Clifford owed much to his father, but he had earned his victory. Would the future fulfil the great promise and reveal the full potential of this young politician? The editor of the *Brandon Sun* thought so. "The Government," he predicted, "has in the election of Mr. Clifford Sifton...an acquisition that will prove more valuable than they at present can have any idea of."[60]

# 3

# "Quite an Addition to the House"
# (1888–91)

Political vultures commonly close in on a leader wounded and defeated in battle. The victor, in contrast, usually has time to savour his triumph. In the muddle of Manitoba politics in 1888, however, precisely the reverse occurred. The Conservative rump restored John Norquay to the leadership of the provincial party in an apparent repudiation of the "pro-Macdonald" forces. And the embers of the government's victory fires had scarcely died down before Liberals were hatching a plot to secure Greenway's head. The conspirators sought to involve Clifford Sifton, who spurned the offer of a portfolio in a reconstituted ministry and rallied to the support of his leader.

The crisis demonstrated that Manitoba political parties were still in a state of flux despite the existence of partisan organizations in local politics for more than a decade. Pressure from Ottawa had helped to force Norquay into a nominal conservatism, but he had never led a wholly united party. His government had cracked under the tension of the provincial-rights and anti-disallowance issues, which resulted in open feuding between "pro-Norquay" and "pro-Macdonald" Conservatives. Similarly, Greenway headed a party that had united essentially on one issue: to provide for construction of railways competitive with the CPR, by defeating Norquay and ending disallowance. Other planks had been in the platform, but this was the one issue which had temporarily papered over the lack of party loyalty among the various factions. Having taken power and ended disallowance, the party could find no unanimity on the best way to establish railway competition.

Premier Greenway himself was a curious man. A former Conservative from Ontario, he liked to pose as "the farmer Premier" from Crystal City, a representative of the predominantly rural class in the province. He had a certain plodding dullness in his public personality which carried the ring of authenticity to his fellow farmers, who had learned to be suspicious of the motives of city lawyers and entrepreneurs. He believed in competent, economical administration; he did not seek to be either moral crusader or social reformer. Greenway was an intelligent, ambitious politician, although he had a side to him that was devious, indeed unscrupulous.[1] He could also be indecisive, even downright obtuse, when confronting difficult problems and certainly lacked firmness in dealing with some of his colleagues. At fifty, he was by a wide margin the oldest and most politically experienced of his cabinet, selecting for himself the agriculture and immigration portfolio.

Of his colleagues, the most celebrated and the most difficult was Joseph Martin, aged thirty-six, the attorney general and railway commissioner. Violent, mercurial, erratic, and ferociously energetic, Martin was a rabble-rousing populist. He had earned considerable notoriety in opposition when he had advocated unconstitutional actions if necessary to secure Manitoba's "rights" and pushing provincial railway construction by force if nothing else could accomplish it. His contempt for Greenway was monumental, and he took few pains to hide his ambitions to occupy the premier's chair.

Lyman M. Jones, former mayor of Winnipeg, became provincial treasurer. He had been appointed to appease the Winnipeg business community. The forty-five-year-old Jones was a representative of the Harris farm implement company, believed in rural Manitoba to be one of the parasitic beneficiaries of the National Policy protective tariff. More respected in rural districts was the minister of public works, James Smart, the thirty-year-old former mayor of Brandon. He proved to be a capable administrator and was judged by a leading Conservative to be "a man of integrity & worth & of great personal character."[2] Of an age with Smart was provincial secretary James E.P. Prendergast, an able lawyer who represented the French constituencies. He was not wholly trusted by the Liberals because he had formerly supported Norquay.

Greenway and Martin took charge of the government's railway policy, and they lost no time in trying to consolidate various railway interests behind them. One group of promoters, including Liberal MLA Rodmond P. Roblin, had seen their Manitoba Central Railway charter disallowed in 1887. Greenway agreed to restore it. More important, if he did not actually promise that they could build the Red River Valley Railway, he certainly promised them running rights over it when completed. Then he moved to pacify the Hudson Bay Railway interests with a small grant of money and vague promises of running rights on the RRVR as well.[3] "Free trade in railways" had become a Liberal slogan, and at the time this was translated into running rights on the RRVR and government charters for all who desired them. Thus, Manitobans envisaged at least two Canadian and one or more American lines competing on the Red River line for prairie traffic, entering into a cutthroat battle over freight rates and forcing the CPR into drastic reductions in order to survive.

It was an impossible dream, as Greenway and Martin quickly discovered. Neither of the Canadian lines had an American connection, which was obviously essential if competition were to result. Only two American lines qualified. One was the St. Paul, Minneapolis and Manitoba line, controlled by James J. Hill. But because it had been closely associated with the CPR in the past and still was in the public mind, it was unlikely to provide the independence and competition required. The alternative was the Northern Pacific, which found little inherently attractive in the Canadian prairie market. The NPR only showed interest because it was competing with the CPR for the traffic of Puget Sound, and a line in Manitoba which could be used to undercut CPR prairie traffic would be a useful lever for forcing the Canadian company to be reasonable on the west coast. Even so, the NPR had no desire to enter into a suicidal rate war with the CPR which neither company could afford.

Forced to deal with the Northern Pacific, the provincial negotiators found little room to manoeuvre. A new company, the Northern Pacific and Manitoba, was to be chartered to complete the RRVR and branch lines to Portage la Prairie and Brandon. It would then negotiate a running rights agreement with the NPR, which otherwise assumed no financial obligations. The NPR naturally refused to countenance competition from other railways on its lines. The agreement did have one saving virtue from the Manitoba point of view. That was the all-important reduction in rates, disappointingly small in face of the wild estimates of the Liberals when in opposition, but significant nevertheless. The NPR agreed to a rate of twenty-one cents per hundredweight to ship wheat from Portage la Prairie or Winnipeg to Duluth, and twenty-two cents from Brandon, three cents less than the prevailing rates of the CPR, which was forced to meet them. In general, freight rates were reduced between 10 and 13 per cent. The Northern Pacific also agreed that its rate schedules should be approved by the provincial cabinet before becoming effective.[4]

A major political storm broke with the announcement of the terms of the contract. A group of friends of the Hudson Bay Railway interests, including promoter Hugh Sutherland, Liberal lawyer and politician James Fisher, and D.J. Beaton and Alexander Macdonald of the *Manitoba Free Press,* attempted to induce Clifford Sifton to join in a revolt against Greenway. Beaton, whom Sifton had known in Brandon, wrote a letter probably offering the attorney-generalship as part of a scheme which apparently was to make Fisher premier and defeat the contract. Sifton promptly killed whatever chance of success the plot had by informing Greenway, who was able to use the intelligence to rally his troops.[5]

After a long and stormy caucus session, most of the Liberal members reluctantly agreed with the premier that the contract was the best that could be secured, even if it fell far below expectations. At a special session called at the end of August to ratify the agreement, Clifford Sifton emerged as the ablest defender, outside of the cabinet, of the government's policy. When he moved the address in reply to the Speech from the Throne on 28 August, he had in mind demands of the *Free Press* for government construction and operation of the Red River line, with running rights for all. There was no evidence, he said, that government operation would produce lower freight rates, particularly given the limitations of the line: "Experience had . . . shown that rates could only be permanently lowered by free, untrammeled competition of private capital against private capital and business interests against business interests." Competition would force the CPR to expand its operations and branch line services. Sifton particularly welcomed the NP & M branch from Morris to Brandon, which would enable western Manitoba to bypass Winnipeg and break the capital's monopoly. He even looked forward to eventual co-operation between the NP & M railway and the Great North-West Central Railway, which had a charter to build beyond Brandon.[6] The prospect of reduced freight rates and a genuine alternative route for shipping grain made the arrangement popular in western Manitoba. "People here are well satisfied with the Railway legislation," reported Sifton upon returning to Brandon, "as indeed they should be."[7]

During the brief first session of the seventh Manitoba legislature Clifford Sifton had created a sensation as the rising young man of the party. "He has a capital flow of language," commented one observer, "is dignified and patriotic in his utterance and rounds up his sentences in good form. In oratory he is quite an addition to the house." Yet another young newsman, John W. Dafoe, later recalled "the orderly sequence of the arguments; the clearness and moderation with which they were expressed; the absence of surplus verbiage; the complete self-possession of the speaker."[8] He was a man set apart, and one who already had put the premier in his debt.

Meanwhile construction on the Northern Pacific and Manitoba line had proceeded apace. Attorney General Martin soon found a way to keep the cauldron of provincial rights and anti-monopoly sentiment at a continuous boil. The NP & M branch line to Portage la Prairie had to cross the CPR main line southwest of Winnipeg, at a location derisively called Fort Whyte after the unfortunate William Whyte, who was in charge of the prairie region of the CPR. The theatrical Martin, who also conveniently happened to be provincial railway commissioner and a director of the NP & M, had evidently decided to try to humiliate the CPR by forcing a crossing without the usual legal formalities. The CPR certainly seemed vulnerable to more public abuse. Both President Sir George Stephen and Vice-President William Van Horne, considered wizards in the world of finance and railways, had proven to be inept politicians in dealing with Manitoba. In 1887 their public threats of dire consequences to the province should the RRVR be completed had stiffened the resolve of the anti-disallowance forces. A year later Van Horne was determined that the irritating, contemptible provincial schemer would not be allowed to override the CPR without due process. Whyte was ordered to prevent the crossing.

Martin recruited a force of special police and a confrontation took place as the CPR ripped out crossings, derailed an engine on the right-of-way, and continuously ran a train back and forth over the proposed crossing point. Martin relished the role of a David taking on Goliath. He achieved only a cheap public victory. The Canadian Pacific had no serious intention of blocking the crossing permanently, but it did want Manitoba to observe the proprieties of making application to the Railway Committee of the dominion government. Martin denounced the ensuing delay, but if anything was the cause, it was his tactics. He had long been the most visible opponent of the CPR in the province, and during the fall of 1888, he made additional threats of retaliation against the company, including repeal of some of their provincial tax privileges and introduction of punitive taxes.

None of this amused Clifford Sifton. The attorney general's questionable methods irritated him. Martin's threatened legislation in particular would be a blow at the sacredness of contracts and would undermine business confidence in the province. "I presume these statements are entirely unauthorized," he told Greenway, "& I trust that the Govt. have no intention of carrying out such a programme." Pointless alienation of the CPR would do no good, and Martin's proposals went diametrically against Sifton's understanding of proper business procedures. He could not support such measures.[9]

Martin's worst threats were not carried out during the second session of the legislature, which began 8 November. Whether Sifton influenced government policy is uncertain, but he supported a compromise bill to permit the branch line of the NP & M to be constructed as a government work, if necessary, to overcome alleged CPR obstruction. The Canadian Pacific, he declared, had been "the enemy of the province," and the government would not allow it to drive out the Northern Pacific. But constitutional and legal means, not force, were the proper way to resolve the issue.[10] Thus early in his political life Sifton showed his independence and risked the ire of one of the most influential men in the party. The two men were of opposite temperaments: Martin was volcanic, dramatic, irascible; Sifton, systematic, calm, and calculating. The enmity which took root exacted a heavy toll from both men, and from the Manitoba Liberal party, for over a decade.

The railway issue subsided quickly from national importance. The local government could take some credit for the reduction in freight rates, the first extensive construction since the completion of the CPR main line, and the prospects for relief from monopoly. Unhappily, however, Martin had been drawn into what proved to be a long, rancorous series of libel suits and countersuits with the *Manitoba Free Press,* which had accused the government, and especially Martin, of all manner of corruption in connection with the railway contracts. Although few of the charges were ultimately substantiated, the confrontation tended to obscure other public issues and spattered a good deal of mud on the Greenway government. A complacent Prime Minister Macdonald sat back confident that Martin would soon destroy the government and force a realignment in local politics much more satisfactory to Ottawa. He was shortly to be disillusioned when Manitoba precipitated a crisis over education policy which had profound national implications.

It began comparatively innocently and almost ignored amidst the ravings of Martin and the *Free Press.* For years western Manitobans had complained about the system of financing education in the province, which they believed was weighted in favour of the older established districts and which in any case left too much to be raised by local direct taxation. Little account was taken of the problems of financing the construction of new schools or the costs of maintaining schools in sparsely settled districts. At first the provincial education grant had been equally divided between Protestant and Catholic schools. The disproportionate influx of Protestants forced a change, and after 1876 the grant was divided on a per pupil basis. This formula obviously favoured older areas with greater concentrations of children. Naturally the older districts—which tended to support Norquay—did not favour a change. It did not take much, furthermore, to reveal the anti-Catholic prejudices of many Protestants. They "knew" that Catholics bred like rabbits at the behest of the Church, a policy of deliberate aggrandizement for which the Protestants had to pay. All this led to considerable resentment in western Manitoba, which was underrepresented in the legislature, and gave rise to the demands for representation by population.

Representative of the sentiment was an attack in 1884 by the *Brandon Sun* on the "ten or a dozen constituencies—insignificant parishes—stretching along the Red River north & south of Winnipeg, with a total vote not greater than that of Brandon alone." These River constituencies were "unprogressive and not remarkably intelligent." The *Sun* made little attempt to veil its contempt for the mixed-blood population, whether French or English:

> The people of these parishes are not in sympathy with the rest of the province; they are a distinct class, depending less on agriculture, and with views and aspirations widely different from those of the rest of the population. Premier Norquay is himself one of that class; and although a

very able man, he cannot understand or enter into the spirit which animates the settlers in Western Manitoba. He is not with us because he is not of us.[11]

At least Brandonites could rest content that Greenway was "one of them." Revision of school financing was one of the planks in the 1886 Liberal platform. With a redistributed legislature recognizing the weight of western Manitoba, there was every expectation that a thorough revision would be carried out, ignoring the past privileges of the older districts. The railway legislation out of the way, the government turned its attention to education as early as the fall of 1888. During the 1889 session Martin announced that the government intended to introduce a consolidation of school legislation at the next session.[12]

The decision could not have come at a worse time. In the summer of 1888 the Québec legislature had passed a bill compensating the Jesuit Order and the Roman Catholic Church for lands taken over by the Crown, the division of money being determined by the pope. It was a matter within the powers, and of concern only to the province; but it was seen by many Protestants as an instance of French-Canadian effrontery and Catholic aggressiveness which had to be halted at all costs. The federal government, they urged, must disallow the legislation. The resulting storm of anti-French and anti-Catholic fury eventually spread from its epicentre in Ontario with decreasing power toward the two coasts. Agitation begun over a specific act broadened into a fearsome nativist attack on French language and culture, particularly under the aegis of the Equal Rights Association. The compact between cultures, if it had ever existed, had simply impeded progress. French culture and Roman Catholicism became the scapegoats for the widespread frustration that the country was not developing sufficiently quickly. Tens of thousands of Canadians were flocking each year to the United States, and Canadian cities were filling with slums. Instead of being wholly "British" and progressive, Canada was torn by internal conflict and held back by the French. Francophobia and anti-Catholicism, strengthened by jingoistic British imperialism and theories of Anglo-Saxon racial superiority, burst out of control early in 1889. A political crisis arose in Ontario over French expansion into the eastern counties and French-language instruction in the schools. The primary issue facing this country, trumpeted D'Alton McCarthy, the renegade Conservative whose great ability lent credibility to the ERA campaign, was whether this nation was to be British or French.[13]

Such sentiments were applauded by many Manitobans.[14] Despite a couple of fairly good crop years, the province was still developing slowly, and every year the tracks to the United States of hundreds of failed homesteaders attested to the difficulty of prairie farming. An enervating malaise hung heavily over the land; a new cause, a fresh sense of direction, was eagerly looked for. Rivalries of race and religion had existed in the province since before 1870. They had been at various times submerged, but not eradicated, and were beginning to reappear even before the Jesuits' Estates controversy reached the prairies.

In November 1888, for example, the Rev. George Bryce, a leading Presbyterian minister and educator, had expressed concern that the "children of foreigners" were failing to attend school. "Whether looked at from the economic, social, political, moral or religious standpoint," he wrote, "such a thing is dangerous." The Brandon correspondent of the *Free Press* was stimulated to add his views: "The great problem for the American statesman to-day is the assimilation of the foreign elements; it therefore behooves our people to profit when they can by the experience of our neighbors over the way by grappling with the difficulty before it assumes larger proportions and [is] beyond being controlled." The *Brandon Sun* subsequently asked, "Is it not in accord with modern social and political ideas that unity of language should prevail" in education? Failure to force immigrant children to attend schools would be to "neglect...the inculcation of proper ideas of citizenship and duty to their adopted country, right sentiments and pure morals."[15] These arguments bear a striking similarity to those later used by Clifford Sifton in defending changes in the Manitoba school system.

To western minds, the French were as "foreign" as any non-British immigrant group. There was plenty of evidence of anti-French sentiment in the West prior to 1888. The North-West Territories had witnessed attacks since 1884 on French and Catholic educational and language privileges. A wave of protest had followed the appointment of Joseph Royal, a French Canadian, as lieutenant-governor. The official status of the French language in Manitoba, previously assaulted in 1879, had again become a public issue in 1886. By January 1888 the French in the province were reported to be "completely demoralized and divided." As a result, Archbishop Taché of St. Boniface sought and obtained assurances of support for French schools and language from Greenway and Martin in return for his aid in the crucial St. François-Xavier by-election. He did so, states one authority, "because he was convinced that a general campaign against Roman Catholicism and French-Canadian culture was underway throughout western Canada."[16] The promises received, Taché would later discover, were meaningless.

Such, then, was the milieu in which James Smart began to encourage a review of the education system. In March 1889, the *Brandon Sun,* the organ of Smart and Sifton, reviewed the problems of building and staffing schools in western Manitoba; by 2 May it was calling for complete revision of the school system and abolition of separate schools, ideas upon which it expanded later in the month.[17]

A denominational or confessional system patterned after Québec's had been established in 1871. It was thought that the 1871 Act fulfilled the spirit of the Manitoba Act of 1870, which sought to protect the educational privileges which Protestants and Catholics held "by law or practice at the time of Union." Prior to 1871 there had been a voluntary school system wherein the Roman Catholics and various Protestant denominations established their own schools which were maintained by gifts and fees. After 1871 the Protestants were grouped into one system, the Catholics in another; both were given government grants; both were substantially independent of the government and, after 1875, of each other. There was a single Board of Education, but in practice it was divided into separate Protestant and Catholic sections. Ontarians settling in the province tended to import their own terminology, referring to the Protestant section as "public" and the Catholic section as "separate," despite the vast differences between the modified national system of Ontario and the dual system of Manitoba. The Catholic schools also tended to be identified in the public mind as the "French" system. This was understandable, though unjustified. The provincial census of 1885–86 had shown 94,000 Protestants to 14,600 Catholics, over 11,000 of whom were French or métis. The Catholics were outnumbered by each of three Protestant denominations, Presbyterian, Church of England, and Methodist. Racially, 73,000 were British, while those of German origin were almost exactly equal to the combined French and métis population.[18] The fairly even division of French and English, Catholics and Protestants which had existed in 1870 was forever destroyed. This was underlined in the Protestant mind by the fact that the French Catholics were grouped mostly in a few comparatively restricted areas, largely in the old parishes near St. Boniface.

The government caucus approved the abolition of the Board of Education and the establishment of a new department, perhaps as early as the end of the 1889 session of the legislature in March. In May and early June the cabinet began plotting its strategy, which may have included the trial balloons in the *Brandon Sun*.[19] At that time the public response was minimal, though fairly favourable to the proposals. Precisely what the government intended at this stage for the Catholic schools is not clear. The ministers were cognizant of the constitutional roadblocks in the way of outright abolition and perhaps anticipated creating a system similar to that of Ontario, with strict government control of public and separate schools. Probably Smart and Martin would have liked to go farther, since they shared radical views on the proper relationship of church and state.

The fat hit the fire in early July. The *Brandon Sun* conveniently discovered that the Catholic section of the Board of Education had managed to accumulate an operating surplus of $14,000. This enraged many Protestants, whose school districts were strapped for funds. The government forced the Catholic section of the board to surrender the money, to general Protestant approbation.[20] The Manitoba and North-West Baptists, meeting in convention at Winnipeg, rushed to condemn both the Jesuits' Estates Act and separate schools as violations of the principle of separation of church and state. No doubt Smart, a former president of the convention in 1886, had some influence in engineering the resolutions. Finally, on 11 July, just in time for the benefit of the Orangemen congregating at Brandon to celebrate the "Glorious Twelfth," the *Sun* printed another vigorous attack on separate schools. The Orangemen obliged with a series of vicious anti-Catholic speeches and resolutions and denunciations of the French language and separate schools.[21]

Symbolically, the sudden and premature death of ex-Premier Norquay coincided with the beginning of this agitation. The discordant trumpet calls of those impatient for change brought to a crashing close an era of relative racial harmony that Norquay had tried to maintain. He was hardly in his grave when a number of Conservatives began to demand new directions for the party. In particular, they urged that it should lead a crusade against separate school and French language privileges. "It has come to this," intoned the *Brandon Mail,* "all distinctions as to class, creed and nationality have got to be wiped out— the dual languages in the Local Legislature must be discontinued, separate schools must be abolished, tax exemptions on churches, schools, etc. must be suspended and all must be brought to the eternal principle of national equality for the sake of building up the country."[22]

The response to the Conservative challenge came quickly. The Liberals had no intention of losing the initiative. At Souris in the heart of western Manitoba on 1 August, and at Clearwater on 2 August, Smart spoke out on the education issue with Greenway on the platform. "The government believes," he said, "that it is decidedly in the interests of the people to have our schools made national at least so far as the qualifications of the teachers and the secular course of instruction are concerned." He attacked the administrative waste arising from two school boards and the inequitable system of distributing the government grant. But he also stressed, "I do not wish to be understood in any of my remarks on this question to advocate the abolition of the separate school system."[23]

The government policy was brought sharply into national focus as a result of a meeting of 5 August at Portage la Prairie, addressed by D'Alton McCarthy. As a major figure in dominion politics, the most formidable opponent of the Jesuits' Estates Act and, more broadly, of the French fact in Canada, McCarthy commanded a national audience. He spoke principally on the Jesuits' Estates issue, but he also expressed approval of Smart's recent statements and suggested action on the French language. The thrust of his remarks was, as he had said in Winnipeg, that "by a persistent effort on the part of the English speaking people," resurgent and aggressive French-Canadian nationalism "can be confined within the limits of Quebec, and bye-and-bye even eradicated there."[24]

Joseph Martin, sharing the platform, promptly sprang to his feet to thank McCarthy and echoed Smart's statements about school reform. But he went farther. He wanted a rigorous application of the principle of separation of church and state by making the schools entirely secular, religious training to be given in the church and home. He also stated that the government was committed to abolition of government printing in French.[25] On both points he exceeded what the cabinet had approved and defended his actions to Greenway simply as logical extensions of the position already approved by the caucus. Greenway was plainly irritated by Martin's actions, and reportedly told two French-speaking members of the legislature that the attorney general's ideas on the French language were "all bosh." Having sampled favourable public reaction however, and after a meeting with Martin and Smart, Greenway later denied having made such a comment and informed Prendergast, the French representative, that the government would proceed generally as his two colleagues had indicated. The disgusted provincial secretary finally acted on his resignation—which had been in the premier's hands for two months—no longer able to forestall the inevitable.[26] Thus, by mid-summer the government was committed to radical surgery upon the school system, if not outright abolition of Catholic schools, and to ending government printing in French. Greenway and Martin, confident of their ability to govern without French support, had jettisoned pledges made to the Catholics only eighteen months earlier. The heather was ablaze; none could foresee the widespread consequences.

Clifford Sifton had missed the rapid spread of the agitation. He had left late in June to visit his parents at their new home in California and did not return until two days after the McCarthy-Martin meeting at Portage la Prairie. Whether he had had much influence during caucus deliberations in the spring, or through his influence with Smart and the *Sun,* is not known. Joseph Martin, who liked to take upon himself the credit for originating the school question, claimed some years later that there was an element of Manitoba Liberals led by Sifton which had always opposed him bitterly on separate schools. "There never would have been a school question if the Hon. Clifford Sifton had had his way," declared Martin, "when that policy was first promulgated by myself in Manitoba."[27] If Sifton did oppose Martin, however, it was probably to question his extreme positions. He agreed with the principle of the policy, but would have advocated doing only what was legally, constitutionally, and politically safe. His commitment to the principle of a single school system grew out of his background and the composition of his political constituency. He was brought up a Liberal in the Clear Grit tradition of western Ontario and a Methodist with a deep-seated mistrust of Roman Catholicism. The policy was tremendously popular with people of all political stripes in the Brandon area, where there was determination that the will of the majority should shape Manitoba society.[28]

Greenway's ministers had announced a general course of action, but they were far from wholly agreed on direction, let alone particulars of policy. Martin kept trying to force Greenway to a radical course, which led to a constant state of tension in the cabinet. At one stage Lieutenant-Governor Schultz suggested to Prime Minister Macdonald that it might be wise to try to engineer Martin's dismissal from the cabinet, in the hope that the government would moderate its school policy.[29] Macdonald favoured a cautious approach. The Manitobans' proposal to tamper with the rights of the French-Canadian Catholic minority, he knew, could have serious national consequences. He encouraged indirect action, the staging of protest meetings, circulation of petitions against the government policy, and passage of popular resolutions supporting the existing school system. But direct interference, such as dismissing Martin, could have damaging results. Greenway, he told Schultz, "must take the consequences of associating with such a man [Martin]—to use the old proverb—'He that lies down with dogs must rise with fleas.' As they came together into the Government so must they depart." He hoped that a policy of non-interference would allow Martin and Greenway to destroy themselves and not "give them an opportunity of posing as martyrs in the eyes of their friends."[30] The ending of railway disallowance had robbed the provincial government of its main device with which to flog Ottawa and divert attention from its other problems. Macdonald was determined that Greenway should not be handed another such issue. Schultz noted that the local cabinet had not decided by December whether or not to go for outright abolition of the Catholic schools. The prime minister was not unduly worried. "The Provincial Legislature has no power to pass an Act diminishing the privileges secured to separate schools and those attending them, by the Constitution," he wrote. Still, he noted dryly, "it is impossible to forecast what the eccentricities of Martin and his subordinate Greenway may lead them to."[31]

When the legislature opened on 30 January 1890, the Liberals seem to have been still divided on school policy. The principle of government control and "national" schools was agreed upon; but some members apparently wanted a completely secular school system, and perhaps outright abolition of all denominational schools. The former was too drastic a change for most Manitobans, who feared the effects of "godless" schools. The latter certainly was much too risky legally and constitutionally. The government therefore elected to begin with the language issue, for which it knew there was general support. Some of the most impassioned speeches of the session were delivered on the resolution to eliminate French-language printing of government documents. The mood was such that the efforts of French members to exercise their legal right to speak in their native tongue "excited considerable laughter in the House." Most English members agreed with the tenor of an editorial in the *Manitoba Free Press* which contended that "whatever privileges custom may encourage, or promote, the law can recognize no French, no Dutch, no

Italian in this country; here we are all Canadians, and when we speak the tongue and write the language of the Canadian Dominion—which is English—there is no call for any other."[32] At one sweep historical, legal, and constitutional considerations were dismissed and the French-speaking people found themselves considered foreigners in their own country. In Clifford Sifton's opinion the issue should be resolved by logic, not by emotion. It ought to be considered as "entirely" a matter "of business." The translation and printing costs were an unnecessary expense. Most Manitobans desired the change, and neither previous guarantees to the French of eastern Canada nor those of Martin and Greenway during the St. François-Xavier by-election should now be considered binding.[33]

The language issue was but a preliminary skirmish. The measure passed was symbolic and had little real impact upon the day-to-day lives of the French-speaking community. The school legislation was wholly different. Every French-speaking Manitoban, and every Catholic Manitoban, would feel its impact. The separate French Catholic schools were a vital element in preserving both culture and religion. An attack on them would raise fundamental questions about the nature of Manitoban and Canadian society. What was to become of the notion that French and English were to be regarded as co-equal founding races of both country and province?

The government introduced two education bills. One abolished the Board of Education and created a department to be headed by one of the existing cabinet ministers. There seemed to be little doubt that this measure was within the provincial powers. It was patterned generally upon the Ontario model, as was the more contentious Public Schools Bill itself. The latter bill was crudely drafted and required repeated amendments to make it workable.[34] Its intent was to create a so-called "national" system of schools, non-denominational and supported by public funds. Religious instruction was not proscribed but would be limited to state-approved opening exercises and the like. There was one very important departure from the Ontario system: there would be no public support for separate or denominational schools. Such schools could still be operated with private financing, but their supporters would have to pay the public school taxes as well. This "double taxation" of course doomed the Catholic schools, as the Liberals fully intended.

The term "national" schools which was derived from the United States was also used in Ontario and generally seems to have been associated with anti-Catholic nativism.[35] Stripped to its essentials, a national system was intended to forge a homogeneous nationality from the disparate ethnic groups comprising the population. In Ontario the separate schools had ironclad protection, both through the constitution and through the political strength of the Catholic element.[36] In the West these constraints were more limited. Moreover, there was popular determination that the will of the majority must prevail and that separate schools should be forever removed as a troublesome element in Manitoba politics and society.

Clifford Sifton delivered the longest speech on the government side during the debate on the legislation, speaking over four hours. His position was firm and clear. The legislation was "founded in justice and equity." Of the bill to create the department of education, he said that the principle underlying it was "that the expenditure of the public money should be under the control of those responsible for the people," while technical matters were referred to specialists. Too much power had hitherto rested in the hands of a single man, the superintendent of the Protestant section of the board. The government now proposed an advisory board which would permit greater input from the government and other concerned bodies and make the system more responsive to public opinion.

That the school legislation was anti-Catholic he flatly denied. Nor would he want to "wound the religious feelings or convictions or sensibilities of his fellow-citizens." Nevertheless, he gravely continued, honourable members should recall that it was the French members of the legislature who had opposed a clause in the municipal bill requiring that reeves and councillors should be able to read and write. What greater condemnation of the Catholic school system could have been offered? The French members "had admitted by their actions that the class they represented were woefully ignorant." The French and Catholic members had contended that the province was legally and morally bound to uphold the provisions of the Manitoba Act, which in turn was the constitutional reflection of a treaty arrived at between the dominion government and the people of Red River. Such an argument, said Sifton, was nonsense, for there could be no treaty between Crown and subject. If the moral obligation were admitted, it could be only to carry out the terms passed upon by the popular conventions held under the provisional government of Louis Riel in 1869–70. But Catholic educational rights had not then been discussed and were later slipped in by agents of the Catholic Church. The government legislation in his opinion "did not conflict with constitutional rights provided in the Manitoba Act." The Catholics in 1890 had precisely the same privileges that they enjoyed in 1870, the right to set up voluntary schools at their own expense.

In this and other comments he was remarkably prescient concerning the future court decisions on the legislation. The highest courts, said Sifton, had been inclined to find "that the clauses of the B.N.A. Act conferring rights upon the provinces should be largely and liberally construed." Education was a prerogative of the provinces. Sifton correctly observed that "the intention of any constitutional instrument cannot be gathered from the outside, but upon the words used in the statute, and these words alone." Even if the Canadian Supreme Court ruled against the legislation, he believed an appeal to the Judicial Committee of the Privy Council in London, the highest court in the Empire, would uphold the Manitoba legislation.

The member for Brandon North also managed, despite his claims of tolerance, to get in a few blows against the Catholic church. The existing separate school system, he declared, "was practically an alliance between a particular church and the state, and detrimental to the rights of other denominations.... Universal education was a necessity to the State for its own preservation, was a necessity to the wisdom, purity and stability of government." Separate schools were "bad and pernicious" in practice and "tended to increase the political power of the priesthood." Why, the pope was practically in charge of Québec politics; he had been told—by a Protestant Québecker—"that the Government of that province existed to register the decrees of the Pope. A proof of this was the Jesuit Estates Act." The Roman Catholics "were not in sympathy with educating the masses; their desire was to educate the higher classes of the population." Against Manitoba in the dominion Parliament were arrayed the solid forces of Québec and other francophones and Catholics across the country. What, asked Sifton, were the tiny forces of "abolitionist" Manitoba against the mighty forces massed like those of the South before the American Civil War? Yet the Manitoba cause, like the anti-slavery cause, was just, and so it must triumph: "All men must be equal."[37]

For a young man still in his second year of political life, the speech had been impressive. Little did Sifton realize that it was but the opening shot in a six-year campaign to defend the national school system, a campaign in which he would emerge as the successful chief strategist for the Manitoba government.

Even his opponents recognized Clifford Sifton's capacity for hard work. He had already a deserved reputation as one of the outstanding speakers on the government side. As one of the few lawyers in the legislature, his talents were in special demand in considering draft legislation, questioning officials in committee, or analysing contracts.[38] Moreover, Sifton's education gave him a great advantage. Many members had little more than public schooling, and few had gone beyond high school. While he was one of the novices in the House, he had a good grounding in rules of procedure and debate and was experienced in other facets of politics. The Manitoba Liberal party itself had only been in existence a few years, and Sifton had been involved in it from the beginning. There was no tradition or party establishment against which he had to struggle to rise to the top.

Yet Sifton seemed strangely reluctant to seize available opportunities. When Attorney General Martin resigned at the end of the 1890 session, Sifton and his friend Isaac Campbell, member for South Winnipeg, were the logical successors. However, both men refused the position, and Greenway was forced to persuade Martin to continue.[39] Evidently Sifton was concerned that his personal affairs would not permit him to assume office. He still carried the main responsibility for his law firm, and his family too continued to grow.

Winfield Burrows Sifton was born on 21 January 1890, and a third son, Henry Arthur (Harry) Sifton, on 26 June 1891.

It is unlikely, however, that the arrival of Winfield dissuaded Clifford from taking office in 1890, for the impending arrival of Harry did not do so in 1891. But it might have been embarrassing to assume office just before his father was appointed to a comfortable government sinecure. Shortly after Clifford had returned from California in 1889, John Wright, senior, arrived back in Brandon, ostensibly to renew acquaintances. He confessed that he enjoyed the southern climate but admitted as well to having "a soft spot yet for Manitoba." A "spontaneous" petition was duly circulated among his friends, imploring the government to offer "J.W." a suitable position, which was accordingly arranged.[40]

In June 1890, a new provincial reformatory at Brandon was completed, and J.W. Sifton was appointed superintendent. It was intended to be a prestigious position. The building itself had cost over $38,000, and Sifton headed a staff of ten, including a matron, a teacher, three guards, two servants, a watchman, and a caretaker. By the following winter this clumsy make-work patronage project had become a minor scandal. The reason was simple. In all that time the courts had sent only one inmate to the reformatory, an eleven-year-old boy sentenced to two months for larceny. Early in 1891 the government eliminated four of the staff, but as the opposition papers pointed out, this still left more than enough to ensure that the hapless inmate was well and truly reformed! The unfortunate J.W. Sifton, described by the *Mail* as "the principal hand plucking the goose," was anxious for a transfer. The government therefore created a new, less controversial sinecure for him, inspector of public institutions. And the reformatory was converted into an asylum for the insane, for which presumably more prospective inmates could be found.[41]

Following the storms and turmoil of the 1890 session of the legislature, Manitoba politics seemed almost becalmed during the remainder of the year. Sir John A. Macdonald briefly renewed his hope that a moderate realignment in Manitoba politics would result from forcing Greenway and Martin out of the government.[42] This strategy was quickly forgotten, however, as the required dominion general election loomed nearer. Called early in 1891, it would be the prime minister's last campaign, fought on the issues of trade and loyalty. Would the National Policy of protective tariffs survive, a policy that Macdonald argued was intended to preserve the British tie and Canadian independence in North America? Or would the continentalist Liberal policy of unrestricted reciprocity with the United States prevail?

Manitoba Liberals responded eagerly to the election call, confident that at least in the West Conservative unpopularity as a result of the disallowance issue, combined with free-trade sentiment among farmers, foreordained a Tory defeat. When the Liberals of Selkirk riding met at Wawanesa on 11 February to nominate a candidate, there was no doubt who they wanted— Clifford Sifton. But Sifton declined. In consternation, the meeting offered the plum to Greenway. He too unaccountably refused. Finally Joseph Martin leapt into the breach and agreed to run.[43] Sifton certainly would have been a strong candidate; even the Conservatives conceded that he would probably have beaten the incumbent, T.M. Daly.[44] Once again, however, he pleaded personal and business reasons as his excuse for not running. Perhaps they were the real reasons. But Sifton also liked to enter a campaign thoroughly prepared and preferably with the odds in his favour. Liberal preparation in the federal constituencies in the West was still woefully inadequate, and the federal government had powerful resources to place behind its candidates. Sifton knew that Daly was particularly well organized and financed. The voters' lists were badly dated. And he well understood the formidable power of the CPR. The prime minister and the CPR, for example, forced the *Manitoba Free Press* to reverse its traditional policy and support the Tory government. Though controlled since 1889 by officials of the hated CPR, it was still the most powerful newspaper in the province. With that symbol of anti-CPR sentiment, Joseph Martin, running in Selkirk, there was little they would not do to ensure Daly's re-election.

Sifton had promised the Liberal convention that he would support whoever was nominated, and he did. On a number of occasions he spoke in Martin's interest. Even the Tory *Mail* reported that he was "a fluent speaker" and had been "received with deafening cheers" as he denounced the evils of protection and forecast the blessings of reciprocity. It was all in a lost cause. Not only were the Liberals once again defeated nationally, but Martin's campaign got off the ground too late, and he was soundly defeated by 3,660 votes to 3,225. At their victory celebration in Brandon, the Tories attempted to burn a symbolic container of "Liberal" garbage marked "Unrestricted Reciprocity." The Liberals were consoled when, despite the Tories' best efforts, it resolutely refused to ignite.[45]

Martin was quickly returned to the legislature in a by-election, but he resubmitted his resignation as attorney general around 1 April. Again Sifton indicated that he did not want the post; and Isaac Campbell, who had resigned his seat and unsuccessfully contested the Winnipeg seat in the general elections, firmly refused to consider office or even to run again provincially. The premier continued to press Sifton, who reluctantly agreed by the end of the month to accept the honour—but only with certain conditions. These included an attempt to strengthen the government by replacing Provincial Secretary Daniel McLean with J.D. Cameron, a young Winnipeg lawyer. He also wanted education to become the responsibility of the provincial secretary, rather than of the attorney general as it had been under Martin. Greenway was agreeable. On 14 May 1891 Sifton was sworn in as attorney general; and on 15 May, as provincial lands commissioner.[46]

He had hoped to be returned by acclamation in the necessary by-election to confirm his appointment. The Tory organization seemed amenable at first, but Charles Cliffe, publisher of the *Brandon Mail*, was determined that Sifton should be opposed and himself entered the contest. The *Mail* began a series of attacks on Sifton and the Greenway government, and by early June Cliffe was holding public meetings at which Sifton refused to appear, much to Cliffe's indignation. Instead, the attorney general was conducting a quiet, house-to-house canvass of the constituency and revising the voters' list before commencing his public campaign.[47] In mid-July Sifton finally announced an exhausting series of meetings, running almost to election day on 8 August. The pace overwhelmed Cliffe. Sifton's platform was the record of the Greenway government. It is indicative of the priorities of his constituents that he considered freight rates, not separate schools or the French language, to be the central issue. The competition induced by the government policy, he asserted, had produced "better transportation facilities and improved rates."[48]

By 1891 Sifton had matured into a masterful public performer. But there were more important aspects to winning elections than public meetings. Sifton contemptuously observed that Cliffe had the "foolish notion that everybody he talks to is going to support him."[49] He held no such illusions. He hoped, for example, that a rapprochement between the CPR and the Greenway government, concluded in the spring, could be used to his advantage. He wanted the vote of the CPR employees, and he wanted to silence the heavy artillery of the *Manitoba Free Press*. Neither was accomplished wholly, but the CPR did provide limited support in the contest, a heavy blow to the Tories.[50] There were other unofficial expenses in the campaign, which caused Sifton to complain that it was "becoming very expensive." He secured a confidential agent to infiltrate the opposition organization and a lawyer to act as a "watchdog counsel" at the meetings of his opponents, to keep track of questionable proceedings and potentially libellous statements. Such techniques enabled Sifton both to secure evidence necessary to unseat opponents should they be elected and to defend himself from a contested election by giving him as much information about his opponents' corrupt practices as they had about any committed by his supporters. He was confident of victory, assuring Greenway, "If I can't beat Cliffe by one hundred on the 8th of August or nearly so I may as well retire."[51] He was too modest; his victory margin was 543 to 361.

The Tory press seethed. The *Mail* had already accused Sifton of distributing free whiskey through his agents in 1888. Now it indignantly detailed the alleged enormities of Sifton's latest campaign. He was accused of manipulating the electoral lists and engaging in a "wholesale purchase" of the constituency. "Chattel mortgages on affects are freely taken, money and other considerations are offered and every device is being employed to secure by strategy what cannot be secured by an uninfluenced expression of the electorate." Whiskey again was said to have been freely available to Liberal voters, government jobs and liquor licences generously offered, and an estimated $5,000 otherwise expended. It was claimed that at least six men were prepared to testify that they had been offered from $10 to $25 for their votes by Sifton's agents. The *Free Press* denounced Sifton as possessed of a "cheap cleverness," "extraordinary vanity," and as "the most unscrupulous member of the government." The Liberals of course denied all the charges and assured the people that Sifton was "of solid, painstaking, industrious character" and "most unpretentious."[52] The attorney general, for his part, simply ignored the charges, a policy that he would adhere to throughout his career.

The exaggerated indignation of the Tory press was partly a response to having been "out-generalled." Sifton had done nothing that others had not done to the Liberals, including his father, in the past; but he was more talented. It would be nearly impossible to prove that he had had any connection with the alleged corrupt action of his agents. But the Tory concern went much deeper. It was dawning upon them that Greenway had taken into his cabinet a resourceful politician whose skills belied his years. Martin's resignation, they had fondly hoped, would break up the government; instead it had found new strength. Before long the young attorney general would be regarded as the real power in the Greenway government.

Plate 1. In 1896, when this photograph was taken, Clifford Sifton was attorney general of Manitoba and vigorously engaged in defending Manitoba's national school system. He was the principal architect of the Greenway government's overwhelming electoral victory in that year.

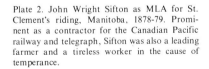

Plate 2. John Wright Sifton as MLA for St. Clement's riding, Manitoba, 1878-79. Prominent as a contractor for the Canadian Pacific railway and telegraph, Sifton was also a leading farmer and a tireless worker in the cause of temperance.

Plate 3. Clifford Sifton's Brandon house, 113 Princess Avenue (from a 1967 photograph). Sifton practised law in Brandon from 1882 to 1896 and represented North Brandon in the Manitoba legislature from 1888 to 1896.

Plate 4. Rosser Street, Brandon, in Sifton's time. The city was founded in 1881 during the CPR boom. It was in the midst of a nearly homogeneous WASP agrarian district and became a centre for farmers' protest movements during the 1880's and 1890's.

Plate 5. Joseph Martin was attorney general of Manitoba from 1888 to 1891. His aggressive attacks on the CPR, and his support of the RRVR and the Northern Pacific and of national schools, won him strong public support. He and Sifton became bitter enemies, a rivalry that be-devilled the Liberal Party in Manitoba through-out the 1890's.

Plate 6. Thomas Greenway, Liberal premier of Manitoba, 1888-1900. During the 1880's he successfully exploited agrarian discontent and provincial rights sentiment to the advantage of the Liberal party. As premier, however, he was neither forceful nor decisive and often appeared to be dominated by stronger personalities like Sifton and Martin.

Plate 7. Greenway and Martin lost no time in rolling up their sleeves and ridding Manitoba of the hated CPR monopoly in the spring of 1888. Their achievement was immensely popular and led to the strong Liberal victory that year.

Plate 8. James A. Smart, from a photograph of 1901. He was dubbed "Sifton's alter ego" by Governor General Lord Minto, serving as deputy minister of the interior (1897-1904) and deputy superintendent general of Indian affairs (1897-1902). Formerly he had been mayor of Brandon and a member of the first Greenway cabinet.

Plate 9. Manitobans confidently, if somewhat naively, expected the Red River Valley Railway to revitalize the provincial economy and lower the cost of living by providing effective competition for the CPR and thus reducing freight rates.

# 4

# Attorney General
# (1891–95)

The civil servants were among the first to sense the style of the new attorney general. Compared to the tempestuous Martin, Sifton was a model of controlled energy and systematic administration. He was in Winnipeg at least two or three days a week, a demanding taskmaster, formal and aloof, brooking no sloppiness or carelessness. He demanded attention to detail in both legal and administrative work. Often his abrupt decisiveness and nervous energy, and perhaps his deafness, made him appear abrasive.

Yet his ability quickly commanded respect. At thirty, he was a solid and handsome six feet tall, with the supple alertness of a man who enjoyed vigorous physical exercise. His hair was always cut short, and he experimented with a moustache, rather larger and droopier than the close-clipped one he favoured in later years. But it was his piercing eyes which both gripped and intimidated those whom he met. Behind them, it was once remarked, were a mind like a steel trap and the memory of an elephant, encased in the hide of a rhinoceros. They were useful attributes in a politician, especially the thick skin, as the opposition press frothed and fumed in unsuccessful efforts to draw him into public controversy.

An Olympian aloofness was also part of his public style. It was a welcome contrast to the ceaseless bickering and libellous confrontations between Martin and his enemies, real or imagined. The government, Sifton realized, needed to put such posturing aside and find a new sense of purpose. Some indeed thought that Sifton had become first mate on a sinking, rudderless vessel, hastily abandoned by his predecessor. The government's railway policy had not been an overwhelming popular success. Immigration was dwindling. Farm prices remained low. High tariffs and freight rates and the baneful effects of the elevator monopoly were merely the most frequently cited causes of the depressed farm economy. Most of these matters were beyond provincial jurisdiction or solution, but a discontented electorate did not augur well for the government, which soon had to seek a renewed mandate. Sifton believed extensive reorganization and much effort were required to seize the political initiative. The planning and execution of his by-election campaign in June, July, and August was really a preliminary skirmish. His great success helped to renew the spirit of the party. Now the planning could begin for the greater battle ahead.

The most uncertain factor when Sifton assumed office was the school question. The constitutionality of the 1890 Public Schools Act was then being tested in the courts. Quite naturally, the Roman Catholic minority had preferred outright disallowance by the dominion government of the offensive legislation. That it was unconstitutional and abrogated rights guaranteed them under the Manitoba Act seemed obvious to the Catholics, who had begun petitioning for disallowance within a few days of the granting of royal assent on 31 March 1890. Prime Minister Macdonald remained firm. "If the bill were disallowed," he wrote to one anxious correspondent, "the game of Greenway and Martin would be played successfully. They would probably summon the legislature again, and carry the Bill over again, and then dissolve and go to the country. The excitement would be tremendous and the question would remain unsettled."[1] Equally convinced that the legislation was unconstitutional, Macdonald preferred the finality of a judicial decision to the renewal of federal-provincial conflict over disallowance.

Accordingly, the dominion government sponsored a test case in which a Roman Catholic ratepayer of Winnipeg, J.K. Barrett, contested the legality of a city by-law requiring him to pay taxes in support of the national schools. At issue was whether the Manitoba Public Schools Act, 1890, contravened section 22 (1) of the Manitoba Act, 1870. The province had been given the "exclusive" right to make laws concerning education, except that "nothing in any such law shall prejudicially affect any right or privilege with respect to denominational schools which any class of persons have by law or practice at the Union." In judgments of November 1890 and February 1891 the Manitoba courts had upheld the Public Schools Act, declaring that the Roman Catholics—or, for that matter, the Anglicans and Presbyterians—had the same right that they had enjoyed prior to 1871 of freely establishing their own voluntary schools. The Manitoba Court of Appeal had held that it would not have been the intent of Parliament to prevent the province from bringing "within the reach of all the children in it the means of acquiring at least an elementary education, such an education as will fit them, when they grow up, to exercise intelligently the duties of citizenship." The state must therefore have the power to fund such a system, which was for the well being of the entire state.[2]

These judgments might well have constituted a warning to the dominion government that the ultimate fate of the appeal was by no means certain. Added to this was the opinion of Edward Blake, the former national Liberal party leader who had been helping to prepare the appeal from the Manitoba courts to the Supreme Court of Canada. He told J.S. Ewart, principal lawyer on the minority side, that he did not regard the "main argument" as particularly sound and suggested that he not be continued as a counsel on the case.[3] But the one-year deadline for disallowance passed quietly in 1891, with officials in Ottawa confident that the more sympathetic Supreme Court would come down firmly on the side of the minority.

When Sifton became attorney general, he wrote to Joseph Martin, who had been, and remained, in charge of the case for the province, requesting details.[4] There was, however, little that could be done in the meantime. Nor was the adverse decision of the Supreme Court at the end of October entirely unexpected. The court held that while section 22(1) of the Manitoba Act was "not an example of very precise or accurate drafting," the general intent was clear. Contrary to the Manitoba courts, they held that intent to be the continuation of the denominational school system in the province after Confederation. The 1890 Schools Act, declared the justices, "prejudicially affected" that right. Catholics were being taxed to support schools of which they could not in conscience approve and were therefore less able to maintain their own denominational schools.[5]

Manitoba, of course, would exercise its right to appeal to the Judicial Committee of the Privy Council, and Sifton now acted swiftly to strengthen his government's hand. If the weaknesses of the minority case had been exposed in the Manitoba judgments, so the deficiencies of the provincial case had been bared in Ottawa. Sifton believed that the Judicial Committee would be more sympathetic to the provincial point of view. He also knew that it was more likely to insist on a strict construction of the wording of the statute and that it would be less moved by arguments about intent arising from the general circumstances surrounding the passage of the Manitoba Act or even the national implications of the issue in Canada.

Still, there was a way to give a useful psychological boost to the Manitoba case. The members of the Judicial Committee would all have remembered the vigorous debate in Britain over established denominational and private interests in 1870 when the state-supported schools had been established. They had lived for twenty years in a situation where voluntary and state-supported schools had managed to co-exist; and by 1891 the principle and desirability of a state-supported system was widely accepted in England. If only their lordships could be made to see a parallel between the English and the Manitoban situations, if only they could be brought to see the dangers of the fragmentation of that system and the difficulty of financing a viable system of education for all Manitobans if that fragmentation took place, the appeal might be successful.

With this in mind, Sifton sponsored a new case, intended to emphasize the possibility of fragmentation. He arranged to have an Anglican ratepayer, Alexander Logan, contest the Public Schools Act as Barrett had done, arguing that the right of the members of the Church of England to establish denominational schools as they had prior to 1871 was prejudicially affected by the act.[6] Could the Judicial Committee fail to agree that Anglicans were every bit as much a "class of persons" under the Manitoba Act as Roman Catholics—or Presbyterians? Would the case not underline the contention of the Manitoba government that the issue was not an attack by Protestants on Catholic rights, but an assertion of the right and duty of the state to effect a viable system of education for all its citizens without regard to special privileges of race or religion? The Manitoba courts quickly ruled that members of the Church of England were indeed a "class of persons" within the meaning of the Manitoba Act. And, in light of the Supreme Court decision in the Barrett Case, they decided in December 1891 that the appeal of Logan should be upheld as well. The Barrett and Logan cases were then appealed together to the Judicial Committee. Pleased with his Machiavellian manoeuvre, Sifton told Martin, "I am quite sanguine that the effect of the two cases coming together will strengthen our argument in favour of the Province very much."[7]

While the school case slowly moved on, the Manitoba government was preparing for the fifth and last session of the seventh legislature—Sifton's first as a member of the government—and for the general election. The government, however, had little fresh legislation to present to the House. Fortunately for Greenway, the divided opposition had even less to offer, except charges of corruption and broken promises.

The government's main legislative goal, in fact, appeared to be to ensure its re-election, which it attempted to do through a new redistribution bill and amendments to the Election Act of 1891. The former, under Premier Greenway's supervision, was nothing less than a blatant gerrymander. It increased the number of seats from thirty-eight to forty, and as Sifton pointed out in its defence, the thirty-seven seats outside of Winnipeg were much more equal in population than had previously been the case, averaging about 3,300 people. But the redistribution also conveniently carved up the constituencies of such leading opposition members as R.P. Roblin (Dufferin), E.J. Wood (Cypress), and A.F. Martin (Morris). To the howls of protest from Wood, part of whose constituency had been transferred to that of Premier Greenway (Mountain), Sifton sardonically replied that the change would give Wood "the opportunity of entering into combat with the premier. To engage in such a contest would result in the hon. member's name being handed down to posterity, and this was one of the prime reasons for making the change in his constituency."[8]

The opposition was even more outraged when confronted with Sifton's amendments to the Election Act. The Liberals already had a history of reversing themselves on this issue. In opposition, they had railed against the evils of allowing the government to place the drawing up and revision of electoral lists in the hands of partisan officials. In 1889 the supporters of the government rolled their eyes heavenward and thanked God they were not as other men as they passed a law placing preparation of the lists in the hands of municipal authorities. As the time for another election drew near, however, they discovered that the other men were not to be trusted at all and that the preparation of the lists must be restored to the government. This had been accomplished by one of the last bills introduced by Joseph Martin in 1891. Now Clifford Sifton proposed further unobtrusive amendments to provide that illegal actions performed without the knowledge or consent of a candidate should not void an election. "It would be unfair," opined the Winnipeg *Tribune* while defending the legislation, "for any candidate who had conducted his election honestly to be unseated because some overzealous friend of his had been guilty of corrupt practices through no connivance of the candidate." Sifton himself had admitted during debate on the Throne Speech that "we all know that in the heat of election times many things are done by both parties which they regret, and it seems to be almost impossible to conduct an election now without it being open to criticism."[9]

Given that sad set of circumstances, it was certainly necessary to protect the innocent candidates. Indeed so obvious was the virtue of this legislation that the government assumed that it required no debate. The chairman of the law amendments committee secured a favourable report on it by adjourning the committee, and later the same day reconvening it without notifying the opposition members. Two days later Sifton had the House reconvened after dinner at 7:30 P.M. instead of the usual hour of 8:00. Unaccountably, someone again neglected to inform the opposition, and the bill passed without a dissenting word or amendment.[10]

The opposition press was now seized with paroxysms of apoplectic fury as it groped for new epithets with which to denounce the government and particularly Clifford Sifton, "the greatest of all the ministerial hypocrites." His "surprising impudence" was too much to bear, given the corrupt actions which the opposition believed had been perpetrated in his ministerial by-election. "Mr. Sifton," declared the editor of the *Free Press,* "is by no means an able man; but he is the most slippery customer Manitoba politics has yet developed." How could it be proven that corrupt actions were done with the advice and consent of the candidates? The new law "will make Mr. Sifton and the whiskey and the dollar bills quite safe. All that it will be necessary to do will be to get his heelers around him at the beginning of the campaign and tell them with a wink that they are on no account to dish out whiskey or buy votes with money. The heelers will know what is meant. There will be whiskey and money as before; but Mr. Sifton had given his 'instructions'; and he would be a sharp counsel who would prove his personal knowledge of anything unlawful."[11] Sifton's explanations that corrupt acts by authorized agents or acts which could be shown to have altered the result of the election would result in voiding the election persuaded few. It could prove very difficult to determine whether an agent was "authorized" or not or whether particular corrupt actions materially affected the outcome of the election.

The government had also been moving to strengthen its position in other ways. The most important of these was a partially secret understanding with the CPR, so recently an object of hatred and scorn. It was, as usual with such cases, an arrangement of mutual convenience. The government had milked the Northern Pacific and its NP & M subsidiary for every possible drop of political benefit. By the end of 1889 it was clear that no further reductions in freight rates could be expected, and a few months later it was equally clear that no new branch lines competitive with the CPR were likely to be built. President Van Horne of the CPR observed that "the Northern Pacific lines which are built in settled country do not earn one quarter of their working expense."[12] New lines into unsettled or lightly settled districts were a risk which the NP & M could no longer afford. The government, badly in need of evidence of new railway construction and action on freight rates, naturally began to revise its attitude to the CPR.

The Canadian Pacific too began to change its view of the Greenway government. It had been forced to act in response to the Northern Pacific by reducing freight rates in 1888, upgrading the line between Winnipeg and Port Arthur, building wagon roads to elevators on CPR lines to draw off traffic from the NP & M, and completing a branch line to Souris to head off any Northern Pacific expansion beyond Brandon. Indeed, the CPR found it advisable to encourage any small independent lines being built to the north of its main line, while discouraging any further construction by other lines—particularly the NP & M— in the south of the province.[13] When Premier Greenway failed to induce the Northern Pacific to build beyond Brandon to the Souris coal fields near Bienfait, NWT, he turned to the CPR, which perceived a valuable opportunity to close out forever the risk of Northern Pacific competition in southwestern Manitoba and the adjacent Territories.

In January 1891, Joseph Martin and D.H. McMillan of the Manitoba government and Major J.M. Walsh, formerly of the North-West Mounted Police and representing the Dominion Coal, Coke and Transportation Company which controlled the Souris coal fields, began negotiations with Van Horne. In an agreement concluded in March, the government agreed to pay the CPR a subsidy of $150,000 for the construction of ninety miles of line to the coal fields. In return, the CPR undertook to guarantee maximum coal freight rates on a scale ranging from $1.50 per ton for the first hundred miles, to $2.25 per ton up to three hundred miles; and Walsh's coal company undertook to supply coal to the railway for $1.75 per ton. The political and economic benefits of this scheme were far-ranging, for these rates would cut the price of soft coal throughout southern Manitoba by 50 per cent.[14] This agreement marked an important new departure in Manitoba politics. Van Horne probably knew of Joseph Martin's impending resignation by the time the agreement was signed, and he may have strongly suspected that his replacement would be Clifford Sifton, who not only conveniently happened to be a close friend of Walsh but who also had already proven himself to be a good friend of the CPR. With the departure of Martin the Northern Pacific had no strong advocate left in the cabinet. Triumphantly Van Horne observed that the agreement had "completed the estrangement between the Local Government and the Northern Pacific."[15]

The weight of the CPR was first felt on the Liberal side, unobtrusively but effectively, in Sifton's by-election in the summer; then in January 1892 in by-elections in South Winnipeg and Manitou. Early in February 1892 the CPR agreed to undertake additional politically beneficial construction by extending its Glenboro branch to Souris and thirty miles beyond. And two months later Van Horne assured Major Walsh—through whom he frequently communicated with Sifton and Greenway—that "We do not wish to do the least thing that will make any difficulty for the Government in their coming elections. . . . If there is anything we can do to give the Government a boost quietly I will be glad if you will let me know. They have treated us very fairly and I will be glad of any opportunity to show that we do not lack in appreciation."[16]

For months the government had been preparing for the election, reviving constituency organizations, arranging nominating conventions, beginning public works projects all over the province, such as colonization roads into the new Dauphin district or an expensive addition to the now-crowded Brandon asylum. Although Greenway was ostensibly in charge of the campaign, Sifton's was unquestionably the guiding hand, his drive and ability gradually giving him effective control of the party machinery. The degree to which Greenway was willing to allow Sifton to take on responsibilities properly belonging to the premier was illustrated during a cabinet shuffle in May. Sifton had long been anxious to strengthen the cabinet, and he was probably the force behind the appointment of his friend Robert Watson, Liberal MP for Marquette, to the post of minister of public works. It took a portfolio of some prestige and power to induce Watson to move from federal politics. The cabinet decided that James Smart would have to be moved from Public Works; and it fell to Sifton, the most junior member, to break the news to Smart.

Smart had sat in the House since 1886. He had been a member of Greenway's original cabinet and had performed his duties well enough to receive even Tory approbation; now his reward was to be the least prestigious post, provincial secretary. Daniel McLean of Virden, the incumbent, was willing enough to be sacrificed, left without portfolio, and promised a patronage plum after the election. But he was not a man of remarkable ability or ambition. Smart, however, was extremely upset, and threatened to resign before he reluctantly accepted the arrangement.[17]

The reconstituted cabinet, undoubtedly stronger, lost little time in opening a full-scale electoral campaign. Sifton toured the province tirelessly, engineering nominations, encouraging the faithful, and appearing—almost always as wind-up speaker—on dozens of public platforms. He answered, or dismissed as unfounded, the repeated charges of governmental corruption and claimed that government pledges had been fulfilled. There had been a redistribution of seats that more nearly approximated representation by population, relief for municipal taxes, and introduction of railway competition. Despite a recession, the government had been able to induce the CPR to build a needed line, the result of which would be vastly cheaper fuel. Indeed the savings realized by Manitobans would quickly more than repay the subsidy granted. Freight rates were undeniably lower than they had been when the government assumed office.

But the Manitoba government was determined to make the school question the central issue. It had been assisted in this endeavour by the Conservative government in Ottawa. A promise had been given the Roman Catholic minority that even if the Judicial Committee of the Privy Council upheld the Manitoba Public Schools Act, the federal government would introduce remedial legislation, as it appeared to have power to do under section 22 (2) and (3) of the Manitoba Act, and section 93 (3) and (4) of the British North America Act, to force the province to restore the substance of separate school privileges. Provincial officials had always been aware of this federal power, but the public promise in February to use it gave the provincial government an excellent campaign issue. Sifton called on the Young Men's Liberal Club of Winnipeg "to stand shoulder to shoulder in the present crisis" and to see that the province gave no "uncertain sound" at the next election.[18]

Over and over again Sifton pointed out that if the Judicial Committee failed to uphold the law, the Conservative opposition was committed to full restoration of the separate school system. The Liberal government would never consent to a return to the old system. The issue before the courts was merely one of taxing powers, and there were other avenues to create the substance of a national school system if need be. The government, however, would require powerful popular support to carry through such measures. In the more likely event that the legislation would be upheld, Sifton contended, it was equally necessary that a strong government be elected to resist federal remedial pressure. If the Conservatives were returned to power, what likelihood was there that they would resist federal pressure when they would depend upon the French and Catholic members for their margin of majority? The people must "rise and say 'We'll stand by you on this question.'"[19]

On election day, 23 July, the Liberals triumphed with twenty-six of the forty seats. The Conservatives, who had gone into the election with ten seats, gained but one, for a total of eleven. Three independents were returned, James Fisher (Russell), M. Jerome (Carillon), and J.E.P. Prendergast (St. Boniface), all of whom opposed the government on the school issue, but otherwise gave it general support. The popular vote was much closer, however, with only 51.9 per cent supporting the government.[20] Clifford Sifton had breezily predicted an increased majority for himself and spent little time in his own constituency. His actual victory margin of sixty-eight votes in North Brandon was uncomfortably close. Furthermore, two cabinet ministers, James Smart and Daniel McLean were defeated.

The Conservatives again raised the cry of corruption and bribery. The *Manitoba Free Press,* which had characterized the seventh legislature as "the weakest in intellect and the least respectable in character that has been seen for many a day," had led the attack on the government with the cry, "Turn the rascals out." When the fray was over, it declared that most of the government constituencies were "bought with boodle" in the most corrupt election ever seen in Canada.[21] Even allowing for exaggeration, the government certainly had spent money freely and had enjoyed the active support of the CPR.[22]

One week following the election the Judicial Committee of the Privy Council rendered judgment in the school cases. An exultant Joseph Martin telegraphed Sifton, "Strong judgment in our favour, adopting our arguments and controverting Supreme Court on every point. Congratulations on double event."[23] The court appeared to have accepted almost all the basic assumptions of the Manitoba government. It agreed that the Barrett and Logan cases were similar, that the national system of schools was non-denominational, and that Catholics and Anglicans had the right to send their children or not, or to withdraw them from the religious exercises. If conscience compelled them to establish their own schools, the law did not hinder them from doing so, and in this respect they had still the privileges which they had had in 1870. But the power of the state to "provide for the educational wants of the more sparsely inhabited districts of a country almost as large as Great Britain" must not be curtailed merely because pangs of conscience prevented the minority from taking advantage of privileges available freely to all Manitobans.[24]

It was a crucial victory for the provincial authorities and supporters of national schools. Yet the decision had only affirmed that the province could establish national schools. The minority and the federal government had served notice that another line of attack existed. Through remedial legislation it was hoped that the province could be forced to restore the substance of the separate system to the Roman Catholics. It promised to be a bloodier battle than the first. The government, declared Sifton, had been elected on a platform of "no compromise," and it would adhere to that promise. In almost the same breath that it announced the court's decision, the Winnipeg *Tribune* defiantly trumpeted, "The people of Manitoba are free and are determined to remain free. We will never submit to have Sir John Thompson force on us the will of the Quebec hierarchy."[25] The gathering storm clouds formed a gloomy, threatening prospect.

In a plebiscite held simultaneously with the provincial election in 1892, Manitobans voted 18,637 for prohibition to 7,115 opposed. There had been a discouraging decade since the Siftons had led the prohibitionist forces in local option contests in Marquette and Lisgar constituencies in 1880–81. Because of a technicality, the Supreme Court had thrown out attempts to enforce prohibition, a blow from which the temperance forces had never recovered.[26] They had been thrown heavily on the defensive during the CPR boom of the early 1880's, quite unable to stem the rivers of liquor that flowed in with the so-called "floating population" as construction moved westward. J.W. Sifton had valiantly led the fight as president of the Dominion Alliance in Manitoba until 1886, but by the time he left the province in 1887, there was almost complete disarray in the prohibitionist ranks.

The enemies of alcohol were numerous, nevertheless. In theory they had two principal weapons. One was to have municipalities rather than electoral districts vote on the local option issue, which had been found to be legal under the Canada Temperance Act of 1878. By this means much of the province had been made officially "dry" by the 1890's. The second weapon was a licensing act which required each would-be holder of a liquor licence in the "wet" districts to have the written approval of sixteen of the nearest twenty householders. Unhappily the laxity of enforcement under the Norquay government was notorious and largely vitiated the efforts of temperance workers, even in many "dry" areas.

Prohibitionists were largely behind Greenway in the 1888 election. The premier himself had for some years been associated with temperance organizations, albeit in a rather loose way, as had James Smart and many other leading Liberals. In 1889 the government consolidated and amended existing legislation.[27] To minimize abuses in the granting of licences, an independent licensing commission was established with strict conditions upon which it might issue or refuse licences. Municipalities were made responsible for appointing inspectors to enforce the Act; and they were empowered to levy taxes upon licence holders not exceeding the provincial fee.

This law had great virtues from the government point of view. It removed the onus of granting licences to a board of commissioners and the onus of enforcement to the municipalities. Strapped as they were for funds, few municipal counsellors were willing to hire the needed enforcement officers, and instead they claimed that proper enforcement required provincial or even dominion government action. Moreover the revenues from licences, ranging from $100 to $250 per establishment, constituted an important source of municipal income. Consequently most prohibitionists believed that anything less than provincial action would fail. But Attorney General Joseph Martin had not firmly enforced the law, although prosecutions were certainly carried on more vigorously than before.

When Clifford Sifton became attorney general, decisive, even draconian action was expected. After all, he came from one of the best-known prohibitionist families in the province. If he had not spoken as widely as his father and brother, he had still a noteworthy record in temperance organizations. And surely his father, once again active in the cause, would wield some influence. Clifford Sifton had come to office at a time of a renewal of prohibitionist sentiment across the Dominion. In 1888 the Dominion Alliance, meeting in Montreal, had committed itself anew to the cause. It had tried to make prohibition an issue during the 1891 dominion election. Thereafter it deluged Parliament with petitions for federal action.[28] The result was the appointment by the dominion government in March 1892 of the Royal Commission on the Liquor Traffic in Canada.

The rising crest of temperance enthusiasm in Manitoba had few obvious indigenous causes. There were no major social disruptions such as the CPR boom; nor were there yet the waves of foreign immigrants who could be denounced as "drinkers" and therefore dangerous to the fabric of society. In fact, many of the Manitobans who testified before the commission, whether supporting or opposing prohibition, admitted that drinking was a less serious problem than it had been a few years earlier. J.W. Sifton went so far as to opine that "we [Manitobans] have improved morally. We think we are the most moral and sober people on this continent. We think we can bear that out by statistics. We think there is no city of the same size so sober as Winnipeg."[29] The Manitoba agitation, now headed by a new generation of capable leaders, was substantially a product of the dominion-wide movement. This, in turn, was part of the response to industrialism, to demographic change, to the new social problems of an increasingly urban society. It reflected rural insecurity and reaction against the problems of urban life spilling over into the countryside. It was associated with the Social Gospel, women's suffrage, and urban and agrarian reform movements. It was, finally, a response long overdue, however inadequate, to a perpetual, debilitating human problem.

As a private member Sifton had had an unexceptionable record from the prohibitionists' standpoint. In 1889 he had generally supported the restrictive liquor licence act, although he had opposed, unsuccessfully, its provision requiring a fee from those who wished to protest the granting of a licence. He also wanted to place a limit on the fees available to municipalities, reasoning correctly that they would become too attached to the revenue to permit them to undertake effective enforcement.[30] The following year he opposed a proposal to lower the number of signatures required for a licence from sixteen to twelve of the nearest twenty householders. He assured the legislature that "the respectable element in his constituency was against the removal of restrictions." After a battle of two days, he succeeded in obtaining a compromise of fourteen signatures.[31]

Then, in 1892, the prohibitionists presented him with a dilemma. They wanted to make prohibition a public issue in the upcoming election. They intended to force the politicians to take a stand and to demand a plebiscite to demonstrate popular opinion. Sifton was entirely ready to take a public stand in favour of prohibition. But a plebiscite was full of hidden dangers. It "introduces a principle unknown to the principle of the British constitution," he told the legislature. "The principle of that constitution is that laws shall be made by persons elected by the electors, and passed in the discretion of those representatives." Whether or not it set an unhealthy precedent, declared the attorney general, a popular vote on the question of total prohibition ran other risks. The people were being asked to pronounce on an issue which lay outside provincial jurisdiction. The province only had definite powers in the area of licensing; the dominion government had the far broader powers of regulating the manufacture, importation, and sale of liquor.[32] "Total prohibition was advisable," in Sifton's opinion, "as there was nothing doing so great a physical and moral injury at the present time as the liquor traffic." But even if the vote resulted in an overwhelming majority for prohibition, there could be no promise of government action until the issue of jurisdiction was finally determined. "The difficulty . . . in connection with laws of this kind," he reminded the legislators, "is that in a moment of moral fervour, some particular portion of the public sanction the law and then utterly fail to strengthen the hands of those who pass the act. In such cases it were better that the law had never passed."[33]

The government only reluctantly supported a private member's bill for a referendum. Rarely had Sifton been so obviously uncomfortable in speaking, supporting the bill out of political necessity. He was right to worry. The prohibitionists avoided supporting either party in the election. They preferred to try to elect a prohibitionist house by forcing candidates to pledge themselves and to reinforce the effect with a solid popular majority in the referendum. Many assumed that the government, by holding the plebiscite, was already committed to action. The *Canadian Northwest Banner,* the temperance organ, apparently shared this assumption when it endorsed Sifton during the election campaign, declaring that "as a Christian gentleman and prohibitionist" he had "kept himself unspotted in his political career from the least toadying to the saloon power either in his private or public life."[34]

The victory of the prohibitionist forces in the 1892 plebiscite was the climax of their fortunes in the first half of the decade. Temperance officials considered the Royal Commission on the Liquor Traffic to be composed mainly of people unsympathetic to the cause who so arranged their meetings as not to give a fair representation of public opinion.[35] The October hearings of the commission in Winnipeg and Brandon were damaging to the provincial government, for practically all the anti-prohibitionists, and most of the temperance men who were not also leading Liberals, agreed that many of the worst problems associated with the liquor traffic could be corrected by strict enforcement of existing law or by the energetic exercise of provincial powers. The "laxity of enforcement" under Clifford Sifton, wrote one temperance advocate after reviewing the evidence of the commission, amounted "in some instances to a scandal and a disgrace." But the assignment of blame was not so simple. The province had charged the municipalities with responsibility for enforcement. And when the Royal Commission reported in 1895, it specifically condemned the failure of municipal rather than the provincial authorities, adding that "the conclusion is irresistible that the people of this province have had it in their power to enforce prohibition of the liquor traffic, if they had desired to do so, to a very much greater extent than they have done or apparently attempted to do."[36]

Whatever the merits of the argument, the commission hearings increased the heat on the government. Now every liquor licence granted, every appearance of illicit sources of liquor, every failure to prosecute—or to succeed in prosecution—was seen as further evidence of an alliance between the government and the liquor interests. Tension between temperance advocates and the attorney general reached a climax in February and early March 1893. A delegation headed by William Redford Mulock, Q.C., president of the Prohibition League of Manitoba, waited upon Sifton and demanded that he take one of two courses: either he must introduce legislation completely forbidding the manufacture, transportation, and sale of liquor or make an appeal to Ottawa requesting the dominion government either to do so or to transfer the powers to the province. Sifton observed that the first course was pointless, since such legislation exceeded provincial powers and would surely be disallowed or immediately thrown out by the courts. The second course would only work if the dominion authorities were willing to act to enforce it across the country, then a most unlikely prospect. He nevertheless did ask the legislature to petition the dominion government to pass a law "prohibiting the importation, manufacture and sale of intoxicating liquor in or into the province of Manitoba." His motion drew attention to the result of the plebiscite and denounced liquor as the greatest cause of vice, disease, and crime, hampering "the moral and material welfare of the province."[37]

Sifton's reluctant attitude left the temperance leaders dissatisfied. He was denounced as two-faced and falsely accused of promising total prohibition in 1892 and reversing himself a few months later. A convention of the Manitoba Prohibition League met in Winnipeg on 24 February 1893 with the express purpose of pressing the legislature to take action. For the zealous delegates

Sifton's motion was a feeble half-measure; nothing less than total, immediate prohibition would be satisfactory.[38] Manitoba, it was said, had challenged Ottawa on railway disallowance and won. She had challenged the Dominion on separate schools and won. Why could she not do it again on prohibition? What was needed was courageous action, not the spineless shilly-shallying which seemed to characterize the attorney general's administration.

On 1 March Sifton delivered a powerful rebuttal. He placed himself squarely in the ranks of the prohibitionists in his attitude to liquor. He had earlier assured the legislature that "he was a temperance man, that he did not know the taste of liquor, and trusted under God that he never should." Liquor, he now declared, was the ultimate cause of nine-tenths of criminal offenses, "although the person might be perfectly sober at the time the crime was committed by him." Simply look at the population of the jails, trace the parentage of those incarcerated, "and it will be found that the criminal class of the civilized world today are bred from the use of liquor." To those who contended that the government had no more right to interfere with a man's drinking habits than with his choice of food and clothing, he replied that drinking was a social disease. It should be compared to the Diseases of Animals Act which permitted the government to kill glandered horses, despite any hardship to the horses' owners. "How" he asked, "can anyone say that the sale of liquor which has proven to be a much worse evil than glandered horses shall not be prohibited because it would interfere with the personal rights of the people?" Unscientific as his analysis may have been, no prohibitionist would have disagreed with it in any particular.

The attorney general then reviewed the efforts of the government to enforce the existing law. The requirement of fewer signatures necessary for a liquor licence and reduced penalties for infractions of the law were not, as prohibitionists thought, a sign of leniency. Rather, the greater reasonableness of the conditions and penalties had greatly increased the chances of securing conviction in the courts. Prosecutions had increased, and the amount of fines collected had nearly doubled between 1889 and 1892. At the same time, between 1888 and 1892 the number of licences issued had declined from 169 to 155, despite the increase in population. All this underlined the government's commitment to temperance. But a bill to introduce total prohibition would be futile. It was not similar to the school issue, in which the government had always taken the ground that its law was constitutionally correct. There was no basis for the belief that the provinces could arrogate to themselves control of the liquor traffic, and Sifton exhaustively cited the series of judicial decisions bearing on the issue. Only the federal government had the power, which, Sifton asserted, it must be asked to exercise or to delegate to the provinces.[39] Not until May 1896, however, did the Judicial Committee affirm, albeit rather fuzzily, that while the main responsibility did in fact lie with the dominion government, the provinces too had substantial powers to limit the liquor traffic within their boundaries.[40]

In Manitoba, dissatisfaction with Sifton's enforcement continued. That he sought to deal with the worst abuses was clear, but he declined to provide the army of detectives that would have been necessary to ferret out every illicit still and source of supply which kept appearing in the "dry" districts. A temperance convention at Boissevain in 1894 demanded many dubious amendments to fill loopholes in the licence law. Sifton chose to ignore them. The most disturbing problem for the government was the rise of the Patrons of Industry, a radical agrarian organization, as a potent political force. Where the Liberals and Conservatives had avoided making temperance a party issue, the Patron platform expressly included a firm commitment to prohibition. There was talk of the formation of a new party of "the three P's: Prohibition, Patrons and Purity." The government worked quietly and effectively to prevent an alliance between the prohibitionists and Patrons, aided by the fact that temperance leaders were still chary of tying the fortunes of their movement to the success of any single political party.[41]

Sifton was not a zealot. Prohibitionists were disappointed because he lacked the ardour of the true moralist. He was a realistic politician, and he did not believe that the public was yet ready to pay the full costs of effective prohibition, particularly as it required national action. Even strenuous enforcement of existing law in Manitoba, beyond a certain level, would have diminishing returns and win few friends for the government. He also believed, correctly, that the divisions in the prohibitionist ranks, the diffusion of their efforts, and the presence of other issues such as the school question in Manitoba politics would allow the government to ignore the extremists. He realized, as did the prohibitionists themselves, that popular enthusiasm was difficult to sustain over a lengthy period.[42]

The office of attorney general in Manitoba was still considered part-time employment in the late nineteenth century. The $3,000 salary and the sessional indemnity of $600 provided a cabinet minister with an income at least three or four times that of the average Manitoban, but it was not expected that ministers would be fully occupied with their duties. Like his predecessors, Sifton regularly found time to devote to his law practice, except during the legislative session. In his capacity as attorney general, he was at once the head of the Manitoba bar and chief law officer of the Crown. Under his jurisdiction were provincial courts and jails, provincial police, registry and land titles offices, and liquor licences.

Sifton did undertake some important reforms in the administration of law, partly in response to both professional and public criticism. Amid the agrarian agitation of the Patrons of Industry in 1893 and 1894 arose complaints that lawyers' fees were among the more onerous burdens placed on farmers. A special committee was appointed to look into the matter, and being composed largely of lawyers, it not unnaturally found that Manitoba lawyers' fees were not exorbitant and were quite in line with those charged in Ontario and the North-West Territories. It did, however, condemn the excessive rates charged by conveyancers, bailiffs, notaries public, and the like—what might be called the "para-professionals" of the Manitoba legal system.[43] These were patronage appointments of men who frequently had little or no legal training, but whose practices brought the whole profession into disrepute. Or so thought the lawyers, who demanded greater professional competence in appointments.

The greatest problems of underqualification were to be found among justices of the peace and magistrates. Sifton continued Martin's practice of housecleaning and upgrading the JP's. In 1895 he also moved to place police magistrates on a footing of some stability and permanence; they now would be paid fixed salaries instead of relying on court fees. If they had no legal training, at least a higher grade of appointment could be made when their posts did not depend on the vagaries of politics and the survival of the government which had appointed them.[44]

A longstanding complaint of many Manitobans, including some lawyers, had been the complexity and expense of civil actions. Joseph Martin had corrected the worst problems of the county courts in 1891, but there remained the awkward division between the common law and equity sides of the Court of Queen's Bench, each side having different rules and procedures. Uniting the two had long been advocated,[45] but there had been no agreement on either procedure or anticipated benefits. England had attempted to resolve procedural problems in her court system with a Judicature Act, later largely copied by Ontario; but a proposal in 1891 to introduce a similar act for Manitoba drew heated protests from the legal profession, with claims that experience under the new system in England and Ontario had shown the cure to be worse than the disease. An even stronger reaction met Sifton's announcement early in 1894 that such a measure would be introduced. Martin took a public stand against the proposal, claiming it would make legal actions more expensive than ever.[46] The attorney general hastily withdrew the bill, entered into more extensive discussions with lawyers, and introduced a considerably amended bill in 1895.

The new bill, "An Act Respecting the Constitution and Practice of the Court of Queen's Bench," was no carbon copy of the Ontario or English laws. Sifton had been asked particularly to study American court procedures, noted for their comparative speed and simplicity, and the bill incorporated several American features. Opposition to the measure seemed to have evaporated, since most lawyers appeared to agree that it suited provincial circumstances. "Attorney-General Sifton deserved great credit," declared the *Western Law Times,* praising the "originality" of the legislation and his "zeal and diligence in attempting to render justice more easily attained."[47] One authority has stated that "this was probably Clifford Sifton's greatest contribution to the province in his capacity of Attorney-General."[48]

The attorney general also administered the three provincial jails at Winnipeg, Portage la Prairie, and Brandon. A fourth jail, at Neepawa, had no inmates, a situation which men like Sifton and his father liked to attribute to the fact that it was in the midst of a dry local option district. Few people had any pretensions about jails as social rehabilitation centres in the 1890's, for incarceration was viewed as just punishment. So long as they were secure, reasonably clean, and untroubled by disturbance, there was little public concern. The modest aim of Sifton's department was said to be "to make the prisons as far as possible self-sustaining."[49] This was to be achieved by requiring the prisoners to raise vegetables, saw wood for public buildings, shovel snow, and like activity. To some degree the province was successful, expending in 1893, for example, only $1,800 on "prison subsistence." Yet the prisoners were chronically underemployed. The further evil of throwing together criminals of all ages and classes was pointed out by J.W. Sifton in his capacity as inspector of public institutions. No action, however, was taken on his recommendation that the three jails should handle different classes of prisoner.[50]

Such suggestions were seen at the time as little more than minor quibbles. Few of Sifton's contemporaries found ground for serious disagreement with his administrative performance, apart from criticism of his enforcement of the liquor licence law. He was not a social reformer. Except for his prohibition sentiments, he did not believe in principle that government action would bring about reform, and in general he was satisfied with things as they were. In 1893, for example, he did not participate in a debate on women's suffrage, but he readily voted with the majority who opposed it. A year earlier he had opposed a bill proposed by Joseph Martin to change the laws on seduction. Existing law, argued the former attorney general, prevented the victim from suing for damages; a suit had to be brought on by her parents or guardian or employer, and not for personal damages, but for "loss of services." Martin described the law as a "relic of barbarism," a product of "the old feudal idea that a woman must go to her master before bringing actions." Sifton defended the existing law, not on the basis that it was inherently just, but on the ground that "the law at present was the same as that in Ontario and in almost every civilized country," and there was no need for radical change.[51] Such was his attitude toward most social reform legislation.

He was not inflexible, however, when popular opinion required action in a direction with which he disagreed. During his term of office there were widespread demands to protect farmers and labourers against the worst abuses of the economic system. The agrarian and labour agitation of the early 1890's reflected a groping toward security and stability. The monied classes had long counted on state aid to implement protective tariffs and to legislate protection for capital invested or loaned. Manitobans still could be, and were, imprisoned for debt. More frequently, farmers could lose all their possessions as a result of one crop failure or excessively low international wheat prices.

"At the present time," commented Sifton early in 1894, "a creditor has all the law on his side."[52]

A principal cause of agrarian irritation was the comfortable relationship existing between farm implement companies, particularly Massey-Harris, and the provincial government. The company aided the government by encouraging its many local agents to support the Liberals actively with time and money and by preventing any agents from joining the Conservative cause. In return, the government facilitated making the travelling agents commissioners for the taking of affidavits.[53] This gave the favoured agents a great competitive advantage. A smooth-talking travelling salesman, addressing the farmer in his own farmyard, might easily persuade him to sign what appeared to be a simple credit agreement for expensive machinery. In fact, the farmer might well have signed a lien on his property, which could be duly entered at the nearest registry or land title office and might mean that he could lose everything at his first defaulted payment. Scandalous abuse of this system led to a storm of public outrage. Reluctantly Sifton allowed a moderate act to pass in 1893, further strengthened in 1894, to prohibit the registration of such lien notes.[54]

Also in 1894 the Patrons' agitation made it essential to give farmers a modicum of protection against seizure of all their assets for defaulting on mortgage payments. The proposed measures angered the financial community, which was increasingly suspicious that the government was caving in completely to the unconscionable demands of the farmers. Such legislation, warned H.D. Cameron of the Hamilton Provident and Loan Society, "makes Capitalists hesitate to invest their money [in Manitoba], where everything is being done to prevent the Creditor from getting his money back." The government should concentrate on "laws to protect the citizen's life and liberty," while "the less legislation in other directions . . . the better for all concerned."[55]

Sifton did not disagree. He himself held a number of mortgages and had arranged many more. He had a deep respect for, and interest in, the rights of capital and property. Indeed, he had consulted with the capitalists about the legislation. In his opinion there was "very little use in endeavoring to protect farmers from the effects of their own contracts by Act of Parliament." "It may be hard to learn the lesson," he added bluntly, "but farmers, like other men who do business will be obliged to learn by experience how to do their business." Despite his own reservations, and whatever the fears of the business community, Sifton regarded the legislation passed "as being very mild in comparison with what we easily might have had considering the spirit which prevailed in the country and we may consider ourselves very fortunate in having been able to restrain the disposition to legislate against capital." In the long run, the new law was probably "desirable in order to prevent men from being totally deprived of the power to earn a livelihood and also for the protection of the wife and family of the debtor."[56]

Sifton's sentiments were widely shared in the cabinet. By the end of 1892 it was essentially urban in composition, Greenway being the only farmer. The defeat of McLean and Smart in the 1892 elections completed the cabinet changes begun earlier, and it now conformed to the design of the attorney general. Smart was succeeded as provincial secretary in January 1893 by J.D. Cameron, the Winnipeg lawyer whose entry into the cabinet was a condition of Sifton's own acceptance of office. The farmer premier seemed to be allowing his energetic attorney general to take over the party machinery and to shape the general policies of the government to a surprising degree.

Greenway may have understood instinctively that only an extraordinary personality could keep a right rein on the ambitious Sifton and concluded that it was best for the party to let him generally have his way. Sifton was sometimes a difficult colleague, occasionally tactless and annoyingly self-assured. Curiously, he appeared to show less deference to the premier than to anyone else. He seemed prepared from the beginning to treat Greenway as an equal, sometimes less. "It seems to me," Sifton once chastised him, "you must be pretty slow about looking after the Electoral Division of Lisgar, and it is time somebody took hold of it and attended to it."[57] Despite several such blunt statements, there was little concrete evidence of friction between the two men.

Sifton did more than anyone else to keep the party organization from stagnation between elections. He spoke often to Liberal organizations and at political banquets, and he contributed heavily from his own pocket to their support. It was essential to keep up appearances, because the rise of the Patrons of Industry as a force in Manitoba politics could have been disastrous for the Liberals. This new agrarian movement began to gather steam in 1892, adapting American models to the circumstances of the Canadian prairies. At first it had been an exclusively agrarian organization focusing on self-education and local co-operation. It was inclined to engage, as had the Farmers' Union, in what proved to be unsuccessful attempts at co-operative marketing of binder-twine and wheat.[58] Clearly hundreds, perhaps thousands, of firm Liberals and Conservatives had joined the Patron cause without the slightest sense of inconsistency or intention of disloyalty to their parties.

Party loyalty was nevertheless weakened by the failure of the Greenway government to implement total prohibition after the 1892 plebiscite. To dedicated prohibitionists, neither the Conservatives nor the Liberals had a satisfactory record. Then too, most of the problems the farmers identified required political solutions. Economic depression in 1893, with its disastrously low world wheat prices, finally convinced the Patrons to take direct political action. To the usual agrarian demands for lower tariffs and freight rates, economy of administration and honesty in government, they added prohibition, women's suffrage, and a general demand that power be restored to the agricultural classes.[59]

Fortunately for the Liberals, the Manitoba Patrons proved to be political amateurs. The movement, furthermore, was divided about the decision to "go political," for many loyal Liberal and Conservative members had no desire for a new party and wanted to retain the non-partisan structure. There were also indications that the prohibition and women's suffrage planks created some enemies and added few friends to their political base.[60]

Clifford Sifton had been inclined to be sympathetic to the movement until it began to take shape as a political party. Even then he preferred to attempt to persuade the Patrons that they could gain nothing even if all forty members of the legislature were Patrons. In what way could such a legislature be more sympathetic to the farmers than the Greenway government? "I presume," he noted with some irritation, "it would be taken for granted that a man's brains are not necessarily any clearer because he is a Patron although they may be." He believed that "most of the influential members of the Patron's society are strong Liberals in politics," and when they had thought through the situation, they would realize that a Patron member would be able to do no more, and perhaps less, than Sifton himself.[61]

The first crisis with the Patrons came in 1894. The depression continued. Sympathy for the movement spread rapidly throughout Manitoba and the Territories, and in Ontario seventeen were elected to the provincial legislature. The Greenway government meanwhile was successful in election protests launched against two leading Conservatives in the local legislature, W.A. Macdonald, who had defeated James Smart in Brandon in 1892; and J.A. Davidson of Beautiful Plains. By-elections were scheduled for 23 August 1894, with the government increasingly nervous about Patron inroads among the Liberal rank and file. The Patrons had no hope of success in the urban riding of Brandon; after Smart declined to run again, Charles Adams, a Liberal friend of Sifton and former mayor of Brandon, was duly elected. But they were determined to contest rural Beautiful Plains. The government knew that Davidson's Conservative support was holding firm and that a Liberal and a Patron would divide the remaining votes, allowing his re-election. To allow a Patron victory, on the other hand, would greatly encourage the movement. Realizing the risk, the government nevertheless decided not to contest the constituency. The Patrons were successful and euphoric. The effect, observed Sifton, "will be to stimulate their efforts in other places and to encourage them to take a still more active part in political matters." The only hope which Sifton saw was that "they have been somewhat unfortunate in the first candidate that they have succeeded in electing. If reports be correct, he will not be likely to shed very much lustre upon the Order."[62] The episode illustrated the difficulties facing the Liberals. In Manitoba at least, defections from the Liberals to the Patrons appeared to be more serious than from the Conservatives. It was an ominous portent for the coming general elections, both provincial and federal. Vigorous government initiatives became essential.

Sifton's immediate and well-grounded fears were of the consequences in federal politics. By June the Patrons had nominated five candidates in

Manitoba in anticipation of an early dominion election.[63] The Liberals were not nearly so well prepared. Indeed, the national organization of the Liberals had been notoriously weak in the past. Prior to 1887, when Wilfrid Laurier assumed the leadership of the party, little was done to widen the base of Liberal support. Not until 1892 did the party create a national directorate which included a Manitoba representative, Robert Watson; and there still were none from the Territories or British Columbia. This was because Laurier centred his organization initially upon a committee of parliamentary members, and there were no Liberal members west of Manitoba.[64] Then, when Watson entered the local government, Manitoba's input into the federal party became informal and irregular at best. Sifton took the initiative to keep open the lines of communication between the federal and provincial organizations. It helped too that Laurier decided to hold a national Liberal policy convention in Ottawa in June 1893 and to involve Liberals from across the country.

The most serious fear that Sifton had was that the national party, having suffered defeat in 1891 on the platform of unrestricted reciprocity, would substitute a policy of gradual modification of the tariff. In the West, declared Sifton, it would "meet with absolutely no response." He wanted a radical revenue tariff plank which would "strike at the root of the evil." "If I were to enter into details to show you how the tariff as at present constructed extracts the blood from this Province," he told Laurier, "I have no doubt that you would be surprised at the fact that the people have not declared themselves upon the question before." The confusing nature of Liberal policy was, in Sifton's estimation, the real reason for Liberal defeats in 1887 and 1891. A simple proposal for a revenue tariff combined with "very radical proposals for the reduction of the expense of government" would probably meet with a "warm and hearty" response among Manitobans.[65]

Sifton also ventured an opinion that must have seemed extraordinary to Laurier, coming from a member of the Manitoba government which had long railed against the privileges of the railways. Some Liberals were mooting a Canadian version of the American Interstate Commerce law, regulating railway traffic. Sifton objected, contending that it would prove to be "entirely impracticable" and ruinous to the through traffic of the Canadian railways. Politically, such a plank would be sheer folly. It would "consolidate all the railroad interests against us in the case of an election, and we are not so overwhelmingly in a majority in Canada now, that we can afford to throw any of our friends into the enemies' hands."[66] The attorney general had learned well the value of such allies in the late provincial elections and had even earlier discovered the unpleasant effects of railway opposition.

Symbolic of Sifton's rising stature among Manitoba Liberals was the fact that he and Watson represented the provincial government at the Ottawa Convention and that Sifton was named vice-chairman of the convention representing Manitoba. He could hardly have been dissatisfied with the platform devised by the party. Appropriately, he seconded the fourth resolution, on economy in government. There was nothing in the platform to antagonize the railways. Furthermore, while the party as a whole was backpedaling furiously on the tariff issue to avoid alienating the business community of central Canada again, a vaguely worded resolution left plenty of room for western Liberals to argue that a revenue tariff would be the ultimate goal of a Liberal government.[67]

With some compromise, the national Liberals could achieve unity on most subjects of popular concern. But no Liberal could forget the fundamental division created by the Manitoba school question. Two opposed visions of Canada confronted one another. Some believed that only a homogeneous, English-speaking culture, at least outside Québec, could produce a strong country. Others, particularly French Canadians, believed that strength could only result from tolerance and mutual respect between the two founding cultures, and they considered the school policy of the Manitoba government a frontal assault upon privileges guaranteed in the constitutions of Canada and of Manitoba. Laurier's tact, aided by the blessing of not having to act when in opposition while the equally divided dominion government agonized over what to do, allowed him time to paper over party differences.

Yet the issue could destroy the Liberal party as easily as the government, as Laurier well knew. There had been some protests from Roman Catholic Liberals over Sifton's appointment as a vice-president of the party. It had worked out because Sifton had the sense to avoid comment on the school issue. However, Laurier viewed the unfolding political situation in Winnipeg in the chilly fall of 1893 with dismay. The local member of Parliament, Hugh John Macdonald, resigned his seat in October, and a by-election was set for 22 November. None other than "Fighting Joe" Martin emerged as the Liberal candidate. Of all Manitoba politicians it was the volatile Martin who symbolized to those in central and eastern Canada the worst excesses of Manitoban anti-French, anti-Catholic intolerance. Having him in Ottawa would exacerbate an already open sore in the party. Anxiously Laurier asked Sifton about "the personality of the candidate in Winnipeg," and Sifton admitted to sharing some of Laurier's apprehensions about Martin's future impact. In the meantime, however, the election was fought principally on the tariff rather than the school issue, and Martin's convincing victory was viewed as a public endorsement of Liberal policy. Sifton excepted, Martin had received the solid public backing of the Manitoba cabinet during his campaign.[68]

Not the least of the problems created by Martin's election was complication over political organization in Manitoba. Laurier had anticipated leaving the major responsibility for organizing the province with Sifton and the local government. But Martin had to have a place on the party's inner councils, if only by default, for he was the only Liberal member from the prairies. Unhappily, Sifton and Martin never worked together easily and gave conflicting advice to Laurier.

One thing all western Liberals could agree upon was the need for a tour of the West by the Liberal leader. If the party hoped to make inroads in the West, it was essential that Laurier show the flag. His tour, which began in Winnipeg on 3 September 1894, extended west to Vancouver and Victoria and ended with a banquet in the Manitoba capital on 25 October, was generally a great success. The elegantly trim figure with his resonant voice and personal charm drew large, usually sympathetic crowds wherever he went.

Although he accompanied Laurier on the platform on several occasions, Sifton spoke only at Brandon when he introduced the leader at a reception on 8 October. After fulsome praise for Laurier, Sifton made a short speech tinged with populist rhetoric. The Liberals, he declared, had worked to eliminate class legislation and to introduce the secret ballot. The Conservatives had set out to restore class privilege, the greatest example being the implementation of the National Policy protective tariff. The country had progressed little since its introduction in 1879, and the chief industry developed had been the manufacture of a select clique of millionaires. What had the Tories accomplished? They had increased the public debt; their government was rotted with corruption; the Maritimes and Québec were being depopulated. Land and railway monopolies had been crushing the West, which was forced to pay both the dividends of the CPR magnates and tribute to eastern millionaires under the tariff. In the best wheat land in the world, with a fine class of farmers, did one find truly independent farms? No. Everywhere one looked were "mortgaged farms and mortgaged chattels." Westerners had "paid tribute to the customs houses and to the banking institutions of the eastern manufacturers and it was God's truth the time had come when they could not pay any longer. (prolonged applause)." The price of wheat then stood at the ruinously low level of thirty-eight cents per bushel, so that the farmer could not even meet production costs. The Liberals were pledged to lower tariffs on the necessities of life and means of production to reduce the costs. They would reject "baneful" class legislation and introduce "legislation for the masses."[69]

Perhaps Sifton spoke with an eye to the Patron sentiment, which centred in the area surrounding Brandon. But his own later wealth and reputation lend a certain irony to his remarks. Even at the time he rarely expressed such opinions privately. It was easy in the midst of a depression to flail a government for doing nothing. Sifton should have realized this. The Manitoba government itself had been forced to curtail expenditures in every direction, and since 1892 it had been entirely unable to stimulate any new railway building or major reductions in freight rates. The government seemed becalmed, taking few of the initiatives required either to relieve the plight of the farmer or to halt the defections from its own party ranks.

   While attorney general, Sifton was always able to find time to devote to his growing family. The oldest son, John Wright, junior, was now in school. And a fourth son, christened Clifford, was born in Brandon on 3 August 1893. There were vacations almost every year, sometimes to the southern United States and often at a retreat on Lake of the Woods, near Rat Portage (Kenora), Ontario. In September 1893 the family went to the World Fair at Chicago, the great international exposition at which the Canadian and Manitoba governments, and the CPR, all had huge displays advertising the bounteous riches of Canada, particularly her western lands. Clifford and Arma were themselves frequently caught up in the whirl of social activity occasioned by his office and their rising status. Receptions for visiting dignitaries, receptions and levées of the lieutenant-governor, balls and banquets were all part of the rewards—and hazards—of the practising politician.
   Sifton still actively participated in sports and was occasionally to be found on the curling rinks, though he never played with the fierce competitiveness of so many of his fellow Manitobans. Indeed, the prudent politician found it wise to avoid scheduling elections and public meetings at bonspiel as well as at harvest time. The Siftons much preferred riding. They joined the Brandon Polo Club, which used to engage in mock hunts after the British fashion, and emulated the habits of a society to which they aspired. Horses, however, were more than a means to pursue admission to "society." Fine horses and horsemanship became one of Sifton's few lifelong passions outside his political career.
   The Siftons did not entirely escape tragedy and misfortune. In 1892 Clifford's sister, Sophia Molesworth, died suddenly. And his father was frequently in poor health, particularly during the spring and summer of 1894. Yet John Sifton remained an active worker in the IOGT and the Dominion Alliance as well as in Grace Methodist Church in Winnipeg, where he now resided. As inspector of public institutions, he visited the jails, hospitals, welfare homes, asylums, and government buildings across the province several times each year, compiling reports on the physical condition of the buildings and occasionally on their administration, with recommendations for changes, which were submitted to the minister of public works. Clifford saw to it that an occasional additional plum was thrown his father's way—auditing the books of various offices under the attorney general's department in 1891-92, for example, or being appointed in 1892 as commissioner to investigate charges of maladministration in the Deaf and Dumb Institute.[70] Possibly J.W.

Sifton's greatest personal satisfaction came when the Brandon hospital opened its doors in the spring of 1892, climaxing a decade of work in which he had been the initiator of the project and a prominent fund-raiser.[71]


Clifford Sifton's principal political concern remained the school question. He was responsible for the continuing defence of the system from federal interference on behalf of the Roman Catholic minority and also for implementing it within the province. The latter task had fallen to him in 1892, when he became minister responsible for the Department of Education. As established in 1890, the Department of Education was to be administered by the whole cabinet, but to all intents and purposes the responsibility had been handed to Joseph Martin. When Sifton joined the cabinet, he had declined the task, which passed to Provincial Secretary McLean; but when McLean was left without portfolio in May 1892, it was reassigned to the attorney general. There it remained while Sifton was in the provincial government.

The department had the power to appoint inspectors and instructors in normal schools, to establish standards for the certification of teachers, and to determine school vacations. An advisory board, appointed by the cabinet, was assigned powers to select textbooks and establish curricula, to determine the qualifications of teachers, and to exercise general powers in areas not specified in the law. The board was, in fact, a regulatory rather than an advisory institution; it was "a statutory body which was given the legislative authority to make regulations for education."[72]

The government was extremely parsimonious when it came to education. The school-age population doubled between 1890 and 1896, from twenty-five to fifty thousand, though the proportion actually registered dropped from 88 per cent to 76 per cent. Yet the legislative grant increased only from $118,000 to $165,000 in the same period. The Liberals had raised the maximum grant per school in 1888 from $100 to $150, to fulfil promises to relieve pressure on municipalities; but in 1893 it was reduced to $130, while municipal taxes continued to rise sharply. The average salary paid teachers actually decreased from $488 in 1890 to $434 in 1896, despite the fact that teacher qualifications showed on average a marked improvement and that the teacher/pupil ratio increased from 1:26 to 1:33 in the same period.[73] The fact was that in a time of forced restraint, the legislature would not accept any new educational expenditure.

Educational opportunity for most Manitobans was limited to a few primary years in a rather haphazard public school system. The Greenway government was trying to bring about some order, but given the pioneer conditions and the monetary limitations, no sudden change could have been expected. It was, consequently, little short of a miracle that many Manitobans emerged with any degree of literacy. No law compelled attendance. Schools were opened at the discretion of the trustees. Some were open during the summer, between planting and harvest, because it was impossible to secure regular attendance during the bitter Manitoba winters, or schoolhouses were not built for winter use, or it was deemed that the price of fuel was too high. Teachers in rural areas were often employed for only a few months in each year, with no security of tenure. Despite departmental pressure to upgrade themselves, many teachers had only third-class certificates, being little more than graduates of the public schools. Pupils were supposed to buy their own books, which many could not afford, and the schools in a number of rural areas were notoriously lacking in even the most basic books and equipment.

The debates in the legislature reflected the prevailing sentiment in rural Manitoba, to some extent shared by Sifton, that a basic public school education, equally accessible to everyone, was all that was required or that could be expected to be furnished by the public. Limited grants were given to the collegiate institutes, or high schools, located in Winnipeg, Brandon, and Portage la Prairie. But such grants were resented in rural areas. Sifton made it clear that he could not countenance a proposal to reduce or eliminate tuition fees for students attending high school. It would be "an injustice to the poorer classes who are not able to, as a rule, send their children to the high schools by reason of the fact that they are compelled to become self-sustaining at an early age," and they should not be forced to pay for schools from which they could derive no benefit. In any case he questioned the value of a high school education. The Ontario experience had been that thousands of young men and women had not been educated for the sorts of jobs which were available to them upon graduation, "and the result of it has been that an immense number of them have left the Province and found their way south of the line where congenial employment could more easily be got."[74] Sifton was opposed to the "tendency...to glorify literary education." In school, he later recalled, "We were taught nothing practical. The faculty of observation was destroyed by persistent and exclusive devotion to literary education." Farm children exposed to high school education learned nothing of agriculture, and "the result is that...we have been educating bookkeepers, lawyers, doctors and school teachers for the United States." The education system of Ontario "was educating young men and women away from the farm, which was the only profitable opening for them in Canada."[75]

In 1892 the government passed a bill to create an agricultural college, but budgetary difficulties made it impossible to fund it. There was public demand for the introduction of agriculture as a subject of instruction in the schools. Sifton would have preferred to provide it at the secondary level, but again funds could not be found, and finally in 1894 it was introduced in the public schools. "The object," he told the legislature, "was not to make farmers in the public schools but to train the pupils['] faculty of observation and to teach them not to despise all means of education except books." In the normal school and through the Farmers' Institutes, the province's teachers were being made acquainted with the subject. Additionally, a number of new and mostly "practical" subjects began to appear in the 1890's, including Canadian history, algebra, physics, botany, Euclid, music, temperance, and drawing.[76]

The University of Manitoba received ineffectual attention at the hands of the Greenway government. All teaching was done in the denominational colleges which together comprised the university; as an institution, the university only had powers to examine students and grant degrees. The colleges were privately funded, and although the university had been endowed with a land grant, it had little income and the provincial grant of $3,500 was scarcely enough to permit it to do more than conduct examinations. The university had ambitions to become a teaching institution, and in 1892 the law was changed to permit it to do so. But no money was provided. In 1893 Sifton sponsored a resolution to grant $10,000 for teaching purposes. The denominational colleges, he noted, could not cover all areas of instruction, particularly those requiring heavy capital outlay and expensive apparatus, such as the sciences. The grant, it was hoped, would allow the university to begin offering courses in mathematics, natural sciences, and modern languages, such courses to be available to all students without charge. The government, rather than the university, was to have power of appointment of professors, office to be held "during pleasure," and government approval was to be required before university lands were disposed of. The University Council was outraged at the provincial assumption of power, not so much over academic appointment and tenure as over the sale of lands. An amended bill which soothed the academic tempers was shortly passed.[77]

But it was an exercise in futility. The government found that it could not bring the legislation into effect, given the temper of the rural members. If needed local improvements could not be provided, if local taxes were rising and the province was cutting back everywhere else, how could it even think of so large an appropriation for an elitist institution that benefited so few Manitobans? Robert Hill Myers, MLA for Minnedosa, declared that he "did not see that the province was called upon to begin the expenditure of this first sum for the University which was bound to rapidly increase until it drew heavily upon the funds of the government." The government should husband its resouces and aid municipalities. Not only did Sifton find that he could not bring his measure into effect, but in subsequent years he had to fight simply to preserve the $3,500 grant.[78]

Underlying the difficulties of provincial education policy in these years was an enervating, sometimes aggravating uncertainty about the future of the school system. The minority counsel, J.S. Ewart, contended before the dominion Privy Council in Ottawa in November 1892 that the Judicial Committee decision in the Barrett case had not precluded an appeal to the

Governor General-in-Council for remedial legislation, under section 22 (2) and (3) of the Manitoba Act and section 93 (3) and (4) of the British North America Act. Not having received any official notice of the hearing, Manitoba did not offer a counterargument. Sifton was firm, nevertheless, in his public reaction. The dominion government had no right "to interfere in the matter in any way whatever." It was wrong in principle. Constitutionally, education "lies wholly within the jurisdiction of the Provincial Government." He believed that the Judicial Committee decision ruled out any appeal. Finally, he considered that any attempt by Ottawa to interfere "would clearly be taken at the dictation of Quebec" and would therefore be doubly objectionable.[79]

Two conflicting strategies were apparent from the beginning of this second phase of the school dispute. The dominion government had promised in 1891 to take remedial action if the court appeal failed. Now it was being pressed in opposite directions by its French and English supporters, and it desperately wanted to make its proceedings appear to be impartial and to create the impression that any decision to introduce remedial legislation would arise solely from legal and constitutional obligations. The Manitoba government was not touched by any such conflicting pressures. Sifton wanted to avoid even the slightest indication of accepting the proposition that the dominion Privy Council could sit as a judicial body. He believed that it was a political body which would reach a political decision. The public must accept this interpretation if Manitoba hoped to win. In a conflict with the Dominion, he told an Ontario friend, "we will be largely dependent upon the support of Ontario." "I have a great deal of confidence," he added, "that when it comes to the point of decision, the independent Protestants of Ontario will see that our position is upheld."[80]

In January 1893, the dominion Privy Council held formal hearings at which the Manitoba government declined to appear. A month later it resolved to send the touchy issue to the courts for an opinion, although it took until May even to complete the questions to be considered. It was necessary to determine, first, whether the decision of 1892 had precluded an appeal by the minority. If not, was there ground for an appeal under the Manitoba and British North America Acts? If so, which statute applied? And if there was a well-founded grievance involving rights acquired after the Union, did the Governor General-in-Council have the power to remedy it?[81]

Sifton's position was that Manitoba would not respond to the federal initiative and would act only if the province's rights were being threatened. Accordingly, the Manitoba government declined to name counsel to present its side of the case when it was argued before the Supreme Court on 17 October. The court therefore selected the eminent lawyer Christopher Robinson to substitute for the respondent. Sifton held that the reference to the Supreme Court by the dominion government was merely "for advice.... It is purely a voluntary proceeding on their part and we are not a party to it in any way."[82] This did not prevent him from succinctly restating Manitoba's adamant attitude:

> Our position with regard to the petition of the Catholic minority is simply this:
>
> 1st—That in our opinion the Governor-General-in-Council has no power to interfere.
>
> 2nd—That if he has power, it is clearly contrary to good policy that he should interfere.
>
> By referring the matter to the Supreme Court to ascertain what the powers of the Government are, the Government has practically intimated that if its powers are upheld it will exercise them. It must, therefore, be understood that upon this question we are at issue with the Dominion Government and we intend to remain so until it is settled.
>
> Should it be held by the courts that the Governor-General-in-Council has the legal power to interfere[,] the carrying out of such interference will involve forcing upon the people of Manitoba legislation which her people have repudiated. It is quite needless for me to point out that such a task would hardly be accomplished in the present generation.[83]

Despite his public belligerence, Sifton was naturally anxious to bring the Catholic schools under the jurisdiction of the Department of Education and the advisory board, and he hoped that a flexible approach would have the desired result. The greatest confrontation came in Winnipeg, where Catholic ratepayers were being taxed like all other citizens for the support of national schools. Lacking physical or geographic separation from the Protestant majority, the Catholic minority in the city found it exceedingly difficult to maintain their own schools. Rural areas were altogether different. Particularly in the French-speaking districts, the Catholic population was grouped in a solid majority. Departmental figures reveal the slow rate of conversion to the national system, as five so-called French, or rural Catholic, schools received the grant in 1891, seven in 1892, and twelve in 1893.[84]

On the surface, it was simple to qualify for the provincial grant; if a teacher had a certificate and was willing to sign a declaration that he or she was willing to abide by the regulations with respect to religious teaching, texts, and so forth, there were few difficulties. In practice, the department was willing to have its inspectors look the other way if violations of the regulations were not too blatant, provided the declarations were in order. The department was more concerned that the French-speaking pupils make progress in learning English than with whether a furtive "Hail Mary" was added to the scripture readings or even whether the school day was slightly pared to permit religious instruction after hours. Archbishop Taché naturally pressed his teachers not to sign the declaration and to struggle along and hold out while the courts and governments were deciding their fate.

In 1892 Sifton hired an inspector, A.L. Young of Winnipeg, to travel among the Catholic school districts along the Red, Assiniboine, Seine, and Rat Rivers to try to persuade them to accept the national school system. Although he could not have official status as an inspector in non-national schools, Young was welcomed as a visitor. He found most of them in good condition, though sometimes short of seating and suitable equipment. Half the teachers held first-class certificates; 20 per cent, second-class certificates; and 10 per cent, third-class certificates. The remainder presumably held interim certificates, which could have been extended under the national system while qualifications were upgraded. "With remarkably few exceptions," observed Young, "English is taught in all the schools. The parents and trustees recognize the desirability of having their children study English, consequently those teachers who have a sufficient knowledge of the English language to teach it successfully are in much greater demand and receive higher wages than those who understand the French language only." He found many of the students quite capable of reading, translating, and clearly pronouncing English but commented oddly that "in regard to French reading there is room for considerable improvement in expression." In most other areas, from arithmetic to geography, he found the schools doing a creditable job.[85]

To the government it all seemed so simple! If only Taché would be reasonable! If only he would let his teachers sign a declaration that they either did not teach religion during school hours or taught according to the regulations prescribed by the advisory board, the government would then be flexible and accommodating. But Taché still hoped to win, to force the dominion government to fulfil its promise of 1891 to institute remedial action. He could not afford to lose the schools before the issue was decided. Besides, it galled the archbishop that the government was so generous with the Mennonites settled in the south of the province since the 1870's. They were allowed a large degree of independence. Their schools were conducted largely in German. They were allowed a Mennonite school inspector and a normal school at Gretna which turned out teachers with third-class certificates, enough to qualify for the grant. They made no religious or linguistic sacrifices, yet, observed Lieutenant-Governor Schultz, "they are accorded facilities which, were the separate school right not involved, would go a long way toward satisfying our R.C. population." What had the Mennonites done to deserve such preferential treatment? Would Franco-Manitobans be treated as generously? Evidently not.[86]

The Catholic schools, particularly those in rural districts, mostly managed to preserve their independence. As long as they could collect municipal taxes, they could survive with a few expedients—by paring budgets, by hiring less qualified teachers or nuns when available, by using the parish priest as a teacher, and by raising funds locally. One way or another the provincial grant of up to $130 per school could be partially made up or dispensed with. With growing irritation the department concluded that if the carrot would not work, the stick also must be applied. Besides, many Protestants were beginning to take notice of the stubborn survival of the Catholic schools. When Frank Schultz, a leading Orangeman, wrote to Sifton demanding action, the government decided to plug the legal loophole during the 1894 session.[87]

This development was ironic and sad, because throughout 1893 Lieutenant-Governor Schultz—no relation of the Orangeman—had been labouring to bring about a compromise. While Sifton and Greenway, on the one hand, and Taché, on the other, were still at opposite poles on the principle involved, the government had reportedly agreed that Franco-Manitobans should at least be treated as generously as the Mennonites and were prepared to modify the Public Schools Act to permit the required administrative flexibility by giving the department greater discretionary powers. They also claimed to be willing to consider restoring the French normal school. All of this, hoped Schultz, would help to cushion the impact of a Supreme Court decision that he expected to be adverse to the minority.[88] Sifton even seemed to be preparing the way for such a solution when he told the legislature that the government school policy "made no distinction between Germans, Icelanders, Mennonites, Canadians or any other classes of the community. All who were willing to conduct the schools on the lines laid down in the act received the grant no matter what their nationality or religion."[89]

Thus, it was doubly crushing to the Catholics when, without warning, the government proposed a few days later to amend the Schools Act to prohibit the raising of taxes by municipalities for schools not recognized by the department. Now there was no hope that the schools could long survive. While the Orangemen professed great satisfaction, Sifton calmly assured the House that the amendments constituted merely minor changes in detail, being intended only to carry out the intent of the 1890 legislation.[90] Recognizing the true danger to the Catholic schools, the French members, led by J.E.P. Prendergast, vented their futile rage. Prime Minister Thompson acknowledged that it made matters "much worse than before"; and added with weary discouragement tinged with bitterness, "I do not know why these people [the Manitoba government] should be so eager to tear this country to pieces, but they seem bent upon civil war."[91]

Still reeling from the blow from the Manitoba government, the minority was knocked to its knees by the decision of the Supreme Court, announced 20 February, just a week after the introduction of the provincial amendments. By a split 3-2 verdict the court ruled in effect that the 1892 decision of the Judicial

Committee·had precluded any appeal by the minority to obtain remedial action for their grievances.

While preparations were being made to appeal the case to the Judicial Committee, Taché petitioned the federal government to disallow the amendments to the Schools Act. He noted bitterly that on third reading the government bill had the unanimous support of the Protestant members, while all four Catholic members opposed it. This, he declared, "proves that the School Question is merely and simply a question of religion and that Catholics are perfectly justified when they say that they are victims to a religious persecution." At the same time Lieutenant-Governor Schultz appealed to Greenway for some show of magnanimity. But the irresolute Greenway was "weak and often overruled by his colleagues."[92]

With pain and despair Taché must have reflected on the conjunction of difficulties which now threatened to destroy his life's work. The separate schools were nearly lost. The courts had ruled adversely once, and now, though not finally, a second time. The federal government, which he had supposed in 1870 would guarantee minority rights, had repeatedly failed to do so. French language privileges had disappeared with hardly a serious scrap. Taché could point to many villains: duplicitous, disloyal politicians, well-intentioned but spineless leaders, Protestant bigots, and Francophobes. He was old, and tired, and sick. The initiative seemed to have passed to the other side, led by an unflappable master strategist.

When Taché died in June 1894, he must have known that the resistance of the Catholic schools was crumbling in face of Sifton's latest assault. By the end of 1894, according to the department, thirty-seven "French schools" had "accepted the public school system," while twenty had been disbanded, leaving forty-four still functioning as separate or convent schools.[93] The effect of the legislation was graphically reflected in the correspondence of the parish priests with the archbishop of St. Boniface. Adolphe Bourret of Sainte-Agathe had been confident in 1892 that the five schools in his parish could survive, but in 1895 they were hanging on only with the proceeds of a local bazaar and some of the profits from a lottery which the archbishop had organized in Québec on behalf of the schools. Or there was the case of Father Dufresne of Lorette, whose school had closed in April 1894 for lack of funds. "C'est le commencement de la fin," he wrote disconsolately.[94]

It was just this trend which made Sifton's inspector A.L. Young optimistic. "There is no doubt that with the exercise of good judgment," he declared in December 1894, "Separate Schools will be practically abolished in this Province before the end of another year."[95] His prophecy was not borne out, since the separate schools received new hope early in 1895 which enabled them to cling tenaciously to their precarious existence. But it was a very close thing.

During 1894 public pressure forced the government into an ever more rigid position. In Winnipeg, where the Catholics had been negotiating in hopes of obtaining government concessions, the representatives of the Catholic schools received a chilly reception in the summer. They had asked for one-year extensions to permits of Catholic teachers; for permission to end the school day at three o'clock to allow religious instruction after school; and for authorization to use non-sectarian textbooks then used in the Catholic schools. Sifton's frigid reply concluded that "the Government cannot consistently with the principles which are embodied in the 'Public Schools Act,' of this Province, make any departures in the direction intimated. The advantages of the Public School System are available to all citizens of the Province for the benefit of their children, and no distinction can be made in favor of any particular class."[96]

Given the progress in absorbing the Catholic schools, there were those who thought that the time had come to make the national schools wholly secular. The Catholics, who complained that the religious exercises prescribed by the advisory board were Protestant, would then have no ground of complaint—or so argued men like Joseph Martin. Without consulting the government, he advanced such a proposal publicly, as the logical conclusion of the policy introduced in 1890. Probably many Manitobans agreed with him. Use of the exercises was optional, according to the decision of the local trustees. Of 786 school districts in 1895, for example, only 433 used religious exercises at the end of the school day, only 396 closed school with prayer, only 295 used the Bible at all, and 205 taught the Ten Commandments. Some 629, however, admitted to giving "moral instruction."[97] Sifton instantly perceived nevertheless that secularizing the schools would be foolhardy, as it would certainly destroy the consensus of support which the government had managed to build. Those who opposed "godless schools" believed passionately in the need for religious instruction in some form. When Laurier anxiously wrote suggesting that nothing be done, because secularizing the schools would not satisfy the Catholics and would only antagonize many others, Sifton assured him that he agreed wholeheartedly and that there was "no possibility of any action being taken in the direction indicated."[98]

It was vital to preserve the government's popular base because, as Sifton knew, the war was far from won. The minority appeal was argued before the Judicial Committee of the Privy Council in December 1894, in a case known as *Brophy and Others vs. the Attorney General of Manitoba.* Despite having secured the strongest available British counsel, Sifton realized that defeat was possible. Early in January rumours began to appear in the press that the Supreme Court decision had been overturned. Sifton read a transcript of the argument before the court and the judges' remarks and concluded that the dominion government's contention would be upheld. "It is a matter of great regret that the decision should be on this line," he told Laurier, "Not from a Manitoba standpoint because I fancy it will make little difference to us here, but from the standpoint of Canadian politics generally."[99]

His prediction proved correct. The Catholic minority rejoiced as the Judicial Committee rendered an unanimous decision on 29 January. The court concluded essentially that the 1892 decision in the Barrett case did not preclude a minority appeal for redress of grievances. The applicable statute was held to be the Manitoba Act, and the court concluded that subsections (2) and (3) of section 22 did not depend for their interpretation solely upon subsection (1), but covered privileges accumulated in law since the union. Given the basic ruling, the court found that the minority did have a legitimate grievance on the basis that both the statute creating a Department of Education and the Public Schools Act 1890 infringed on rights enjoyed by law prior to 1890. Finally—and crucially—the dominion government was held to have the power to remedy such grievances as the minority might appeal to it.

Having decided as much, the court also made a number of curious and confusing comments which clouded the political issue now before the Canadian public. Some parts of the judgment could be read as implying that almost the whole of the Manitoba legislation of 1890 created a grievance for the minority, who naturally seized on these words and looked forward to a return to the system which had then existed. But the court also denied that its decision was inconsistent with that of 1892, which must have meant that the Public Schools Act had some validity. After a tortuous discussion of the problem of "intent" and of the history of the dual educational system between 1870 and 1890, the court concluded that action could be taken to remedy the grievances, although "it is not for this tribunal to intimate the precise steps to be taken." The old system need not be entirely restored, however. "The system of education embodied in the Acts of 1890 no doubt commends itself to, and adequately supplies the wants of the great majority of the inhabitants of the province. All legitimate ground of complaint would be removed if that system were supplemented by provisions which would remove the grievance upon which the appeal is founded, and were modified so far as might be necessary to give effect to these policies."[100]

The decision did not produce a spirit of compromise on either side. The jubilant Catholics were given new reason to cling to their faltering schools. The dominion government now would be pressed to see that the Catholics obtained their "just rights," declared Adelard Langevin, the young, emotional, and temperamental archbishop-elect of St. Boniface.[101] For him this meant nothing less than the substantial restoration of privileges enjoyed prior to 1890.

There was no less rigidity, and greater hostility, in the provincial government response. James Fisher, long a supporter of the minority cause, proposed a compromise on the Ontario model. That drew a heated rejoinder from Sifton. He moved that the legislature affirm Manitoba's loyal acceptance of the Brophy decision. At the same time, she must assert her determination to control her own educational policy, resisting "by all constitutional means" and "to the utmost extent" of the powers of the legislature any attack on the school system established in 1890. Where was there evidence that the Catholic Church would agree to such a compromise? Catholic officials in Manitoba were, after all, demanding a full return to the old dual system. But the Catholic people of Manitoba were not a unit on the school issue. Was this not shown by the fact that nearly half of the former separate schools had chosen to enter the public system? Further, while Sifton had administered the schools, "Roman Catholics had come to the office, and with tears in their eyes, stated that they wished they could have their children educated like the other children of the province" but were prevented by the clergy. The Catholics, he flatly asserted, had no legitimate grievances. The national school system was available to all freely, equally, and without prejudice. Its schools had been declared by the Judicial Committee itself in 1892 to be non-denominational rather than Protestant. No one forced Catholic children to attend the schools or to take religious instruction in them. The dominion government was being asked to determine general education policy within the province and would likely try to act against Manitoba, not because the Catholics had a legitimate grievance, but because the voice of Québec counted for more than that of Manitoba.

The Catholics should consider themselves fortunate to have the national school system available. With statistics and reports Sifton attempted to show that "the old separate schools which had pretended to educate did not educate." It was a line of attack which was to assume prominence in coming months as Manitoba took its case to the public; it also flew in the face of much contained in the confidential reports of Sifton's own inspector, A.L. Young. Sifton quoted from the requirements for first-class teachers' certificates under the old Roman Catholic system in which teachers were expected to demonstrate mostly theological knowledge. He also cited statistics purporting to show that Catholic countries had higher illiteracy and crime rates.

Fisher, concluded Sifton, must surely "be blind to history when he spoke of compromising with the church of Rome, whose educational policy was as enduring as the seven hills of the Eternal City. Rome never compromised, but pressed on and on, until she had as much control of education as she could get." Sifton did not want to be unjust "to any section of the community, and no one was worthy of being called a man who would not accord religious freedom to all, but he supported this system because he believed it was in the best interests of the whole people of the province." The government was therefore determined "to fight the case to the last ditch, and to maintain the rights of the province so long as they remained on the treasury benches."[102]

Each side now had won important victories, and the battle lines were drawn. Even as the dominion cabinet had begun to hold hearings on the dispute and to devise new strategy, a defiant challenge from Manitoba served notice that the war would forthwith be carried to the people.

# 5

# Schools and Politics
# (1895–96)

The Manitoba school legislation of 1890 has been described as a "profound attack on the terms of the composition of Canada."[1] If it is accepted that one of the basic principles of Confederation was federal protection of minority rights and, even more fundamentally, that Confederation entailed a compact between two founding races, the proposition is true. According to this theory, Confederation entailed not only constitutional guarantees for minority rights, but an understanding that both founding races would be accorded equitable treatment throughout the country. The guarantees for minority educational and linguistic rights incorporated into the Manitoba Act, 1870, and the North-West Territories Act, 1875 and 1877, are held to be proof of the continuing commitment to these principles by the dominion government.

Whatever the merits of this theory,[2] a great many Canadians, including Clifford Sifton, did not accept it. Men like John Wright Sifton in western Ontario had not suddenly shed their animus toward Roman Catholicism and their dislike of French Canadians as a result of Confederation. Their mistrust of French Canada had been forged in the Union of the Canadas when French-Canadian votes forced separate schools on Canada West; by French-Canadian denial of representation by population; and by French-Canadian hostility to the acquisition of the western British territories. Backward, corrupt, French-Canadian grafters were perceived as a millstone around the necks of those who wanted to get on with building a progressive, transcontinental, and "British" nation.

Confederation, they understood, relieved them of this burden. It allowed

French Canadians to protect their culture in Québec, while the rest of Canada—principally Ontario—occupied itself with nation-building. Federal guarantees of limited minority rights in Québec, Ontario, and certain federal institutions were not construed with magnanimity. They were reluctantly conceded as essential to the achievement of Confederation; and they were considered maximum and final concessions, not to be extended. Mean-spirited as this attitude may appear, thousands of Upper Canadians would have contended that over a quarter-century of experience under the Union of the Canadas had demonstrated that a dual nation would not work. A further quarter-century of unrelieved French-English discord and sluggish national progress after 1867 only reaffirmed the problems of duality. In the opinion of many English Canadians, French Canadians had aggressively sought to extend their privileges beyond the framework of 1867, and their efforts were particularly questionable and ill-advised in the case of the prairie West.

This issue greatly irritated many Manitobans. Not only had the incubus of dualism been fastened on the province by the Manitoba Act, but it had been done underhandedly. Although the people of Red River had requested official status for French and English during the second convention in 1870, they had specifically rejected provincial status and had not even discussed or requested a dual school system. One of Sifton's most effective points when speaking on the school issue was that the minority's principal guarantees had been obtained by Louis Riel and Bishop Taché, not openly, but in secret. Taché had pulled strings in Québec to obtain the concessions and counted on the political power of Québec to maintain them. What moral obligation could Manitobans feel toward guarantees so obtained?

Manitobans like Sifton had also developed their own peculiar ideas on Canadian nationhood. They found themselves in a hinterland, removed from the centres of power and resentful of the economic control of central Canada. Sentiment toward "the East" became ambivalent, often hostile. Manitobans sensed that the school question was another great federal-provincial confrontation in the tradition of the railway disallowance issue. The province was already excessively constrained by monopolies, tariffs, federal control of  public lands, and other economic hindrances. She must withstand the attempts of the dominion authorities and their Québec allies to interfere in educational matters and impose a social structure which, whatever its merits in central Canada, had no proper place in the West.

Manitoban thought, furthermore, was strikingly influenced by the United States. The completion of the CPR had by no means ended intercourse between Manitobans and their southern neighbours. Many Manitobans continued to use American routes to the East. The business communities of St. Paul and Winnipeg were in regular contact, and a great deal of trade crossed the international boundary. The provincial press was constantly filled with American news. The farmers were unfailingly aware of Chicago livestock and grain prices. Agrarian groups organized on American models and studied the efforts of American farmers to cope with railways, elevator operators, millers, the courts, and state legislatures. While they could be fiercely nationalistic, Manitobans were not hesitant to borrow ideas from the American experience.

This was certainly true in education. Manitobans believed the educational problems facing them resembled more closely the American than the Québec experience. A dual system seemed irrelevant, for Manitoba was no longer dual in character, but was becoming multiracial. Already the Germans and Mennonites were as numerous as the Franco-Manitobans; there was a large Icelandic community; the first Ukrainians were beginning to appear. Would each require a separate school system? What would be the result? The protest that the question was of no consequence, that only the French Canadians had constitutional guarantees, that they were part of a national community of French-speaking people, was impatiently dismissed. The issue was, what was right for Manitoba? When one of Sifton's opponents argued that it was impossible to "have national schools in a free country," the attorney general promptly referred him "to thirty or forty states of the neighboring Union" where "from the Atlantic to the Pacific they have national schools, and national unity."[3]

In the United States the schools had been a major instrument in forging unity from diversity. Duality had caused divisions in Canada long before 1890, and Sifton indignantly rejected the charge that it was Manitoba that had "thrown the apple of discord into Dominion politics."[4] Sifton and his followers agreed wholeheartedly with the efforts of the Equal Rights Association, formed in 1889, to eliminate the constitutional guarantees for minority cultural rights outside Québec. It seemed a clear and simple proposition that national unity could only arise from cultural uniformity, while the way of duality or diversity could only lead to disunity.[5]

On another level, the debate centred on two distinctly differing philosophies of education. "A Catholic," writes one authority, "starts with an assumption that religion is the central concern of human existence. A Catholic believes that his purpose in life is to learn to live in such a way as to prepare himself for an immortal supernatural destiny." The Church is the visible institution established by God to help mankind in seeking this transcendent objective, and the Church must therefore control the education of a Catholic child. The public schools, by contrast, have to take a "neutral" position on many moral and theological issues because of the diversity of beliefs encompassed in the public system. But from a Catholic perspective a public system cannot be neutral; its very assumptions and goals are at odds with Catholic belief. "By default, civic or political virtue has become the primary goal of public school education. In other words, these schools must exist primarily to produce good citizens." Such a system is "incapable" of providing adequate care "for the moral side of a Catholic child's education."[6]

The dual system established in Manitoba in 1871, and patterned on that of Québec, exactly suited the philosophy of the Church. It had nearly absolute control of the education of Catholic children. The role of the state was merely supportive, raising taxes and encouraging attendance. The Church could establish curricula, approve texts, set standards for teachers, and inspect its own schools. All subjects were taught in a religious context consistent with Church dogma and interpretation of revelation. Sifton was quite right when he stated in 1895 that the Church was unwilling to compromise and that those who suggested a compromise on the Ontario model had no hope of obtaining the willing consent of the Church. When the St. Boniface authorities later reluctantly agreed to approve an arrangement in 1896 which allowed some state control, they clearly believed that they were being defeated on this basic issue.[7]

Protestants, for their part, began with the assumption that the state was, or ought to be, at bottom essentially Christian; that a diversity of interpretations of the Christian gospel existed; and that the Christian consensus which underlay the society ought to provide the possibility of agreement on a common set of moral and religious values which could be taught to all children in a common school system. The Catholics could maintain their distinctiveness outside the schools, just as the Protestant denominations did. Furthermore, the Protestants tended to assume that subjects such as science or music were, or could be, essentially secular and that the moral lessons of subjects like history and literature ought to be less religious than patriotic. Most Protestants agreed that religion ought to be taught separately from school work and that it should be optional. The extremists wanted all religion deleted from the curriculum. Either solution was intolerable to the Catholics. As J.S. Ewart, the leading advocate on the Catholic side, wrote, "the Protestant and Catholic methods of education are irreconcilably discrepant. It is often argued that all children may well be taught together every subject but religion ... [but] the Roman Catholic idea of education is that the religious element ought to pervade even the studies that are usually termed secular."[8] In a sense, the Protestants resented and objected to the undemocratic side of Catholicism which held that there was only one right interpretation of truth. The Protestants claimed liberty of conscience as a democratic right, contending that the Church through the schools ought not to be the prime, and certainly not the sole, arbiter of beliefs and moral values.[9]

How, then, did Sifton view the proposition that parents ought to be able to select the kinds of education they wished for their children without being financially disadvantaged? Why, he often asked in reply, were Roman Catholics the only ones to be so favoured? If these principles were right for Catholics, why were they any less right for Mennonites, Icelanders, Anglicans, Jews, or atheists? To him the constitutional guarantees for Catholics amounted to special privileges. Most westerners accepted the proposition that such special privileges either should not exist or must be available to all equally, which in turn would destroy the ability of the state to provide a basic level of education and inculcate a common set of values.

Sifton believed that the state's basic educational goals were to create national unity out of cultural diversity and to enable each child to have the opportunity to function effectively in a progressive, individualistic society. The Catholic educational system, in the opinion of Protestants, did neither. It perpetuated cultural differences and left most of its students permanently disadvantaged. In part this reflected only Protestant prejudice, the widespread belief that the Catholic Church turned out nothing but unthinking sheep, subject entirely to the orders of the Church. It also, however, reflected the opinion of thoughtful men who realized that the Catholic philosophy of education differed fundamentally from the competitive individualism which they believed essential.[10]

In this intensely fought struggle, then, each side considered that it was acting in defence of principles which the other side endangered. These involved concepts as basic as the purpose of education and of national existence and the meaning of life. The issues of the respective jurisdictions of dominion and provincial authorities, of church and state, and of whether the state in its actions was infringing upon or upholding the civil liberties of individuals remained at the core of the school question.

That the battle was fought out on a more mundane level is scarcely surprising. Prejudice and questionable tactics were unhappily found on both sides, though perhaps more notably on the side of the Manitoba government. Leaders of each side were appealing to men who had little philosophical understanding of their own strong passions. Neither side held quite so rigidly in practice to the diametrically opposed principles which they proclaimed in public; yet there was never enough flexibility for a weak and indecisive dominion government to force them together.

Led by Clifford Sifton, the Manitoba government skilfully parried each dominion manoeuvre and adeptly rationalized its actions. Untroubled by serious internal division, the provincial Liberals could calmly observe the contortions through which the issue put the Conservatives at Ottawa. The prime minister, now the well-intentioned but indecisive Sir Mackenzie Bowell, was badly equipped for an extended war of nerves, and his divided followers continually undermined him. Archbishop Langevin too was a weaker leader of the Catholic Church in Manitoba than Taché had been. He was rigid, inexperienced, and unrealistic in the political arena, and he did not carry the requisite weight with his fellow prelates in Québec or the rest of Canada. The Church, already badly situated for a battle with a strongly entrenched provincial government, was constantly divided on tactics and on the question of compromise.[11]

Early in 1895 the direction of Manitoba policy was entirely in Clifford Sifton's hands. Premier Greenway was stricken with erysipelas and unable to undertake any serious work between January and April, during which period Sifton was acting premier. On 16 February, just two days into the legislative session, the Manitoba government was advised that the dominion Privy Council intended to hold hearings on the school case, commencing on 26 February. Sifton could not take time to go to Ottawa to present the provincial side of the argument, so he authorized D'Alton McCarthy to represent the province and seek an extension until after the session. This concession was bluntly refused, and McCarthy was given less than a week to prepare to defend the province's interest.[12]

That the dominion cabinet would find in favour of the minority was practically predetermined. Sifton's main concern was to score points which would be valuable in the coming campaign. He was now prepared to concede that the dominion government had the legal right to interfere with Manitoba schools; but morally it had no right, he told the legislature, to interfere with the will of the people. McCarthy picked up this theme when he told the Privy Council, "It is trifling almost with the people of Manitoba to tell them that because 10,000 half-breeds passed a separate school law in 1871 the province was for ever bound down to that system. Now according to the last census [1891] there was a population in Manitoba of 152,506, of whom 20,571 were Roman Catholics."[13]

The second major objective was to undermine the dominion government's attempts to appear to be acting judicially and aiding the minority solely as a legal and constitutional obligation. Sifton was delighted that in the Ottawa hearings of 4 to 7 March, McCarthy succeeded in getting Mackenzie Bowell virtually to admit the provincial contention.

> From the first [he told McCarthy] I anticipated difficulty in making it clear to the public that the legal aspect of this question had passed away and that it was now purely a question of Government policy. I do not think the other side yet realize how important it is to us to make this clear. If they did I fancy the Premier would not have given the case away as he did in reply to you. However I think that we have sufficient ground now to go upon and they have gone so far in admitting our contention that they cannot very well get back.[14]

Down in Ottawa the prime minister was desperately trying to avoid having to make a decision. He promptly blundered again. He believed, as had his predecessor, that Lieutenant-Governor Schultz wielded some influence over Premier Greenway; he also accepted Schultz's reports—eagerly concurred in by other Manitoba Conservatives—that at heart Greenway was a moderate and opposed to Sifton's extreme position. Both beliefs were ill-founded. The agitated prime minister wrote to Schultz, however, suggesting that he approach Greenway to make some "slight concession" as a means of settling the question, rather than submit to extreme and irrevocable remedial legislation by the dominion Parliament.[15] Perhaps the prime minister hoped to drive a wedge between premier and attorney general. Certainly he wanted to test the firmness of the Manitobans' resolve. He had acted on his own, however, with no indication that many of his colleagues would have accepted as adequate any "slight concession" which Greenway might have made, let alone the Québec members or the Roman Catholic Church. Most important, he had revealed his bluff, his personal indecision, and the division within his cabinet. Sifton was able to take the measure of his opponent and thereafter moved with astonishing assurance.[16]

This line of attack having led nowhere, the dominion cabinet finally issued a remedial order on 21 March. There was no hint of compromise, as the province was directed to modify its legislation of 1890 in such a way as to restore to the minority the substance of the separate school system. The Catholics were to be given "the right to build, maintain, equip, manage, conduct and support" their schools as they had prior to 1890; they were to share proportionately in public education funds and to be exempt from supporting any other schools.[17] The order provoked an instant response. Protest meetings were held all over Manitoba, with calls for burning both the remedial order and the dominion cabinet in effigy. Major Stewart Mulvey, a former grand master of the Manitoba Orangemen, heatedly demanded, "If it cost $8,000,000 to subdue about 300 half-breeds on the banks of the Saskatchewan, how many millions will it take to make slaves of the 200,000 inhabitants of Manitoba, the bone and sinew of the Dominion, by subjecting them to the teachings of the hierarchy for another century? Let the government count the cost."[18]

Sifton avoided incendiary comments. Instead, as he had promised McCarthy, he adjourned the legislature until 9 May to "consider" the province's response. He also had promised that the response would be negative, but the delay would serve to place additional strains on the unhappy dominion cabinet, now facing a general election. Meanwhile, he suggested to Laurier, the Liberals could put pressure on the government by reminding Quebeckers that the remedial order was not itself of any legislative effect. It should be argued that the remedial order was a purely political delaying tactic to avoid remedial legislation prior to an election and that there was no guarantee that the government if returned to power would introduce the legislation.[19]

The provincial legislature had not long been adjourned when an opportunity arose for Sifton to put even more pressure on the dominion authorities. In the solidly Conservative riding of Haldimand, the Liberals had chosen not to nominate a candidate during a ministerial by-election, but representing D'Alton McCarthy's nascent third party was Jeffery A. McCarthy, a partner in D'Alton McCarthy's Barrie law firm. Realistically there was little hope that he could win. Yet when D'Alton McCarthy asked Sifton to speak in the campaign, he held a hasty conference with McMillan, Cameron, and Watson and concluded that it was too good an opportunity to miss. Coming so soon after the issuance of the remedial order, Sifton's speeches would secure an attention throughout Ontario that otherwise would be impossible to obtain. What more dramatic way could there be to present Manitoba's case in the province which would be crucial in the forthcoming general election?[20]

Sifton, recalled one of his contemporaries, "was a speaker of unique ability, cogent in his reasoning, and delivering his arguments in such continuous and aggressive sequence that they seemed to batter down all opposition."[21] Rarely was he in better form than in his Ontario tour which began in Hagersville and Caledonia on 11 and 12 April and concluded with a grand rally in Massey Hall, Toronto, on 24 April. He played easily and skillfully on the prejudices of his audiences. On one level, he presented the issue as fundamental to national unity. Using the figures of the 1891 census, he argued that only 12,000 of the 20,000 Catholics in the province were French-speaking. It was for these 12,000 people that special privileges were to be created, privileges to which most of the 150,000 people in the province were opposed. By what right did the French population demand special privileges? After all, there were 15,000 Mennonites; were they not more deserving? And if the Mennonites and the French, what of the thousands of Icelanders, Jews, Hungarians, Roumanians, Finlanders, and other nationalities? Where would it end? Something had to be done with "all those foreign elements." It was "upon the English and Protestant people," who had largely come from Ontario, "that most largely rests the duty of developing that Province in a manner consonant with British institutions." They had to be able "to take all this heterogeneous mass and make [it] into one, bring the different elements together."

On another level, he was determined to destroy the contention that the Catholics had any moral right to their own schools. The schools had been secured by underhanded means in 1870 and had failed to educate ever since. He alleged that parish priests who had doubled as paid teachers—a self-evident evil to many Protestants—had made inaccurate and misleading returns about the number of pupils in attendance, that schools were not kept open more than a few days a week or a few weeks a year, and had low standards and inadequate inspection, with the result that "throughout that section of the country where the separate School districts were in existence the people have grown up in a state of absolute ignorance and illiteracy." Such had been the result of the old system which the dominion government wanted to restore.

One could go from one end of Manitoba to the other, and he would not find among the business or professional men a young man from any of those [French métis] families. The children of such families remained on the farm where they were born. There was no idea of progress among them. If this system were imposed upon them permanently it would simply make them hewers of wood and drawers of water.

The thrust of Sifton's argument was that the French Catholic minority was counting on Québec sympathy and political power to restore a corrupt and inefficient system. This would fragment the school system, perpetuating divisions of class, race, and language. The government was already spending one-fifth of its revenue on education and was straining to provide a basic education for all children in the province, even in sparsely settled districts. Fragmentation would render this system impossible to maintain. Look for example to the United States—"to Minnesota, where Dane and Swede and Norwegian and German, people of all nations, were brought together in the National Schools and welded into one people. That was what they were trying to do in Manitoba."[22]

Sifton's point, declared the Toronto *Globe,* was that "the Manitoba laws of 1890 were passed, not to gratify bigots or to tyrannize over the minority, but to give to every child in the Province, French or English or Mennonite, Protestant or Catholic, an equal opportunity for a good education, a fair start, an equal chance in life."[23] It was magnificent propaganda, superbly packaged, a forthright appeal to the progressive liberalism of the day. But many criticisms of Sifton's remarks quickly appeared. Catholics and their sympathizers pointed out that the pre-1890 system could have been modified and improved to correct the worst abuses. They disputed Sifton's figures as misleading and his examples of French-Catholic illiteracy as chosen from the most backward métis settlements. They contended that the recent decision of the Judicial Committee had been that the minority was both morally and legally entitled to redress of its grievances and that Ottawa had had an unavoidable obligation laid upon it. They argued that Roman Catholics were constitutionally entitled to privileges not promised to other minorities and that the American example was not applicable.

Nevertheless, Sifton had scored many telling points. Not the least was his demonstration of the division between at least some English-speaking Catholics of Winnipeg and the French-Catholic communities. Many of the former, while desirous of their own schools, had little real sympathy with the cultural aspirations of their French co-religionists. Another of his points had been that the Church was uncompromising on the issue of complete restoration. Several defenders of the minority rushed into print to declare that the remedial order meant a great deal less than the full privileges of the pre-1890 system. Archbishop Langevin, however, hastened to inform his chief counsel, John S. Ewart, that "we would accept changes in the details" only. He denied a report in the Toronto *Mail and Empire,* a leading Conservative organ, that the Church would permit the province to "prescribe the school books, certificate the teachers, and inspect the schools." "I will never accept an arrangement," wrote Langevin, "by which we have not the control of books and of teachers." He would accept provincial nomination of inspectors only after the names had been presented by the "Separate School Board." If the remedial order meant anything at all, "we should be able to control our own schools."[24]

The Manitoba legislature reconvened on 9 May, only to be adjourned again the following day. Greenway, Sifton, and Langevin had all been summoned to Ottawa by Governor General Lord Aberdeen in a last-ditch personal effort to arrange an acceptable compromise. Nothing came of the talks, both sides remaining intransigent. Sifton and Langevin returned to Winnipeg from Ottawa in the same railway car. But they had never met, even during the negotiations, and consequently did not converse during the entire trip. When queried upon arrival at Winnipeg, each evinced surprise at learning the other's identity, Langevin adding that he had "always imagined that Mr. Sifton was an old man." Nothing could have illustrated more graphically the tragic distance separating the two solitudes in the province.[25]

Once again Sifton was practically in charge of Manitoba policy, Greenway being stricken with another bout of illness. The premier managed to return from Ontario in time to make a short address on the reply to the remedial order, but it was the attorney general who had drafted the reply and defended it at length in the legislature. He made it clear that the dominion government had been given the power to act and that the province would not relieve it of the responsibility. Sifton repeated the substance of his Ontario speeches and added that it was the dominion government which was being inflexible, which had rejected a policy of negotiation or compromise. The reply maintained that there was a serious question as to whether the federal government could interfere with the province's taxation powers and implied that there would be another drawn-out court battle if Parliament passed remedial legislation. Finally, it recommended another thorough investigation.[26]

Passed on 19 June, the Manitoba reply sent the dominion cabinet into near-fatal convulsions. The province's refusal to act had been anticipated since the failure of the negotiations with Lord Aberdeen, and efforts had begun to draft a remedial bill which would have the approval of the minority.[27] Such a bill, generally along the lines of the remedial order, was accepted by Langevin early in July. Parliament was in session, and it might well have been introduced. On the very brink of decisive action, however, prodded forward by his Québec ministers and tugged back by those from Ontario, Bowell flung himself into the tempting embrace of yet another compromise. Once again he hoped that the threat, now explicit, of remedial legislation would compel the province to act and save his government from utter collapse. On 6 July the prime minister announced that if Manitoba did not redress the grievances of the minority within six months, Parliament would be recalled to do so. Three weeks later, on 27 July, an order-in-council was passed to formally advise the provincial government of the threat and to suggest that legislation along the lines of some unspecified "middle course" would be deemed sufficient.[28]

Bowell had barely held his government together. The expedient by which he did so, however, was to prove fatal to the minority's cause, as Sifton instantly perceived. The intended six-month stay of execution put pressure on the dominion government, not the province. Gleefully Sifton observed, "The Government has made a much more serious blunder than any of the numerous ones which they have made hitherto." Bowell's pledge would only antagonize Ontario, "and the Government would have stood a much better chance of getting a bill through before adjournment or prorogation than they will at any time in the future."[29]

Having been handed the initiative, Sifton did not intend that Manitoba should lose it. He certainly would not reply any sooner than absolutely necessary. During the summer and fall, meanwhile, the Liberal government's troops across the province were being readied. In October the Liberal press and supporters were provided with a lengthy and persuasively written summary of the government's case for national schools by F.C. Wade, a Winnipeg lawyer who had worked closely with Sifton in its preparation.[30] Wade attempted to document Sifton's assertions concerning the inefficiency of the schools and added statistics to demonstrate the higher rates of illiteracy and crime among Catholic populations. He dwelt on the evils of church-dominated schools, the violation of the principle of separation of church and state, and the problems of perpetuating duality. J.S. Ewart attempted to point out the most obvious fallacies in Wade's arguments in a hastily produced reply, but it was not very effective in approach or timing.[31] In any event, few people on either side of the question were any longer amenable to persuasion.

With his preparations in Manitoba finally made, Sifton journeyed to Montreal. On 15 December he conferred at the Windsor Hotel with Wilfrid Laurier and James Sutherland, the principal Ontario organizer of the national Liberal party.[32] Precisely what commitments were made remains unknown; but the purpose of the meeting was to co-ordinate policy between the national and provincial organizations.

Sifton had scarcely returned to Manitoba before a reply to the dominion government, formally refusing to implement any concessions to the minority, was issued. It was couched in the relentless logic of the attorney general. It was obvious, he wrote, that "no concession which does not admit the principle of... separate schools and embody the same in the Educational Statutes of the province will be regarded as an adequate measure of relief or accepted as a solution of the difficulty." The dominion government would be flexible on the degree of clerical control, but not on the principle of separation. It was precisely that principle which Manitoba did not intend to admit. "The issue is therefore very clearly defined." The province would adhere to "the principle of a uniform non-sectarian public school system."[33] To underline the provincial defiance, the eighth legislature was dissolved the same day, 21 December, with an election called for 15 January 1896. "We have our coats off," Sifton told reporters, "and intend to win."[34]

Sifton opened the government campaign on 31 December at Douglas, the centre of a wheat-growing area in the eastern part of his constituency. He recounted with pride the record of the government—a government, he would later recall, that "speaking generally" was "the most honest, economical and businesslike government that I have ever known anything about."[35] He noted the government's efforts to establish cheese factories and creameries and introduce agriculture into the schools, its attempts to secure lower freight rates, its improvements in the administration of justice, and its continued rigid economy in administration.

It was the school question, however, which his listeners had come to hear him expound. They were not disappointed; the attorney general gave a virtuoso performance. He had already blanketed his constituency with copies of the provincial reply to the second remedial order, and, waving a copy of Wade's pamphlet, he delivered a succinct summary of the events. "The Dominion government," he asserted, "has stated its intention of forcing separate schools upon us and we are determined that it shall not. This is our stand and it is to ascertain if it is also the mind of the people that we are now before you." Why should the Roman Catholics have special privileges? When they had had their own system, the results had been disgraceful. "I have proved it on the floor of the house that the people of the districts where separate schools have been in existence for years are so illiterate as to be a disgrace to Canadian citizenship." In making up Wade's pamphlet, he said, examples had been taken "at random" from departmental files, so as to constitute "a fair sample of all the [teachers'] reports sent in." In facsimile was produced one teacher's list of subjects taught in the school:

1. CATTECHISM.
2. RELIGION.
3. THE GOLDEN PRIMER.
4. WRITING AND READING.
5. SPELING.
6. ARITMETIC. .
7. GEOGRAFY AND HISTORY.

The list was received with roars of laughter, and Sifton observed, "After this from the teacher, what would you expect from the pupils[?]" The policy of 1890 had been effected because there was no justification for special privilege and because "the schools were useless, and the money spent on them was being wasted."

Sifton further demonstrated that Catholic schools received on average more than Protestant schools, but he naturally did not add that the basis for distribution of the grant was the number of pupils, not the number of schools. "The system," he claimed, "was permeated with inequalities and irregularities." The only thing to do was "to wipe out the old system and build up a new." To satisfy the minority, the government was prepared to do "anything in reason. If we can settle this matter without compromising principle, then we will do it, but not otherwise." But always discussions showed that "the minority wanted their pound of flesh; they would be satisfied with nothing less than separate schools."

That the dominion government was neither legally nor morally bound to pass remedial legislation was, Sifton believed, readily demonstrable. The real reasons for dominion action were political. "I want to ask you this: If we had 65 members in Manitoba, and Quebec had five, would this [remedial] order ever have been made? (Laughter and no, no.) Well then, just because we are small and young are we going to submit to an injustice done to gain over a section of the community? (Applause and no, no.)" It was indeed Manitoba, not the dominion government, which had acted constitutionally throughout, "because the spirit of confederation is that as far as possible a province is not to be interfered with in managing those affairs entrusted to it by the constitution." Only a "great wrong or gross injustice" could justify dominion interference, "but in this case they have never attempted to give any such reason."[36]

It was a bitterly cold winter campaign. This time Sifton did not repeat his error of 1892 and spent a great deal of time in his own constituency. Once, indeed, he was lost for a while in a blinding snowstorm while driving between towns. The only issue raised in the campaign which seemed to cause him serious concern was the charge—first raised in the *Brandon Sun*—that his trip to Montreal had been for the purpose of making an arrangement with Laurier to settle the school dispute with some kind of compromise after the federal election, in return for which Sifton would be named minister of the interior. Although remarkably prophetic, there is no corroborating contemporary evidence. Sifton, of course, vehemently denied that there was any direct or indirect understanding with anyone.[37]

The Liberals had timed the election skilfully. Since 1894 the major question had been the strength of the Patrons of Industry in the province, for they had been greatly encouraged by their victory in Beautiful Plains. By 1895, however, the movement was having difficulty concealing its internal strains.[38]

Even so, they remained a dangerously uncertain quantity. They were more likely to take Liberal than Conservative votes, and the results of three-way contests were distressingly unpredictable. Nine Patrons were nominated, but two soon withdrew. Sifton was willing not to oppose W.F. Sirrett, the Patron nominated for Beautiful Plains, in order once more to defeat the Conservative there. Elsewhere, however, he concluded that "the first sign of giving way and allowing a Patron to bluff our candidate out of the field" would result not only in losing a government seat where the Patrons were strong, but would encourage Patrons to run "in a lot of other constituencies where they have really no chance to be elected."[39]

Fortunately for the Liberals, the Conservative party was also in serious disarray. They were without an able spokesman in the legislature and were caught unprepared by the election. Nine of the forty constituencies had Liberal acclamations, including two of the three Winnipeg seats. Many of the Tory candidates were weak. The party waffled on the school issue, a majority of the English-speaking members declaring more or less in favour of national schools. Even the Patrons had managed to be more decisive in their support of the schools.

The result of the polling on 15 January was a solid victory for the Greenway government. Thirty-one straight Liberals were returned, with two independent Liberals, two Patrons, and five Conservatives.[40] Sifton was especially pleased with his strong personal victory of 434 to 190. He smugly observed that "some of the Opposition candidates did not make much of a fight and showed signs of being very weak. As a result the revenue of the government will be increased by about $1,000 from forfeited deposits." The opposition, in his view, "had no arguments to advance" except for allegations of corruption, which they could not substantiate. As a result, "they simply went to pieces on the platform in all directions."[41] The government's opponents had been thoroughly discomfited, the Patrons in particular, by its aggressive tactics.[42] Greenway and Sifton had proven their point. Outside of the French-speaking districts, the province seemed solidly in support of national schools and opposed to dominion coercion.

One of the extraordinary aspects of the provincial election of 1896 was the ability of the government to make it to such a degree a one-issue campaign. No one seemed to notice that for four years there had been almost no railway construction and that in the eight years the Greenway government had been in power less than 275 miles of railway had been built.[43]

In the summer of 1892 there had been a promising outlook for the liaison of convenience between the Canadian Pacific Railway and the Greenway government. Both anticipated the systematic completion of a few short branch lines in southern and southwestern Manitoba and even expected construction to open up the Dauphin country to the northwest. Sir William Van Horne was exceedingly pleased with his Manitoba ally. "I wish we had some of his [Greenway's] practical sense at Ottawa," he told Major Walsh.[44]

The financial panic of 1893, however, destroyed any hope of further CPR construction. "The present times," Van Horne told his Winnipeg solicitors in 1894, "are the worst I have ever experienced, and I can see no sign of a turn for the better; indeed I believe that the worst is yet to come."[45] He reacted during the depression like any sound businessman concerned with maintaining investor confidence in his enterprise. His financial restraint and persistent fight to maintain dividend payments may have won him plaudits in the community of international finance. To western farmers, however, who were being devastated by the lowest international grain prices in years, the CPR seemed to be expecting them to carry its creditors and investors on their backs. Van Horne stoutly maintained that wheat rates had been steadily reduced and compared favourably with rates anywhere in North America.

> The fact the Company is earning dividends is pointed to as a reason why we should reduce our rates; a good many people evidently think that a railway company ought not to pay dividends, and most people overlook the fact that a prosperous railway is the most important factor in the success of any district. If we were not paying dividends we could not get any money for branches, extensions, &c., and the advantage to the country of the expenditure of millions each year would be lost. It will be a very bad day for our North West when the Canadian Pacific Company ceases to pay dividends.[46]

So the CPR plunged lower and lower in the estimation of westerners. One of the most repeated charges against the Greenway government was that it was too friendly with the company and not inclined to work on behalf of the farmers to secure lower freight rates. Sifton admitted that he believed that the CPR was very ably managed, but he also pointed out that he had always been critical of its rates.[47]

Within the Manitoba cabinet there were two opposing philosophies of railway development. Premier Greenway favoured construction of the Manitoba and South Eastern line, with the ultimate goal of giving the province yet another competitive line and an outlet at Duluth. His attitude reflected the position of the well-settled southern part of the province which he represented. In the west and northwest parts of the province, however, the need was for branch lines and extensions rather than competition. Sifton represented these areas and insisted that the limited resources of the province should henceforth be applied in the new districts, as there were already sufficient outlets to meet existing needs. He prevailed, and during the time he was in the cabinet the southeastern project was quietly shelved.[48]

It was one thing to agree on a general line of policy; it was quite another to sell it during a depression. Although he had visions of eventually building into the Dauphin country, Van Horne would not touch branch line construction in Manitoba after the spring of 1893. Even when there were signs of an upturn late in 1895, he resisted pressure from Winnipeg and Ottawa. "So far as the Canadian Pacific is concerned, it has got to recover its lost ground before it can undertake any new lines," he wrote. "It is very certain that nothing can be done for another year at least."[49] Attempts by the Manitoba government to interest the Northern Pacific or Great Northern in the lines were equally unsuccessful.

In 1893 Greenway and Sifton had on foot a rather shaky scheme to build the Dauphin line, but it would have depended upon bonds secured by a land grant. Western lands were already tied up in commitments to railways to such an extent that Van Horne predicted that no suitable lands could be obtained south of Peace River, and the project was reluctantly dropped. The CPR president did state, nevertheless, that he thought the Dauphin line could be built for $8,000 per mile, information which the provincial authorities would shortly find very useful.[50]

Faced with discouragement at every turn, Sifton had to use his ingenuity. With its tiny resources, Manitoba could not afford a direct subsidy for so long a line. The usual alternative method hitherto employed was to guarantee the interest on railway bonds secured with land. But the land was no longer available. Sifton therefore concluded that the best way to proceed was to use the credit of the province as a guarantee for both the principal and interest of the railway bonds, so that they would sell at or near par. In 1895 Sifton was able to sell this concept to Donald Mann, and then to William Mackenzie, a couple of rather obscure but able railway contractors who shared the attorney general's optimism and vision about the future of the Dauphin region. Negotiations were not sufficiently advanced to be announced during the provincial election of 1896, but shortly thereafter an agreement in principle was reached which could be presented to the new provincial legislature. The dominion authorities were happy to co-operate with various concessions, believing that they would reap the credit for any railway construction at the forthcoming general election.[51]

Under the terms of the agreement reached with Mackenzie and Mann's Lake Manitoba Railway and Canal Company, the government agreed to guarantee the principal and interest at 4 per cent on thirty-year bonds at a rate of $8,000 per mile to a maximum of 125 miles. Mackenzie and Mann committed themselves to build and operate for thirty years such a line, running from Portage la Prairie or Gladstone to the Dauphin district. They also agreed to permit other railways reasonable running rights, to allow loading of grain from farmers' vehicles and flat warehouses, and—most important—to submit to government approval of freight rates.[52] It was the proposal to regulate freight rates, so politically essential, which had horrified the Canadian Pacific. But Mackenzie and Mann believed that in their own self-interest the politicians would not dare to set the rates too low, for an unprofitable line would mean that the province would actually have to pay on the interest and principal.

The prospect of the railway defaulting captured the imaginations of the opposition. To their mournful predictions about the awful consequences of the contingent liability about to be laid upon the province, Sifton replied that there was no alternative if the line was to be built. Furthermore, he maintained, the credit of the province was such that provincial bonds were selling at par, and even at 106 per cent, so that Mackenzie and Mann would obtain the full face value of their bonds and would not be paying "interest on discounts."[53] All being well, the line would cost the province scarcely a cent. Mackenzie and Mann had their crews in the field by the spring. Their line was a great success and the beginning—along with Sifton's apparently painless method of financing railways—of a new era of railway expansion.

Manitoba's reply to the remedial order on 21 December was an invitation to decisive action on the part of the federal government. Bowell might well have been expected to have mustered his courage and prepared a remedial bill to present promptly to Parliament upon Manitoba's refusal to comply. There was, however, no spark of greatness in the bewhiskered, egotistical old Senator who with unsteady hand and clouded eye was attempting to guide the battered ship of state. The obligation to act now lay with the dominion government, nearly paralysed at its darkening prospects. A cold adverse wind from Québec and Ontario in by-elections late in 1895 demonstrated that the Tories' dithering had undermined their strength among Roman Catholic voters and antagonized many in Ontario. Parliament met on 2 January to find a cabal of ministers determined to replace Bowell with the wily, pugnacious Sir Charles Tupper, then Canadian high commissioner in London, but an experienced, decisive leader who would restore morale. The prime minister, however, proved unexpectedly tough when his position was at stake and forced a compromise by which he could cling to office until the end of the session, when he would yield to Tupper.

Faced with the deadline of 25 April, when the seventh Parliament would expire, the government frittered away the remaining time. Not until 11 February did A.R. Dickey, minister of justice, introduce the remedial bill, still incomplete, and second reading was not moved until 3 March. The bill did not completely restore the pre-1890 system. It did, nevertheless, accept the premise of the minority that nothing less than the establishment of a fully separate system would be considered just. There would be an end to double taxation. Catholics would be taxed only for the separate schools, although they had the option of declaring that they wished to support the public system.

The Catholic board would control curricula, teachers, and inspectors; school texts could be chosen from those in use in either Manitoba public or Ontario separate schools. There would also be inspectors appointed by the lieutenant-governor-in-council of the province, whose sole function was to ensure that the separate schools met provincial standards of "efficiency." Finally, although the government recognized that it would undoubtedly raise a serious constitutional quarrel, Catholic schools were to receive a proportional share of the legislative grant. The purpose of the bill was to go as far as possible in redressing the grievances of the minority, while meeting the objections of the Manitoba government that previous proposals to restore the old system had provided no guarantees about the efficiency of the schools.[54]

The dominion government was trying to act consistently. Any attempt at serious compromise would have undermined its contention that it was only fulfilling its legal obligation to redress the grievances of the minority as outlined in the decision of the Judicial Committee in the Brophy case. It obtained a declaration from Archbishop Langevin that the bill was an acceptable measure which "gives us a real control of our schools and an immense relief in our long agony."[55] But whether the government had the integrity to maintain its resolve and the ability to see it through was still in doubt.

On the other side, Wilfrid Laurier was scarcely less apprehensive than the Conservatives about the potentially disastrous effects of the school question, both upon his party and upon dominion politics generally. The astounding gulf which still separated the Liberals of Manitoba from those at Ottawa was revealed late in January, when Laurier anxiously wrote to Sifton appealing for a settlement to remove the issue from politics. What concessions, if any, was the Manitoba government prepared to make?[56] Sifton was concerned only with the Manitoba situation. The local government had just made stern pledges to uphold the national system; it had always contended that the minority would accept nothing less than the pre-1890 system, and if there was to be compromise, the Church and dominion authorities must abandon this stand.

Some Tories hoped, and some Liberals feared, that faced with parliamentary legislation the Manitobans would seek a compromise. Sir Donald A. Smith, who owned vast tracts of land in Manitoba, and whose long connection with the province gave him some influence with men on both sides of the dispute, ventured out to Winnipeg on 16 February to seek some common ground upon which a compromise might be based. After several days of shuttling back and forth between the archbishop's residence and the legislative buildings, he was forced to concede that Greenway and Langevin had been rather obdurate, though he took some comfort from the fact that neither was willing to close altogether the door to further talks.[57] In fact, the leaders on both sides were being little more than politely deferential.

Less than a week later Sifton left no doubt about Manitoba's continuing intransigence. He introduced a motion of protest against dominion coercion, declaring that it would not resolve the problem and that it was "an unnecessary and unjustifiable attack upon the constitutional rights of the legislature and people of Manitoba, and indirectly upon the rights of the legislatures and people of every province of the Dominion, and a violation of the principle of provincial autonomy which is without precedent in the history of the Dominion."[58] In a fiery speech, the attorney general practically dared the Bowell government to pass the legislation. By now the national Liberal party was beginning to scent victory. They were no longer worried about the passage of the legislation, which they believed could be successfully obstructed. They were more concerned that the province would weaken and compromise, relieving the Tories of the burden of attempted coercion and of the ignominy of failure. They therefore could hardly have been more pleased at Sifton's defiant resolution. Exulted J.D. Edgar, a close confidant of Laurier, "Sifton *has behaved just as we wished.*"[59]

The danger of compromise was by no means over, however. Some in the Bowell government preferred almost any negotiated settlement to entering an election campaign as the perpetrators of coercion. Sir Charles Tupper, now in Parliament and in charge of Tory strategy, was prevailed upon to make one last attempt by sending a delegation to Winnipeg. He reluctantly consented. On the understanding that proceedings on the remedial bill would be suspended during the negotiations, Premier Greenway agreed to meet the commissioners, Sir Donald Smith, A.R. Dickey, and Senator A. Desjardins, minister of militia. After having introduced strong remedial legislation it was, as Provincial Secretary J.D. Cameron said, "humiliating" for the dominion authorities now to come to the province begging for concessions.[60] However, anticipating that the talks would only waste rapidly dwindling time, Tupper resolutely pressed on with the bill. This angered Premier Greenway, who conveniently "fell ill" and sent his two most inflexible colleagues, Sifton and Cameron, to meet the commissioners when they arrived on 25 March.[61]

With barely a month left in the term of the Parliament and the passage of the remedial legislation in serious doubt, the greatest fear of the united opposition at Ottawa was that the Conservatives would finally make generous concessions that would prove irresistible to the Greenway government. They bombarded Sifton with pleas to hold fast. McCarthy observed that second reading had been obtained by a very narrow margin and that there was practically no question that opposition obstruction would prevent the bill from ever emerging from the committee stage. He added that "it will be a very bitter disappointment to the friends of Manitoba who have fought for its rights if there is any substantial yielding on the part of the Manitoba Government."[62] The opposition desired that the talks be as protracted as possible and that Sifton should ensure that there would be a public record of exactly what took place.[63]

On one point the fears of the opposition were justified. The commissioners were prepared to make heavy concessions. All pretense of approximating the separate school privileges extant prior to 1890 was abandoned. There was not even an attempt to compromise on the basis of the Ontario system. All that they asked was that the Manitoba government agree to give *in law* substantially the same educational privileges which Nova Scotian Catholics enjoyed *by practice*. Indeed, the Tories were prepared to meet almost every major objection which Manitoba had hitherto raised: there would be no separate school board; no separate taxation; and Catholics would have to meet government standards with respect to curricula, texts, teacher certification, and inspection. What they did request were principally administrative modifications to benefit the Roman Catholics. Where there were at least twenty-five Catholic children in town and village schools, or fifty in city schools, it was asked that the Catholic children be brought into a separate building, or separate rooms in the school, and taught by a Catholic teacher. They further asked that any ten Catholic parents should have the right of appeal to the advisory board in the event of abuse or neglect of this provision by local trustees. In schools where a majority of children were Catholic, it was requested that there be an exemption from the regulations concerning religious exercises—that is, that in such cases the Catholics would be free to devise their own religious exercises. Textbooks should not be offensive to Catholics, and there should be a guarantee of Catholic representation on the advisory board and on the board of examiners which certified teachers. A publicly assisted Catholic normal school was requested, and a two-year extension of the permits of "non-qualified teachers in Catholic schools . . . to enable them to qualify."[64]

The dominion commissioners had agonized over these terms and had tried to secure Langevin's consent. The archbishop was deeply troubled. After an intense debate with his closest advisers, Langevin concluded that he could neither support nor reject the terms. For one thing, he did not believe that the Manitoba government would accept the proposals; and naturally he did not want to abandon the rapidly dimming prospect of obtaining the provisions of the remedial bill.[65] The gloomy outlook was emphasized on 27 March, when in a steady downpour some two thousand citizens of Winnipeg and a band turned out to conduct a mock funeral procession to cremate and bury a symbolic remedial bill. By the time the mourners reached the legislative buildings, the soaked paper refused to ignite, and the frustrated crowd instead tore it to shreds.[66]

Sifton and Cameron shredded the dominion commissioners' proposals just as effectively. Rather than regarding them as a basis for discussion, they dissected the terms as they would an incompetently drawn bill in the law amendments committee. Their fundamental objection was that the Catholics would still be accorded "distinct and special privileges as against the remaining portion of the people. It would establish a system of state-supported separate schools for the Roman Catholic people." Separate schools "in any form" would not be allowed. Beyond that, Sifton and Cameron claimed that the federal proposals would increase costs and reduce efficiency since more teachers would be needed to handle the same number of pupils. "Grading of classes and mutual competition would be destroyed," resulting in lower standards for separate schools. The federal proposals, furthermore, would make establishment of separate schools compulsory, whether Catholics or local trustees wanted them or not; and Catholics would be deprived of the option of sending their children to public schools. In this hostile spirit, they attacked each proposal, except to concede that some accommodation on textbooks might be obtained and to point out that there had long been a standing offer to the archbishop of St. Boniface to sit on the advisory board. The Manitobans were prepared to make two counterproposals: either the schools could be completely secularized, or religious exercises could be conducted during the last half-hour of the school day, between 3:30 and 4:00 o'clock, by any Christian clergyman acceptable to the trustees, with the privilege of exemption for pupils whose parents so desired.[67]

Obviously the archbishop and the dominion commissioners could not accept such proposals. Smith, Dickey, and Desjardins, who seem to have held some genuine hope for success in the early stages of the conference, replied in weary discouragement, mainly for the public record. They refuted many of Sifton's points in detail, conceded that even a Catholic normal school was not essential, and pleaded for a reconsideration of the inflexible provincial response. Following a further negative reply from the Manitobans on 1 April, the negotiations ended.[68] "The conference," a satisfied Sifton told McCarthy, "has proven entirely abortive." It was now essential for the opposition at Ottawa to ensure that the remedial bill was either defeated or "deliberately talked out."

> I am satisfied that the Government's position will be most materially weakened by the publication of the proceedings of the conference. We have not conceded any point of principle, but we have made an offer which would have removed all practical grievance. The proceedings will show that the cause of failure of the conference was not that we were unreasonable, but that the Dominion Government were tied to the Church, and the Church insisted upon legally established separate schools. This it appears to me should have the effect of making it impossible for some Ontario members who supported the second reading of the Bill to continue their support. Undoubtedly it will strengthen the feeling in our favor in the Province of Ontario.[69]

McCarthy replied that he was "well pleased" with Sifton's conduct and added that he "was somewhat surprised with the moderation of the demands of the Dominion Commissioners." This, he believed, would provide new ammunition with which the opposition could attack the stringent provisions of the bill. "Unless a change comes over the spirit of the Opposition," he assured Sifton, "you may rely on it that the bill will not pass." Indeed, he suggested that Sifton should now turn his attention to political organization in Manitoba to ensure that "in the next House there will not be more than one [Manitoba] member in favor of Remedial Legislation."[70]

After two more weeks of heroic effort, during which he kept the Commons in almost continuous session, Sir Charles Tupper finally abandoned the remedial bill on 16 April. A week later, after dealing with essential business, the House was prorogued, two days before the expiry of the parliamentary term.[71] There was no time for the politicians to lick their wounds or catch their breath. The struggle was fast moving toward its climax on election day, now set for 23 June.


Tupper fired the opening guns of the campaign in Winnipeg on 8 May. The indomitable prime minister was determined to strike back at his enemies in the heart of their own territory. Few Canadian elections have witnessed a scene so audacious as the seventy-five-year-old Tupper rallying his troops and restoring morale from within so hostile an environment. His daring actions were matched by the skill of his platform. He did not ignore or apologize for the remedial legislation, and he exploited Liberal inconsistencies with great effect. Even more important was his determination to broaden the issues of the campaign, to meet the principal demands of the farmers, and to portray the Tory government as responsible for brightening prospects and prepared with programmes for prosperity. One of his most effective planks was a pledge to build a Hudson Bay railway. The Tories were not slow to take some credit for the fact that Mackenzie and Mann's construction crews were in the field, building what was expected to be the first stage of the new route.

Plainly the Liberals in Manitoba were caught off balance. The fury of Sir Charles's attack had allowed the Tories to seize the initiative, and there was no spokesman of the national Liberal party available to counter him effectively. Laurier and his lieutenants were all occupied in central and eastern Canada, apparently confident that Manitoba would vote as a unit against the Tories. Provincial Liberals rendered good service, but none could act as an authoritative spokesman on national policy. It was critically important that some such Liberal representative should appear, but none did. Tupper spoke of further compromise, though he was pledged to remedial legislation. Few Manitobans could have seriously thought that any terms more severe than those offered by the dominion commissioners would ever be imposed. Tory spokesmen argued that these terms maintained the principles of a national school system unimpaired, while rendering the minority its due. The Liberals, by contrast, had to contend with the fact that Laurier, speaking at St. Roch in Québec, had pledged himself to use the full federal power if negotiations failed to produce justice for the minority. In Ontario he played a very different tune about the virtues of upholding provincial rights and minimized the rights of the minority.[72]

The Liberals were further hampered by ineffective organization. When Laurier had toured the West in 1894, Manitoba Liberals had been confident of great success. Their only reservations concerned the possible influence of the Patrons.[73] However, given the mutual lack of respect between Greenway and Sifton on the one hand, and Martin on the other, since 1894 the party had never developed a smoothly running machine. The irritating problem of the Patrons, furthermore, did not diminish after the provincial election of 1896, as Sifton had confidently predicted. The Liberals in Ontario had reached agreements with the Patron and McCarthyite parties to minimize diffusion of the opposition vote there,[74] but nothing comparable seems to have been attempted in Manitoba until much too late. Then Sifton found that "they have no leader of any capacity so that an arrangement with them is impossible." The Patron lodges were determined to nominate candidates in most rural constituencies, generally weak men who would draw more Liberal than Conservative votes. "The result," Sifton informed McCarthy, "is that it looks as though we would be defeated in three or four seats on account of the vote being split."[75] By "making the fight practically on the School Question alone," Sifton hoped that "we can save our position to a very material extent." To achieve this, he asked McCarthy to run in a Manitoba constituency, preferably Brandon—the seat of Minister of the Interior T.M. Daly, who had voted for the remedial bill—as well as in his fairly safe seat of North Simcoe in Ontario. Not only would this enable the anti-remedialists to carry Brandon, where the Patrons were particularly stubborn, but "it would assist us very materially in the other seats as well."[76] After some hesitation, McCarthy agreed.[77] The question remained whether he could serve as the champion the Liberals needed to offset Sir Charles Tupper.

There also remained a question about Sifton's personal interest in this strategy. If he was elected for two constituencies, McCarthy would choose to represent his Ontario riding, thus reopening Brandon. Was Sifton using this device to leave his options for the future open? When one of his supporters suggested that the attorney general run for Brandon, he declined, but he did not altogether shut the door. "It is quite impossible for me to leave the Government here while the school question is unsettled," he wrote. "I became a member of this Government five years ago principally because of the difficulties arising out of this question and having conducted the fight for five years I propose to stay with it until it is through."[78] Yet if the school question were settled and a Liberal government were in power after 23 June, what then? Few political observers believed that Sifton would long be satisfied to remain in his post. The rumours that he had the promise of a dominion cabinet post should the Liberals be elected and the school issue be subsequently settled resurfaced. Alternately, the rumour was scouted that Greenway was to advance to the dominion cabinet, and Sifton to the premiership.[79] Both Greenway and Sifton vigorously denied the speculations and plunged into the campaign. As the premier put it, "the Tories are going to make a desperate effort to capture the Province but we will try and stay with them if we can."[80] The provincial government chose to assign its members to different parts of the province. Sifton concentrated on the Brandon and Marquette constituencies of western Manitoba.

Their backs to the wall, the Tories fought tenaciously. Tupper persuaded Hugh John Macdonald to come out of retirement and contest Winnipeg as minister of the interior: T.M. Daly, who had supported the remedial bill was now a political liability, and he was dropped. This meant much more to the government campaign than the lustre of a great Conservative name. As a long-time CPR solicitor, Macdonald was able to count on the company's support against Joseph Martin. Equally important, the influential *Manitoba Free Press* was controlled by Sir William Van Horne and Sir Donald Smith, and during the campaign Smith vented his anger at the Manitoba Liberals for having failed to accept what he conceived to be a reasonable compromise on the school issue. From its formerly fairly independent stance the *Free Press* turned to outright support of several of the Tories, and of Macdonald in particular.

In the rural seats the Tories were scarcely less skilful. They realized that their only chance was to keep Patron candidates in the field to split the opposition vote. Evidently Patrons received active support to remain in contention in Lisgar, Marquette, Macdonald, and Brandon. Desperate Liberal efforts to persuade the Patrons to withdraw were mostly unsuccessful. In Lisgar the Patron did withdraw at the last moment. In Marquette, the Patron also abandoned the contest, but the Tories immediately brought out another. In Brandon, Sifton arranged for the Liberal candidate to withdraw in favour of McCarthy, but he was unable to exercise any influence with the determined Patron, W. Postlethwaite.[81]

Apart from delivering a few speeches on behalf of J.H. Ashdown, the Liberal candidate in Marquette, Sifton spent almost all his time in a detailed canvass of Brandon to secure McCarthy's election. The Tories had complicated his strategy somewhat by removing Daly from the cabinet, for he would have been an easy target. The Conservatives fielded W.A. Macdonald, Sifton's long-time opponent, who was firmly in favour of national schools. However, he had to contend with the pledges made by Tupper in Winnipeg. In what was possibly the most committed district in the province on the issue of

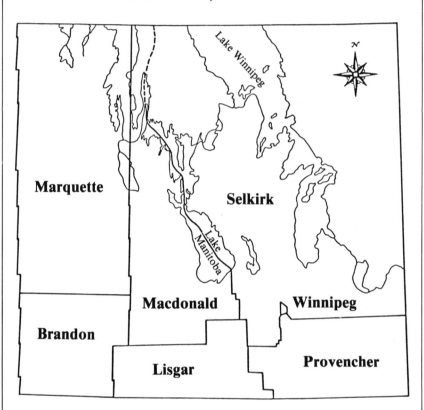

## Manitoba Constituencies, 1896 and 1900

Lake Winnipeg

N

Marquette

Selkirk

Lake Manitoba

Macdonald

Winnipeg

Brandon

Lisgar

Provencher

Source: *Adapted from Electoral Atlas of the Dominion of Canada as Divided for the Revision of the Voters' List made in the Year 1894* (Ottawa: Government Printing Bureau, 1895), Index Map, Manitoba Constituencies.

national schools, it was not difficult for McCarthy, a former Conservative, to secure the support of a number of the leading Tories in the constituency.

The highlight of the campaign was a four-day blitz of the constituency by McCarthy at the end of May. It was a carefully orchestrated running road show which entertained thousands of the electors. As was the custom, meetings were organized as public debates of heroic endurance, to which the candidate's opponents or their representatives were invited.[82] The Conservatives and Patrons were outmatched. Commencing with a triumphant meeting at Brandon on 26 May, at which Sifton and McCarthy addressed some 2,500 people, the Liberals held several meetings a day crisscrossing the constituency. On 28 May, for example, McCarthy began to address a crowd at Wawanesa at 10:00 A.M. Before he had finished, Macdonald appeared, and a joint debate continued to mid-afternoon. Sifton, meanwhile, had gone ahead to Boissevain, arriving about two hours late for a scheduled 3:00 P.M. meeting, informed the crowd of the reason for the delay, and spoke for two hours. After a short adjournment, Macdonald rushed in and had time to make a short speech before McCarthy arrived. The attorney general did not pause, as he headed for the scene of the evening meeting at Deloraine. F.C. Wade had begun the speeches at 9:30 P.M., followed by Sifton, and then by an exhausted Macdonald when he rolled in on his hand-car. A Patron then took the floor until McCarthy arrived at 1:30 A.M., speaking to the still-enthusiastic throng for another two hours. A few hours' sleep and they were all at it again.[83]

In Brandon, if not in the rest of the province, Sifton was able to have things pretty much his own way. McCarthy did make the school issue and the national character of Canada the principal question, and Sifton was mainly concerned with justifying his support for an outsider and a renegade Tory. He did attack the protective tariff and joke about more than a decade of broken Conservative promises to construct the Hudson Bay railway. But it was the school question which transcended party considerations. "When we remember," he told the crowd at Brandon, "that this is no ordinary contest in which we engage, that we are not fighting about a little railway, nor a division of a county, but a question of principle which will determine the future of a country for all time to come, surely the question of a man's residence is of no importance."[84]

Near the end of the campaign, on 19 June, the Liberals staged a mass rally in Winnipeg in a desperate attempt to salvage Martin's seat. Premier Greenway, Sifton, and all available prominent Liberals were summoned to aid the cause. The attorney general responded with one of his ablest addresses. Eighteen years of Conservative rule, he declared, had served only to increase both public expenditure and the public debt greatly. Dominion fiscal policy bore especially heavily "upon the farmers, the backbone of this country." The land policy, too, "was enough of itself to kill any new country. The need was for a statesman capable of grappling with this question." Joseph Martin, he implied, was a strong candidate for such a post in a Liberal government.

Following his by now authoritative, patented review of the Manitoba position on the school issue, Sifton concluded with an appeal to Winnipeggers to stand fast for his version of tolerance and of civil and religious liberty:

> We may value money, we may value material interests, but the people who won't fight for their civil and religious liberties are no good. That is the first thing to get settled in any country. You have to get it settled and keep it settled. Not only your own religious liberty, but that of your fellow citizens. We cannot allow this to be done in one part of the nation without it re-acting on ourselves. The government has not bought the people of Quebec by promising to restore separate schools in Manitoba[;] they have got the hierarchy to coerce the Roman Catholic voters. We must stand up for the rights of our Roman Catholic fellow subjects. I wish my Roman Catholic fellow citizen to have every right in the exercise of his religion that I enjoy. I respect his religious convictions, and I say the crime of coercion is greater there than here. I characterize this thing which they are doing in the name of Her Gracious Majesty the Queen, as the most nefarious compact ever entered into. Three times in Winnipeg you have given your verdict. I ask you have the people of Winnipeg gone back on that verdict?[85]

The result of the polling on 23 June was a solid national victory for Wilfrid Laurier and the Liberal party. Yet it was a verdict replete with apparent contradictions. Québec, which had exerted the greatest pressure for remedial legislation, voted heavily for Laurier, who had opposed the measure. There Laurier's open appeals to the sympathies of his fellow French Canadians, his promises to do more for the minority than the Tupper government, and the skilfully manipulated Liberal machine operated by Joseph Israel Tarte, Laurier's lieutenant, combined to crush the dissension-torn Tory organization. In Ontario, by contrast, a province supposedly strongly opposed to an imposed settlement on Manitoba, Tupper's strenuous battle enabled the Conservatives to pull even. At dissolution there had been 134 Conservatives and 78 Liberals in the House of Commons; the 1896 election saw 88 Conservatives returned to 118 Liberals—and yet the Liberals received 1 per cent less of the popular vote than the Tories.[86]

In Manitoba the contradiction was most pronounced, and the Liberals were both surprised and disappointed. Of seven seats, four went Conservative, two Liberal, and one—Brandon—went independent, electing McCarthy. From the Liberal party point of view, that meant three victories and four defeats, a serious embarrassment when a strong contingent opposed to remedial legislation had been anticipated. The Liberals, including McCarthy, took only 35 per cent of the popular vote, to 47 per cent for the Tories, and 18 per cent for the Patrons, who had run in only three constituencies.[87] Many explanations for this astonishing result have been offered, ranging from voter apathy, to stronger Tory candidates, to the success of the Conservatives in diverting attention from the school question. Clifford Sifton argued, as have later observers, that there was an innate Conservatism in the Manitoba populace.[88] Clearly two of the Conservative victories—in Macdonald and Marquette—resulted from the Patron splitting the vote; and it is probable that the main reason that McCarthy rather than a Liberal was run in Brandon was because of the Patron. Comparing voting trends in previous and subsequent elections, it is apparent that Sifton was correct in his analysis that the Tory vote held firm in 1896, while the Patrons cut deeply into the Liberal ranks.

Conservative control of election machinery, heavy dominion government spending in the province, and corruption were also significant. Two Conservatives were subsequently unseated for electoral irregularities, Nathaniel Boyd in Macdonald and Hugh John Macdonald in Winnipeg. The minister of the interior had narrowly defeated Joseph Martin, but according to the *Tribune* the Tories among other things had spent at least $50,000 to purchase their victory.[89] Sir William Van Horne, a master of colourful metaphor, repeatedly denied that the CPR had intervened, though he despaired of being trusted. "In the last election," he told Robert Jaffray of the Toronto *Globe* a few weeks later, "we were somewhat in the position of a girl who had once been whoring, but who had reformed and was trying to lead a correct life—it was difficult to make everybody believe it."[90] Unfortunately, the evidence was that the reform was less than complete and that in Winnipeg, at least, the young lady had not been able to resist blatant soliciting.[91] Once again was kindled the bitter hatred of western Liberals toward the CPR.

Whatever explanations might be offered, Manitoba had not spoken with a united voice. This would certainly weaken the position of the province in dealing with the new dominion government and the new prime minister, Wilfrid Laurier, who had pledged himself to achieve a settlement of the troublesome question.

Laurier moved immediately to settle the school question, and he did so with a sure touch and political realism which too long had been absent from Ottawa. He had little room to manoeuvre. Manitoba's position had not been strengthened, but the new Parliament was no more likely than its predecessor to be able to pass remedial legislation. Such a course could only destroy Laurier's government, create a new wave of racial and religious animosity throughout the country, and commence another round of legal and constitutional fighting. The issue had to be removed from the political arena if the minority was to have any relief. This could only be done, Laurier realized, by accepting the basic principles of the Manitoba public school system and seeking some modifications in detail.

Shortly after the election, Laurier sent out feelers to Archbishop Langevin, who made it clear that he still clung to the principles embodied in the remedial bill. Thereafter the prime minister concluded that the archbishop would have to be outflanked. Emissaries were sent to Rome to instruct Langevin's superiors on the realities of Canadian politics. Divisions within the Catholic church in Canada were seized upon as Laurier sought to prevent a unanimous condemnation of his proposed settlement. Some bishops, especially those who were English-speaking, might be prevailed upon to accept the settlement in silence, while a few prominent Catholics might be persuaded—sometimes with the judicious use of patronage—to voice a qualified approval. Until these and other arrangements were concluded, no settlement could be announced; and as Laurier particularly wanted to avoid parliamentary debate on the subject during the fall session, negotiations were not rushed.

The essential thing, however, was to reach an agreement with Manitoba— that is to say, with Clifford Sifton. Shortly after the election, Van Horne wrote to one of the Liberal leader's closest advisers, "I hope Mr. Laurier will realize that Sifton is the only man who can settle the school question and that he will make sure of having him in his cabinet." He later added that he considered Sifton to be "the ablest man in the Liberal party."[92] Of course the CPR president was not entirely disinterested, but he appears to have been preaching to the converted. The prime minister may even have made up his mind prior to the election that he should attempt to secure Sifton.[93] When he completed his cabinet in July, he left open the position of minister of the interior, allowing several ambitious candidates to raise their hopes. It is certain, however, that Laurier never seriously considered anyone but Sifton for the post and that Sifton himself entertained little doubt but that he would have it. The two men simply agreed that it would be impossible for Sifton to leave his provincial office until the school question was officially settled.

While Sifton confidently awaited developments, Joseph Martin mounted a furious campaign to secure the vacancy. Although defeated in Winnipeg, Martin believed that it was he, not Sifton, who had the general support of western Liberals. A few were backing Sifton, he told J.S. Willison of the Toronto *Globe,* "on account of the course pursued by me in the local government of preventing any kind of boodling amongst our friends. The section of the party, a very insignificant one, which desires to keep me out, consists of those who expect to have their pockets filled by the new government and they dread my hostility to anything of that kind."[94] This paragon of virtue then organized popular meetings to support his candidacy, encouraged his friends to write Laurier on his behalf, and repeatedly recorded at length his claims to office.[95]

Sifton mounted no such campaign. Several Liberals, perhaps in response to Martin's efforts, wrote Laurier to suggest Sifton's name. Robert Hill Myers, for example, stated that the Manitoba attorney general "is the best and most successful politician in Manitoba to-day and as clever as any in Canada. ... Do not fail to choose Sifton. He is of more value than any public man in Canada and quite young and a great worker."[96] His reputation had gone far beyond the borders of Manitoba, for the Toronto *Star* declared that Sifton was "recognized as a clever politician and administrator, and is regarded as a second John A. Macdonald for political shrewdness."[97]

The tenor of these remarks conveys some of the reasons that Laurier should prefer Sifton. Martin was capable and energetic, but he was also emotional, irascible, and uncompromising. Despite his self-assessment, he had not emerged from Manitoba politics with a reputation of unusual political purity, and he remained the principal symbol to Catholic Liberals of the excesses of the Manitoba legislation of 1890. By comparison, while Sifton had few friends among French Canadians, his name did not generate the same heated response. Laurier may not have approved of the principles underlying Manitoba's school system, but as a politician he could appreciate the surefooted and resourceful defence which he had watched Sifton conduct for five years. He had been a reliable member of the provincial government. And the prime minister could not have failed to notice Sifton's organizational skill, the energy which he imparted to the local government, and his ingenuity in securing railway development. Most important, Sifton was already a man with definite ideas about the needs of the West, the policies necessary for Canadian development, and the proven capacity to carry them through.

It suited Laurier's purposes, nevertheless, to allow Martin to believe that he would be seriously considered. He was used as the first intermediary between the Manitoba government and the prime minister. By the end of July he was able to outline proposals which foreshadowed the final settlement: religious education from 3:30 to 4:00 P.M., a Roman Catholic teacher to be provided when there were at least sixty Catholic pupils in a school, school texts not offensive to Catholics, and a provision for bilingual teaching in schools with ten or more French-speaking pupils.[98] Thus the bases of the settlement were agreed upon quickly. Laurier was prepared to abandon altogether the principle of separation in secular instruction; and Manitoba was prepared to recognize, albeit in a minor way, that Roman Catholics could have privileges distinguished in law and to accept in law the idea of bilingual instruction.

All that remained was to negotiate the details. Laurier summoned Sifton to a conference in Ottawa on 13 and 14 August. Curiously for a man who could behave so diplomatically when he chose, the prime minister completely ignored Greenway, whose pride was injured. Sifton informed his premier of the conference, adding, "If you care to be of the Conference you should be in Ottawa by the 13th or 14th. Suite yourself about coming but I would as you know be pleased to be with you in it." Greenway irritably declined: "It appears to me that if they cared much for my views there, I should at least have heard from some of them before this. The Elections over nearly six weeks ago and not as much as a scratch of a pen from that quarter."[99]

Cameron and Watson accompanied Sifton to Ottawa. They met with a sub-committee of the dominion cabinet headed by Sir Oliver Mowat, minister of justice and former premier of Ontario. At the same time Sifton wrote to Greenway that Laurier had formally offered him the ministry of the interior and that Martin would be excluded. "The matter now depends upon the settlement of the vexed question. I think their offer is pretty reasonable."[100] It was less easy to convince some of the key men among the rank and file. Eventually the prime minister and his intended minister of the interior agreed that pleasing everyone was impossible and that the extremists would have to be met head on.[101]

Joseph Martin remained dangerous. He was furious at being denied the cabinet post, which he claimed had been promised him prior to the election. He was equally outraged at being excluded from the settlement of the school question, an issue which he proudly declared had originated with him and which had been a major factor in the outcome of the late election.[102] Should Martin choose to organize opposition to the school settlement, he could thoroughly undermine its credibility. Laurier's intention apparently had been to offer Martin the chief justiceship of British Columbia, or of the North-West Territories, as a consolation prize. But the prime minister did not get around to making the offer until September, by which time it had become public rumour and Martin had vehemently denied that he ever would accept such a second-best position.[103] When, with a couple of prominent Winnipeg supporters, Martin swept into Ottawa to buttonhole Laurier, he was decidedly heated. The prime minister remained unfazed. "It is understood," wrote one observer, "that Mr. Laurier went into the whole situation with him, and spoke so kindly and reassuring and frankly, that Mr. Martin's softer nature was touched, and he said that he would no longer resist what seemed to be his leader's decision, and which seemed to be reached with such reluctance and deep regret."[104] Martin thereupon announced his retirement.

It was all a charade to obscure some hasty and bitter political bargaining. Neither the selfless image nor retirement from politics suited Martin very well. Even before he went to Ottawa, he had laid down the conditions for his continued silence in federal affairs, and some hurried secret negotiations produced a CPR solicitorship for him in British Columbia.[105] Because he understood, perhaps from Laurier himself, that the real reason for his exclusion from the cabinet had been the objections of certain members of the Manitoba government, Martin immediately returned to the province with the avowed intention of supporting a Patron in a by-election and announced that he would oppose Greenway everywhere in the province. Possibly Laurier's strategy was part of a plan suggested by Sifton to divert Martin's wrath from the school settlement.[106] If it was thought, however, that Martin's impending removal to British Columbia would eliminate him as a force in Manitoba politics, it was a sad miscalculation. Martin's hatred for Sifton, and for those other Manitoba Liberals whom he believed had sold him out, would bedevil politics in the province for years to come.

Once the parliamentary session was over in early October, Laurier bent every effort to achieve public acceptance of the settlement, the general outline of which had been determined by the beginning of September. A few details and changes of wording remained. Once again the CPR placed the government in its debt by arranging through Vice-President T.G. Shaughnessy to meet some of the obligations incurred by the Catholic Church and its counsel, J.S. Ewart. Laurier also sent his minister of public works, J. Israel Tarte, to Manitoba to complete these sub-rosa arrangements and to help placate the French-speaking community.[107] When Tarte did trouble himself to visit Langevin, however, it was not to negotiate with the archbishop or even to seek his support. Rather, he told Langevin in effect that the Church would have to accept what the government offered and that confessional schools were impossible to obtain. Indeed, Tarte boasted that Québec would remain loyal to the Laurier government even if nothing were done to settle the school question. Langevin forlornly and stubbornly insisted that only separate schools would be acceptable.[108]

While the archbishop may have considered his demands the least that could justly be offered, they were far removed from reality. That became apparent when the terms of the so-called Laurier-Greenway compromise were finally announced on 17 November. By an order-in-council of 12 November drawn up by Sifton, one of his last acts as attorney general, a "final settlement of Questions" between the dominion and Manitoba governments in connection with the Public Schools Act of 1890 was approved. The agreement was to be implemented by legislation at the next session of the provincial legislature. Religious instruction was to be permitted during the last half-hour of the school day, between 3:30 and 4:00 P.M., upon the resolution of a majority of school trustees or upon the petition of the parents of ten or more children in a rural school, or of twenty-five children in a city, town, or village school. Such instruction was to be by a local clergyman or his appointee, with the privilege of exemption for children whose parents so desired. Children could be segregated by denomination for religious instruction, but not for secular studies. Where a minority, Catholic or Protestant, had at least forty children in a town or city school, or twenty-five in rural schools, a teacher of the minority denomination must be employed. Finally, wherever ten or more pupils had a native language other than English, they were to be taught in that language and in English "upon the bi-lingual system."[109]

Pleased with his handiwork, Sifton promptly issued an appeal to the electors of the dominion constituency of Brandon, in which he declared that the terms were "in strict accord with the principle of national schools" and constituted a final rejection of the demand for separate schools. "The conduct, management, regulation and control of the public school system remain substantially unaltered." There would be more efficient religious instruction, very much as the Manitoba commissioners had offered in the spring, and "all denominations are placed upon an equal footing." The settlement, therefore, was "a complete vindication of the course pursued by your provincial representatives" and a "condemnation of the co-ercive policy of the late Federal Government."[110]

On one point at least Langevin and Sifton were in agreement: the province had scarcely compromised at all. Forgotten altogether, apparently, were even the moderate demands of the dominion commissioners the previous spring. There were to be no separate school buildings or rooms for Catholic children during secular instruction; there was no exemption of Catholic children from the religious regulations of the Schools Act; there was no guarantee of textbooks not offensive to the Church; there was no guarantee of Catholic representation upon the advisory board; there was no mention of a publicly assisted Catholic normal school; nor were the permits of non-qualified Catholic teachers to be extended. Only the guarantee of minority teachers was granted on terms more generous than those requested in the spring; but from the Catholic point of view much of the effectiveness of this concession was vitiated by the denial of separation of minority students for secular instruction. Langevin was only told of the terms after their official announcement. He lost no time in denouncing them. The Church, he raged, had not approved, and could not have approved, the settlement.[111]

He was no more impressed with the concession of bilingual instruction, insisted upon by Laurier. The prime minister had asked for French-language instruction, which Sifton realized would have been represented as giving in to dictation from Québec. In line with Manitoba's stand that there was no reason to regard the French-speaking minority as possessed of special rights or privileges, Sifton modified the proposal to instruction in any native language and English. This was not lost on the furious Langevin, who referred to the settlement as "miserable crumbs that they have thrown derisively at us," not concessions but odious restrictions. "We who came as the pioneers into the country, who discovered it, have no more than the last arrivals; we whose rights are guaranteed by the constitution, are placed on the same footing as those who came from Ireland or the depths of Russia, we are not better apportioned than the Chinese and Japanese." "As a bishop and a Frenchman I protest. They are making a sport of the nationality."[112]

Little did Sifton and Laurier imagine that their settlement would provoke problems in Manitoba public education for twenty years. From their point of view, the terms removed the issue from public attention. They did not inform the public that the so-called "final settlement" was in reality only the first stage in seeking further concessions for the minority. Approval of the terms by several French Canadians and Catholics, however, had only been obtained on this understanding.[113] Although he had to absorb much criticism of the settlement as a sellout of Catholics and French Canadians, Laurier still hoped that his "sunny way" of negotiation would secure more for the minority than attempted coercion.

In Winnipeg J.D. Cameron, who succeeded Sifton as attorney general, complacently observed, "The school settlement has taken very well here. Amongst our own friends we have only fallen foul of the radical wing of the Baptist Church. The volcanic eruptions in and around the cathedral across the river have convinced the Protestants generally of all denominations that the best has been done."[114] Despite Cameron's confidence, there were several Protestant protests at the concessions offered, including an "indignation meeting" at Hargrave, Manitoba, on 21 November, where Laurier and Sifton were burned in effigy "amidst hoots and groans and cheers for the national school system. Men who for years had supported the Liberal cause expressed their determination of never again casting a Grit vote."[115] These were expressions of discontent which the Greenway government would ignore at its peril. At the very time that the compromise was shaking loose the coalition which had so long supported the Liberals on the school issue, the provincial government was losing its ablest member. Nevertheless the protests from Protestants were as yet few. For the time being Sifton's triumph— which the settlement surely was—simply brought the retiring attorney general unprecedented popularity and acclaim.

Early in September D'Alton McCarthy had abandoned Brandon, choosing to sit for his Ontario constituency. On 20 October at Souris, a convention of Liberals unanimously nominated Sifton to contest the expected by-election. And on the same day that the school compromise was announced Sifton was formally sworn in as minister of the interior and superintendent-general of Indian affairs.[116] He promptly returned to Brandon for the election campaign, but his prestige and strength in the wake of the announcement were such that on nomination day he was accorded an acclamation.

Clifford Sifton's removal to Ottawa symbolized the new realities in Canadian politics. His had been less a triumph of provincial rights than a victory for a particular view of Confederation. He symbolized an aggressive new nationalism, certainly capable of intolerance and prejudice, but also fiercely determined to encourage an active role for the state in shaping society and in coming to terms with the needs of a modern developing country. He would find himself allied with an immensely able prime minister, but one whose deepest beliefs were often in conflict with his own. Laurier had an instinct for politically essential compromise, which may have been his greatest asset. His new lieutenant would not infrequently test it to the full.

6

# A New Ministry
## (1896–97)

The problems confronting the government of Canada were, in Sifton's opinion, purely practical. He told Laurier the government faced three major issues. The first was revision of the tariff. The second was "the immigration question, the question of securing a large addition to the agricultural population of the West." The third was "the transportation question, the question of getting their products to market." "I said then," he later recalled,

> that to place a large producing population upon the Western prairies and to inaugurate a system whereby the products of their labours should be brought to the seaboard through exclusively Canadian channels and shipped from Canadian ports would of itself be enough glory for one Government, and would bring such prosperity to the Dominion of Canada as to wholly transform the financial difficulties of the country.[1]

Ambitious as Sifton undoubtedly was, he was not to be contented merely with holding office and wielding power. He believed that the government must be committed to certain broad goals of national development. He had confidence in his assessment of the problems facing the Dominion and in his ability to contribute to their solution. The objectives he outlined to the prime minister remained his future concerns, both in and out of power.

It was in this context that he viewed his responsibilities as minister of the interior. Hitherto the portfolio had ranked rather low in the Ottawa hierarchy. Invested as it was, however, with responsibility for immigration and settlement policy, it fitted squarely in the middle of Sifton's scheme of national development. He knew what he wanted, and he did not accept office unconditionally. For years he had seen the portfolio handed to men who neither knew nor cared to try to understand the West or who had insufficient weight in cabinet to carry their points. Sifton demanded and received from Laurier an undertaking that he would receive the full backing of the government for his policies for western development. On the whole Laurier fulfilled the promise faithfully. Given this commitment, Sifton realized, there would be no escaping the blame if his policies failed.[2]

Sifton's duties went well beyond departmental administration. Under his charge was to be the organization of the Liberal party machinery in Manitoba, the North-West Territories, and British Columbia, then together comprising seventeen seats. His main goal naturally was to ensure a solid Liberal majority from the region at the next general election. There were also many lesser chores: administering patronage, arranging by-elections, organizing propaganda, and attempting to settle intra-party quarrels. Such political problems were not new to Sifton, but the stage was far more vast and the demands on his energies unabating.

Created in 1873, the Department of the Interior was intended to be a clearing house and co-ordinating body for dominion administration of the vast western domain acquired in 1870.[3] The department was charged with supervision of the settlement process, its main duty being to administer public lands—or "dominion lands"—policy. Because negotiation of Indian treaties and administration of Indian lands were inextricably bound up with settlement, Indian affairs came under the jurisdiction of the minister of the interior, first as a branch of his department and then, after 1880, as a separate department of which he became superintendent-general. Settling the aboriginal land titles of the mixed-blood population also fell to the Interior Department. Equally concerned with public lands, but from a different direction, was the Geological Survey Department, which also was assigned to the minister of the interior.

Thus, by various accretions to his duties, the minister became responsible for an enormous range of tasks. All the native people of Canada came under his jurisdiction. So did responsibility for exploration, mapping, and mineral surveys throughout the Dominion. He controlled a vast fiefdom, ranging west from the Ontario-Manitoba border to the Rocky Mountains and north from the United States boundary to the Arctic Ocean, over which he held more power than any other person, administering homestead, railway, school, forest, mineral and grazing lands, and national parks policy. When the relatively small and ineffective immigration branch was transferred from Agriculture to the Interior Department in 1892, the stage was set for an able man in the right circumstances to realize the department's tremendous potential.

Following his acclamation, Sifton began a careful investigation of what might be termed the "field operations" of his department in the West, known as the "outside service." At the same time he was accorded a triumphal series of banquets at Brandon, Moosomin, Winnipeg, and Hartney, at which he spoke of his tentative ideas about the tasks before him. He saw himself partly as a missionary called to renew eastern Canada's faith in the possibilities of the West. It would be difficult, but eastern Canadians had to be made to understand that their future prosperity depended heavily upon continued investment in western development. At the same time, he had to try to persuade those in power that excessively high tariffs and freight rates and poor administration of public lands had driven thousands of settlers from their lands.

Sifton refused to predict large numbers of immigrants in the near future; he did promise that the whole question would "be studied anew from top to bottom, and a radical change made." The most pressing need, however, was to effect changes in land and other policies directly affecting the West in order to retain the farmers already there. No miracles should be expected, but if administrative changes in personnel and organization would be likely to effect the desired results, Sifton would carry them out. He promised that "the details of his department, instead of being pigeonholed as in times past, would be looked into and dealt with. The people would find a radical change in the interior department, that instead of the department running the minister, the minister would run the department."[4]

By mid-December Sifton's preparations were completed, and the press of work at Ottawa could no longer be put off. Clifford, Arma, and the four boys bade farewell to their many Brandon friends and left to take up permanent residence in the national capital. It was a city of dull buildings and muddy streets, distinguished for its humid summers, bitter winters, and the sharp, sour odours of its pulp and paper mills. "Ottawa," Laurier had once observed, "is not a handsome city and does not appear to be destined to become one either."[5] On 21 December, more than a month after being sworn to office, Clifford Sifton arrived in the department offices to confront several months' accumulated backlog of files and correspondence.

"The distribution of patronage," observed one historian of this period, "was the most important single function of government."[6] This truth was irritatingly real to Sifton. Eager to get on with his departmental duties, he found that everywhere he turned "the job-hunters descended upon him, singly, in droves and in battalions."[7] The grass roots membership of the Liberal party was in a singularly vindictive frame of mind. Not only had they had no tangible reward for their labours on behalf of the party for the last eighteen years, but most of them believed that the Mackenzie government had been brought down in 1878 by a partisan Tory civil service. Instead of rousting out enemy enclaves, the Mackenzie government had naively trusted in the. ideal of the political neutrality of civil servants. Never again would the Liberals be so betrayed. "Remember Mackenzie!" was the cry which rang repeatedly in the ears of Laurier's besieged government after 23 June.

Along with the departments of Public Works, Railways, the Militia and the Post Office, the Department of the Interior was one of the great patronage portfolios. Awaiting Sifton were hundreds of letters from hopeful applicants across the country, recounting, often at awesome length and in numbing detail, their unstinting sacrifices over long years on behalf of the party. Now they wanted their reward. Sifton also encountered lists of recommendations from Liberal MPs, anxious to placate constituents and friends. Administering patronage entailed everything from disposal of government supply contracts to Liberal businesses, to ensuring that government advertising was carried on only in Liberal newspapers, and to directing department officials to patronize Liberal hotels and transportation companies. Confronted with a civil service accustomed to things running in well-known grooves, the minister had to be constantly vigilant.

Civil service positions, however, generated the greatest demand. For every available post, it seemed, there were ninety and nine supplicants who had to be turned away. Soon Sifton, like his colleagues, was taking refuge in the apostolic plaint, "I only had five loaves and two fishes, and what are they among so many[?]" "The trouble in the North West," he noted. "is that the service is so overmanned that I am compelled to occupy myself in dismissing men instead of dispensing patronage."[8] One way and another, despite this disclaimer, Sifton quickly gained a reputation as a thoroughgoing reformer. The most immediate weapon was the outright accusation of "offensive political partisanship." Unfortunately for their careers, a number of officials had worked actively for the Tory cause in the late elections. A letter from a Liberal member outlining such activities was regarded by Sifton as sufficient cause for dismissal. Other officials were notorious drunkards or incompetents who hitherto had preserved their positions by political connections; they too were dropped. Those whose shortcomings were less obvious could be removed or encouraged to resign in a number of ways: by superannuation, by demotion or transfer, by withholding promotions or salary increases, or even by decreasing salaries. Sifton freely used all these methods.

He began at the top. A.M. Burgess, deputy minister of the interior since 1883, must have trembled when he learned who his new political master was to be. Sifton had not forgotten his abrupt dismissal at their interview in 1884 and had long believed Burgess guilty of arrogant incompetence. At the same time he was determined to replace Hayter Reed, deputy superintendent-general of Indian affairs since 1893. Reed was intensely unpopular in the West, where he was regarded as a partisan Tory who had achieved office solely through connections. Sifton believed it would increase the efficiency of the departments to bring them both under one deputy. His choice was James A. Smart, his crony from Brandon, who was completing a second term as mayor in 1896. Smart had generally been recognized as an admirable administrator, if not a strong politician, while in the Greenway government. Most important, Sifton trusted him, and they worked well together.[9]

Nevertheless, it was not accepted practice for an incoming minister to unceremoniously turn out his deputy, let alone two of them; and it would not be easily accomplished. Social Ottawa was soon a-twitter with the audacity of Laurier's young colleague. Both Burgess and Reed set about to use all their connections to subvert Sifton's plans.[10] For weeks the issue was not resolved as the battle was fought out in cabinet. Finally in mid-February reluctant approval was given. The appropriate orders-in-council were passed early in March, and Smart assumed his dual office on 1 April 1897. An agitated Joseph Pope, deputy to the secretary of state, wrote that "Sifton has triumphed over Laurier [who had resisted the move] and . . . Burgess and Reed are to be offered as a propitiatory sacrifice to the new Minister of the Interior. This is a bad business and creates great disquietude in the service especially among Deputy Heads. It is felt to be destructive of the feeling of permanence and stability which attached to the office in the past."[11]

It was exactly for this reason, however, that western Liberals thoroughly approved of Sifton's victory, as foreshadowing significant new departures. "The West," reported J.H. Ross of the North-West Territories Executive Committee, "is with you in the changes you have made in your department and are pleased to note that you had strength enough to withstand the pressure brought to bear by those who wish to allow things to run along in the old grooves and actually put their lives into the hands of their enemies."[12] Still, the knowledge that the mighty had fallen carried little cheer to those who failed to obtain expected favours. The Macleod Liberals, backed by Alberta MP Frank Oliver, for example, vigorously protested the fact that their local nominee had not been selected to replace an Indian agent transferred from a nearby reserve. Retorted Sifton, "If it was necessary for me in the case of a vacancy immediately to make a fresh appointment of a local man I do not see how I could improve the efficiency of the staff or carry out any intelligent scheme of reformation." In another instance, the sensitivities of Winnipeg Liberals were acutely pricked when Sifton decided to grant financial aid to the Western Canadian Immigration Association, a non-partisan association whose secretary was a Conservative. "I think that in a certain line the Association is doing good work," he wrote, "and I want its friendship and not its enmity in the work in which I am engaged." Even the Liberal Winnipeg *Tribune* took exception when Sifton promoted an alleged Conservative in the Interior Department and when he took a Roman Catholic as his secretary in Indian affairs.[13]

Not only did the minister of the interior believe that a hard line on civil service salaries might induce some government employees to reconsider their positions, but he also believed that it was a way to effect economy and induce efficiency. For years the Liberals had denounced Tory extravagance, and now they faced the necessity of trying to locate the $3 million or $4 million of surplus which they had claimed could be trimmed from dominion expenditure, then about $44 million annually. Of course by the time the Tory fat had been replaced by Grit, the saving was not nearly as great as anticipated.[14]

When Sifton presented his departmental estimates to the House of Commons in 1897, he had decided to withhold the automatic annual salary increases of $50 provided for in the Civil Service Act. Some of his employees who seemed to merit it were awarded considerably larger increments; most received nothing. Former Conservative Finance Minister George E. Foster demanded an explanation, declaring that such a policy "completely changed the basis upon which additions are to be made to the salaries of civil servants in this country." That was precisely Sifton's object. "It is not conducive to the efficiency of the service," he told the Commons, "that every man who is in the service shall know that he is going to get $50 a year increase whether he is efficient or not. It is not conducive to efficiency that there should be no special recognition of merit, or ability, or diligence." He carried his policy and thereafter consistently employed incentives to improve the standards of his department.[15]

The attention which Sifton devoted to the three departments under his charge clearly reflected his priorities. The Geological Survey suffered nothing more than severe restraint on salary increases and general expenditure. The great ability and prestige of its deputy, G.M. Dawson, allowed the Survey to continue its largely scientific functions of searching out, mapping, and informing the country about Canada's mineral resources.[16] It was the Department of Indian Affairs which Sifton attacked most vigorously. He arrived in Ottawa with little more to guide him than the conventional theories of his day about Indians. It was widely known that the Indian population was declining. Indeed, faced first with starvation and then with the appalling conditions on reserves, the western tribes in particular had been declining sharply for twenty-five or thirty years. Were they dying out altogether? No one knew. What the Liberals did know, however, was that the Tories had not seized the opportunity to cut back on staff; nor had they attempted to reduce expenses in areas such as Indian education and medical attendance or to place on the market large tracts of Indian lands which remained undeveloped. Sifton's declared intention was to "see that we either had more Indians to look after or less officials, for at present there were nearly as many officials as Indians."[17]

Such was the spirit in which he set about applying his knife to the Department of Indian Affairs. A peculiar imbalance in the budget made his task extremely difficult. Approximately three-quarters of the Indian affairs budget was spent on the Indians of the Northwest, who comprised about one-quarter of Canada's total Indian population. The numbered treaties negotiated on the plains in the 1870's required heavy government aid in the form of education, farm instruction, food, annuities, medical attendance, and so forth. The budget for the more settled and peaceful Indians elsewhere in Canada was already stretched so thin as to have little flexibility. If there were to be significant reductions, therefore, they would have to be made in the organization and personnel of the Northwest.

Sifton centralized the administration in Ottawa, and several agencies were closed down altogether.[18] This scheme was expected both to improve efficiency and to reduce manpower. There were 144 employees in the department when Sifton arrived; within two years some 57 had been dismissed or resigned from the Northwest service alone. Liberals were appointed to some of the vacancies, but in 1897-98 the department budgeted for only 115 officers, a decrease of 29, or 20 per cent. The department claimed that this amounted to a saving of over $27,000 in salaries. On top of this Sifton imposed a general reduction in salary levels for all categories, although some individuals were promoted. As a result the average annual salary dropped by 4 per cent.[19]

Before he was through Sifton must have appeared a tyrant to his staff. The savings were marginal—less than 3 per cent of the departmental budget—and did nothing for morale. More importantly, there is no evidence that the Indians were better served. For the foreseeable future the superintendent-general had no apparent objective but to hold the line on expenditure. "My present impression," he told a supporter who had requested additional aid for an Indian school, "is that there will be no substantial increases in these items in the next four years."[20]

By contrast, the Department of the Interior suffered much less. It was Sifton's principal interest, and while he wanted to make a number of short-term changes, he preferred to institute organizational changes more cautiously. Given the range of departmental activities, such restraint was not surprising. "I am just beginning to realize the extent of the contract I have taken hold of," he told Smart on Christmas Day, 1896, after just four days in his Ottawa office. "I can assure you it is somewhat appalling."[21]

A flurry of orders rapidly emanated from Sifton's desk. Smart was instructed to make a thorough inspection of the western offices to familiarize himself with their operations and personnel before coming to Ottawa. Dominion mining regulations were to be reviewed, because "there are violent complaints made to the effect, that [they] are practically prohibitive of mining, and are such, that prospecting and locating of mining claims is practically an impossibility." The policies of grazing leases, reservation of timber berths on the eastern slopes of the Rockies, and water reservation in southern Alberta must also be reviewed. There was a series of outstanding issues long in dispute between the dominion and Manitoba governments, especially with respect to swamp lands and "applications for patents for half breed claims," which Sifton lost no time in attempting to resolve. He also completed agreements with the Greenway government to share the costs of certain immigration promotion programmes.[22]

Sifton presented to Parliament legislation which attempted to facilitate settlement and registry of land titles. Registrars in land titles offices were given powers of attorney. Second homesteads could be acquired under some circumstances without the residence requirement. Ranchers could obtain title to their lands without fulfilling cultivation requirements intended for homestead lands. Settlers were permitted to nominate an agent to register their homesteads. The minister was given powers to decide when to grant grazing rights, to determine when a woman should be adjudged to be the head of a family, to deal with people whose homesteads were too poor to provide an adequate living, and even to dispose of patented lands whose owners had died before actually receiving the patent.[23] In a rare spirit of non-partisan co-operation, Sifton included in his bill reforms suggested by Nicholas Flood Davin, Conservative member for Assiniboia West, and by Rev. J.M. Douglas, Patron-Liberal member for Assiniboia East. Few of the changes were momentous, but they did solve several problems which had long irritated westerners. In his first legislative acts, therefore, Sifton received the approbation even of the opposition. It was a honeymoon that would be very short-lived.

Desirable as it was to make it as easy as possible for a settler to select, locate, patent, and succeed on his land, there were some suggestions which Sifton was not prepared to accept. One was the popular demand to permit second homesteading on the same terms as original homesteading. Where the land was too poor, or water was unobtainable, or there was some similar clear-cut case, he would consider it. There would be no sympathy, however, for those who had patented their lands, sold them, and wished to move on to seek another free homestead. Nor would those who lost patented lands through bankruptcy caused by crop failure or bad management receive consideration.[24] Sifton's solution was to permit second homesteading only when the settler had not received the patent for the original homestead. Related in principle, in Sifton's opinion, was the issue of squatters' rights. "There is no way in the world, the Department can recognize a squatter by giving him any legal right," he told Frank Oliver.[25] Such actions reflect his philosophy that the sort of settler wanted in the West was a man who was determined to make a success of his homestead at any price and who had respect for the rights of property. The government could not permit temptations which might weaken this resolve.

As minister of the interior, Sifton was trying to make the existing system work more efficiently rather than trying to impose any new philosophy. That is not to say that he agreed with the policy established in the Dominion Lands Act, 1872. The Conservative government then and in the 1880's had tried to fuse two conflicting concepts into one administrative system. They hoped to attract immigrants by the offer of a free quarter-section of land. For a ten-dollar registry fee and fulfilment of a three-year residence and certain cultivation requirements, a settler could obtain title to 160 acres. At the same time, the government attempted to defray the costs of opening up the West by granting alternate sections of land to the railways, which served as collateral for railway bonds and which might be sold to help meet construction expenses. There were several other reasons for withholding land. One-twentieth of all western lands was reserved for the Hudson's Bay Company as part of the settlement of 1869–70 which resulted in the transfer of Rupert's Land to Canada. The government reserved up to two sections in each township as school lands to be sold at high prices to defray educational costs. In both Manitoba and the Territories large tracts of land had been granted to the mixed-blood population to extinguish aboriginal title, but a large proportion had never been developed, and much of it was tied up in disputes over title, tax sales, or by speculators. The government also had granted large blocks of land to colonization companies and speculators, most of whom were making little effort to attract settlers, preferring to wait for the value of their lands to rise. Finally, many whites increasingly considered the Indian reserves as part of the process that tended to withhold good lands from immediate and efficient exploitation and to disperse white settlement.[26]

The result was that considerably less than half of the lands of the prairie West were available for free homesteading. In some districts, moreover, it was already obvious that a viable farm could not be created on only 160 acres; some land was almost totally non-productive or unsuited to intensive grain or mixed farming, and much of it was still located too far from railways to permit development. The dispersed settlement frequently resulted in high taxes and inadequate services. "The cause of nearly all the difficulties we labor under," Sifton told a Liberal gathering at Souris, "is the sparseness of our population in so large a territory. The system of settlement in alternate sections was the root of the evil. Every farmer knows that each homesteader has been improving in value the railway section alongside of him as well as his own." He concluded that "the old policy had completely failed."[27] Imputing blame, nevertheless, did not solve the problem. Sifton realized that he was unable to change overnight a system which had been in effect for a quarter of a century. Thus in his first few months, he concentrated on modifying existing regulations, while preparing a broad assault on the more important hindrances to settlement.

One scheme which Sifton had in mind to put large tracts of the reserved lands on the market cheaply was to purchase at a low price all the CPR lands east of the 103rd meridian, at Grenfell. This constituted some 1,850,000 acres controlled by the CPR proper and an additional 767,000 acres of the Manitoba South Western land grant acquired by the CPR. It would give the CPR needed capital and encourage the early settlement of the eastern prairies, long an object of the Manitoba government. But President Van Horne was not very favourable. There were signs, he told Sifton, of increasing immigration and a consequent rise in prices after a long period of depressed markets. Besides, while the CPR had mortgaged all its lands to some extent, the massive nature of its landholdings was an important factor in strengthening the company's credit when seeking to borrow funds abroad. So large a sale would weaken the company's credit. Van Horne then made an observation which, had it been made in public, would have been roundly condemned as blasphemy against the sacred doctrine of the free homestead. The experience of the company's immigration workers in Britain and Europe, he wrote, had been "that the offer of free lands is not nearly so attractive as most of us over here suppose it to be. People in Europe are not accustomed to getting anything of value for nothing, and they cannot understand free lands except on the supposition that they are worthless." The government, he thought, would do better to finance its immigration schemes by selling its lands at one dollar an acre, on easy terms and low rates of interest.[28]

Such a policy would have been a political disaster, whatever its practical merits. Still, Van Horne had been in the business of promoting immigration for longer than most people in the government, and the minister of the interior found it valuable to consider his ideas. Officially immigration had been the responsibility of the minister of agriculture until 1892, but government promotional efforts had been weak. The government seemed to expect first the offer of free lands, then the completion of the railway, as well as the efforts of colonization companies, and the anticipated exhaustion of the supply of free or cheap lands in the United States, to produce a steady influx of immigrants into Canada. It never happened.[29] Shifting immigration to the Department of the Interior in 1892 did little good. T.M. Daly, the new minister, had plenty of enthusiasm; but, predicted Van Horne, it "will have to stand the test of a good deal of ice water." The chilly response by the cabinet quickly stalled Daly's plans. A year later Van Horne noted, "The efforts of the Government towards inducing immigration seem now to be confined chiefly to asking us for passes for people who wish to go home to 'advertise the country.' "[30] Immigration fell off sharply in the 1890's—by no means wholly the fault of the government—and in 1896 less than seventeen thousand immigrants arrived, the fewest since 1868.

So concerned was Van Horne that immigration would receive the same short shrift under the new Laurier government that he mounted a campaign to have it "administered by a special commission of three men in whom the entire country would have confidence, removing this work from the jurisdiction of

any individual minister and from the soporific influence of the civil service."
Laurier would have none of it. Eventually Van Horne found that he was
pleased with the new minister. After an interview with Sifton in January 1897,
he wrote, "I have now, for the first time in years, confidence that something
worth while will be done."[31]

Sifton had always taken an interest in Manitoba's small programme of
immigration promotion, confined chiefly to Iceland and Britain, although it
was Premier Greenway's responsibility. On the only occasion when he had
spoken publicly on the subject, at an immigration convention in Winnipeg in
February 1896, he stated that he considered it hopeless to expect to fill the
country with "farmers with capital who could comfortably support
themselves." He considered that "experience has shown that those who make
the best settlers are those whose condition in the land from which they come is
not too rosy, and who are content in coming here to get along in a humble way
at first."[32] Sifton's policies would only partially conform to this objective after
he reached Ottawa.

His first concern was to establish an effective organization to keep
immigrants in the country from the time they reached Canadian ports until
they were located upon their land. Lacking effective guidance, thousands of
immigrants drifted into cities or into the United States. If they reached the
West, they often gave up in face of the difficulty of obtaining a suitable
homestead. Sifton promptly established a bureau in the Northwest "which has
for its particular object the locating and settlement of people there." His next
concern almost directly contradicted his statement to the immigration
convention. He focused attention on the American West, attempting to
attract farmers—including former Canadians—whose experience and capital
would make them successful in Canada. He removed the headquarters of the
work from Chicago to St. Paul, and within a few months put immigration
officers to work in Michigan, Minnesota, Kansas, and the Dakotas. "I can
only say," he told the House of Commons, "that the system has been carefully
organized, and we hope that good results will flow from it." Finally, he hoped
to overhaul the neglected British and European services, but he predicted that
it might be some time before "the tide will turn and we shall have a stream of
immigration poured into the north-western portion of Canada such as we
have not seen of late years."[33]

The immediate task, in Sifton's mind, was to revive the moribund
immigration staff. After another round of firings and restructuring, he
extended the principle of payment of agents by commission for immigrants
actually placed on the land, rather than payment by salary. "The pall of death
seemed to have fallen over the officials," Sifton later observed. "They were not
doing anything and . . . they seemed to be convinced that it was not worth while
to do anything because they could not succeed."[34] Such pessimism would no
longer be tolerated. With aggressive, positive salesmanship, Sifton was

Plate 10. Manitoba legislature building, Kennedy Street, Winnipeg, 1899. Horses, carriages, bicycles, and railways still dominated transportation.

Plate 11. The Manitoba government carried on its own programme of immigration promotion. The optimism and exaggerated promises of the literature appear ironic in light of the economic slump of the early 1890's.

Plate 12. An unusually relaxed formal photograph of Sifton in 1900. The minister of the interior was at the height of his power and influence in the Laurier cabinet.

Plate 13. Hugh John Macdonald (standing) and Sir Charles Tupper, probably ca. 1899. In provincial and federal politics they were among the most powerful of Sifton's Conservative foes.

# DOMINION CABINET, 1899.

HON. SIR LOUIS H. DAVIES, M.P.,
Minister of Marine and Fisheries.

HON. W. S. FIELDING, M.P.,
Minister of Finance.

HON. A. G. BLAIR, M.P.,
Minister of Railways and Canals.

HON. CLIFFORD SIFTON, M.P.,
Minister of the Interior.

RT. HON. SIR WILFRID LAURIER, G.C.M.G., M.P.,
Prime Minister and President of the Council.

HON. J. I. TARTE, M.P.,
Minister of Public Works.

HON. DAVID MILLS, Senate,
Minister of Justice.

HON. WM. MULOCK, M.P.,
Postmaster General.

HON. SIR RICHARD CARTWRIGHT,
G.C.M.G., M.P.,
Minister of Trade and Commerce.

Plate 14. A portion of the Laurier government, including some of those most friendly to Sifton (Davies, Mulock, Cartwright), and some with whom he most frequently disagreed (Tarte, Mills, Blair).

Plate 15. Employees of the *Manitoba Free Press*, 1886. Standing in the front row in front of the steps may be seen F.C. Wade (...
left), W.F. Luxton (third from left), and J.W. Dafoe (on Luxton's left).

Plate 16. The presses of the *Manitoba Free Press*, probably much as they were when Sifton purchased the newspaper in 1897.
It was for him both a political and a business investment.

convinced that a new image of Canada could be created abroad and the floods of Europeans diverted increasingly toward Canada.

At thirty-five Sifton was the youngest member of Laurier's famed "Ministry of the Talents." His was not the only new broom sweeping away layered dust and hidden cobwebs. The ministry was determined to put a new face on the dominion government. Although some changes were merely cosmetic, many others cut more deeply. In the exhilarating first months of power the new ministers plunged with vigour into their reforms, ranging from those of William Mulock in the Post Office and those of Dr. Frederick Borden in the Militia to those of W.S. Fielding in Finance. Sifton did not suffer by comparison with his illustrious colleagues. Within a few months he was generally recognized as one of the most influential in cabinet deliberations, being described, according to the phrenological predilections of the day, as "a long-headed man" who was "steadily growing in the estimation of both sides" of the House of Commons.[35]

Apart from Laurier and Israel Tarte, the minister of public works, Sifton had little contact with his French-Canadian colleagues. Laurier's great abilities commanded his respect. But Sifton and Tarte seemed to be always at daggers drawn. Tarte was convinced, correctly, that Sifton had little sympathy for promoting immigration in French-speaking countries and that he was reluctant to hire French-Canadian civil servants. Sifton was convinced, equally correctly, that Tarte had too little concern for the political and public benefit of public works projects in the West, preferring to concentrate on Québec.

Even among his English colleagues Sifton formed few real friendships. He was perhaps closest to Louis Davies, minister of marine and fisheries, a former premier of Prince Edward Island and active for some years in the Liberal opposition at Ottawa. Collector of Customs William Paterson, renowned for his leather lungs and fortissimo platform delivery, was also comfortable with him. One of the senior Liberals in the cabinet, Sir Richard Cartwright, minister of trade and commerce, often evinced an avuncular interest in Sifton, whose political skill and aggressiveness he much admired. With most of his colleagues, however, Sifton tended to be distantly formal, occasionally cordial, but too often abrupt and impatient.

In his first months in office he was concerned with establishing the government's authority in western Canada and with developing effective politicial machinery. Politics, for Clifford Sifton, was a continuous war. The Conservative party was, simply, "the enemy." Each battle or skirmish required serious preparation. Independence and idealism therefore had little place among the troops. If it appeared that western interests were occasionally being sacrificed, the rank and file were expected to accept the assurances of their leaders that the government was acting in the national interest. The Liberals had a fairly good base on which to build in western Canada. Popular support for the Conservatives had dropped sharply between 1891 and 1896, and for the first time the Liberals had outpolled their opponents in British Columbia and the North-West Territories. Many voters had abandoned the traditional parties in 1896, voting for Independents or Patrons. With the Conservative machinery in disrepair, an excellent opportunity arose to entrench the Liberals' position. In a close election, as Laurier knew, the vote in the West could be decisive. He wanted his western lieutenant to be able to overcome the regional propensities for independence, idealism, western chauvinism, and mistrust of central Canada and traditional political structures which were already distressingly apparent.

Sifton's immediate objectives were to consolidate the Liberal victory of 1896 and to meet some popular western demands as an earnest of the government's responsiveness to Western needs. It was essential to begin in Manitoba, where the goal was to turn the Liberal minority of 1896 quickly into a majority. Within weeks of the June election Sifton had begun investigations which would lead to contesting three Conservative victories—in Winnipeg, Macdonald, and Marquette—with a view to unseating the incumbents. Suspecting "a fraud of some kind," Sifton lost no time in putting "skilled detectives" to work. He told Laurier he had obtained "conclusive evidence of an organized system of tampering with ballots which constitutes the most colossal crime against honest elections which I have ever had any knowledge of." He hoped that the dominion government would bear the necessary expenses. The prime minister promptly agreed to do so, anticipating that Sifton would "unearth the most odious conspiracy which has taken place for many long years."[36]

Prosecutions launched shortly before Christmas, 1896, resulted in the unseating of Hugh John Macdonald and Nathaniel Boyd in Winnipeg and Macdonald. The Marquette case was thrown out on a technicality. A bill of over one hundred separate charges of bribery and corruption was presented to the courts in connection with the Winnipeg election. In Macdonald, the principal charge was stuffing of ballot boxes. It was shown, for example, that the Conservatives had run a sort of night school to instruct returning officers in the subtle arts of ballot manipulation. J.D. Cameron reported that "one Herman[,] a professional gambler and cardsharper of this city [Winnipeg] was taken out to the rural constituency of Macdonald and there as a Deputy Returning officer practiced his three card monte tricks before the innocent farmers with an ease and success that simply astounded all hands when the result of the poll was made known." One of Sifton's methods in establishing his case was simple, though costly and time-consuming. Knowing the political sympathy of practically every voter, he calculated the expected totals at each poll, compared it with the actual result, and where the tallies differed significantly, sent men around to obtain a statutory declaration from each voter as to how he had cast his ballot.[37]

Having unseated two Conservatives, it was imperative that the Liberals unite behind their candidates in the consequent by-elections. In Macdonald there was no serious problem. The defeated candidate, Dr. J.G. Rutherford, a veterinarian, was renominated. Winnipeg was more difficult. Joseph Martin was manoeuvering in the background, attempting to secure the seat. On 11 January he was elected honorary president of the Winnipeg Liberal Association, while the executive consisted of both Sifton's and Martin's friends. For the moment Sifton held the trump card. The Liberals, he told Robert Watson, had better not let Martin "ride over them again." If he received the nomination, it would be revealed during the campaign that "he is at present in the employ of the Canadian Pacific Railway Company, and, as you know, that would be fatal to his candidature.... Just fancy yourself in the middle of an election campaign having a charge made on the platform that your candidate was an employee of the Canadian Pacific Railway Company. The probability is he would lose his deposit."[38] Sifton's point was driven home a few weeks later when the story was leaked to the Winnipeg *Tribune*, hitherto a strong supporter of Martin. In shocked disbelief Martin's supporters read of his apparently turncoat arrangement, that even he had been bought off by his former enemy.[39] The Machiavellian ploy of the previous autumn had again brought a rich harvest. The news helped to rally support around Sifton's chosen candidate, former Winnipeg mayor R.W. Jameson.[40] Friends of both Sifton and Martin could unite in Jameson's support, which might help to heal the widening breach.

The Liberals carried the two seats in by-elections of 27 April by comfortable majorities. Within ten months of the 1896 dominion election Manitoba had become a solidly Liberal province, government supporters holding five of the seven seats. Yet the victories had been extracted in a pugnacious style in which the minister of the interior neither asked nor yielded quarter. When Laurier and Sir Charles Tupper attempted to "saw off" election protests in late 1896 and early 1897, Sifton would have no part of it. Tupper was especially concerned about the humiliation being faced by Hugh John Macdonald, who had only reluctantly agreed to run in Winnipeg and who probably bore little direct responsibility for the corrupt campaign organized on his behalf. Rather than have Macdonald's reputation sullied, Tupper wanted Sifton to allow him to retire quietly. But Sifton steadfastly refused to drop the prosecutions. If the corruption were not exposed, he maintained, the Tories would be tempted to do the same thing again. Macdonald promptly turned his attention to aid in the recovery of the provincial Conservative party; and in future he and Tupper were determined to repay the minister of the interior in kind.[41]

Sifton's diplomatic mettle also was put to the test in the North-West Territories throughout his first months in office. In local politics the Territories adhered, formally at least, to the ideal of non-partisan politics. Led by F.W.G. Haultain, member for Macleod and an able lawyer, the local assembly had been pressing for a measure of autonomy and self-government, which the Conservative governments had obstinately refused to grant. With growing frustration, residents of the Territories began to realize that voting for the government in power, as they had by large majorities in the dominion elections of 1887 and 1891, by no means guaranteed that Ottawa would be responsive to local needs. The Liberals had sought to take advantage of growing discontent in the 1890's which, along with demographic change, was gradually eroding the Conservatives' traditional support. So too, however, had the Patrons of Industry been active, especially in the populous southern District of Assiniboia.

In Assiniboia East the Liberals had co-operated with the Patrons in electing Rev. J.M. Douglas; in Assiniboia West similar co-operation had brought them within one vote of defeating Nicholas Flood Davin, the sitting Tory. Patron influence was less pronounced in the District of Alberta, where Independent Liberal Frank Oliver had been elected. His victory arose from a situation peculiar to Alberta, where the solidly Conservative ranching community south of Calgary had always dominated politics. Oliver had been a vigorous spokesman, both through his *Edmonton Bulletin* and as a member of the local assembly, for the interests of the homesteaders to the north. Conservative organization was weakening, while expanding settlement in the north turned the scales in favour of the Liberals. However, the Grits were not sufficiently sure of themselves to run on a straight party ticket.[42] Consequently, the outcome of the 1896 election in three of the Territorial seats mainly reflected discontent with the Tories. All of Sifton's skill would be required to preserve these victories.

His most immediate problem, unexpectedly, was in the fourth Territorial constituency, the District of Saskatchewan in the north and east. It was a vast, sparsely populated riding, distinguished, according to J.D. Cameron, as "the most poverty stricken and corrupt constituency in Canada." Laurier had agreed to run there as well as in Québec East in 1896 because the Saskatchewan Liberals were so badly divided. He won a narrow victory over two Conservatives, subsequently abandoning the constituency in favour of his home riding.[43] Electing another Liberal should have been an easy task. Appearances were deceiving. T.O. Davis, a merchant and former mayor of Prince Albert, had laboured for years in the riding in the Grit interest, contributing heavily in time and money. He had the métis vote in his pocket, particularly through promises of settlement of long-outstanding land claims, and was the most popular Liberal in rural districts by a wide margin. Davis was an outcast, however, so far as most Prince Albert Liberals were

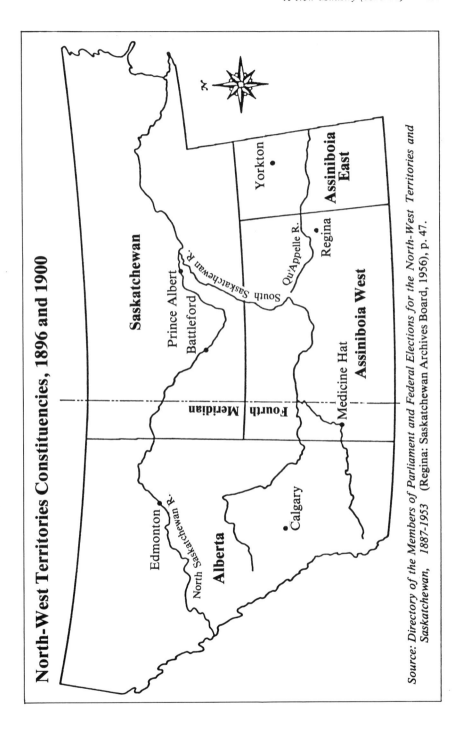

## North-West Territories Constituencies, 1896 and 1900

Alberta

Saskatchewan

Assiniboia West

Assiniboia East

Edmonton

Prince Albert

Battleford

Yorkton

Medicine Hat

Calgary

Regina

North Saskatchewan R.

South Saskatchewan R.

Qu'Appelle R.

Fourth Meridian

*Source: Directory of the Members of Parliament and Federal Elections for the North-West Territories and Saskatchewan, 1887-1953* (Regina: Saskatchewan Archives Board, 1956), p. 47.

concerned. They did not like the class of people whom Davis represented, and they objected to the rough and ready politics of which he was an undoubted master. Davis was determined to have the nomination; the Prince Albert Liberals were determined that he should not.

It was very embarrassing for the federal Liberals. Sifton sent his brother Arthur from Calgary to Prince Albert, where he had resided for two years, to try to iron out the situation. The Conservatives were induced not to contest the seat; and Davis's leading Liberal opponent, H.W. Newlands, was bought off with a civil service appointment. It was all in vain. The Prince Albert Liberals were determined to oppose Davis, even though he succeeded in obtaining Laurier's personal endorsement. Finally on 19 December Davis emerged the victor in a bitterly fought by-election over his Independent Liberal opponent, J.R. McPhail. It appeared that Davis had employed his full bag of tricks to obtain his triumph, and McPhail promptly contested the election. "Never will there be even a comparatively clean election in Saskatchewan," McPhail told Sifton, "unless there is a stop put to such corrupt practices as have been carried on here." He believed that "Davis has bought his seat," and McPhail owed it to himself and his supporters to expose Davis's practices and to disqualify him from running in future.[44]

Only a few months earlier Sifton told Laurier, when pressing him to support the protests in Manitoba, "I cannot conceive of any more urgent public duty resting upon you as Premier of the Dominion than to leave no stone unturned to expose these frauds and punish the perpetrators." It was one thing to expose the Conservatives in such activities; it was quite another to expose fellow Liberals. Davis wrote frantically to Sifton practically admitting all the charges and explaining that he would certainly be unseated if the protest ever reached the courtroom. Sternly Sifton told McPhail that his petition was "an act of deliberate hostility to the Government" and demanded its withdrawal. At first McPhail refused; then in March 1897, for considerations not wholly explained, he too caved in.[45]

At the beginning of December, 1896, prior to the Saskatchewan by-election, N.F. Davin had offered to ensure that no Conservative would enter the contest if a protest against him by the Liberals and Patrons of Assiniboia West was dropped. Laurier was agreeable. Sifton, however, believed that the Conservative abstention could be engineered without Davin's help. More important, he and his fellow Grits had been aching for years to unseat Davin. Naturally such sentiment was strongest in Assiniboia West, and any attempt to "saw off" the protest could be complicated by the fact that many of the petitioners had no loyalty whatever to the Liberal party. "Impossible to abandon Assiniboia without local consent," wired Sifton to Laurier, and Davin's offer was spurned.[46]

Davin wasted no time in launching a libel suit against Walter Scott, a young Liberal journalist who had recently assumed control of Davin's former organ, the Regina *Leader*. Scott had accused Davin of being a "boodler" and believed the government could supply the evidence to substantiate the charge. Sifton was asked not only to have the necessary information searched but also to pay the deposit required when the election protest was entered. "Davin," wrote J.H. Ross, "we must get rid of no matter what it costs."[47] In the firm belief that they could win both the protest and the libel case, the Liberals of Assiniboia West proceeded. Then early in June the word came from Ottawa that the protest must be dropped. Sifton blamed Laurier for having reached an agreement with Tupper to "saw off" remaining protests. The prime minister, conveniently, had just left for England and was not available to field angry western protests. Sifton portrayed himself as simply carrying out the immutable orders of his leader and upholding the honour of the Liberal party. In reality, Sifton had apparently been given an ultimatum by Hugh John Macdonald. If the protest against Davin were not dropped, the Conservatives would proceed with cases against the Liberals in Selkirk and Lisgar, where they stood a strong chance of winning. Even the defeat of Davin was not worth the loss of two Liberal seats. Sifton probably asked Laurier to conclude the arrangements.

Appealing to Scott to undertake to "get the protest against Davin dropped," Sifton assured him that "Mr. Laurier was impelled by the most powerful reasons in the interest of the party and Government to make the arrangement which he did make." "You are one of the men, unfortunately too few in our Western Country," he told Scott in a rare gesture of flattery, "who are able to rise above petty local feeling or personal feelings however strong, and look to the interest of the party and the interest of the Country as a whole." Careful instructions followed outlining the nature of the diplomacy required. The defeated candidate, J.K. McInnis, for example, would have to be offered some position. The lawyer who had entered the protest could be assured that Sifton would remember his services and "to a young man practising in Regina the friendship of the Government is not an unimportant matter."[48] Scott was reluctant but successful, and on 14 August the protest was withdrawn. But Sifton had to absorb the expense personally, including the costs of the petition and even an additional payment of $1,200 which McInnis demanded. "The Regina matter has now been arranged," wrote Sifton in exasperation, "but I am told it will take the rest of my salary for the year to clear the cost. Life to me appears to be very real and earnest."

So it was. The minister of the interior had personally absorbed $18,000 in expenses incurred in connection with election frauds cases in Manitoba and the Territories. While the government reimbursed him for some $7,000— which the Conservatives loudly and bitterly protested—he still had lost far more than his annual $7,000 salary as a minister.[49] When the dust finally settled, the Liberals appeared to be firmly established across the West, with eight of eleven prairie seats, and four of six in British Columbia. But the foundation was unstable. Not only did the divisive spirit of Joseph Martin continue to plague the party in Manitoba, but also Martin himself entered on a new and equally stormy political career in British Columbia. Nor were all Liberals in Saskatchewan and Assiniboia West entirely reconciled to Sifton's course. Finally, there was a stubbornly independent core in all regions which would never wholly accept the rigidly partisan and highly centralized framework that Sifton was trying to impose. He was willing to delegate authority but rarely to release it.

Such was the case with his attitude to the movement for autonomy for the North-West Territories. From the Territorial point of view, Ottawa was far too remote to appreciate local needs. The local assembly had few of the taxing powers of a provincial government and no revenues from public lands, yet Ottawa stubbornly refused to grant sufficient funds to meet the great demands for public works. From Ottawa, however, the Territories seemed unlikely to be able to exercise full provincial powers with so scant and scattered a population.

The Liberals had promised to deliver more. Were they not, after all, the party of provincial rights, the champions of the underdog against the overweaning power of Ottawa? At Moosomin, prior to going to Ottawa, Sifton announced that "the swaddling clothes plan of treating the North-West had come to an end." There were certain affairs which were better run by "the people of the North-West...themselves than by the people at Ottawa."[50] But the view from the minister's desk at Ottawa rapidly modified Sifton's opinions. When the territorial negotiators, F.W.G. Haultain and J.H. Ross, arrived in Ottawa, they discovered that the minister, like his predecessors, was inclined to see many virtues in retaining control of lands and other matters. One important point the Liberals did concede: there would be responsible government. The lieutenant-governor would in effect choose a premier, who in turn would select a cabinet or executive council that enjoyed majority support in the elective assembly. Under the legislation introduced by Sifton in the 1897 parliamentary session, the territorial assembly gained few new powers of significance. Essentially it maintained the status quo, simply recognizing in law those powers acquired in practice in preceding years. Worse still, the Liberals proved to be as tight with the purse strings as the Tories. Here too were sown seeds of future dissension.[51]

There seemed to be no escape for Sifton from the Manitoba school question. He had been aware that the Laurier-Greenway compromise was not viewed in Ottawa as a final settlement. Few of those concerned, however, could have foreseen the endless delays which ensued. Archbishop Langevin continued his energetic opposition to the settlement. He considered it a betrayal of the French and Roman Catholic population. He desperately needed the united support of all Canadian Catholics, both to bring pressure on the dominion and provincial governments and to secure financial aid for his schools. They were suffering terribly. Israel Tarte had noted in November 1896 that over fifty Catholic schools had closed since 1890. Only a few parishes had reasonably strong schools; most of those which survived did so only with the help of religious orders who could provide some staff and facilities.[52] Thousands of Catholic children remained without educational facilities or in pathetically poor schools, and gradually more and more Catholics were accepting the public school régime.

Langevin had always maintained that the question was one of conscience and principle, not of party, and that voting for anyone opposed to separate schools was, for a Catholic, unacceptable. When the provincial riding of St. Boniface was opened early in 1897 for a by-election, Langevin was determined to make the contest a minor plebiscite in which the French Catholic voters could register their disapproval of the settlement. Every effort was made to elect the Conservative by a large majority. The schools offered to Catholics by the settlement, declared the archbishop, were schools "without the crucifix, without Catholic books, where the teacher cannot speak of God, whence Christ is banished." During the campaign priests reportedly made a house-to-house canvass of the constituency, threatening that those who voted Liberal would find "the crucifix...taken from the wall, the confessional closed to them and burial in consecrated ground refused, in fact all the consolations of religion would be denied."[53]

The solid Conservative victory in St. Boniface made Langevin's point. But the nature of his campaign also made it very difficult for those who wanted to aid the Catholic cause. Moral outrage, however justifiable, could never restore the former school system. The war had been lost, and realistically it was time for the Catholic Church to try to gain as much as possible in the peace. The Church in Québec was already losing some of its fervour for the Manitoba cause. The Ontario clergy, led by Archbishop Walsh of Toronto, did not like the settlement but feared that continued agitation would rouse Protestant prejudice against them in their own province. With the promise that future concessions would be sought, they accepted the compromise.[54]

To help quell the agitation, the Liberals were anxious for Greenway to make a public commitment to administer the school system with generosity and goodwill toward the Catholics. His speech at a banquet for Laurier in Montreal on 30 December 1896 was conciliatory, offering a Catholic member of the advisory board, a Catholic inspector, and consideration of Catholic views on textbooks.[55] But Greenway's gesture, followed by passage of the compromise in the Manitoba legislature, was met only by Langevin's defiance. The result was a marked stiffening of Protestant attitudes.

Nor was this the only difficulty. Greenway's promise of additional concessions came with several strings attached. Manitoba had a series of outstanding financial claims against the Dominion, extending as far back as 1879. The province calculated that over $280,000 was owing on a public buildings account, over $110,000 on the subsidy account, and accumulated interest of nearly $319,000. Additionally, some $300,000 was claimed on the school lands fund, and agreements were desired on the province's claims for compensation with respect to swamp lands.[56] The province was not inclined to expedite the school concessions until at least some of the money was paid. Conversely, the Dominion was reluctant to pay until they were granted. On balance, it was plainly Greenway who would run political risks by benefiting the Catholics, and he had no desire to do so for a prime minister who had ignored him in the negotiations of 1896.

Clifford Sifton was caught in the centre. Laurier supposed he had great influence with Greenway, and Sifton had to be loyal to his new chief. On the other hand, he knew the political sensitivity of Manitoba and how little room Greenway actually had to manoeuvre in. And he neither agreed with nor could he consistently defend demands for substantial changes in the system. He believed that the by-elections in Winnipeg and Macdonald ridings could be viewed as public pronouncements on the Laurier-Greenway compromise. "It is...important that a constituency generally Protestant should not show any lack of confidence in Mr. Laurier while the School question is under fire," he told J.G. Rutherford. "He is at least entitled to the support of the Manitoba constituencies after what he has done."[57]

That was a proposition about which Greenway was becoming increasingly dubious. Summoned to Ottawa in mid-May, Greenway was pressed to agree to several important concessions. Sifton intervened and a more moderate list was approved. These included the appointment of a Catholic inspector, the appointment of Langevin and another Catholic nominee to the advisory board, permission to use Ontario public school texts as well as those authorized by the advisory board, and three-year interim certificates to allow Catholic teachers to upgrade themselves where necessary.[58] In return the Laurier government agreed to the provincial claim for $280,000, and to provide $100,000 a year for three years on the school lands claim, while reserving judgment on other matters.[59]

At this point everything began to break down. Greenway had understood the dominion financial offer to be firm and immediate and announced it as such to the press before going to New York on railway business. The dominion authorities had acted on a similar assumption about Greenway's offer of concessions. Laurier was anxious to have the matter cleared up before he left late in the month for the Jubilee celebrations and Colonial Conference in England. At the earnest request of the Canadian government, Rome had sent a papal delegate, Merry del Val, to Canada in April to look into the whole question and inform himself concerning the Canadian political situation; it was hoped that he would support Laurier's position and suggest that Rome press the Canadian hierarchy—especially Langevin—to acquiesce. Laurier had promised del Val that the concessions agreed upon with Greenway would be carried out. The papal delegate wanted a definite letter of commitment from Manitoba that the concessions would be executed by order-in-council.

Laurier wrote Greenway that there had been "some misapprehension" concerning the dominion commitment. No money would be forthcoming until the next (1898) session of Parliament, mainly because the prime minister did not want to risk a debate on the school question during his absence. At the same time the Manitoba government made it clear that the concessions could not be implemented by order-in-council, particularly since the agreement had been leaked to the press.[60]

Sifton was still hopeful that the situation could be retrieved. The importance of the proposed settlement was made plain in his correspondence with Laurier. Once the concessions were effected, del Val was willing to recommend that Catholic opposition to the public school system should cease. In practice, Sifton pointed out, this could mean that most Catholics and Protestants would still be able to have their own schools, because patterns of rural settlement had left the denominations substantially separate from one another. He estimated that there would be about one hundred schools which would be exclusively Catholic, eight hundred or eight hundred and fifty which would be Protestant, and "a very few cases—in all—I should say not more than ten or fifteen—where there will be mixed schools in which the Roman Catholic or Protestant minority of children will not be sufficient in number to have a teacher of their own religious faith." Such cases would have to be ignored. Because existing public school facilities were already crowded in Winnipeg, Sifton was optimistic that the local school board would decide to rent the buildings used by Catholics, allowing the Catholic children to continue to attend their own schools and be taught by teachers of their own faith. It was further expected that the advisory board would be encouraged to devise separate Protestant and Catholic religious exercises. Such arrangements, of course, would have to be made quietly as administrative practices, not as law, because of the political risks.[61] The federal Liberals had tried to sweeten the pill for Greenway by agreeing to proceed with resolutions to give Manitoba the school lands money once the concessions agreed to in May had been formally passed.

Nervous because of public agitation and angered by what he considered Laurier's deception, the Manitoba premier persistently refused to take action. Sifton tried frantically to persuade him. Increasingly acrimonious telegrams passed back and forth, culminating in a bitter exchange in mid-June: "Essential you should wire contents papers [orders-in-council] tonight," wired Sifton on 16 June. "Cannot advance your interests a step until satisfactory settlement." Retorted Greenway, "In view of your threatening message tonight deem it best to discontinue further correspondence upon the subject."[62] Plainly Sifton's influence was no longer decisive in Manitoba politics. He was immediately apologetic and rushed out to Winnipeg to attempt to repair the damage. But the dominion government had overdrawn its small fund of Manitoba goodwill. Added to the difficulties over the school question and financial claims was the obvious hostility in Ottawa to Greenway's pet Winnipeg-to-Duluth railway scheme, which he had revived shortly after Sifton left the provincial cabinet. Greenway was irritated too at Sifton's failure to exercise his influence with the CPR to dampen the hostility of the *Manitoba Free Press* toward the provincial government. Finally, and possibly most important, the recently announced tariff policy of the Laurier government had been an embarrassing disappointment to western Liberals. All in all, Greenway did not consider himself obligated to take any further risks for Laurier and Sifton.

The parliamentary session ended with no action taken respecting the school lands fund. Catholic opposition, in face of Manitoba's intransigence, would have been too great. Sifton continued to press the province to embody one or two concessions in an order-in-council. The local government considered that it had done enough by making some of the changes by administrative fiat. Greenway finally told Sifton that he had been humiliated by the "want of action, on the part of the Government in settling the financial claims of the Province" as Laurier "had verbally and by letters promised to do." The local government had made financial commitments on the basis of Laurier's word and had been left stranded.[63]

Before returning to Rome to make his recommendations, Merry del Val took seriously ill, an illness, it was claimed, brought on by the anxiety and disillusionment occasioned by the negotiations in Canada. None of the principals, including Sifton, had looked at all impressive. The minority was still no better off than it had been under the Laurier-Greenway compromise. For the rest, there was nothing but broken promises. Could any faith be placed in vague assurances that more concessions would yet be negotiated? At the same time, would continued agitation by Langevin and the Catholic Church generally serve the best interests of the minority? Such were the questions that del Val had to weigh in his recommendations to the pope. On his conclusions rested the hopes of the Laurier government for an early end to the protracted dispute.

In the long litany of western grievances no refrain was more recurringly persistent than that of the evils of the protective tariff. No Liberal had raised his voice more eloquently in praise of free trade, nor railed more harshly at the tribute exacted by manufacturers from the farmer than Clifford Sifton.

Western Liberals confidently expected that 23 June 1896 would mark a watershed in Canadian history. The new government could promptly begin its great task of dismantling the dykes of protection, allowing prosperity to flow in on the tide of free trade. The new minister of the interior would surely play an active role in putting forth western views and holding the government to its promised course. It must have been something of a shock, therefore, when, a scant four months after Sifton had been sworn into office, one of his constituents received a letter from him stating, "I not only would not retire from the Government because they refused to eliminate the principle of protection from the tariff but I would not remain in the Government if they did eliminate the principle of protection entirely from the tariff."[64] How is it possible to account for this astonishing reversal?

First, the Liberal party itself had changed, though this was little understood in the West. It had been defeated on the issue of Unrestricted Reciprocity in 1891, when many powerful business and transportation interests had contributed to the success of Sir John A. Macdonald and the loyalty cry. Continued commitment to an extreme free trade position would effectively hobble the Liberals in contests with the government. It was essential, therefore, to modify party policy, which was done at the Ottawa convention in 1893. In place of the firm promise of immediate free trade were substituted pious phrases about exchanging a revenue tariff for the protective tariff and the desirability of having the tariff rest as lightly as possible upon the necessities of life.[65]

It was a marvellously worded platform. It permitted the Liberals to retain the support of those who favoured free trade, but it also allowed party leaders to make definite promises to the business community that there need be no fear of stringent free trade measures. As a result the Liberals enjoyed extensive business support in 1896. Sir William Van Horne, for example, commented that it had been the expected dire consequences of Unrestricted Reciprocity that had caused the CPR to support the Conservatives in 1891. "The Liberal leaders," he wrote in March 1896, "understand the matter very well and I do not think they will make the same mistake again." In 1898 Lyman M. Jones, farm implement manufacturer and former provincial treasurer in the Greenway government, told Sifton, "Before the last election manufacturers believed they understood the [tariff] policy of the present Government, and upon that understanding they of course acted."[66]

A second reason for Sifton's position was that in 1894 the Conservatives had substantially modified the tariff in response to public opinion. The duty on farm implements, for instance, had been reduced from 35 to 20 per cent. This had softened business support for the Tories. However, it also meant that once in power the Liberals had to move within narrow confines. No dramatic assault on protection was possible without endangering a large segment of the manufacturing community. The Liberals thus had to defend the basic structure of the existing tariff and were able to make only relatively modest alterations. Finally, Sifton himself was changing. His perspective was broadening, and he accepted the position of the national party from the time of the 1893 convention. He thereafter tended to avoid making promises of specific or extensive tariff reductions.[67] The party, he would say, was committed to a general review of the whole matter and to making reductions where they could be carried out fairly and equitably, still leaving the manufacturer a reasonable margin of profit, while easing the burden on the consumer.[68]

Thus it was that Sifton could, at least from the point of view of some of his constituents, unblushingly repudiate the beloved doctrine of free trade. "I would consider that so to construct the tariff as to wantonly destroy the industries that have been built up under it would be utterly unjustifiable from any possible standpoint of reason." The principle of free trade was fine, but the fact was that for eighteen years Canadian business had grown up under protection. To throw it off suddenly would be catastrophic for the entire country. "I have a profound distrust of the wholesale application of theories to business." He would work to relieve the burdens of westerners resulting from tariffs and freight rates, "but I do not intend to insist that the business of other Provinces shall be destroyed and thousands of good Canadian people turned out of employment for the sake of carrying out a theory."[69] A convinced pragmatist, Sifton contended that government policies ought to be viewed as a whole. The tariff was but a part of a broad series of policies which would benefit the West. These included modified customs regulations, negotiated changes in railway freight rate structures, improvements in the St. Lawrence canals to lower shipping costs, and the adoption of a British preference in trade policy.

Prime Minister Laurier's diplomatic talent was shown to advantage as he worked to achieve a Liberal consensus on the tariff question. Immediately after the election, he informed businessmen that no new tariff would be introduced for eight or nine months, and in the meantime they would be fully consulted. He appointed W.S. Fielding of Nova Scotia, a moderate on the tariff question, as minister of finance, while relegating Sir Richard Cartwright, the party's senior financial expert but a doctrinaire free trader, to the then comparatively minor portfolio of trade and commerce. To mollify the free-trade wing of the party, he sent out feelers to the Americans concerning a possible reciprocity agreement, which he was certain would not be favourably received. "We must hold our hands free to deal in any direction which the interest of Canada may demand," he told John Charlton, a Liberal MP and lumberman who was ardently pushing free trade in Washington; "and, whilst, for my part, I am strongly impressed with the view that our relations with our neighbours should be friendly, at the same time I am equally strong in the opinion that we may have to take the American tariff—if conceived in hostility to Canada—& make it the Canadian tariff."[70]

Laurier was pragmatic too. He bluntly told J.S. Willison, editor of the Liberal Toronto *Globe,* "I wish the Globe would stop urging reforms. Reforms are for Oppositions. It is the business of Governments to stay in office."[71] When it came to the tariff, that philosophy certainly held true. No longer were the Liberals going to go to Washington to plead for reciprocity. The answer to American protectionism was retaliation in kind—a startling about-face for a man who only five years earlier had been preaching precisely the opposite solution. Events would show, however, that the apparent similarity in the views of the prime minister and the minister of the interior was only superficial. Sifton had in fact experienced a conversion to moderate protectionism. Free trade remained Laurier's ideal, but he was willing to sacrifice principle when, and as long as, circumstances required it.

After the autumn parliamentary session of 1896, a tariff commission consisting of Fielding, Cartwright, and Paterson was established. At once the eastern bias of the party become evident. The commissioners were prepared to travel to major centres in central and Maritime Canada to hear local representations, but had no intention of visiting the West. Naturally, representations to the commission in industrial and manufacturing centres leaned heavily to protectionism. When Sifton arrived in Ottawa, he immediately insisted that the commission must make at least a token appearance in the West. A failure to entertain western views would be politically calamitous, particularly in light of the conclusions which Sifton knew the commission was going to reach. Reluctantly, the commissioners agreed to venture as far as Winnipeg.[72]

The West was by no means unified on the tariff. Most farmers agreed that the removal of the tariff on the necessities of life, ranging from coal oil, lumber, and clothing to farm implements and binder twine, was desirable. But the evils of the tariff depended upon whose ox was being gored. Various western interests, including many farmers, wanted certain items in the tariff schedule retained—on grain, flour, cattle, horses, and so forth. Sifton concluded that the West could be induced to swallow the tariff if concessions were made on three items—agricultural implements, binder twine, and barbed wire. He was equally determined to protect the duty on wheat and flour, because it was "a material benefit to the farmer of the North West." Despite strong demands in central Canada for removal of these duties, Sifton promised to "fight that question all the way through."[73]

As the general direction of government policy started to drift down to Liberal backbenchers and party members, there began to appear a marked restiveness. Robert Lorne Richardson, MP for Lisgar, owner and sometime editor of the Winnipeg *Tribune* and a committed free-trade Liberal, wrote anxiously to Sifton, "In a measure you have our political lives in your hand, unless we break [with the party]; and you must try and make it possible for us to justify any position which we may be called upon to take. A few concessions to the west on several articles would I think enable us all to hold our jobs, and help the Govt. hold its."[74] By far the single most important item was the duty on agricultural implements, then at 20 per cent. "I sounded Greenway on the agricultural implement question," wrote Richardson, "and he thinks if 10 per cent could be settled upon it would be quite satisfactory." Indeed, "inasmuch as there will be no great scaling down on other lines, implements ought to be placed at 10%[.] Then we could all I think unite in justifying the changes."[75]

What Richardson did not know was that the implement manufacturers had organized a lobby for exactly the opposite purpose. Business had been so bad for them since the Conservatives lowered the tariff, they claimed, that an immediate increase in the duty to 25 per cent was essential. Of course, their past services to the Liberal party were not forgotten. Because an increase in the implement duty would kill the party in rural districts, a compromise was suggested: lower the tariff on the raw materials of the implement industry, particularly on pig iron and steel. Under the circumstances, Sifton told Richardson, "I am afraid that ten per cent is completely out of the question. There is no doubt it would bankrupt every implement concern in Canada and I doubt that there would be any justification for it."[76]

When Fielding presented his budget speech, it was apparent that Sifton had secured almost all that he had asked. There were a few rhetorical bows toward the principles of free trade and a revenue tariff and assurances that the new tariff was but a "first instalment of tariff reform." In fact, there was no new principle adopted. As sops to the western farmer binder twine and barbed wire were placed on the free list, and coal oil and a few items of clothing were slightly reduced. Iron and steel duties were lowered. But duties on implements were unchanged, lumber duties were increased, and the clothing and textile industry remained heavily protected. It was exceedingly difficult for western Liberals to justify the tariff, given their past attacks on the principle of protection. The only ray of sunshine was the popular introduction of a British preference.[77]

Western farmers lost no time in protesting. Replied Sifton to one petitioner, "I think if you will look at the change made in the tariff you will find that the people in Manitoba have secured enormous reductions in their taxation." What difference did it make if the saving was not concentrated on one item, such as implements? "The endeavour has been to equalize the duty," and "the duty on mowers and binders is still below the average of the other duties." He anticipated that reducing the cost of raw materials would enable "the dealers [to] reduce the price of implements very materially." "The people of Manitoba," asserted Sifton, "have profited more largely by the revision than the people in any other portion of the Dominion." Besides, could not westerners appreciate the fact that deepening the St. Lawrence canals between Buffalo and Montreal would reduce carriage rates for grain by four cents a bushel from the Lakehead? Could they not understand that the government had shaved $1.5 million from its total expenditure?[78]

Apparently not. The Winnipeg *Tribune* spoke for thousands of western farmers when it referred to the "great disappointment" resulting from "the failure of the government to meet western expectations in the revision of the tariff." Surely implement duties could have been reduced "without killing the industry. In addition, however, from our point of view, we are not much concerned about the demise of these 'industries' provided our settlers get cheap implements." Premier Greenway complained to Sifton of finding "so many old-time tried friends declaring that they will never again cast a Liberal vote on account of the action of the Dominion government with regard to their tariff policy"; and he added that he sympathized with them. In the end Sifton concluded that the government would have to ride out the storm. "I have no doubt the boys out west are all right," he reassured Richardson. "They will stand a disappointment on the tariff. I sympathize with them in their feelings and was sorry I could not do better for them. I think, however, our general policy is having its effect on the country and Manitoba will share with the rest."[79] As Sifton would shortly discover, his optimism was misplaced.

It has been said that "it was the farmer's misfortune that his demands for freer trade brought him so directly into conflict with National Policy objectives."[80] These included preserving the domestic market for Canadian producers and manufacturers and carrying Canadian trade by Canadian routes. Sifton wholeheartedly endorsed these goals and in the process of contributing to the formulation of government policy developed the strong tinge of anti-Americanism which cropped up so frequently in later years.

Shortly before the tariff was announced, he wrote to Laurier advocating an export duty on "saw logs." For years Canadian timber had been exported to the United States, where it was processed into sawn lumber or pulp and paper. When Canada raised the possibility of placing a substantial export duty on the logs to promote processing in Canada, there were rumours of American retaliation. "I have a strong feeling," he declared, "that if we, to speak very plainly, lie down under the bluff that the Americans have made on the lumber question, it will be regarded throughout the Country with great disapproval." Existing conditions were "a great reflection upon our legislation. Immense quantities of logs as you know, have been taken to Michigan, and cut up by Canadian labor. They have taken our property and our population as well and I believe the country would back us in endeavoring to bring about a different state of things." He also argued for an increase in the Canadian duty on cattle, observing that "it would be a most foolish mistake to leave the cattle duty at 20%, when the American duty has been put up to 40%. I hope the free trade theory, which has already been shattered, will not be permitted to stand in the way when it is plainly not in our business interests. Building the [Crow's Nest] Railway to the Mining regions of British Columbia, and doing everything we can to get the trade of the Country, and prevent it from going South-ward we should also help ourselves by the tariff law as much as possible."[81] It was a statement which Sir John A. Macdonald himself might have applauded. It also would have been a revelation to Sifton's rural constituents to discover that their representative in the cabinet considered the free trade theory to have been "shattered."

Preserving the trade of the mining districts of southeastern British Columbia from the greedy clutches of the Americans had certainly been a principal consideration in the agreement made in the spring of 1897 to construct the Crow's Nest Pass Railway. Negotiating the contract was perhaps the single most important event of Sifton's first months in office and illustrates his rapid rise to power. Even before he entered the government, Sifton had advocated the railway. It would, he had declared, make "every miner in British Columbia...a customer of the merchants of Winnipeg, Toronto and Montreal. Then we shall have taken one step towards securing Canada for the Canadians."[82]

Discoveries of valuable mineral ores in southeastern British Columbia had taken place in the 1880's. As early as 1889 the Canadian Pacific began seriously to consider a Crow's Nest line, but President Van Horne concluded that development of the region was ten or fifteen years premature.[83] Competitive pressures from the Great Northern and various smaller Canadian and American lines nevertheless forced the CPR to move more quickly than he desired. The CPR spent a good deal of money locating and surveying the Crow's Nest line, and only the financial stringency of 1893 to 1895 forestalled actual construction. The company's commitment was so great, wrote Van Horne in 1894, that the directors "feel bound to use every means in their power to prevent any subsidy being given to any·other Company proposing to occupy that ground." The CPR intended to build "as soon as circumstances will permit." In February 1896 Van Horne still considered the company's financial picture too unfavourable, despite signs of general economic improvement.[84]

Meanwhile, the CPR president had sniffed the political breezes, concluded that the future of the Conservative government was at best shaky, and began an active programme of building bridges to the Liberal party. He concentrated on two politicians, J.D. Edgar and L.H. Davies, both close associates of Laurier, and on the most influential Liberal journalist in Canada, J.S. Willison of the *Globe*.[85] They were entertained as only an epicure of Van Horne's stature could arrange; they travelled with him in his opulent private car and became his confidants; they toured the West either at CPR expense or with the company's active aid; and Van Horne repeatedly assured them of the benevolent neutrality of the CPR in matters political. Thus when the Liberals came to power, Van Horne had several important pipelines to the party leadership, his position being further improved when Clifford Sifton arrived in Ottawa.

By April 1896 Van Horne was telling Willison that the Crow's Nest Pass line "should be built without delay if the permanent diversion southwards of the greater part of the ores of the Kootenay and adjacent districts is to be prevented." Less than two months earlier, Van Horne had assured two Conservatives that the CPR still could not afford to undertake the line. Now, he was urging the Liberals to endorse a subsidy for it. In case the Liberals were uneasy about supporting CPR construction, he cheerfully added, "if somebody else can be found to build this line, it will suit us even better than building it ourselves."[86] Not only did that contradict previous and subsequent CPR policy, but it is likely that Van Horne believed that no other private company would undertake it under the conditions which any dominion government would be likely to exact. A few days later, Van Horne submitted a proposal to Sir Charles Tupper in the dying days of Parliament, when any possibility of serious consideration was past.

It was hardly a coincidence that on the very day that Laurier was sworn in as prime minister, the *Globe* launched a series of articles promoting the Crow's Nest Pass railway and that the CPR and the newspaper jointly sponsored a vigorous publicity campaign.[87] In September Vice-President T.G. Shaughnessy visited Laurier. The government, he reported to Van Horne, was "very favourably disposed" to the line and willing to take up the matter once the parliamentary session was over. Van Horne promptly resubmitted the plan which he had informally proposed to Tupper, essentially requesting a direct subsidy of $5,000 per mile and a twenty-year loan at prevailing interest rates for the remainder of the cost.[88]

The new government had not decided on any basic principles of railway policy. It had to contend with a heritage of Liberal hostility to the CPR, to the very idea of railway monopoly, to railway subsidies in general, and to allegedly high freight rates. Yet in its first few months of office it was being asked to approve a plan which would inevitably be interpreted as wholly for the benefit of the CPR, subsidized and financed by the Canadian public. Obviously Van Horne's scheme as it stood was politically impossible and must have been intended as an initial bargaining position.[89]

By the time Sifton joined the cabinet any hope of securing an alternative private company to build the line on terms acceptable to the Canadian government had proven to be chimerical. The most basic requirement was a guarantee to preserve the trade of the region in Canadian channels; as Van Horne convincingly demonstrated to the cabinet, any such line would simply be a dependency of the CPR. Therefore, the logic of the situation dictated construction by his company.[90] Sifton agreed. Dissenting, however, was A.G. Blair, minister of railways and canals, who favoured government construction through a syndicate. Mainly because Laurier and most of his colleagues were opposed in principle to government construction, and also because they suspected Blair of having a personal interest in his proposed syndicate, his plan was doomed to failure.[91]

At the same time Public Works Minister Tarte, who incidentally ran much of the political machinery in Québec, reported on an interview with T.G. Shaughnessy about the Crow's Nest affair. The future of the government, wrote Tarte, would depend largely upon the wisdom of its railway policy. Conservative power in the province had rested upon the support "des grands intérêts matériels" and the influence of the Church. Being unable to count upon Church support (in light of the schools settlement), "il faut attacher le plus solidement possible à notre char les influences terrestres, la puissance du capital." In particular, the government needed to secure the support of both the Grand Trunk and the Canadian Pacific railways. "Avec ces deux grands compagnies de chemins de fer derrière nous, nous pouvons faire face à l'orage clérical."[92] That was the sort of practical politics which Laurier, and Sifton, well understood. Having made up his mind to favour CPR construction, Laurier told Van Horne and Shaughnessy "that he will be guided largely by Mr. Sifton's views, he being best acquainted with the situation in the West. Mr. Sifton is very friendly to us [CPR] but insists that we must make such concessions in the matter of rates as will reasonably satisfy the Western people."[93]

The prime minister was not so inferior a poker player, however, as to give away everything to the CPR quite so simply. He was not inclined to rush an agreement, especially since no legislation could be introduced into Parliament until after the conclusion of the debate on the tariff. He did not wish to humiliate Blair, though he was prepared to differ with him. And a little uncertainty on the part of the CPR would not hurt. Accordingly, in the third week of February a sub-committee of the cabinet, consisting of Mowat, Blair, and Sifton, was established to investigate and report upon the Crow's Nest Pass line. Blair was thus given a forum to continue to push for his scheme. Angrily, the impatient Van Horne made private threats to proceed with construction between Ft. Macleod and the summit of the pass. The CPR had the power to do so under its charters and could thus have destroyed the viability of an alternative scheme. The public agitation against the Canadian Pacific, fumed Van Horne, was being worked up by the Great Northern and by those who hoped to profit from a scheme for private or government construction. "We are not paupers yet," he wrote indignantly. "We can build the Crows Nest Pass line without Governmental assistance if we see fit. But in view of what the Company has tried to do towards building up the interests of this country it is disappointing, to say the least, to be treated as a public enemy or as a public menace."[94]

Van Horne himself was a gambler of no mean experience. This revelation of the strong financial situation of the company did not reach the cabinet. He instead appealed to Sifton for a final settlement before the parliamentary session, claiming that the delay was attributed in financial circles to hostility on the part of the government and the public. The result was depressing the value of the CPR stock, making it difficult or impossible to borrow for improvements or additions.[95] A month later, however, negotiations were still plodding on. Van Horne and Shaughnessy interviewed Sifton and painted a bleak picture of the fortunes of the company. The agreement should be completed at once, Sifton told Laurier. "I thought they had begun to feel that there is a chance that the transaction may not be consummated this Session. Their stock is going down and they feel much discouraged."[96]

The persistent attacks on the CPR continued. Sifton was inclined to be blunt in response. He ruled out government construction because "the sentiment of the more capable business people of the East is very much against it." "I do not understand why you are so bitter against the C.P.R.," he told one correspondent. Sifton had lived with the CPR for years and did not believe it merited the abuse directed against it.

> Of course I perfectly understand that the Railway Company is not a philanthropic institution, that it makes all the money it can make and I have no doubt its officials form rings and work things to their own advantage in out of the way places like Kootenay, but if you think, my dear friend, that Government officials would not do the same thing on a Government railroad you will be very much mistaken and you will find that, whereas you can get the railroad company's official dismissed by proving that he has been guilty of improper conduct you cannot always get that done with a Government officer. Experience shows that in the past the most guilty and rascally officials have been kept in place by political influence. I do not think that there is anything connected with the C.P.R. service that is half as bad as what has been taking place in my own Department.[97]

Sifton was the principal negotiator with the CPR, and his success was only mixed. He seems to have taken at face value the word of Van Horne and Shaughnessy about the dismal financial situation of the company. The freight rate reduction which he negotiated was no great coup. "He has...come down to rather moderate views in this regard," noted Van Horne in February. Sifton was asking for a reduction in grain rates from prairie points to the Lakehead of 3 cents per hundred pounds or 1.8 cents per bushel. But, said Van Horne, this was merely "a reduction which Mr. Shaughnessy and I believe will be forced upon us by other causes" by the time the line was completed. This situation was appreciated by some Winnipeg businessmen, who believed that under the circumstances the Canadian Pacific could be forced to make a reduction greater than 3 cents. Sifton disagreed, finding the western demands "too extreme" and "unreasonable." "There are," he told J.H. Ashdown, "a great many things to be considered in connection with matters of this kind outside of the simple desire of our people to get their freight carried more cheaply, a desire with which, I may say, I am in full accord, but I do not by any means admit that there is any obligation on the part of the Government to drive the railroad company into bankruptcy during the first year or two of its exercise of its powers of office."[98]

A second, and related, demand was that the company and the government should agree upon "maximum through and local rates" and government regulation of the rates thereafter. Here Sifton did hold firm. The CPR had no objection to an initial agreement on rates but strenuously opposed any subsequent interference. The third principal demand made by Sifton was that the government should be empowered to permit other railways to use sections of the Crow's Nest line in places where a second line was impracticable. Again Van Horne was agreeable.[99] Finally, Sifton was determined to use the agreement as a lever to pry loose the railway lands east of the 103rd meridian. He introduced it into the Crow's Nest negotiations shortly after the CPR president's initial cool response. Van Horne now apparently decided that it would be best to humour him. Sifton had offered $2 per acre; after discussions with the CPR president, he raised the offer to $2.80, which he was informed the company probably would accept. Convincing his cabinet colleagues would be a much greater task, as Van Horne realized. He sagely remarked to Sir Donald Smith, "I do not believe...that Mr. Sifton's ideas about the purchase of the lands will prevail." He was correct. The cabinet was not prepared to accept an expenditure which would exceed $7 million for lands on top of a subsidy for the railway which would exceed $3 million.[100]

Sifton urged Laurier to conclude the agreement and to promise to place it before Parliament immediately after the tariff debate. The work could then begin "at once." "The disturbance of trade incident to the introduction of the tariff would be at once counteracted by a monthly expenditure of $500,000.00. The effect of such an expenditure on the trade of Canada in its present condition would be tremendous." In fact, it would "bring about a general state of prosperity." Furthermore, the project would employ thousands of labourers in a province where there had been high unemployment. "The importance of the whole matter cannot be easily over-estimated, and it should in my opinion be dealt with promptly and decisively."[101]

The agreement was concluded at last by early June. The government agreed to a subsidy of $11,000 per mile, up to $3,630,000, for the line between Lethbridge and Nelson. In return the CPR agreed to reduce rates by one-third on green and fresh fruits, by one-fifth on coal oil, and by one-tenth on a series of consumer goods vital to the farmer: cordage, binder twine, agricultural implements, iron, wire, glass, roofing and construction paper, construction felt, paints and oils, livestock, woodenware, and household furniture. A reduction of 3 cents per hundred pounds on flour and grain freight rates from points in the North-West to Fort William was accepted. Half the rate was to be implemented by 1 September 1898 and the remaining 1.5 cents a year later. These were thereafter to be considered maximum rates.[102]

"All of us here feel well satisfied with the bargain," Van Horne told Smith. The company thought the grain and flour rate necessary in any event. The freight rates on specific goods, negotiated by Sifton to try to offset western disappointment on the tariff, were, said Van Horne, "merely nominal, because the new tariff forces most of these changes upon us without regard to the other matter."[103] Although popular myth has it that the CPR officials were staggered at the government demands and that Sifton had bound the railway hand and foot with his tough terms, the company plainly obtained pretty much the agreement it wanted. It was prepared to let the government take the credit for freight rates which it believed would have come about sooner or later in any case.

The real hook, however, was hidden in the statement that "no higher rates than such reduced rates or tolls shall be hereafter charged by the Company...between the points aforesaid." Neither Sifton nor Van Horne and Shaughnessy seem to have placed much emphasis on this wording, certainly at the time. They unquestionably were influenced by the fact that the historic pattern of development for fifteen years had been a constant downward revision of rates, made possible by new technology, growing efficiency both of scale and organization, and competition. By no means was the new Crow's Nest rate seen as a "bottoming out" of the rates. The seventeen-cent rate from Winnipeg, for example, became fourteen cents in 1899 under the new agreement; four years later, with fresh competition, it became a ten-cent rate, with further reductions from points further west as well.[104] The Crow's Nest rates, writes the most recent historian of the CPR, "inflicted no great hardship on the railway; the lower rates yielded a modest profit and continued to do so until the First World War." Only when costs and prices began to rise did the railway discover the disadvantages of the statute, which was interpreted as fixing the maximum rates "in perpetuity." Only then did the Crow's Nest freight rates, and Sifton's prophetic acuity in respect of the agreement, acquire their mystique.[105]

"I believe," wrote Van Horne when advocating the agreement in 1896, "that it should be the policy of every country to horde money in good times, and expend it in bad times."[106] Indeed, the expenditure of so large a sum on a construction project which would employ thousands of labourers and generate thousands more permanent jobs in the British Columbia mining and forest industries helped to make the agreement popular. The government had been forced to adopt an alien labour law in 1897 in retaliation to American labour legislation and was determined that the line should be built only by Canadians or by immigrants intending to settle in Canada. It was equally determined that as far as possible Canadian contractors should be employed. These provisions, Sifton told Col. McMillan of the Manitoba government, should be politically advantageous for the Liberals:

we are doing much more than has ever been attempted by any Government in the past. Our people do not want to let themselves be put in a false position in regard to the matter. In all the work that has been done in the past on the Canadian Pacific Railway and work upon the canals both in Eastern and Western Canada, American contractors have had the lion's share. Onderdonk, Grant, Langdon and other American contractors have made millions out of our work and employed alien labour to a great extent. The late Government never made the slightest attempt to protect our people to the utmost possible extent. We do not expect to be able to prevent the difficulty altogether.... I think you should enlighten our press in Winnipeg upon this question and see that they take the matter up in the proper way. We can claim the credit of having been the first Government which made an attempt to protect Canadian laborers and Canadian contractors.[107]

Sifton hoped that the project would give a boost to his immigration schemes. He made arrangements to have two thousand men sent from Scotland and Wales, specifying that he wanted only those "intending to become farmers in the West and requiring work [to] enable them to get a start and learn the conditions of the country." The workers were needed immediately, he told his officials. The CPR "are in full sympathy with the idea of not bringing in Italians and other foreigners [from the United States], but . . . if we do not furnish them with men in time they will have to get them elsewhere."[108]

Flexibility was essential, Van Horne told Sifton. The CPR was agreeable to the general objectives, but "insistence upon such special conditions after an agreement has been clearly reached would not be looked upon as, shall I say it, honourable." Sifton faced tremendous pressure from both Canadian contractors and labour unions and could not concur with the CPR president. Reports of violations of the understanding were such that he had the minister of justice grant power to W.F. McCreary, the immigration commissioner at Winnipeg, to enforce the alien labour law. The power was to be employed with discretion—he was not to proceed against every visible offence, nor to hinder the work of Canadian immigration agents in the United States who might be sending up farmers who might take employment on the line. "The purpose of giving you authority to act," Sifton informed McCreary, "is to prevent bodies of laborers, such as Italian railway navvies and similar people, coming into the country to secure work upon the Crow's Nest Pass line." It was essential "to prevent our people from being displaced in the employment which is legitimately theirs, by foreigners."[109] The scheme backfired, however, because the Welsh workers not only refused to tolerate the low wages and poor conditions in the CPR camps, but proved articulate in venting their grievances. One MP went so far as to accuse the railway of "White Slavery." It was found that immigrants from central Europe were more docile, while the adverse publicity hindered the promotion of Canadian immigration in Great Britain.[110]

Such reverses were temporary. Sifton believed that the West would forgive the government its disappointing tariff record in face of the apparent advantages of the Crow's Nest Pass agreement. The ogre of CPR monopoly which long had stalked the West was now under government control. Could not the government permit other railways to use the Crow's Nest line? "To all intents and purposes," declared Sifton, "it is a government railway, although operated by the C.P.R., and it is under the control of the government and the people of Canada, whose servants the government are." He calculated that the savings to the West from the rate concessions would amount to about $700,000 a year; based on this, "in five years . . . I believe Canada will have got back the entire bonus that was paid for the railway. We will have the railway, running rights, and incidental privileges, control of freight rates, and will actually not have paid a cent for it." The benefits were even more far-reaching. Cheap coke would permit the investment of millions of dollars and the employment of thousands of men in the mining and smelting industries:

> And, sir, one thing will react upon another, cheaper smelting will result in the production of more ores, and the production of more ores will result in a greater volume of smelting, and a greater volume of smelting will result in the establishment of a refinery, and we will have within ten years the precious metals mined in Canada, smelted in Canada, minted in Canada to as great an extent as is done in any other country in the civilized world.[111]

Six months in office had left Clifford Sifton physically and mentally drained as never before. Once an admirer had written that he "could drive about the country all day interviewing electors, make speeches all night, live on a diet of shingle nails and sleep on the nail kegs." No more. Sifton desperately felt the need to renew his energies, to escape from the unceasing political and administrative demands. Then too his deafness was troubling him as it had not in several years; perhaps his new surroundings made him more acutely aware of his handicap. He hoped there would be time to seek treatment abroad.

Except in a political sense, Brandon no longer made demands upon him. Within weeks of assuming office, he had severed his connection with his old law firm, after more than fourteen years. His family was all with him in Ottawa. A fifth—and last—son, W. Victor, was born there, and the rest of the boys were young, energetic, and demanding. They looked forward to a holiday together. After the interminable months of being almost consumed by his duties, Sifton longed for a time alone with his wife and children. As Ottawa sank languid into another humid summer, members of the government began to drift out of town. Laurier was abroad at the Jubilee celebrations, and nothing of great moment seemed likely to require attention until his return. In happy anticipation the Siftons busily began to plan a lazy vacation on Lake Champlain.[112]

# 7

# Klondike Gold
# (1897–98)

The tranquillity of the Ottawa summer was shattered in mid-July. Within days of each other two unheralded ships, the *Excelsior* and the *Portland,* arrived at San Francisco and Seattle, respectively, laden with gold from the Canadian Yukon. The *Portland*'s arrival on 17 July produced screaming headlines across the continent. Not one, but two shiploads of gold, brought from an unknown land where apparently the precious metal was strewn broadcast in numberless creek and river beds, readily available to any willing adventurer!

So began the madness of the last great North American gold rush. The psychological impact was tremendous on a continent where fresh frontiers were already becoming memories rather than ever-present realities and where men still dreamed both of high adventure and of the chance to "get rich quick." A new California? or Cariboo? Thousands of men abandoned their stores, their boats, their mines, their clerkships, their homes, families, and friends and embarked on a journey in heed of a call that defied reason or description.

The mad rush caught official Ottawa off guard. News of the great gold discoveries on one of the tributary creeks of the Klondike River in 1896 had reached the government and the press gradually and unemphatically during the winter and spring of 1897. Only a few thousand miners were expected to go in; and although administrative changes would be required, they did not appear urgent. The unforeseen massive popular response to the *Portland* threw all previous calculations askew.

The Yukon was a remote, scarcely known provisional district of the North-

West Territories, thus coming under the jurisdiction of the minister of the interior. Its administration was complicated by several problems, the most obvious of which was general ignorance of the region. Communication was difficult, requiring several weeks, if not months, to transmit messages between Ottawa and its distant reaches. The Americans controlled all the immediately practicable routes to the Yukon, although the actual location of the Canada-United States boundary remained in dispute. The population which began to flow into the Yukon was an ominously unstable company of adventurers, predominantly American. Pressure arose at once for implementation of strictly nationalistic policies in order to prevent "foreigners" from carrying off the spoils and to keep the profits of the trade as far as possible within Canada. Whatever action the government took, it had to be immediate. The flood of people required many government institutions, and supplies had to be moved in before the onset of winter.

Gone were Sifton's hopes of a trip abroad to seek treatment for his deafness, and holiday plans were sharply curtailed in face of the new crisis. The problem, he later reflected with a touch of self-congratulation, had been "to organize a new district, organize a Government, think of everything that has to be thought of in connection with the Government, take a new country and a new people, with nothing done, and think of everything and provide for everything. . . . Any such avalanche of responsibility as we have had in connection with the Yukon never was thrust upon a Government before."[1]

The first prospecting in the Yukon began in the 1870's. During the next decade several hundred miners were washing up a few thousand dollars' worth of gold annually from the rivers and streams. The small trade of the region was largely American-dominated. Two Alaska companies, the Alaska Commercial Company and the North American Trading and Transportation Company, supplied Yukon residents via the Yukon River from western Alaska.

Canadian government authority was finally asserted in 1894, when Inspector Charles Constantine of the North-West Mounted Police was sent in with a sergeant to exercise a broad range of powers. Constantine reported that Canadian customs regulations were being ignored and that some $300,000 in gold had been taken from Yukon watercourses in 1894. As a result, in 1895 the government decided to send Constantine back in, heading a force of twenty men, to establish a permanent post, impose dominion authority, regulate the liquor traffic, and act as agents of the Interior, Indian Affairs, and Customs departments. Comptroller F. White of the NWMP cautioned his superiors that "it is most important that the Officer charged with the establishment of law and order among a community of not less than 2000 miners of various nationalities, many of whom have hitherto known no law but that of their own making, should be clothed with discretionary authority."[2] It was good, even necessary, advice. To round out the government services, William Ogilvie, government surveyor and explorer, was sent to sort out mining claims and make other required surveys.

No change in these arrangements was possible in 1896. By the time the great debate on the school question had staggered to its unhappy conclusion, the Tory government barely had time to get essential estimates through Parliament. These did not include provision for additional manpower in the Yukon. Even the modest request of the Police for ten additional officers and a patrol boat could not be met. As a result, Constantine was forced to concentrate his men at Fort Cudahy and regulate the trade up the Yukon River from Alaska into the gold district, while leaving totally unsupervised a growing volume of trade which was entering via Juneau and over the mountain passes.[3] Such conditions were worrisome but did not constitute an emergency. It was not unreasonable to expect that the matter could be taken in hand after the election.

The postponement of the appointment of the new minister of the interior until mid-November, and subsequent events pressing upon him, meant that reports of conditions in the Yukon did not command his attention until well on in 1897. Gradually it had begun to dawn on Constantine and Ogilvie that the discoveries would materially transform the Yukon. Late in 1896 they wrote that the government should expect perhaps ten thousand people to arrive within a year or two. This, they informed Ottawa, would necessitate the establishment of civil government: a gold commissioner, registrar, civil courts, and improved efforts to regulate the liquor trade. Constantine again requested a steam launch and a force of seventy-five men. The large force was essential because the men "are so far away from Head quarters, and the population is chiefly alien and of a class requiring firm handling."[4]

Given the advice received, there is every indication that the government responded adequately. A memorandum of 3 February by Comptroller White, based on these reports, recommended merely maintaining the police force "as at present" and establishing a proper legal apparatus. He also estimated— incredibly, in retrospect—that gold production for 1896 would not exceed $300,000, or the level of 1894. White nevertheless did touch on what would prove to be the key problems. Under the Treaty of Washington, 1871, Canada had the right to navigate the Yukon River through Alaska for commercial purposes. The provision had proven to be of little use in practice, because "transhipment from Ocean to River boats has to be made within U.S. territory, and serious obstacles have been thrown in the way of transhipment in bond." Shorter routes had been found over four mountain passes, the Chilkat, Chilkoot, White, and Taku, of which only the second was much used. But all began in American-controlled territory and were useless as they stood for transport of heavy objects or large quantities of supplies. As a result, the government had begun to explore a route between the Stikine River and Teslin Lake. "If a feasible trail can be found," wrote White, "we shall then have a Canadian route independent of the United States, and from Teslin Lake there is a fair navigation for flat bottom boats direct to Fort Cudahy."[5]

At the beginning of April, Sifton was informed that it was necessary to appoint an officer of the department to register mining claims and settle disputes concerning claim boundaries; to establish a registry office, civil courts, and judicial authority for cases beyond the jurisdiction of a justice of the peace; and to provide for regulation of the liquor traffic. Six weeks later, White requested permission to increase the strength of the Police by ten men, "if necessary"; Laurier promptly approved.[6] Upon investigation it was discovered that both Ogilvie and Constantine had recommended the appointment of a surveyor to act as agent of the Department of the Interior in the Yukon. Accordingly Thomas Fawcett, a careful and capable surveyor with twenty years' experience, left Ottawa on 1 May to serve as gold commissioner, surveyor, and land agent. As chief executive officer of the department in the Yukon, Fawcett was in effect the head of civil government, wielding extensive powers. He and his staff of two more junior surveyors and four other men arrived in Dawson on 15 June. No one could complain about Sifton's lack of despatch in sending up the officers required.[7]

Delay did occur in the appointment of judicial authorities. In April, Sifton recommended to Justice Minister Sir Oliver Mowat that "a Stipendiary Magistrate should be appointed with authority to administer the law in criminal matters," who would also act as registrar under the Land Titles Act. This was important, he told Mowat, because of the unstable character of the mining population, the small size of the police force, and the possibility of insurrection over disputed claims in the absence of judicial authority. The elderly minister of justice unfortunately was no more moved to prompt action on this than on most other problems demanding his attention. By mid-July there still was no action. But there was no sense of impending crisis, and Sifton told Mowat on 15 July that while the matter should be considered before the next session of Parliament, it seemed possible that "we can get along all right in the meantime."[8]

On 21 May, well before the beginning of the gold rush and without the benefit of first-hand knowledge of conditions, Sifton and his colleagues passed a series of regulations to govern placer mining on the Yukon River and its tributaries.[9] Rapidly changing circumstances later led to frequent alterations, creating grievances among the Yukon population. For the time being, however, all the rivers and streams in the district could be claimed freely. The regulations defined the size of various types of claims and specified that after being properly staked out they could be registered for a $15 fee and $100 a year thereafter. No miner could secure more than one claim as a grant, but any number could be purchased; and miners were free to sell, mortgage, or otherwise dispose of their duly registered claims. No "surface rights," such as control of timber, were included. Finally, any claim which remained unworked for seventy-two hours "shall be deemed to be abandoned and open to occupation and entry by any person," except in the case of illness or with the permission of the gold commissioner.

Thus the government was not wholly unprepared when the crisis struck. It had done most of what seemed necessary. "I have [been] working, eating and sleeping with the Yukon Territory for the last three weeks," wrote Sifton a few days later, "but I have found no difficulty in mapping [out] a plan of organization and administration. The whole difficulty is in regard to the transportation. If we could bridge the mountains between the head of the Lynn Canal and the head of the waters of the Yukon [River] in some way, the problem would be extremely simple."[10] Events soon demonstrated that the problem of the Yukon administration was not susceptible of any "simple" solutions.

The rush for gold in the summer immediately brought about in Canada an eruption of long pent-up anti-Americanism. It seemed the United States was inclined to regard the Yukon gold discoveries as practically under American control. Americans had no compunction about excluding Canadians from mining in their states and territories, while preparing to arrogate for themselves the trade and gold of the Canadian Yukon. The newspaper press of the Dominion united in its demand that the government must take steps to keep both under national control. "Canada for the Canadians!" once more became the cry.

The Dominion cabinet agreed. Because Canada had obtained "no benefit whatever" from more than $1 million of Yukon gold taken out by the Americans in 1896, the government decided in July to restrict mining licences "to residents in Canada" and "to reserve a large royalty" from the gold production. The force of NWMP in the Yukon was to be doubled, a measure deemed essential "if we are to get any benefit in either Customs or royalty from the great gold gind."[11]

Within days of the *Portland's* arrival at Seattle, it was apparent that the lemming-like rush to the gold fields was assuming alarming proportions. Both Sifton and the American secretary of the interior issued unheeded warnings of the impossibility of supplying large numbers of miners with food. Starvation was a real possibility.[12] Consequently, the government had to make some difficult and hurried decisions. One was to authorize a further increase in the NWMP in the Yukon to one hundred men. Sifton, in charge of the Police during Laurier's absence, had to reverse the government's expressed intention to curtail the size of the force, if not eliminate it altogether. In that sense the gold rush saved the Police, whose reputation was much enhanced by its subsequent excellent record in the Yukon.[13] The government also considered opening customs posts on the White and Chilkoot passes. Their purpose would have been to collect the duty on non-Canadian goods entering, to check on the gold leaving the Yukon, and generally to prevent smuggling of liquor and other goods. Unfortunately, however, the government inexplicably failed to carry forward this idea and only attempted to levy the duty farther inland on indisputably Canadian territory. This led to many problems within a few months.

Both human and administrative needs forced the government to look into improving communications over the mountain passes. The appalling misery of the miners attempting to stagger with their goods over the fifteen miles between the head of the Lynn Canal and the summit of the White Pass has become one of the enduring epics of Canadian history. Through mud sometimes knee-deep, over and around the bodies of dead horses, clinging to narrow paths over sheer precipices, and crawling up the steep inclines through rain, mist, and snow, over and over again until they had moved a half ton or more of gear and supplies to the top—so it continued in the summer and fall of 1897. By late July the government realized that a telegraph and at least a wagon road, if not a railway, would be absolutely necessary.[14]

The most controversial and ill-considered decision was to make a radical change in the mining regulations. First, every alternate claim was reserved for the government, such claims to be disposed of "at public auction, or in such manner as may be decided by the Minister of the Interior." This provision gave Sifton an extraordinary discretionary power. It was also decided to levy a royalty of 10 per cent on the first $500 per week gross production from each claim, and 20 per cent in excess of $500.[15] In retrospect these regulations appear naive. Evident in them is the mentality that lay behind the Dominion Lands Act: why not defray the expense of opening up and governing the region by taking direct profits from every other claim? Then too, since miners were not like homesteaders, setting down roots and making a permanent contribution to the economy, and particularly since many were aliens, why not impose a royalty so that all Canadians could benefit from the wealth of the Yukon? The alternate claims regulations presumed some sort of orderly development, as on the prairies, where surveys more or less preceded, or at least kept pace with, settlement. But by the time the new regulations were passed, many of the best locations had been thoroughly staked and registered, and not always in the neat, contiguous configurations anticipated. The provision for a royalty took no account of the enormously high cost of production; the new tax could in fact wipe out profits. Also, as time would show, it would not be easy to obtain honest declarations about the amount of gold mined and subject to taxation.

Nevertheless, Sifton had been studying the problem for two or three months and stuck obstinately to his conclusions. He believed that the gold fields constituted a national resource, the benefits of which should accrue to the dominion as a whole. He rejected a proposal of government development as unenforceable and undesirable;[16] but there seemed to him no reason why the dominion should be required to underwrite the entire cost of government.

Sifton told Fawcett that the regulations might prove difficult to enforce and left the methods of implementation to his judgment. The miners were to be informed clearly and exactly about the nature of the regulations. They had been carefully considered, Sifton wrote, "and so far as it is possible to do so, must be enforced to the letter." With two additional surveyors and a clerk, as well as the further police support, Sifton apparently believed that Fawcett could put the regulations into effect.

> You will understand [he advised] there is nothing in Canada that is receiving more attention at the present time than this particular matter, and the success of the policy which has been announced, and which as far as I can learn meets with unanimous approval will depend very largely upon your tact, firmness and discretion. Miners should be given to understand that the Government is assuming considerable expense in providing for the due administration of the law, and the protection of the persons and the property of the people who go in. The difference between mining under conditions which will prevail in the Yukon Territory and which prevailed for instance in the western States where the Government took no expense and left each man practically to protect himself, is you will understand very great. The Government undertaking these responsibilities have a right to expect loyal support and assistance from people who may be permitted to profit from the mineral wealth of the District, in the carrying out of the laws which are framed in reference thereto.[17]

Canadians had long prided themselves on the comparatively non-violent and orderly development of Manitoba and the Territories and the absence of the "lawlessness" of the American frontier. This principle was now to be consciously extended to the Yukon. The government believed that early assertion of Canadian authority would prove the easiest way to keep the district under Canadian control. Nevertheless, given the independent and often rough character of the miners, it seems an exceptional act of faith to have assumed that one hundred policemen and a handful of civil servants could successfully carry out Sifton's objectives.

His claim of unanimous support for his measures was entirely unfounded. From the moment the new regulations were announced, they were perceived to be unworkable. The government was deluged with complaints from its own supporters and from businessmen, as well as from the Conservatives; and press comment ranged from ridicule to vitriol. Opined the Liberal Winnipeg *Tribune,*

> we are at a loss to see how alternate claims can be retained by the government. Suppose two men go into a district and stake out adjoining claims, must one of them give his claim up to the government? And if so, which one? We can understand how, if the government should prospect the whole country and stake out claims, it might sell every alternate one, but it passes our comprehension how they can talk about every alternate claim now. Suppose a man finds a claim at the mouth of a stream and there is

not another claim within five miles of it, will the next claim be retained by the government? The proposition seems on examination to be such an impossible one that we can hardly think any attempt will be made to carry it out.

As to the proposed royalty, it is so enormous that it can never be collected. Gold is easily smuggled out of a country. . . . and unless the government is prepared to station an officer on every claim it would be impossible to collect the amount. If the report from Ottawa is correct, one is almost justified in considering that the government has lost its head over the gold craze. We tell them very frankly that if they attempt to enforce regulations for the reservation of alternate claims and the collection of excessive royalty, they will bring about a state of anarchy on the Yukon.[18]

A writer to the *Victoria Times* perhaps summarized widespread opinion when he wrote, "It is possible for the government to adopt a right principle and still apply it wrongly. . . . The government has recognized the rights of the whole of Canada to share in the wealth of the Yukon, but has not been practical in the method of distribution and allotment of shares, so to speak."[19]

No longer did Sifton speak of "simple" solutions to the problems he faced. The administration, he wrote, "is most complicated and beset with difficulties."[20] Stubbornly he reiterated that the government policy was "correct," and "having perceived good reasons for the policy we are following, we intend to adhere to it." It was time, he told R.L. Richardson, that the friends of the government should "stop apologizing for that which needs no apology."[21] "The Yukon is not the same as any other gold mining country in the world," he remarked to Frank Oliver, "and the difference consists in the fact that it is good for nothing except mining, which in all probability will be temporary." The miners were not going to reinvest their profits in developing the country. There would be no long-term benefit for Canada unless some of the profits were skimmed off at once.[22]

One advantage of Sifton's methods was that the American government could take little exception to them. In spite of the Canadian government's apparently firm intention of mid-July to prevent Americans from mining in the Yukon, a few days' reflection served to show how difficult it would be to implement the restrictions. The United States took a keen interest in the welfare of its many citizens in the Yukon. At the same time, Canada was trying to negotiate with the Americans about running a telegraph line, and perhaps a road or railway, across that part of the disputed territory which the United States firmly controlled. Tens of millions of dollars' worth of trade was at stake. Officials at Ottawa were repeatedly assailed for failing to restrict the mining licences as promised. Sifton pointed out in reply that Canadian access to the Yukon depending upon American goodwill so long as the boundary was in dispute and that a confrontation would mean virtual closing of the territory to all miners. He thought that existing relations between the two countries were fairly harmonious, and "if Canadian and American papers would hold their tongues we would manage the business all right."[23] Unhappily the newspapers would not. Canadian-American relations soon became sharply discordant, and these affairs preoccupied Sifton in the months ahead.

Meanwhile, the strain of these weeks in July and August took its toll. Details of planning, constant public abuse, and the unremitting demand for patronage appointments to the Yukon soon left the minister of the interior seized with nervous tension. "I feel used up and am troubled with insomnia, my old enemy," he wrote. "I am getting into a state where I can neither eat, rest nor sleep."[24] At last in late August and early September, he slipped away for two desperately needed weeks of solitude at Lake Champlain.

Sifton returned to Ottawa "very much refreshed" and "as fit for work as I ever was, with the exception of the fact that I presume the work of the last year makes it necessary for me to be more careful."[25] If he planned to relax his rigorous work routine, it did not show. He now plunged into preparations for a well-publicized trip to the Yukon, in part to offset the adverse publicity of the summer, in part to answer criticisms that he was unfamiliar with actual conditions and therefore incapable of devising adequate policies, and in part to investigate possible routes for a railway into the Yukon, and especially to discover if possible an "all-Canadian" route.

Sifton recovered some public esteem when he announced two of the officials whom he had appointed to high posts in the Yukon. One was Major James Morrow Walsh, a personal friend, late of the NWMP, and the man who controlled the Souris coal fields; now, at age fifty-five he was to become commissioner of the Yukon, or the head of the territorial government. To the public he was a living hero. He was remembered for the tact, initiative, and courage with which he had dealt with Sitting Bull and his Sioux followers while they were in Canada to escape the United States Army between 1877 and 1881. His public image, certainly, was that of a capable, decisive man. His term of office in the Yukon, however, would shed little lustre on either Sifton's reputation or his own. But for the time being his selection was undeniably popular.[26] A second strong choice was Judge T.H. McGuire of the North-West Territories. He was titled judge of the Courts of the Yukon Provisional District, to serve one year until new laws and a more settled form of administration could be devised.[27]

Sifton intended to accompany these two gentlemen and many of the police reinforcements to their new Yukon posts, reaping attention along the way. Rounding out the party were several men whose appointments were but a foretaste of the future. One was Sifton's old intemperate political ally from Winnipeg, Frederick Coate Wade, once introduced to a Liberal rally as "the cyclone of the party." He was given the triple role of crown prosecutor, registrar of lands, and clerk of the court. Once in the Yukon he would also run a profitable private law practice on the side. His name spelled trouble from the beginning.[28] There were two inspectors of mines: J.D. McGregor, horse dealer, cattle rancher, and swine farmer from Brandon, and a good friend of the minister of the interior; and Captain Harwood, a Nova Scotian whaling captain and a friend of Dr. Borden, minister of militia. Neither had any ascertainable qualifications for their posts except the most important— political connections. T. Dufferin Pattullo, stenographer to Walsh and a future premier of British Columbia, was included because of his father's valued contributions to the Liberal cause in Ontario. And Arnott J. Magurn, "commissioner's secretary" in the official party, was in fact the paid publicist. He was the Ottawa correspondent of the *Globe* and sent back reports to his Toronto paper which became fodder for the Liberal press of the country. Altogether the party must have been quite a sight, fitted out as an Arctic expedition and armed "with Colt revolvers, 45 calibre, precise and deadly weapons, and 100 rounds of ammunition each," worn by every man outside his clothing. Doubtful as it is that many of them had ever handled such weapons before, it is possible that a party of fifty armed men would intimidate even the roughest characters at the seamy port of Skagway.[29]

Leaving Vancouver by the steamer *Quadra* on 3 October, the expedition sailed to Dyea, where Sifton and Walsh, accompanied by William Ogilvie, rode on horseback over the Chilkoot Pass to Lake Lindeman, some 140 miles inland, and then returned via Lake Bennett, Tagish, and the White Pass to Skagway. The round trip took ten days. Upon traversing the White Pass, mostly on foot because of the treacherous conditions resulting from heavy traffic and steady rain, Sifton was shocked. He told a reporter that he knew "no man of whom he thinks so little that he would send him over the White Pass."

The Yukon expedition was now divided. McGuire, Wade, McGregor, and a few others pushed on to Dawson, while Walsh remained behind with his staff to supervise the forwarding of supplies. On 21 October Sifton left the Lynn Canal to investigate the Taku Inlet and the Stikine River, both proposed as possible railway routes. The former was not practicable. Sifton was able to sail part way up the Stikine, however, and was impressed with its potential. By the Treaty of Washington, 1871, Canada had rights to commercial navigation of the river through the Alaska Panhandle to British Columbia. It was navigable six months of the year up to Telegraph Creek, from which point a railway could be run north to Teslin Lake, at the head of the Yukon River system. Could this not be the means of avoiding the troublesome conflict with the United States which was so complicating matters at the head of the Lynn Canal?[30]

The difficulty with the United States was not over gold, but trade. Any astute businessman realized that while many were lured by dreams of a fabulously wealthy placer mining operation, few would be successful. Sifton himself advised friends not to invest in Yukon gold ventures: "I expect the money will nearly all of it be lost."[31] It would be lost to those who controlled the trade of the district: food, liquor, mining and camping gear, or even "dens of wickedness." As it became apparent that the trade was going to reach substantial proportions—tens, or even hundreds, of millions of dollars—the cry went up from the business and transportation interests in the United States and Canada that action must be taken to retain the trade exclusively for their respective nationals.

Canada had had commercial shipping rights since 1871 on the Yukon and Stikine rivers, but they remained theoretical. The Americans had made it difficult to transship goods from ocean to river vessels and to carry them in bond. When the North American Trading and Transportation Company had ventured to send goods purchased in Canada up the Yukon River to Canadian territory, the Alaska Commercial Company lobby in Washington succeeded in persuading the American Customs to hinder the trade. English and Canadian vessels were forbidden to unload at St. Michael's on the Alaska coast. Canadian goods brought in on American vessels had to be accompanied through Alaska to Canadian territory by an inspector whose expenses had to be paid, in advance, by the NAT&T Company.[32] The Canadian government had known of these activities at least since 1894, but had not protested. Nor had Canadian merchants evinced much interest in the northern trade until it became valuable in 1897. The Americans were hardly likely to relinquish their control or change their practices just when the trade assumed substantial proportions.

A further problem for the Laurier government was the unsettled boundary between Alaska and the southern Yukon and British Columbia. The immediate crisis hinged to a large extent on the wording of the Anglo-Russian Treaty of St. Petersburg of 1825, dividing Russian and British territory in northwestern North America. The same statute was held to apply after the Americans purchased Alaska in 1867. The southern boundary of Alaska was to follow a presumed chain of mountains running parallel to the coast, which chain was later found not to exist; and the boundary was in any case not to exceed ten marine leagues, or about thirty miles, from the sea. How did this apply to the critical area of the Lynn Canal, thrusting northward ninety miles from the general coastline and giving the easiest access to mountain passes and the Yukon River system? The Americans naturally held that the treaty envisaged an unbroken strip of land and that the boundary should follow the sinuosities of the coast, running back thirty miles from the innermost point of every bay and inlet. But thirty miles inland from the head of the Lynn Canal would have given the United States control of all land to Lake Bennett and effective control of the entire trade. The Canadian contention was that the boundary should follow only the general direction of the coast, and therefore should bisect the Lynn Canal at a point not exceeding thirty miles north of the general coastline. This would give Canada control of the head of the inlet and, therefore, of the great bulk of the trade. The territory between the two extremes was held to be in dispute.

Unfortunately, the Canadian government had not bothered to protest the establishment of American settlements in the disputed zone prior to the gold rush. As a result, the Americans were effectively in control of the head of the inlet. In the early days of the gold rush, however, the Laurier cabinet naively hoped that the United States would consider the entire region to be in dispute and hence equally open to the nationals of both countries. Within weeks the Canadians were disabused of their illusions. The first Canadian feelers to Washington reflected the inexperience of the government in international negotiations. R.W. Scott, Paterson, and Sifton met, during the absence of most other ministers in July, and agreed to try "to obtain consent from the Washington authorities to our sending in goods in bond from the head of the Lynn inlet." "I presume they will consent," Scott wrote to Laurier, "we undertaking to pay the cost of sending an American officer with every transport until they reach a point that is undisputed Canadian territory."[33] A more extraordinary case of giving the game away in the opening moves would be hard to discover. Apparently there was no attempt to protest previous American actions imposing such a system on the rivers or its applicability in disputed territory. American settlement in the region and American assumption of control were accepted. More seriously, the Canadian proposal would prove to be a substantial hindrance to Canadian trade, establishing a system that would cause no end of headaches for the government before it was eliminated.

It was only when the Canadian government began to contemplate the difficulties of establishing telegraph and road communications that a different approach emerged. A proposal was made to run a road and telegraph eighty miles from the Lynn Canal over the White Pass to Fort Selkirk and to maintain dog teams in winter to carry on a mail service. To do so would require Washington's consent to a Canadian right of way over the disputed territory. The British opened negotiations on behalf of Canada but warned of "the extremely jealous spirit with which any action on the part of the Dominion Government, in any way connected with the territory of Alaska is regarded by a considerable and influential section of the American public." The times were not propitious. At last on 14 September President McKinley agreed to the construction of the proposed telegraph line, "without prejudice, however, to the boundary or other claims of either country and with the reservation that its right to revoke the license at any time be admitted."[34]

Building a wagon road, or even a railway, from the head of Lynn Canal remained very much in question. Andrew Blair, minister of railways, pressed for boldly forging ahead with a wagon road. Initially, the cabinet seemed willing to approve the expenditure of $100,000. But the proposal seemed less and less attractive as it was examined more carefully. Sifton had spoken to one of the proposed contractors and found a disturbing "vagueness and indefiniteness about what he is in a position to do." The route was not even fully known. Most important, it was becoming apparent that none of these proposals would do anything about growing trade difficulties in the region or give Canada independent access to her own territory.[35]

The wagon road project had been shelved, therefore, until Sifton could report on alternative routes following his trip. By the time he returned to Victoria in November, he had become a firm convert to building a line in British Columbia from Telegraph Creek to Teslin Lake, with a possible southern extension from Telegraph Creek to Canadian territory on the Portland Canal at the south end of the Panhandle. Publicly he remained neutral, but while he was in British Columbia he sought and obtained the approval both of the provincial government and of Opposition leader Sir Charles Tupper, who was visiting the province.[36] Apart from any decision on the railway, Sifton told reporters, his visit had only confirmed him in his decision to secure the royalty. He had been persuaded, perhaps by Ogilvie, that the policy of reserving every other claim would be unworkable, and therefore he intended to substitute a policy of reserving alternate groups of claims.[37] It remained to be seen whether this would constitute any substantial improvement.

Sifton's trip, then, served to inform him about conditions on the passes, some of the problems faced by Canadians passing through American-controlled territory, and the possibilities of an all-Canadian transportation route. His efforts did not go unappreciated by his colleagues: William Mulock, the postmaster general, wrote in praise of Sifton's "industry, zeal, and self-denial." "No Canadian minister," he declared, "has ever before taken hold of the work of his Department as you have done and manifested such entire self-abnegation and I feel that the Government is greatly indebted to you." He added, "there is no public question today before the Canadian people receiving anything like the amount of attention that the Yukon one does and your name will in the public mind be associated with the establishment of peace, order and good government in that heretofore terra incognita. Lack of skill in dealing with the Yukon problems might have been disastrous for the Government—at least would have cost us the loss of some prestige."[38]

Commendable energy certainly had been exhibited by the minister of the interior; but in retrospect Mulock's judgment appears premature. During the fall of 1897 the complexities of the Yukon problems—internal administration, border problems, and the "all-Canadian" access route—were being compounded. Within a year, Sifton would suffer his first severe political and administrative setbacks in all three areas.

Sifton was principally responsible for determining the policies of the Laurier government in the Yukon. The duty had fallen naturally to him as one of the few ministers in Ottawa during the critical summer of 1897; and, perhaps with the aid of the favourable publicity resulting from his trip to the Yukon, the initiative remained his even after Laurier and his colleagues had returned to the capital.

Sifton had hoped that the Americans would prove co-operative about allowing Canada some rights in the disputed coastal strip until the boundary was settled. Such rights should, he believed, include free and untrammelled passage for Canadian trade. Failing that, he hoped that the Americans would be willing to recognize Canadian rights under the Treaty of Washington, so that Canadian trade could continue freely on the designated rivers. Both expectations proved ill-founded.

As reports of the gold discoveries exposed and then exaggerated the riches of the Yukon, the rising nationalist clamour in both countries for exclusive control of the trade made co-operation between the governments exceedingly difficult. The problem was compounded by the favourite son of all accounts of the Yukon gold rush, William Ogilvie. Born in Ottawa in 1846, Ogilvie was related to Mrs. Sifton, a fact suggestively explored by the Opposition in later years. Well before the gold rush, however, his remarkable services as a surveyor, astronomer, and explorer had established his reputation. He was unquestionably one of the men best acquainted with the geography and mineral resources of the region, and his opinion carried great weight both with the government and with the public.[39]

Ogilvie spoke enthusiastically to reporters about the unlimited riches to be found in the north. None of the newspaper reports about gold finds in the Yukon—of which he could have seen very few—were exaggerated, he grandly announced. No other placer-mining area ever discovered could compare to its fabulous quantities of gold. The gold-bearing region, he continued excitedly, was five hundred miles long and up to one hundred miles wide, or some seventy-five million acres. Why on just two small creeks, Eldorado and Bonanza, he predicted that 140 claims alone would yield $70 million to placer miners, or an average of $500,000 per claim. There were many other creeks only slightly less productive, and probably very much more gold yet to be discovered. He did admit that mining in the region was difficult and complex. He believed that no permanent development would succeed the placer-mining community. But the wealth of the Yukon was at least sufficient to maintain the burgeoning city of Dawson for ten to twenty years and perhaps up to two or three generations.[40] Having toured Canada, where he repeated this intelligence to eager reporters at every stop, Ogilvie took a leave of absence from the department and went to Britain. There he was lionized. Men marvelled at his resistance to the temptation to cash in on the gold finds. Ogilvie basked in the public attention and regaled many an audience with tales of exploration in, and the riches of, the Yukon.

The great explorer's observations reflected neither caution nor good judgment. His estimates influenced government policy in the next crucial weeks. And the effect on public opinion can readily be imagined. The staid Toronto *Globe,* after solemnly considering Ogilvie's statements, suggested that "if half a million people go to the Klondike during the coming spring and summer it will mean an investment of about $300,000,000 in that gigantic mining venture. That is what gives the new industry its greatest economic importance."[41] Probably not a tenth that number ever reached the Klondike, but the spirit which produced such exaggerated statements underlay the events and tensions of this period.

Sir William Van Horne was a little more cautious in his estimates, which were nevertheless wildly optimistic. He predicted that not less than a hundred thousand men would go, generating trade of $100 million; and, he wrote, "we [the CPR] are enlarging our money boxes with the view of getting a fair share of that. We are getting all the locomotives and freight cars we can but still I am afraid we will be smothered by the avalanche of business which promises to come in the spring and early summer." He also added several boats to the Canadian Pacific's west coast fleet to profit from the trade northward.[42] Hundreds of Canadian entrepreneurs and merchants were making similar plans.

The results of American customs policy—originally suggested in part by Canada—now angered Canadian merchants. Goods purchased in Canada had to pay an inspection fee and then be carried in bond across the American-controlled strip of land at the head of the Lynn Canal, accompanied by a customs officer. The fee for the officer was $6 per day, plus $3 expenses; and as it took a minimum of six days to transport the estimated one to two thousand pounds of gear and supplies for each miner to Canadian territory, the cost could be prohibitive. Because the practice was well advertised, it had the expected effect of encouraging intending miners to purchase their supplies in American coastal cities, Seattle and San Francisco.[43]

Exclude all Americans and American goods from Canadian territory was the cry now dinned into the ears of the Canadian government. Retaliatory action, replied Sifton, would be "suicidal" until "every resource of diplomacy is exhausted."[44] Diplomacy might have been the key. While undertaken with commendable despatch, however, Sifton's first attempt was at best a mixed success. A peculiar coincidence of circumstances drew him to Washington late in December 1897 to try to resolve the outstanding issues. At the same time as both governments encountered a hailstorm of petitions demanding control of the Yukon trade, a widespread concern arose that many miners would face imminent starvation without a massive relief effort. The United States government was particularly exercised because so many were Americans and because sensational stories in the press had aroused the public, and consequently Congress, to demand action.

The reasons for the shortages extended well beyond the flood of miners.

Owing to the unusually low level of the Yukon River, boats were only able to ascend with partial loads, in some cases one-third of capacity. Those that did arrive, reported Inspector Constantine, were of little help. One steamer arrived with a load of furniture; another had a cargo of rotten eggs; a third arrived laden only with whiskey, having put off needed supplies of flour and lard to lighten its load. The Yukon Chamber of Mining and Commerce believed that hoarding and speculation in food supplies were driving up prices to prohibitive levels. Sifton had responded to Constantine's recommendation that the government begin sending supplies in over the passes, and by late fall Canadian officials had concluded that the situation might be tight, but not critical. "The amount of supplies now going over pass is sufficient for immediate necessities," Sifton wired Premier J.H. Turner of British Columbia on 18 December. "I am forwarding additional supplies and men on thirty-first Decr and fifth January. I do not think a special expedition would help matters as food is going over as fast as possible now."[45]

This did not meet the political needs of the American government. Congress had voted $200,000 to send a relief expedition to the Yukon and also to reportedly destitute miners in parts of Alaska which had to be reached via the Yukon. The American secretary of war, R.A. Alger, had intended to come to Ottawa to negotiate the passage of the relief expedition. When he fell ill, however, Sifton quickly seized the opportunity to go to Washington and discuss trade problems as well. Sifton even told Alger that "the necessity of relief for the Yukon miners is urgent," at the very moment when he was privately informing Canadian correspondents that the expedition was probably unnecessary.[46]

Agreement was reached quickly. The United States relief expedition would be allowed to go, though it was subsequently decided that an NWMP escort would have to be substituted for the American armed guard originally proposed. Some Canadians were outraged at the prospect of moving in so large a quantity of American supplies. Sifton had little patience with such carping. The United States government, he declared, had been most co-operative:

> They established Dyea and Skagway as sub-ports upon a telegram at our request. They have now made arrangements in accordance with our suggestion and they have always been liberal in their treatment of us. In addition to this our Police officers and supplies have been going over American territory during the season without even the formality of asking for permission and no objection has been raised. In view of this fact when they asked us to agree to allow them to take provisions into the country for relief purposes without payment of duty, in other words, donated from their treasury $200,000 for the purpose of supplying provisions to their people in the territory, we would have placed ourselves in a ridicu-

lous position if we refused to agree to it. As to whether there is any necessity for it or not is another question. . . . You can imagine the position I would be in had I gone to Washington and, after discussing the matter with the Secretary of War, declared that we would not allow them to send relief to their own people who are in our territory, and then called upon the Secretary of the Treasury and asked him to meet me in a liberal spirit in making bonding arrangements.[47]

For more than three months into the new year, the United States authorities continued planning to forward the expedition, which finally proved abortive. Eventually, as it became evident that starvation was not rampant in the Yukon, public pressure subsided.[48]

Sifton had not, as the Conservative Opposition charged, gone begging to Washington, although he had circumvented the usual circuitous diplomatic channels of negotiating through the governor general, the British Colonial and Foreign Offices, and the British ambassador in Washington. The situation required an immediate decision, and he presented the Canadian case concerning trade and bonding privileges both to President McKinley and to Secretary of the Treasury Lyman Gage. As a result the Americans agreed to eliminate their inspection fees for goods travelling in bond. Those transporting goods through American-controlled territory were then to be given an alternative. They could pay the fees for a customs officer to accompany the goods as before; or they could put up a bond or cash equivalent to the customs fee that would ordinarily be charged on imported goods, the bond to be cancelled or the cash refunded at the point of exit after satisfactory proof had been given that the packages had not been opened or consumed en route. There was no doubt that this would be a great relief to the miners. Finally, there was evidently some understanding respecting Canadian privileges of transshipment from ocean to river vessels at Wrangell, near the mouth of the Stikine River, the importance of which would shortly become apparent.[49]

Personal, direct diplomacy may occasionally have its advantages. In this case undue haste and Sifton's inexperience paid off in spades for the Americans. Sifton left Washington with no agreement on paper and no definitions as to precisely where American jurisdiction ended and Canadian jurisdiction began—nothing, in short, but verbal assurances. With jaunty optimism he returned to Ottawa early in January and wired his critics on the west coast that all had been favourably settled. American customs officers were expected to receive the new regulations forthwith. On 5 January he anxiously wired W.B. Howell, assistant secretary of the Treasury, requesting expeditious action, telegraphing the new instructions to Dyea and Skagway if necessary. Howell replied that they should be issued "in a day or two." On 8 January Sifton wrote again; Howell replied in a friendly tone four days later, stating that the regulations were "nearly" completed. On 20 January Howell wired that he had to wait "2 or 3 days" more in order to confer with the collector of customs for Alaska. "Will forward you copy at earliest practicable moment."[50]

The delay was caused by the fact that the proposed new regulations had become public and had raised a storm of protest in the western states. It was acutely embarrassing to Sifton, and irate politicians, including the premier of British Columbia and boards of trade, lost no time in venting their anger. Two steamship agents in Victoria wired, "daily steamships, sailing ships & scows go from Seattle, while Canadian boats get nothing entirely owing to United States customs regulations across disputed territory." The secretary of the British Columbia Board of Trade advised that American regulations were "simply paralizing the trade of Victoria and Vancouver." Demands arose for immediate closure of the mountain passes to all traffic until the new regulations were promulgated.[51]

Sifton admitted that his expectations had "not been fulfilled." But he declined to take the "drastic" steps being demanded, because the "evil consequences" would fall more heavily on Canadians than Americans. Irritating as the delay was, he pleaded for "a little patience." To E.G. Prior, MP for Victoria, he wired in exasperation, "Trust in God and keep your powder dry." At the same time he wrote rather sharply to Gage, recounting the delays. Canada, he observed, had for "some time past [been] affording every facility to the transit of American goods from Alaska through the Yukon territory without expense or trouble. I think we agreed when the matter was under discussion that it would be very unwise to run the risk of exciting international friction or bad feeling in connection with this matter, and I am now writing in the hope that for the purpose of avoiding anything of the kind you will be able to have the necessary instructions sent to your officers immediately."[52] The United States government responded by issuing new regulations on 2 February, and for the moment Sifton believed that the crisis was over and the major problems practically solved.

Late in January, writing to reassure the president of the Toronto Board of Trade concerning the customs difficulty, he added, "Before this will reach you it will be a matter of common knowledge that the Government has succeeded in bringing about an arrangement for the immediate opening of an all Canadian route, the result of which, when properly advertised, will be a distinct advantage to our merchants and manufacturers in overtaking the trade of the Yukon district."[53] "Success" was to prove as elusive as ever. The "all-Canadian" route was, of course, to be the rail link between Telegraph Creek and Teslin Lake. The intention was to ship Canadian goods from Vancouver or Victoria to Wrangell, transship them to river boats, sail up the Stikine, proceed by rail to Teslin Lake, and thence by a system of river boats to the centre of the mining operations at Dawson. It was anticipated that Canada would enjoy the right of free transshipment at Wrangell under the Washington Treaty, thus circumventing American customs duties and bonding fees.

One enduring myth from this period is that the railway proposal was hasty and ill-conceived. Even Sir William Van Horne wrote, "There never was a proposition for the construction of a railway in a district about which so little is known, or one presenting so many difficult problems."[54] Given the routing changes and construction problems during the building of the CPR, the statement seems ridiculous. Compared to the blind faith of the CPR directors as their line pushed through little-known country to an unknown pass in the Selkirks, compared to the monumental difficulties of pushing the line of steel above the Great Lakes and through the Cordillera, the government proposal in 1898 to build 150 easy miles of railway through the comparatively gentle mountain valleys of northwestern British Columbia was, despite its serious shortcomings, a model of rectitude and thorough planning.

This route had been under consideration for some years. The government first became seriously interested in it in 1894 and despatched William Ogilvie to explore the route in the winter of 1894-95 as part of his general duties in the Yukon. At the end of 1896 he still had filed no conclusive report. After Sifton had been in office but a few weeks, he determined to send out a separate expedition to provide a detailed report. The British Columbia government had expressed concern that the route should be developed; and the dominion government even had a proposal before it from an American company to develop a railway north from Vancouver as a joint Canadian-American venture.[55]

Thus, when the gold fever struck in the summer, there were already crews out surveying possible routes to provide the basis for a rational railway policy.[56] A great outcry began in mid-summer to persuade the government to adopt an overland route from Edmonton, an idea which Sifton rejected because of the great distance and cost. He did obtain an estimate of the cost of running a trail from Edmonton suitable for packing and for driving cattle, and it was begun in 1898 as a sop to the public clamour. Under the circumstances, however, a railway or even a wagon road could not have been built in time to meet the immediate need.[57] The choice had to be between the Stikine route or no independent route in time to meet any of the requirements of the miners in 1898. When it was shown by the end of 1897 that the Stikine route was feasible from an engineering standpoint, that a wagon road could be constructed in weeks, and a railway during one summer, the choice was practically made for the government.

Was so costly and permanent an enterprise really necessary? That is a question asked more readily with the benefit of hindsight. In the fall and winter of 1897-98 few doubted that the waves of people attacking the mountain passes were only the first in what promised to be an ongoing flood for several years at least. For reasons of controlling the trade alone, the line would be justified. The government also had to face reports of the probability of trouble in controlling the unruly, alien population. It believed that it was absolutely essential to secure a route by which armed forces could be moved quickly and easily into the Yukon, without having to seek permission from a possibly reluctant or hostile American government.

Thus the government believed that the Stikine line was both feasible and justified. The only serious difficulty was whether the United States would attempt to interfere with privileges of transshipment at Wrangell. Sifton believed it would not. The hindrances to the Canadian Yukon trade which had been imposed at St. Michael's—and which Canada had not protested—had never been employed at Wrangell. Moreover, they plainly were contrary to the spirit, if not the provisions of article 26 of the Treaty of Washington:

> The navigation of the rivers Yukon, Porcupine and Stikine, ascending and descending from, to, and into the sea, shall forever remain free and open for the purposes of commerce to the subjects of Her Britannic Majesty and to the citizens of the United States: subject to any laws and regulations of either country within its own territory, not inconsistent with such privilege of free navigation.

The practice at Wrangell had been for transshipment to take place under the supervision of United States Customs officials, without any attempt to hinder the trade. Sifton came away from Washington with verbal assurances that this practice would continue. "It was arranged that there should be no regulations at Stikeen that would harras[s] our trade," he wired to an anxious British Columbian, "but not specificially provided that same regulations adopted at Dyea and Skagway should apply to stickeen."[58] This qualification would prove crucial. It should be added that there was no reference either in the Treaty of Washington or in Sifton's dealings with the Americans to movement of troops, so United States policy remained undetermined. Nevertheless, Sifton believed that he had widespread political support for his actions. On his return from the Yukon to British Columbia, Sir Charles Tupper had brusquely told him that it was his duty to see that an all-Canadian line was built. The Opposition leader indicated approval for the broad outlines of Sifton's policy.[59]

The minister of the interior had opposed any appropriation even for a wagon road, let alone a railway, without prior parliamentary approval. By the beginning of 1898, however, easy passage of any reasonable measure to build a railway was anticipated, and the imperative requirement was to secure a contract which could be presented to the House of Commons with confidence that the contractors would be able to complete the line in the coming summer. There was no time to call for tenders. Sifton favoured William Mackenzie and Donald Mann, the contractors who had performed so ably in Manitoba and who had a reputation for completing their work on schedule. A second group centred in Montreal and Toronto was considered, but withdrew on 23 January, unable to secure the financing which they anticipated.[60] The Canadian Pacific Railway evinced no interest in securing the contract; and to award it to the CPR would have been impossible politically. Van Horne nevertheless sought a Canadian charter for an enterprise headed by an American promoter, Hamilton Smith, who had a United States charter to build from Chilkat Inlet to Selkirk. The government would allow no more charters which might be competitive with the Stikine route, Sifton told Van Horne:

> my judgment is, after consulting with my colleagues and going into the matter carefully, that a road from Observatory Inlet to Stikeen River and thence to Teslin Lake and, should the country warrant it, down the Hootalinqua River as far as necessary is the one safe Canadian route. As long as the terminus of the Chilkat line was in American territory we would feel as if we were suspended over a volcano and enquiries elicit the undoubted fact that there would be an immense amount of opposition to the Chilkat route by reason of the fact that it is not an all-Canadian route. I believe Sir Charles Tupper, the Opposition and everybody in Canada will unite in supporting the route I suggest as it would make us perfectly independent and give us absolute control. The Stikeen portion should be built this year.[61]

Thus it is obvious that from the beginning Sifton never conceived his full policy in the limited terms of the Stikine-Teslin line set out in the contract. That was merely the first stage, the first emergency part of a considered long-term policy which would extend the line to a Canadian port on Observatory Inlet. The cabinet also had decided at an early point in its deliberations that no cash subsidies would be given the railway. It must be financed out of the region itself by land grants, which, it was hoped, would attract British investment capital.[62]

The government closed with Mackenzie and Mann on 25 January. The contractors undertook to build a wagon road over the route in six weeks and to complete the railway by 1 September. They were required as well to provide a steamship service from the northern terminus of the railway to Dawson City. The sum of $250,000 was deposited with the government, to be forfeited if they did not meet the specified deadlines. In return, they were to be given a land grant of 25,000 acres of northern lands per mile of railway; their line was to be granted a five-year monopoly; for ten years they were to have first option on government subsidies to extend the line; and the land grant was to be free from taxation for ten years. The government was empowered to fix the tolls on the line for seven years. When the railway was completed, an incorporated subsidiary of Mackenzie and Mann was to take over all the responsibilities and obligations of the contract. Any gold produced from the approximately

3,750,000 acres of the land grant was to be taxed at a royalty of only 1 per cent. The company could not select its lands in one large block, nor along major rivers or lakes, nor could it select arable land. As elsewhere in the Yukon, alternate blocks of land would be reserved for the government.[63] Sir William Van Horne thought the terms were "extremely reasonable in view of the very large amount of money which has to be risked by the contractors." "Macken-zie and Mann," he told Senator R.W. Scott, "are the only people in Canada with the necessary knowledge and facilities for putting the work through in time and I think the Govt have acted very wisely in closing with them." But Sir William was not exactly an unbiased observer; he evidently held a block of stock in the Yukon railway enterprise.[64]

Sifton was jubilant. "You will be able to take a steamboat on the river next September and come out by railway and steamboat like a Christian," he told Major Walsh. "I am having a tremendous amount of trouble with Customs officials in Alaska but when all the trade switches to the Canadian route, Canadians will have the inside track. The construction of the railway will be the quickest piece of work ever done in Canada and will, I think give a great deal of satisfaction to all parties."[65]

If ever Clifford Sifton counted his chickens too soon, this was the occasion. A conjunction of circumstances and faulty planning began to undermine his optimistically laid schemes. Though Sir Charles Tupper warmly applauded the contract, opposition to it was immediate and vigorous.[66] The serpent of opposition even raised its ugly head in the Liberal caucus and cabinet.

The first difficulty concerned the undefined boundary. In spite of its announced intention in 1897 to collect customs duties at the summit of the passes north of the Lynn Canal, the Canadian government had been timid and hesitant about asserting its authority. The customs posts had been established at Lakes Lindeman and Bennett, where there was little doubt of Canadian sovereignty. Not only was this less efficient for ensuring the collection of duties from all entering miners, but it also appeared to accept the United States' argument that it owned all the intervening land. Miners were being forced to pay the fee for the accompanying customs officers for an extra fifteen miles past the summit of the White Pass. The American contention, observed a Canadian official, "is of course preposterous: the utmost they can claim is the summit of the pass." The government had not yet taken an official stand, but intended to claim that the boundary bisected the Lynn Canal, leaving Dyea and Skagway in Canada. In mid-January 1898, the NWMP was ordered to establish posts at the summits of the passes, although they were not to hoist the British flag to avoid irritating the Americans. Both A. Bowen Perry and Z.T. Wood, the NWMP officers on the spot, delayed and recommended a compromise boundary at the lakes as "the one safe way in this matter." Their "one safe way" of course amounted to caving in completely to the Americans. Sifton exploded with blunt instructions: "Boundary is at the summit or farther *seaward. Instruct your officers that provisionally the boundary is at the summit & to act accordingly.* The shantys should be put up as instructed just inside the summit."[67] This decisive, if belated, action resulted ultimately in the preservation of all the region beyond the White and Chilkoot passes for Canada.

At the same time, a concentration of American troops at Portland, Oregon, intended ostensibly to maintain order at the notorious sub-port of Skagway, was viewed with apprehension by Sifton. He believed that their real purpose was to back up the territorial claims of local customs officials. Therefore, he decided to rush fifty NWMP reinforcements secretly to the Yukon. In a despatch which he drafted for transmission to the British government, he requested British support for Canadian claims; but he also asked for no British communication concerning the subject with the United States for eight days, because "when the disputes are known at Washington it is possible that we may be forbidden to send goods or men through Dyea or Skagway." "In another ten days," Sifton later wrote, "they would have been in possession of the territory down to Lake Bennett and it would have taken twenty years of negotiating to get them out, in fact I doubt if we would ever have got them out.... It is a case of possession being ten points in the law, and we intend to hold possession. The United States authorities have now been communicated with through diplomatic channels, and we intend to hold the territory if we possibly can."[68]

On 11 February Sifton made the Canadian position official when he stated in the House of Commons, "our contention is that Skagway and Dyea are really in Canadian territory, but as the United States have had undisputed possession of them for some time past, we are precluded from attempting to take possession of that territory." Nevertheless, "we have taken the position that there can be no doubt raised as to the Canadian territory beginning at the summit." The claim was neither deniable nor debatable, "and we have instructed our officers to establish posts as near the boundary as physical conditions will permit." No official protest was made by the United States government, but for another two months Canadian officers had to contend with their angry American counterparts and importers who thoroughly tested their resolution and patience.[69] Finally, in the midst of the escalating border tension, Canada felt constrained to send some two hundred troops of the permanent militia force to strengthen the hand of the NWMP in maintaining order and to counterbalance the presence of several companies of American regulars in the district. It was no accident that this "Yukon Field Force" was sent via the Stikine route to demonstrate its practicability.[70]

These and other incidents bred a determination in the minds of British and

Canadian authorities to arrange an early settlement of the boundary with the United States. If the Americans had succeeded in controlling the territory to Lake Bennett, they would at the very least have been able to control the Yukon trade as well. The practicability of the all-Canadian railway would at once have been destroyed. Canadian authorities feared that American miners would seize on any pretext to stage a rebellion and call in American military support.[71]

Meanwhile, the Yukon Railway bill had received an inauspicious start. The minister of railways and canals, A.G. Blair, introduced the bill to Parliament in an admittedly incompetent speech. His performance was later termed "treachery" by supporters of the policy. As with the Crow's Nest Pass line, Blair had not been intimately involved in negotiating the contract and never seems to have been a warm supporter of the policy adopted. Then Sir Charles Tupper funked on his promise to support the measure. He had given it initial support, but his irate followers forced him to spearhead opposition to it.[72]

Opposition arguments centred generally on a few key points. Of the first importance was whether the proposed route was indeed "all-Canadian" or still subject to American customs regulation. If subject to American control, the whole rationale and economic viability of the line was brought into question. Second, did the contract give Mackenzie and Mann a fabulously wealthy fiefdom through their alleged massive monopoly of land, trade, and gold production? Naturally, the Opposition portrayed the contractors as securing millions of acres of rich gold-bearing lands, which would return their investment many times over. Third, why had the government not called for tenders? Were there other viable offers? What of Hamilton Smith, who claimed to represent Rothschild interests and to be willing to build the road for one-quarter of the land subsidy offered Mackenzie and Mann? Did the contractors obtain the contract solely because the minister of the interior wished to reward his friends? Fourth, was the contract drawn too much in the interest of Mackenzie and Mann? Were the guarantees that they would fulfil the terms of the contract and operate the railway sufficiently ironclad? Finally, opposition arose from those who had their own axes to grind: those who believed in government ownership; those like Frank Oliver, who vowed to oppose anything that would detract from the Edmonton or some other favoured route; those who espied malevolent CPR influence lurking behind Mackenzie and Mann; and certain central and eastern Canadian MPs who saw nothing in the contract for their home provinces.

After the contract had been handled roughly for several days, Sifton finally rose in an expectant House on 15 and 16 February to deliver his first major address in the Commons.[73] Ably and aggressively he defended the contract. He roasted Sir Charles Tupper for his abrupt change of posture. He outlined and sought to justify his administration of the Yukon since the previous summer. On he swept, putting the issue into the context of the exigencies of trade, the difficulties of administration, the problems with the Americans, the reasons for selecting the Stikine route. The Conservatives were arguing that the route was not "all-Canadian." For that they had themselves to blame. They had been patting themselves on the back as they praised the virtues of the Treaty of Washington of 1871, negotiated by the revered Sir John Macdonald. Had not this treaty conferred on Canada the navigational privileges for commercial purposes on the Stikine? Quite the reverse, maintained Sifton. The 1871 Treaty was a poor bargain, for it reduced a proprietary right to all rivers crossing the disputed territory, under the Anglo-Russian Treaty of 1825, to a privilege of navigation for commerce alone and that only on the Stikine River. Despite that gross Tory blunder, and the growing clamour in the United States to defeat the Canadian policy by impeding the trade at Wrangell, Sifton argued that the Americans would not actually go so far as to attempt to violate Canadian treaty rights. Unfortunately, he had no concrete evidence: his assurances at Washington had been verbal, and the American customs regulations of 2 February had not included Wrangell. Sifton was probably correct that the United States administration had no intention of interfering, as later events showed, but it was certainly not going to confirm that publicly or in writing. This silence in face of public and congressional agitation for action was as a dagger thrust at the heart of Sifton's project.

Sifton attempted to defend the "all-Canadian" features of the route by pointing out that if the Americans should attempt to interfere, transshipment could be carried out at Port Simpson. It would be more troublesome and expensive, but travel by river boat on the protected inner passages of the coast was feasible. The Canadian public was not prepared, it would seem, to believe that this would be a successful method of circumventing the Americans, and the Opposition was successful in creating the impression that any interference at Wrangell would be entirely fatal to the scheme.

Sifton was perhaps least convincing when he tried to persuade the House that, despite the five-year ban on competition, "there is no monopoly of any kind whatever" in the Yukon railway contract. Obviously any line from the head of the Lynn Canal would have a strong commercial advantage, being shorter and enabling goods to be carried much farther by cheap ocean-going shipping. Only with a monopoly could the Canadian line be viable, and presumably before the five years were up, the decision would have been made whether or not to extend the Stikine line south to a Canadian ocean port.

But—and Sifton warmed to the opportunity to strike a cutting blow at the Tories—did the Conservatives dare to attack the government for endowing the railway with a land subsidy? Was there a Conservative-built line which had been constructed without a cash subsidy of any kind as the Yukon line would be? Not only had the Tories generously ladled out cash subsidies, but they had been lavish with land where such a policy made a tremendous social and economic impact—in the prairie west. Ogilvie had estimated the gold-bearing lands of the Yukon at 75,000,000 acres; out of that, what was 3,750,000 acres? Compare that with the munificent railway endowment created by the Tories in the prairie region. He held up a map:

> Sixty-seven million acres—the whole fertile belt and much that is not is now a land monopoly reserved for the benefit of railway companies. Do Hon. gentlemen opposite think it is the white portions of this map that show the land reserved? No, it is the black part. We mourn over that in the Northwest, and therefore I had it marked in black on the map.

All that land was reserved; a great deal of it was unearned; and yet not a single homestead could be granted on it. Where had been the Conservative critics of land grants when their own party was granting handsome concessions?

> What we have in the shape of a land monopoly is this. We have millions of acres in that country owned by railway companies, and these companies are not required to do any work or spend any money. They sit down; they toil not neither do they spin. But the farmers toil and the farmers spin.
>
> The farmers do their work: they cultivate their lands and make their roads and bridges and pay their taxes and improve their land. And the land goes up in value for the benefit of the railway companies.

In the Yukon there would be no prior reservation of lands pending selection as there had been on the prairies. Every acre of land had to be earned; it could be claimed only as every ten miles was approved to be in running order. The first such block could not possibly be taken until mid-June at the earliest, by which time the inrush of miners would have had an opportunity to stake the best land. Even then the railway could not take over an entire district or locate simply along creek beds. It was required to select its lands in alternate blocks six miles wide by twenty-four miles deep. And Sifton naturally played down the likelihood of the contractors securing much gold. The company's risk was enormous because so little of its land was likely to produce gold. Sifton demonstrated that the syndicate of H.M. Kersey had been unable to meet the conditions imposed by the government. As for Hamilton Smith, no offer had even been broached to the government. The Smith proposal could not now be taken seriously, for it was but a patent attempt to embarrass the government. Finally, Sifton was prepared to be conciliatory with respect to legal changes which would improve the contract, particularly with respect to the obligations of Mackenzie and Mann.[74]

The speech was a brilliant parliamentary performance and did much to establish Sifton's reputation in the House of Commons. As would be typical, however, it glossed over inconvenient facts and obscured the government's own ineptitude and inexperience in international relations. The Treaty of Washington, for example, did not cover the movement of military personnel across American territory, but Sifton continued to insist that the Stikine route would facilitate independent Canadian movement of military personnel in case of emergency. And aggressive posturing over the all-Canadian route diverted attention from the fact that the government's incompetence had reinforced American control over the Lynn Canal region.

By the time the Yukon Railway bill cleared the House of Commons and was passed on to the Senate on 16 March, events in Washington had further clouded its already gloomy future. Hardly had the bill been presented to Parliament when retaliation appeared in the United States Senate in the form of a threat to obstruct Canadian trade. This took concrete form early in March when as a provision in the Alaska Homestead Bill the Americans specifically proposed to interfere at Wrangell unless certain outrageous conditions were met. These entailed abandonment of the all-Canadian route, construction of a Canadian line joining an American one from the head of Lynn Canal, free admission of American miners' outfits, removal of any restrictions on Americans obtaining mining licences, restoration of certain Atlantic fishing privileges to the United States which were contrary to the Convention of 1818, and granting of most-favoured-nation trade status to the United States.[75]

Understandably these preposterous demands produced an irate response in Canada. The Canadian government rushed two well connected men to Washington to seek some modification: President Van Horne of the CPR and Edward Farrer, the able, ubiquitous, and notorious journalist. The United States officials must have been confused and a bit bemused by these two unofficial diplomats. Farrer, who was on the scene first, seems to have represented Laurier. And Laurier was a politician whose first instincts in a tight situation were to compromise and get out with as much grace as possible. Van Horne communicated with Sifton, who preferred to call the other person's bluff and fight when necessary.

Upon reaching Washington, Farrer promptly negotiated a tentative compromise with congressional officials. Agreement was reached on reciprocal bonding privileges for ten years and reciprocal military transport privileges in the Alaska-Yukon region. Conditions of entry for miners' equipment and licence privileges for Americans were to be put to an arbitration commission. Finally, it was proposed that Mackenzie and Mann should drop the Stikine-Teslin line and join with American promoters in building the White Pass line favoured by the United States government. Farrer's negotiations also revealed that Hamilton Smith had lobbied very hard for the offensive American bill, just as he had lobbied the Canadian Senate to defeat the Yukon Railway bill. His Rothschild backers evidently wanted to discredit the Stikine route so that Canada would be forced to abandon it and take up the Lynn Canal line in which they had an interest. In accordance with the understanding reached by Farrer, the offensive clause in the American legislation was to be redrafted in the belief that the Canadian government approved of the compromise.[76]

Not all of Laurier's ministers, and certainly not Sifton, would accept such a total capitulation. Van Horne told Sifton a week later that he had succeeded in convincing the Americans that they "had been grossly deceived" as to Canadian opinion. In all of his discussions with the Americans, he wrote, it was made clear that there would "be no trouble about the navigation of the Stikeen, for nobody raised the slightest question as to Canada's rights in that regard; and I do not believe that there will be any trouble either about the transfer at Wrangel, for nobody seemed to have any serious thought of interfering with it, and all seemed to regard it as a matter covered in spirit by the right of free navigation." In other words, if Van Horne is to be trusted, the United States officials as much as admitted privately that which Sifton had contended from the very beginning—in effect, that the threats of interference at Wrangell had been a grand bluff. The British government held the same view, that privileges of transshipment could not be interfered with, and accordingly on 17 March instructed the British ambassador in Washington to make this clear.[77] How much trouble Sifton would have saved himself and the Laurier government had he undertaken to get this British opinion in the first place!

Further negotiations produced another redrafting of the American legislation. For weeks it had been evident that the Conservative-dominated Canadian Senate would throw out Sifton's Yukon Railway Bill. Once that event had taken place, the United States was to amend its Alaska Bill to provide for reciprocal bonding and transshipment privileges and reciprocal mining rights for Canadian and American citizens in Alaska and the Yukon. It was assumed that Canada would co-operate on a railway from Lynn Canal. The Canadian government requested that the new measure not be announced until after the Canadian Senate vote. On 30 March the Upper House administered the *coup de grâce* to the Yukon railway bill, 52 to 14, and the Americans proceeded with their legislation which came into effect in mid-May 1898.[78]

The compromise with the United States had made few concessions to Canadian nationalists of Sifton's stripe and simply capped the crushing Senate defeat. The Liberals had been campaigning against the negative Senate sentiment since the contract had first been announced in January, even enlisting Van Horne's energetic aid. By early March it was apparent that the battle had been lost. Perhaps some senators voted against the bill for what they believed were its inherent defects. Much more likely is that it was principally a party vote. It must have seemed unlikely that men as astute as Mackenzie and Mann and Van Horne would have invested in a venture that would be as risky as Sifton claimed. Joseph Pope, who was well placed to know, recorded that certain Tories had opposed the bill for the very "practical" reason that "if the bill passed the contractors would have given the Liberal Machine such as large 'rake-off' as to have assured them power for 20 years. That may be so."[79]

Where did these events leave proposals for an "all-Canadian route? The British government, on whose support Canada had to depend in disputes with the United States, was in no mood for Canadian militancy. Colonial Secretary Joseph Chamberlain, with more than a touch of that supercilious condescension that so often antagonized dominion authorities, recommended that Canada recognize defeat, abandon her nationalistic pretensions, and gracefully join hands with the Americans, especially since the boundary remained unsettled. All that Congress required, he suggested, was the abandonment of the Dominion's policy of monopoly. But since monopoly was, after all, the very rationale underlying the "all-Canadian" route, this would amount to unconditional surrender. In one last spurt of nationalist ardour, the Canadian government replied that such a course was impossible on two counts. First, the Americans had dropped the reciprocal military transport privileges spoken of in the early negotiations with Farrer. Because unrestricted access for military personnel was deemed essential, the government concluded that the "all-Canadian" route was still necessary. Second, any such road would have little economic value if linked to a line from Lynn Canal. Because of its superior commercial value, noted the government, a road from the Lynn Canal "would from the moment of its being built, impair [the] value of [the] Canadian road." The message concluded, weakly, that "these considerations seem to make it expedient that no hasty action should be taken in the matter."[80]

The government took this curious stand in early April, after the informal agreement with the United States and after the Canadian Senate vote—in other words, after the death of the Yukon railway policy. Sifton and the remaining nationalists in the cabinet had probably insisted on a vigorous reply to the British, in the vague hope that somehow the project could be resurrected. But any such expectations were futile. Two weeks later, after vain attempts to devise an alternative scheme, Sifton bitterly commented,

> The difficulty about the Yukon transportation question is a very serious one. I spent an immense amount of time and trouble in working out a solution of it which would have cost the country nothing at all, and after a year or two blundering people will find out that the course suggested was the right one. In the meantime I find a very great deal of difficulty in

finding any other course which could be carried into effect. The delay which has already been caused will double the cost of the administration of the country during the next year.[81]

The American customs regulations, finally put into force in May, along with the compromise agreed to in March, put Canadian trade into the Yukon on an equal footing with that of the United States. There was no great public pressure for the Stikine-Teslin line, which had been so discredited and now no longer seemed essential.

Prime Minister Laurier later denounced the defeat of the Yukon Railway bill as "a piece of wanton, senseless partisanship," a "gross treason to the business interests of this country," and "a crime against Canada."[82] These were fine rhetorical flourishes. However, he in effect had forced a compromise in face of impending defeat. The government never thereafter publicly advocated a White Pass line but seemed simply willing not to oppose it as it was built during 1898. The railway reached the waters of the Yukon River system in 1899 and Whitehorse the following year.[83]

With hindsight Sifton's scheme has been regarded as ill-considered, and it did have serious defects. Nevertheless, it was a policy devised to meet anticipated conditions. Most believed that a huge and continuing influx of people into the Yukon would take place, which would perpetuate intense international rivalry for the resulting trade. Given this competition, the uncertainty of the boundary, and the instability of the population, there seemed to be imperative commercial and administrative justifications for the proposal. Finally, there was no other route which could even approximate the requirements of the emergency. The spring of 1898 produced radical changes. By the end of March, the United States was aroused by impending war with Spain in Cuba, which soon diverted attention, and men, from the Yukon gold fields. The trade of the district in fact fell off rapidly.[84]

Mackenzie and Mann eventually had to be compensated for work done prior to the defeat of the bill. The episode was a serious blow to the prestige of both Sifton and the government. The Opposition had succeeded in raising serious doubts about the whole Yukon administration, an opening which would be fully exploited in the near future. There was, too, a certain popular exasperation at the way Canadians had been forced once again to give in to American bluster and arrogance. Sifton and several of his colleagues were determined that the United States would not again find Canada so pliable.

The internal administration of the Yukon remained a constant preoccupation for the minister of the interior. When public attention was diverted from trade and railway problems, it seemed merely to focus on one or another aspect of alleged misgovernment and injustice committed by uncaring and greedy dominion authorities in the far-off gold fields.

Changes in February 1898 in the mining regulations had been in gestation since Sifton's Yukon adventure and discussions with Ogilvie. The government had altered the regulations at least three times in the preceding nine months and hoped that this new, extensive revision would not only meet certain specific problems, but would also provide a lasting answer to charges that the government's apparent lack of direction in policy had left the entire mining community in a state of confusion. Sifton determined upon a 10 per cent across-the-board royalty on gross annual production exceeding $2,500. He limited all claims to 250 feet of creek or gulch frontage, and settled miners' licence fees at $10. Every alternate ten claims were to be reserved for the government.[85] At first the new regulations seemed to be well received by the miners.[86] Sifton was hopeful that a more flexible approach would permit him to maintain the principles which had underlain his policy from the beginning.

On one principle, however, he had made a fundamental departure. It was little noticed at the time, but it signalled a change which would have serious economic, social, and environmental repercussions in the Yukon, with attendant political upheaval. In July 1897 Sifton had written to a prominent New York businessman who had expressed an interest in large-scale corporate development in the district,

> There is no possibility of any mining companies getting a group of claims. A policy of that kind would simply blanket the whole country and stop development. It was a similar policy which spoiled the North West, by blanketing it with claims which practically shut out settlers. The parties that are being formed are operated on the grub-staking principle. They hire men to prospect and locate claims, having a written agreement with them that the company has a specified interest in the claims.[87]

Such a policy focused on individual claims as the means of development; it would be difficult, if not impossible, to consolidate a large group of claims in such a manner as to permit large-scale development.

Less than six months later Sifton reversed himself. It had become apparent that large parts of the gold-bearing districts could never be efficiently exploited by placer-mining methods. Equally important, powerful business and political pressure was being exerted to allow such development since it would result in monetary and patronage benefits for the Liberal party. In January 1898, therefore, Sifton presented to the cabinet proposals to permit the granting of twenty-year leases "to persons or companies...to dredge for minerals other than coal in the submerged beds or bars of rivers in the Provisional District of Yukon." Such leases were to extend to five miles along a river, and an individual or company could hold up to six such leases or a maximum of thirty miles. The lessee undertook to have a dredge in operation on each five-mile lease within two seasons of the issuance of the lease, to pay an annual rental of $100 per mile of river so leased, and a 10 per cent royalty on output exceeding $15,000. Failure to fulfil the regulations could, at the discretion of the minister of the interior, result in cancellation. The first such lease, or "concession" as they were known, was issued in that same month.[88]

Without fully realizing it, Sifton had helped to establish a conflict between two irreconcilable methods of development. Large-scale mechanical mining was the way of the future, but it doomed the spirit of adventure and individualism which had thus far permeated the gold-rush community. Sifton had apparently concluded that the parallel that he had drawn in July 1897 between development in the Yukon and that in the Northwest no longer applied. Yet before long many would consider the results of his policy to be as baneful as the picture he drew of the unhappy Northwest.

The parliamentary session of 1898 was the first opportunity since the outbreak of the gold rush to legitimize the government in the Yukon. Technically, the dominion government had had no legal authority to treat the Yukon as a district separate from the North-West Territories, and Sifton readily admitted that Major Walsh's commission was "in some respects ultra vires," having been issued to meet an emergency. The peculiar nature of the problems of a remote mining district made it desirable to create a separate jurisdiction from that of the agriculturally oriented territorial government at Regina.

A growing dispute over control of the liquor traffic in the Yukon underlined the need to establish a separate district. Among the powers assumed by the North-West Territories government in 1897 was licensing and regulation of the liquor traffic, with essentially the same powers as any provincial government. Since the laws of the Territories applied in the Yukon, it naturally had an eye on the sizeable revenues to be realized from the Yukon trade. On the other hand, the dominion government was paying to provide an administration for the Yukon, and the minister of the interior, who had hitherto issued the liquor permits, was not easily persuaded to release his grip. The situation was somewhat complicated by a deluge of hundreds of petitions from church groups and temperance societies pleading that the Yukon be kept dry to save the young men from degradation and perdition. Both governments, however, operated on the assumption that total prohibition was utterly unenforceable. It seemed best to control the traffic by allowing a reasonable number of permits and to realize a comfortable profit while so doing.[89]

The Yukon Territory Act, assented to on 13 June 1898, established the district as a separate territory. It was to be administered by a commissioner and appointed council, responsible to the dominion cabinet or the minister of the interior. On speaking to his measure, Sifton showed that he had simply taken over the philosophy of the Macdonald and Mackenzie governments in organizing the West a quarter-century previously. "The only radical departure from that is," he told the Commons, "that we have not provided for any elective members of the council." He considered it a "tentative measure," designed to serve until the permanent character of the community was established. A system of popular representation would be premature, "especially as all the information we possess goes to show that perhaps nine out of ten persons in the district are aliens, totally unacquainted with our method of representation, and the population will in all probability be a very nomadic character, at least for the present." Later on, "as a matter of course, if a permanent population establishes itself in the district, some representative system similar in principle to what was given to the North-West Territories" would have to be provided.[90]

There was at first glance a certain logic and some common sense involved in Sifton's approach. Yet there was a danger as well. Sifton's paternalistic policy was, as he saw it, both necessary and in the British tradition. He had no desire to let the excitable "grass roots"—mostly Americans—develop institutions through which they could noise their grievances. The council's job was to implement Ottawa's wishes and to impose a certain form of government. It was not to act as a channel through which the local populace could appeal to Ottawa. The effect was rather like trying to clamp a lid on a simmering pot without a safety valve. The members of the council—judges, NWMP officers, government officials—neither represented nor understood the problems of the miners, labourers, and others. The steam had to escape somewhere, and Sifton's efforts to cap it simply led to heightened frustration on both sides.

The most immediately frustrated party, however, was the territorial government. It had issued permits for fifty thousand gallons of liquor to enter the Yukon, at a fee of $2 per gallon. It also had sent an agent, G.H.V. Bulyea, to Dawson to establish a licensing system for liquor outlets, without informing Sifton. Bulyea planned an annual fee of $2,000 per establishment and anticipated that this would yield a revenue of between $30,000 and $50,000. Sifton stunned Premier F.W.G. Haultain with his announcement that the Yukon would be made into a separate district and that in the meantime the liquor traffic would remain under dominion jurisdiction. "Now we stand in the position of having had our authority over-ruled, and our self governing rights invaded," wrote Haultain angrily, "and we shall be obliged to protest as strongly as we can against what we consider an unwarrantable and unnecessary diminution of the self governing rights which we were so grateful to you for having procured for the Territories last year."[91] His protests were of no avail. Sifton simply raised the fee for a licence to take liquor into the Yukon from 25 cents to $2 per gallon, in line with the fees set by the Territories and turned the responsibility for issuing permits and licences over to the Yukon commissioner-in-council. There the authority remained so long as it was politically advantageous, and Sifton could piously reply to those who upbraided the government for failing to implement prohibition that the matter was altogether out of his hands.[92]

Of no little concern to Sifton as he tried to put his Yukon house in order was the attitude of Major J.M. Walsh. It had been well understood that Walsh had consented to become commissioner only for one year, but his term would not expire until the end of the summer. Sifton was dismayed to hear early in April that Walsh was anxious to leave his post as soon as possible. The commissioner had not been a conspicuous success, and Sifton had been forced to defend him in the House of Commons. Walsh had never gone to Dawson and was intensely unpopular among the NWMP. Sifton told Walsh that quitting before his task was completed would destroy his public reputation and harm Sifton and the government as well. "I would rather lose $20,000 than have you come back without going to Dawson," he added.[93] The minister of the interior knew his man. To one so enamoured of his reputation as Walsh, Sifton's comment took the form of an imperative.

There had been little choice for Sifton but to press Walsh to stay on. William Ogilvie, designated in January as the new commissioner, was in England, and Walsh's authority and organizational ability were required to cope with the expected influx of new miners. The commissioner did venture to Dawson, but his visit had the reverse of the expected effect. Walsh shortly became the centre of a storm of controversy amid allegations that he had used his official position to benefit his friends and relatives, if not himself, in the manipulation of gold claims.

In the late spring of 1898 those problems still lay ahead. Sifton hoped that at last he had a grip on the Yukon administration. The first few months of the gold rush had been both a frustration and an embarrassment to him and to the Laurier administration. Admittedly, he had been working under great pressure and in exceedingly difficult circumstances. But great energy and the best of intentions could scarcely conceal the fact that he was attempting to provide an administration tailored less to the requirements of the Yukon than to political exigencies at Ottawa. While there was a certain cogency in his Yukon railway scheme and while he had immensely impressed all sides with his speech on the question in the House of Commons, the failure of the policy was a major blow. Finally, both Sifton and the Laurier government had proven woefully inexperienced at international relations, compounding the weakness of the Canadian case concerning the Alaska boundary and appearing unable to protect Canada's trading and commercial interests. The Opposition was confident that on the Yukon administration the government was exceedingly vulnerable. Unfortunately, a great many Liberals thought likewise. The government, and particularly Sifton, had lost a great deal of ground.[94] It would be an uphill battle to regain mastery of the situation.

# 8

# Stalemate: The Ogilvie Commission and the International Joint Commission (1898–99)

Lake of the Woods is one of the brighter jewels in Canada's vast treasury of resort areas. Its myriad islands scattered through the crystal blue waters have long made it a favourite retreat for the wealthy of Winnipeg; and Sifton took his family there for several weeks in August 1898. It was a typical Sifton working vacation: more relaxed than the pace at Ottawa, but never long escaping political and administrative concerns. He received several of his colleagues, including Sir Wilfrid Laurier, at his island near Rat Portage. His correspondence continued to pour out in a steady stream, and there was invariably a daily pile of newspapers so that he might never lose touch with the country's political pulse.

On 1 July, still at his desk in Ottawa, Sifton had cheerfully written J.S. Willison, "I am having a quiet Dom. day. Work will be in pretty good shape when I leave."[1] It seemed reasonable to suppose that nothing more than routine matters would arise now that the Yukon administration had been taken in hand. A duly constituted civil government and revised mining regulations should settle the domestic side of the administration, while an International Joint Commission was to try to settle outstanding Canadian-American disputes, including the Alaska boundary, in a series of meetings scheduled to begin at Québec in late August.

For a second consecutive summer, however, the Yukon burst through to occupy the centre of the political stage. Charges of corruption and incompetence on the part of Yukon officials became a full blown attack on the government for systematic maladministration of the Yukon. To Sifton's dismay, the charges were indiscriminately picked up and repeated by the credulous Liberal press. Almost before he knew it, even his colleagues were collapsing before demands for a commission of investigation into the charges, which Sifton steadfastly maintained were entirely without foundation.

The public debate on the Yukon administration reached the boiling point in June 1898. Late in May the first Yukon newspaper, *The Klondike Nugget,* was founded, and it quickly became the implacable opponent of the government and the chief organ for the interests of the predominantly American population. A few weeks later a government organ, *The Midnight Sun* (later the *Yukon Sun*), was established and sustained by government patronage. The *Nugget* was far more popular and reflected the mood of much of the Klondike population as it struck out fiercely at the government.[2] Reporters were sent out into the streets and bars of Dawson to record the complaints of whatever disappointed miners were hanging around, and little attempt was made to separate embroidered rumour from hard fact. The most common allegations fell into three or four categories. One concerned the closing of Dominion Creek to any further claims transactions because of the confusion arising from attempts to impose the mining regulations. Government officials were said to have manipulated the reopening of the creek for their own benefit. A second group of charges surrounded the ownership of and speculation in claims by government officials. Though legal, it was bitterly resented. Then there were accusations that entry to the gold commissioner's office and the post office was to be arranged principally through bribes. Finally, it was claimed that the new regulations respecting leases or concessions were primarily for the benefit of friends of the government and were detrimental to the progress of placer mining. These charges were not only printed and circulated among the miners, adding to dissension, but they were also assiduously reprinted in the Canadian Conservative press, in some Liberal papers, and internationally. The editor of the *Nugget* made no secret of his collusion with correspondents of *Collier's Weekly,* the *San Francisco Examiner,* the *New York Times,* and *Reuters* of London.[3]

Sifton was bitter at the spreading attacks: "I see the [Toronto] Mail has a more than usually hysterical attack on Yukon administration," he wrote Willison from Ottawa. "The Citizen here has another this morning. I find that Rich, of the Tribune with his usual propensity for treachery & mischief has printed an article totally unjustifiable in its tone which the Tory papers are reprinting." What angered him especially was that his enemies had "fulminated for some months before Parliament met & had not a word to say to me while the House was sitting. Now the House has risen they are starting to manufacture a new set of lies." His initial response was to meet the attacks with refutations in the columns of the *Globe.*[4]

Sifton's explanations did not quell the agitation. When Senator William Templeman, proprietor of the Liberal *Victoria Times,* wrote to suggest that there might be some substance to the Yukon charges and that they should not be ignored, he received a heated response. For over a month the opposition press had been filled with slanderous charges against Yukon officials, replied Sifton, and yet they had been careful to avoid levying one specific charge against any single official.

> What I complain of is, the liberal press have reprinted articles [from the *Nugget*] which have been prepared for the express purpose of damaging the administration without asking for any specific proof that these general charges are well-founded, and I do not see that any liberal paper has a right to refer, in its editorial columns, in general terms to charges against Yukon officials without knowing what charges have been made. The Government is quite prepared to do anything possible to meet the exigencies of the administration in the Yukon district, but for my part I do not see why men, who have gone up there and have faithfully endeavored to do their duty, should be held up by the Liberal press as being under a cloud and charged with corruption when not even the most worthless loafer in Dawson City has yet come forward and made a statement charging any one of them with improper conduct.... I do not intend to pre-suppose that men who were honourable men in their former positions have suddenly become scoundrels and are to be put upon their trial until they are so charged and the specific acts of malfeasance of office are laid before me.[5]

When Laurier proposed a commission to investigate the rising chorus of complaints, Sifton replied tersely: "There are no complaints to investigate. To appoint a commission to investigate would place [the] Government in an indefensible position." Any alleged grievances should be investigated at once by the commissioner on the spot.[6] For the time being the prime minister backed off.

Sifton hoped to brazen out the attacks until William Ogilvie, the new commissioner, had a chance to calm the disputes raging in Dawson. Ogilvie had been instructed in detail about the course he was to pursue, for, whatever his virtues, he was an inexperienced administrator. His was not a trained legal mind, nor had he shown any particular aptitude for decisive leadership. Such qualifications were eminently desirable under the circumstances. When Ogilvie arrived in Dawson in August 1898, he was plunged into an incessant stream of political controversy, backroom conspiracies, charges against a demoralized civil service, and a frankly chaotic administration resulting from the indecision and incompetence of Commissioner Walsh and Gold Commissioner Fawcett. Ogilvie himself became the subject of unfounded rumours of corruption even before he arrived in Dawson, and Sifton wrote consolingly, "I have no doubt that if the Angel Gabriel went to Dawson City he would be reported the next day to be a boodler."[7] At least Ogilvie was spared responsibility for the North-West Mounted Police. Sifton directed that when Walsh departed, Lt. Col. S.B. Steele was to assume charge of the force. But with the government at Ottawa under great pressure, there were endless other duties to perform. In frequent letters Sifton issued directions and offered advice. Most important, he sent up every charge of corruption to which there seemed to be the slightest substance and demanded a careful investigation and immediate report.[8]

Sifton's attempts to forestall a commission of inquiry were destined to fail. On 25 August a meeting of miners in Dawson signed a petition for an investigation into a list of fairly specific charges; and just over a month later the prestigious *Times* of London carried an article by its enterprising colonial editor, Miss Flora Shaw, roundly condemning the Yukon administration.[9] Sifton now found his colleagues, and even his friend J.S. Willison of the *Globe,* insisting that a commission be appointed.

Despite this defeat, Sifton proved to be an adept infighter when it came to shaping the commission. Ogilvie was on the spot; he was still widely admired; and Sifton had always insisted that the commissioner should investigate charges as they arose. Why not assign the task to Ogilvie? The Conservatives naturally wanted an independent judicial commission empowered to investigate every complaint raised against the administration. Sifton was determined that there should be no general fishing expedition. His colleagues eventually concurred, and on 7 October Ogilvie was instructed to investigate the specific charges laid by the miners' meeting.[10]

Once the commission of inquiry had been decided upon, Sifton wanted it carried out strictly and thoroughly. The frame of reference was clear: the miners' charges of 25 August, and only those charges, were to be investigated. Other grievances would be dealt with separately. "You will understand that your report will be published and entered upon the records of Parliament," he cautioned Ogilvie; "you cannot, therefore, be too careful as to the terms in which you express yourself.... The Government have no desire to make a scape-goat of anyone, or to improperly condemn any person for actions that may have been unavoidable." Sifton requested a full report, definite conclusions about each charge, and a transcript of the evidence taken, all to reach Ottawa before the opening of Parliament in 1899. Confident that the charges contained little substance, or at least little that would be politically damaging, Sifton believed that the report would serve to exonerate the government and by association to discredit many of the other allegations.[11]

When evidence pertinent to the inquiry surfaced, Sifton forwarded it to Ogilvie. He added that in justice to the government and to the officials concerned he would require those who had come out to return to Dawson and face the charges against them. Ogilvie was reminded that "it is the desire of the Government that the investigation should be altogether thorough, and that no official should be permitted to shield himself behind any kind of a subterfuge or excuse. Parliament when it meets is entitled to a clear and specific statement which will satisfy every reasonable man that the facts have been thoroughly brought out and investigated." Sifton's own questioning of officials led him to conclude that while they had probably been speculating in gold claims, any actual corruption or dishonesty remained to be proven.[12]

Ogilvie's conduct of the case won few contemporary plaudits. Those opposed to the government considered that he was too narrow in interpreting his powers. The report, which found wrongdoing on the part of only one minor official who had accepted bribes was dismissed by the Conservatives as a whitewash. Supporters of the government, by contrast, thought that Ogilvie had been too informal, too lax in the kind of evidence he allowed. Probably the best assessment is that while Ogilvie was no model judge, he did conduct as thorough an investigation as his instructions permitted. He found that few of the charges could be pinned down with specific evidence and that witnesses who had been prominent in denouncing the government either vanished altogether or became tongue-tied, vague and contradictory under questioning. Technically it could be argued that Sifton's administration had been duly exonerated.[13]

The victory carried little moral conviction. The Yukon officials may have done little that was actually illegal (at least little could ever be proven), but the attitude displayed by the government—and several of Sifton's colleagues were also culpable—was a gross affront to the moral dignity that ought to have accompanied the assertion of government control in that region. Sifton's correspondence with Ogilvie reflects an awareness that government officials must not only *be* upright, but ought to *appear* to be upright as well. That principle was applied by Sifton to some junior officials, who were banished merely because of widespread suspicion of corruption or incompetence. But in senior posts, where special government favourites had been appointed, it was not adhered to at all. A great number of these officials not only used their offices to make money, but displayed it in flagrantly immoral lives. Concerning this the evidence is overwhelming.[14]

It was exactly these issues that most irritated Yukoners. They justifiably resented seeing government officials transported to the Yukon and maintained in comparative luxury at public expense, all the while being free to speculate in gold mines and engage in other forms of profiteering, openly prodigal with their earnings in Dawson gaming houses, and unblushingly traipsing the streets with notorious prostitutes in tow. Sifton was less than convincing when he contended that there was no reason why government officials in the Yukon should not have the same privileges of making investments as they had elsewhere in Canada. The practice was a major source of ammunition for the opposition and was often debated in cabinet. Sifton had always prevailed. He was, however, furious when Postmaster General Mulock sent one of his officials to the Yukon and pointedly publicized the fact that the man had been instructed not to speculate in gold mines. Although in the fall of 1898 he too had privately forbidden a few of the Yukon officials to continue the practice, Sifton concluded that this public announcement called his administration and his defence of his officials into question. Finally in February 1899 he was forced to consent to a general order forbidding such activities, an order that was many months overdue.[15]

The use of inside information for personal gain was a common practice of the day. Yet in the Yukon the abuses were open and highly concentrated in time and space. For thousands of disappointed miners, who often had staked all their savings on a Yukon adventure and the quest for wealth, the spectacle put on by government officials was bound to breed discontent. As Ogilvie put it, "Many of the officials seem to think an appointment to the Yukon Territory a stepping stone to immense wealth."[16]

Optimistically awaiting the results of Ogilvie's report, Sifton told Willison, "I think we have the Yukon business in train to wind up satisfactorily when Parliament meets." All that was likely to turn up were "trifling lapses on the part of the subordinate officials," some of whom might "have been tempted a little beyond their strength." That would not constitute grounds, at least in Sifton's opinion, for condemning either the senior officials or the general administration. The minister of the interior did not think that the Conservatives would want to be responsible in Parliament for the charges being bruited in the Tory press. Indeed, he claimed that nothing would please him more than to see the Conservatives repeat the charges in the House. "In that event," he wrote, "we will be able to get them out in the open where we can fight them and I have no fear of the result."[17] It was a wish that he would see amply fulfilled.

The border tensions of early 1898 had persuaded Prime Minister Laurier and his colleagues that further procrastination in the settlement of the Alaska boundary would be risky. A new discovery of gold, especially in disputed territory, or internal unrest in the Yukon, could provoke a volatile international situation. Partly as a result of Edward Farrer's negotiations in Washington, the Canadian and American governments had agreed in principle by May 1898 that a frontal assault should be made on the long list of outstanding problems between the two countries, including the Alaska boundary, fur sealing in the Bering Sea, Atlantic fisheries, bonding privileges, possible readjustment of the tariff, alien labour laws, mining rights, and several lesser issues.[18] Beginning in August at Québec, and moving subsequently to Washington, an International Joint Commission was to carry out protracted negotiations in hope of producing a formal convention and definite proposals for action by the two governments on each of the issues.

The British side comprised Lord Herschell from England, Sir James Winter of Newfoundland, and Laurier, Sir Louis Davies, Sir Richard Cartwright, and John Charlton. The Canadians were in constant touch with their cabinet colleagues, and in this way Sifton had a not inconsiderable influence on the course of the negotiations. His advice was also important in the preparation of the Canadian case on the boundary and mining issues. Canada still relied on British diplomatic expertise and to a substantial degree on British documentary resources to flesh out her case. Nevertheless, the initial work on the Canadian position on each issue was assigned to different departments, and the drawing up of background memoranda for the boundary and mining cases fell naturally to the Department of the Interior and the Geological Survey.[19]

As a very interested observer, Sifton was guided in offering advice to the Canadian commissioners by the solutions he perceived to be most politically advantageous to the Liberal government. Laurier could ill afford to appear weak in dealing with the Americans; the mood of the country was anti-American, and Sifton readily admitted to sharing such sentiments. He believed that a poor arrangement would be worse than none at all. The two most politically sensitive issues were, in his opinion, the tariff and the Alaska boundary.

Sifton had presented a summary of Canada's case on the boundary to the cabinet within weeks of assuming office. It had been a constant preoccupation ever since. He accepted an extreme interpretation of the St. Petersburg Treaty of 1825 which would have given the United States only a string of disconnected promontories and peninsulas along the coast, while leaving the whole north end of the crucial Lynn Canal to Canada. One of Sifton's staff privately considered the official Canadian case to be "utterly untenable and dishonest."[20] It overlooked the failure to protest American occupation of the disputed territory, and a number of Canadian maps had tacitly acknowledged United States control of a much more generous boundary. But Sifton never seriously believed that the United States would be completely dislodged from territory which she occupied. He presented an initial bargaining position, one from which concessions could be made. The United States, after all, also presented an extreme case, one which would have confirmed American control several miles down Lake Bennett.

Concerned that the Canadians would give in too easily, Sifton journeyed to Québec at the end of September to interview Laurier and Davies. He feared particularly that the boundary question might be referred to arbitration, which he expected would give Canada nothing more than she already possessed—that is, possession north from the summits of the White and

Chilkoot passes. He suggested tying the pelagic sealing dispute, on which the Americans were most anxious for a settlement, to the boundary.

> I would [he told Laurier] insist as a provision antecedent to the reference of the Boundary question to a Commission that whatever the decision of the Commission might be respecting the territory at the head of Lynn Canal we should have undisputed ownership of a port and territory leading to a port upon the canal, either the Chilkat Harbor or Skagway Bay. Dyea would be of no use.
>
> I do not think any contracts for the bonding arrangements will be satisfactory. We require the privilege of using the port for military purposes and for the transport of arms and munitions of war. Besides we wish to build up a town or city which will be a Canadian town or city and a Canadian port where Canadian vessels will have the preference. I need not enlarge upon the desirability of getting a port upon the Lynn Canal.

If the sealing and boundary questions were not tied together, Canada would have no leverage. "The acquisition of a port on the Lynn Canal is the only method we have of getting back the trade of the Yukon District, which has been entirely lost owing to the failure of our railway policy of last Session."[21]

When the meetings resumed in Washington in November, the Americans offered Canada equal commercial privileges on the Lynn Canal and across the disputed strip of territory, provided the British side would concede full American sovereignty. Canada rejected the offer, as it was worse than the status quo, where sovereignty at least remained in dispute. In reply, the British side substantially adopted Sifton's proposal: Canadian control of Pyramid Harbour and a strip of land back of it along the Chilkat River to the Chilkat Pass. At first the Americans seemed disposed to agree, subject to restrictions on fortification and a nominal American title to sovereignty. Apart from this concession, the boundary would be settled as it was. Sifton told Laurier in January 1899 that these proposals seemed satisfactory, if hardly perfect, and reminded him that great care was vital when negotiating the terms on which Canada would assume control.[22]

Then Sifton received a disturbing letter from Davies. The Americans were trying to impose a time limit on Canadian control, and the Canadians were attempting to resist, "insisting that it must run as long as we maintain proper Customs Houses & police protection." Sifton immediately informed his colleagues David Mills and Sir Richard Scott. Both promptly told the commissioners that if Canada could not secure virtual sovereignty, it would be best to drop the negotiations. Sifton vigorously added that he had not understood Laurier to refer to any time limit. "I took it as a matter of course that the arrangement was to be perpetual. If it is not I would not make it. . . . I think a time limit to our concession ... would simply put us in a ridiculous position. Who would build a railway on a Canadian charter under such circumstances?" The objection had been recognized, replied Davies. He and Laurier still proposed Canadian control as long as police and customs posts were maintained, "—in other words, practically until we abandoned the port. Would that not be satisfactory if we can obtain it?" Beside the query Sifton penned a blunt "No." Undoubtedly he did not believe that such an arrangement would sit well with the Canadian electorate.[23]

By this time negotiations were bogged down on trade issues as well, Reciprocity had not received serious discussion until the commission met in Washington. Even then the Canadian government showed no interest in a broad agreement, but merely on a narrow list of specific natural products. When asked about putting horses and horned cattle on the free list, Sifton replied that it would be detrimental to western interests, which expected to have the British Columbia market when the Crow's Nest Pass line was complete. Would he approve a lowered tariff on lumber, rather than free lumber? "I would not compromise in any way," he answered. "If they will not give us free lumber I would advocate preserving our own independence and dealing with the subject as we may see fit hereafter."[24] Free lumber would have been extremely popular in the West, but if the Americans did not agree, Canada must be in a position to protect her own lumber industry and develop her own markets. His ideas on mineral ores were based on the same principle, and in some cases, such as pig iron, Sifton believed that protective tariffs would allow the quick development of a viable Canadian industry which would be killed by reciprocity.

Of greatest concern to him and his western constituents was the possible removal of the duty on flour. His views had not changed from early 1897 when he had promised, "I will fight that question all the way through." The question was basically political. Eastern Canadians and small millers believed they would benefit from removal of the tariff, because they expected it would lower prices and stimulate competition for the two companies which monopolized the industry in Canada, Lake of the Woods Milling Company and the Ogilvie Company. Removal of the duty, wrote Sifton, would "bring upon us serious political injury. The large millers would be rendered determindedly hostile to us, and the small millers would never be heard of in our defence." He added that "as a matter of fact the large millers always control the small millers so that the political influence is all in favour of retaining the duty."[25]

Perhaps the best example of Sifton's hard-headed political realism and suspicious anti-Americanism arose in connection with a proposal to settle disputes over bonding privileges on Canadian railway lines in the United States and American lines in Canada. Laurier proposed an international tribunal or a court of arbitration, but the CPR was hostile to such an arrangement and was vigorously supported by Tarte and Sifton. The minister of the interior told Laurier that it would be impossible to reach any such treaty in a form that would be fair to Canada:

> I do not believe that an international tribunal can be constituted which will be satisfactory, and I regard with very great fear the constitution of such a body where the United States would constantly appear for the purpose of driving us into a corner and compelling concessions on an unfair and strained constructions of the Treaty. Moreover such a treaty would give the United States to some extent territorial rights in Canada with the privilege of asserting the right of the stronger power to insist upon what they would claim to be the fair interpretation of the treaty. It would be the thin edge of the wedge, which would ultimately result in seriously injuring us. Moreover, the American Railway Companies are desperately anxious to have this matter taken up. It is quite clear that they see the advantage it would be to them, consequently it would be very likely to be a disadvantage to us. I do not think myself that there is any danger of the [existing] bonding privileges being abrogated. I know the sentiment of the North Western States pretty well: the sentiment there is extremely strong against any interference with free transportation across Canada and through Canadian waters. I doubt if any political party in the United States will be able to abrogate the bonding privileges against the determined opposition of the New England and the North Western States. There is a bare possibility that they might do so, I think it is extremely improbable, and I would rather take the chances than get the worst of it in a treaty, which I think we would unquestionably get if a treaty should be made.[26]

By the end of November, Sifton was thoroughly put out with the American proposals. "Looking over all the suggestions which have been made in connection with this treaty very carefully and very deliberately," he told Laurier, "as far as I can remember every suggestion which has come has seemed to be that Canada should give away something that was of value to her, no intimation being thrown out that we were to get anything worth while in return for it." He was prepared "to make the best of things" and support whatever the majority of the cabinet decided upon. Nevertheless, "I feel that I ought to say to you that it will be a frightful mistake for us to make any concessions to the United States in the proposed treaty for which we do not get the most ample returns. I am further convinced that the Americans will not make the treaty unless it is altogether jug-handled in their favour."[27]

Throughout the negotiations Sifton had maintained an attitude that might well have pleased Sir John A. Macdonald himself. He emerged as a full-fledged moderate protectionist, willing to seek reciprocity only in hay, potatoes, eggs, mineral ores, and lumber, and virtually nothing more. By late January some momentarily bright prospects of achieving a rather thin treaty had vanished. "Don't you think you have given the Americans long enough to let you know whether they want to make a treaty or not?" Sifton asked Laurier.[28]

In Washington, however, Laurier was under some pressure to reach a settlement of the boundary issue on the American terms. Several ministers believed again that he might give in and present Sir Charles Tupper with a major election issue. Hurriedly Sifton, together with Mills, Blair, Fielding, and Tarte, rushed to New York to confer with Laurier, Davies, and Cartwright. Ironically, about the same time that the Canadian ministers were meeting, news of the suggested compromise on the Lynn Canal was somehow leaked to the American press. Instantaneous and violent public reaction, especially from the west coast, forced the American authorities to withdraw their proposals.[29]

For Laurier and Davies this was a bitter disappointment. Yet the two sides probably had never really been close to agreement. Each was precluded by nationalistic political pressures from conceding more. The Americans could not allow permanent control of a port, an access strip, and the Yukon trade to Canada; Canada could accept nothing less. Laurier's proposal amounted to perpetual control, and he probably would have signed a treaty along these lines despite Sifton's reservations. But the Americans insisted upon a time limit. The Liberals had attacked the Conservatives for giving away in 1871 what had been Canada's under the 1825 treaty. To concede a time limit, along with American sovereignty on the Lynn Canal, and to put the rest of the boundary to an arbitration in which Canada was likely to gain very little would leave the government open to a similar but politically much more dangerous attack—that of giving away in 1899 what the Conservatives had secured in 1871. Referring the entire boundary, including the Lynn Canal, to arbitration was politically much safer and might take the onus of an unsatisfactory settlement off the government.

On his return to Ottawa, Sifton was in a somewhat better frame of mind. Still the negotiations dragged on. Laurier badly wanted a treaty of some sort or a reasonable excuse for breaking off the talks. Even if the Americans were to sign a treaty conceding Pyramid Harbour, advised Sifton, it would be in the full knowledge that such provisions would never pass the United States Senate, given the temper of the people. He complained again of "the condescending willingness of the American people to take everything Canada has got and give nothing in return." In mid-February Laurier summoned Sifton and Fielding to Washington. Agreement, he told them, could not be reached, even on terms of arbitration. With no settlement on the boundary, Canada was not prepared to sign on any of the other issues. Sifton was delighted. "The matter is in very satisfactory shape," he wrote, "and the best evidence of that is the furious wail from Tupper, whose campaign thunder is entirely destroyed."[30]

The conference had been a failure in terms of its announced goals. Virtually nothing was concluded between the two countries. From the point of view of the Liberal government, however, the failure itself could be portrayed as a virtue. Canada had not given in to the United States. Despite pressure to settle from both the United States and Britain, Laurier could argue that he had bargained in good faith but was unwilling to accept anything less than equitable treatment.

Sifton had made a number of specific recommendations which influenced the course of negotiations. His most significant contribution, however, was the vigilant anti-Americanism and suspicion of American motives which he inspired in his colleagues. None of his Ottawa-based colleagues even approximated the steady stream of vehement and sometimes trenchant commentary which he sent to Laurier, Davies, and Cartwright at Washington. Without Sifton, Laurier might have given in and signed a treaty. Had he done so, he might have been in serious political difficulty. Canada lost little, even along the boundary, by the delay.

By the spring of 1899 a stalemate had been produced on two fronts with respect to Yukon policy. Along the Alaska boundary the existing holdings of the two countries were confirmed as a *modus vivendi*. The territory along the boundary remained in dispute, and the two sides were still searching for an acceptable arbitration formula. Nor did the Ogilvie Commission remove all the questions raised concerning the internal administration of the Yukon.

Most Canadians took satisfaction in the failure of the International Joint Commission. The Opposition found it much harder to attack a failure to agree than to criticize the specific provisions of a treaty. But they believed the government was vulnerable on the Yukon administration and anticipated uncovering an enormous scandal which would altogether erase the memory of the seamy McGreevy-Langevin affair with which the Liberals had assaulted the Tory government in 1891, when Hector Langevin, a leading Tory minister, was driven from office. Even as Sifton spoke smugly of the destruction of Tupper's campaign thunder, the Opposition leader and his son, Sir Charles Hibbert Tupper, were preparing a massive assault on Sifton himself.

While several members of the government shared in the responsibility of Yukon administration and were the objects of opposition censure, Sifton was plainly the principal target. The air was thick with charges of nepotism, ministerial and official corruption, and incompetence. The frequently changed mining regulations were held to be ruinous to Yukon development and to the development of placer mining in particular. The government had not moved fast enough to establish a reliable mail service and other essential systems of communication; and patronage had been blatantly abused.

The Conservatives believed that there must be some substance underlying the torrent of charges. The Ogilvie Commission simply was too restricted in scope to satisfy them. And Sifton insisted on keeping it so. The report must not contain any personal opinions, or comments on public policy, or anything falling outside the limits specified in the commission, he had written Ogilvie:

> No question of public policy such for instance as the advisability of Officials holding claims or anything of that kind has any place in the reports. The investigation is simply as to whether Officers of the Government have or have not acted honestly in the discharge of the official duties with which they were charged by the Government. It is not a question of the opinion of anyone at all. Specific charges being made against any person accused and all proof being given of such charge is what should be in the report. It is not your business to conduct an inquisition.[31]

An inquisition was precisely what the Tuppers had in mind. When they launched their attack at the end of March and early April, their object was either to force the government to accept a full judicial inquiry into all aspects of Yukon administration or, failing that, to suggest by listing the profuse charges that the government had a great deal to hide. The two Tuppers, and Sifton in reply, each tested the patience of their fellow MPs and the Hansard reporters with seven-hour addresses.[32]

In his speech of 30 March, cannily timed for the day preceding the Easter recess so that it would have maximum impact in the country before Sifton had opportunity for reply, Sir Charles Hibbert Tupper charged blackmail, bribery, unfair and fraudulent use of information by officials, conflict of interest and abuse of power on the part of the dominion lands agent (F.C. Wade), poor postal service, lack of attention to sewage disposal at Dawson, and abuse of liquor permits. A great many of the officers were the objects of individual censure.

Evidently nervous before Tupper's speech, Sifton was visibly relieved when it was over.[33] The Tories, it seemed, had little concrete evidence for their allegations, certainly little that the minister of the interior could not answer effectively. While he would not claim that his administration had been perfect, Sifton was prepared to declare that "we have exercised care, forethought, diligence, promptness and circumspection from beginning to end, in every possible respect." The government had made mistakes, but had learned from them, for the Yukon was a region of unique, unprecedented needs. The officials appointed to the Yukon were competent to do what was required, and each of the senior officials was vigorously defended. If the Opposition wanted to make specific charges against specific individuals, Sifton was prepared to allow the fullest possible investigation. Meanwhile, there seemed to be a great deal of unwarranted inference which placed all the officials under a cloud. Finally he noted in Tupper's speech "a continuous trend of suggestions that there was some improper or corrupt connection between myself or some member or members of the Government with the Klondike district." He challenged any Tory to place a specific accusation before the House; "he will get his investigation, and I will be able to convince the hon. gentleman who makes that charge that discretion on his part would have been the better part of valour." Sifton's speech was well received, and Laurier congratulated him on it as "a complete vindication of your administration."[34]

The Opposition hardly concurred, though momentarily discomfited. Perhaps J. Ross Robertson, publisher of the *Toronto Telegram* and Tory MP for East Toronto, best summarized his colleagues' sentiment when he observed, "I cannot for one moment believe that there could be so much smoke without some fire."[35] Sir Charles Tupper attempted to salvage the situation by denouncing the Ogilvie Commission as a "farce." "It is no answer to the charges which are ringing over three continents of incapacity and mismanagement and corruption in regard to the Yukon administration." There was a dark cloud hanging over Canada's international reputation which could be dispelled only through an open judicial inquiry. It might mean the loss of the minister of the interior, but it would save Canada's reputation and, perhaps, even the government itself. "Had they granted such a commission, *whether the charges were found too true or not,*" declared Tupper, "it would have disposed completely of any suspicion of complicity on the part of the Government."[36]

Sir Charles had practically admitted Sifton's contention that there was no factual basis in the hands of the Opposition upon which charges could be laid, though he still pressed for a broad inquiry. The minister of the interior chose simply to ignore the speech in the House of Commons. Privately he felt the elder Tupper was getting soft in the brain. "I certainly do not think it would be wise to answer the fool according to his folly," he wrote with unwarranted arrogance. "I fancy that the old man will fall into quiet oblivion within the next two or three years."[37] Prophetic in the long run, Sifton was ill-advised to dismiss Tupper so readily. Believing that public opinion was aroused and that Sifton, if not the Laurier government, was vulnerable, the Tuppers held tenaciously to the issue.

In mid-May they varied the fare slightly by attacking Sifton for receiving government funds as a partial reimbursement for costs incurred in the electoral frauds cases of 1896–97.[38] Then as evidence appeared from Ogilvie's investigations and as continued complaints filtered down from the Klondike, Sir Charles Hibbert Tupper warmed up to yet another assault. On 27 and 28 June he exhausted the House with a nine-hour barrage attempting to meet Sifton's demands for particulars of the charges being levied.[39] He reiterated many of the earlier accusations, but now both Walsh and Ogilvie came under attack, as well as Sifton for compliance in the wilful exploitation of the country by officials. Tupper asserted that Sifton had recommended the appointment of officials "who were incapable, incompetent, inefficient and corrupt, to positions requiring experience, technical knowledge and integrity of character." He also declared that "the Honourable Clifford Sifton, the Minister of the Interior has been guilty of favouritism and partiality in the administration of the laws and regulations applicable to the district of the Yukon in the North-West Territories." Specifically, he said that Sifton's former law partners, A.E. Philp and A.D. Cameron, had obtained four dredging leases directly, and several others indirectly, and that Sifton and Walsh had had an interest in them. Something of the tenor of Tupper's speech is indicated by a passage which he quoted from Francis Parkman's *Montcalm and Wolfe,* implying an obvious parallel with the condition of New France near the close of the French regime:

Canada was the prey of official jackals—true lion's providers—since they helped to prepare a way for the imperial beast, who, roused at last from his lethargy, was gathering his strength to seize her for his own. Honesty could not be expected from a body of men clothed with arbitrary and ill-defined powers, ruling with absolute sway an unfortunate people who had no voice in their own destinies, and answerable only to an apathetic master 3,000 miles away.

In calling for a royal commission, Sir Hibbert Tupper declared that if, after a full investigation, his charges were not substantiated, he was fully prepared to resign his seat.

Devastating as the charges appeared at first glance, Sifton was untroubled, and he replied with cool aplomb.[40] He pointed out that almost all of Sir Hibbert's claims were framed "in such language that no possible information upon the subject can be gathered." In other words, they remained ill-defined and vague. For this reason he dismissed most of them out-of-hand. As to the specific charges concerning himself, he demonstrated with withering sarcasm that Tupper did not even have his facts straight. There was nothing to prevent his former law partners from applying for leases on the same basis as anyone else, and that was all that they had done. The return to Parliament from which Tupper had gleaned his information regarding mining leases showed clearly that while they had applied for leases, they had secured none. Similarly, he defended Major Walsh by exposing the weakness of the evidence. Sir Hibbert had held up as an example of good policy Macdonald's appointment of a royal commission to investigate allegations of corruption in connection with the building of the CPR. With irony and some personal bitterness, Sifton commented, "That great statesman, in the generosity of his heart and in the desire for purity of administration, issued a royal commission. What was it to investigate? It was to investigate the conduct of his political opponents. It was not to investigate the administration of his own officers." By contrast, when charges of corruption were levied against the Tory government, had these been looked into by any royal commission? They had not. Instead, the government sent its own officers to investigate, and any indictable offenses were laid before the courts. That was exactly what Sifton proposed to do.

By destroying many of Sir Hibbert Tupper's arguments and dismissing the rest as too vague to merit serious consideration, Sifton not only saved his position, but also enhanced his reputation as one of the ablest debaters on the government side. His course was politically astute, for he recognized that the public is rarely impressed by massive marshalling of detail—especially when some of it can be shown to be erroneous or misleading. For their part, the Tuppers now prepared to carry the issue to the public platform, where they hoped to keep it alive as a major issue in anticipated general elections.[41]

The editor of *The Canadian Magazine*, by no means a supporter of the government, concluded that "not much has been brought forth to substantiate the charges made by the London *Times* and by the Canadian Opposition." Sifton had not always exercised the best judgment, and some minor acts of corruption had been exposed. "On the whole, however, the honourable gentleman has come through the ordeal fairly well, though perhaps not with increased public respect." This last cavil was important. Those less willing to be generous would perhaps have agreed with Governor General Lord Minto, who told Queen Victoria, "The Government . . . have weathered the attacks, though I am much inclined to think the management of affairs in the Gold Districts would not bear very close scrutiny."[42]

9

# A Party Organ:
# Sifton and the *Manitoba Free Press*
# (1897–98)

The constant criticism from Winnipeg Liberals, particularly their repetition of the Yukon charges, greatly troubled Clifford Sifton. From almost anywhere else it might have been bearable, and even slowly and quietly overcome. But coming from the heart of his supposed bastion of power, it was intolerable. Winnipeg after all aspired to be the metropolitan centre for the vast district from the Lakehead to the Rockies. The attitude of its newspapers and politicians coloured political debate across the West. Long before the Yukon administration emerged as the central topic of political debate in the summer of 1898, Sifton had determined upon drastic action to counter and if possible to silence his critics: he would take the politically risky step of securing his own newspaper to form a reliable base for defending government policy. In the future, he hoped, it would provide a solid rallying point for all western Liberals. Nevertheless, there first would be a bitter internal battle in the party against those who opposed Sifton's policies in principle or out of self-interest.

Robert Lorne Richardson, MP for Lisgar and publisher and sometime editor of the *Winnipeg Tribune,* was an industrious, ambitious, and foolhardy journalist. Born in Lanark, Ontario, in 1860, Richardson had served with the Montreal *Star* and Toronto *Globe* before going to Winnipeg, where he acted as city editor of the Liberal *Daily Sun,* which folded in 1889. Indeed, such was the rate of mortality among Winnipeg newspapers that for a few weeks early in 1890 the *Manitoba Free Press* had the field to itself as it trained its guns on Greenway and his colleagues. The Liberals of course could not allow such a situation to continue and gave Richardson's *Tribune* heavy support when it first appeared on 28 January 1890.

Richardson had within his grasp the opportunity to make his paper the leading journal of western Canada, and he fumbled it. There was no effective Conservative paper, and the *Free Press,* with some justice, was regarded as the organ of the CPR and the business community. Richardson was never able to realize that necessary fusion of the metropolitan aspirations of his city with the concerns of the rural population that would have won his paper broad acceptance. That it survived at all was apparently the result of government patronage and the flogging of the daily and weekly editions throughout the province by the Liberal party machinery. But there was little weight in the paper's declamations. Richardson saw himself as a populist, giving voice to popular grievances and attacking the CPR, all kinds of monopoly, the protective tariff, and separate schools. His principles, of which he made much, were exceedingly flexible. He could flail the CPR on the one hand and accept a railway pass from President Van Horne with the other.[1] He could pose as a supporter of purity in politics and use corrupt methods in his own campaigns. He could spew forth a fountain of verbiage in praise of free trade and plead with Sifton for a tariff compromise suitable to help save his seat; he would defend the Fielding tariff in one editorial and claim widespread western disappointment in another.

Although Sifton pushed the *Tribune* as much as anyone in the Greenway government, he had never been much impressed with it.[2] It merely constituted the best available partisan propaganda. But Richardson had not the wit to perceive that 23 June 1896 had changed the position of his paper. Not only was he now a government MP, but he had also been appointed a party whip. In September 1896 the paper plunged recklessly along in maintaining that there could be no compromise on the school issue when it was well known that Sifton and Laurier were trying to arrange one. Did Richardson and his editor, J.J. Moncrieff, not realize the need to accommodate the new political realities? Could they not understand that they would shortly have to reverse themselves? Sifton was furious. "I cannot conceive the management of the paper being so silly as to permit an article of that kind being published," he fumed. "They ought to understand that the time has arrived when they cannot afford to use their editorial columnes for the purpose of fads."[3] The *Tribune* and its owner, in other words, would have to learn the difference between being an opposition organ in national politics, enjoying the considerable latitude possible in the position, and the discipline of being on the government side. As a member of Parliament, and of the Liberal caucus, Richardson would have to fall into line. However, he saw matters differently. "I certainly would not think of allowing my position as a member to interfere with the newspaper," he told Sifton in the course of a minor dispute.[4] (Time would demonstrate that this was but another dispensable principle.)

The *Tribune* was not about to be a tractable party organ. The "hope of the country," Richardson wrote, lay "in honest outspoken papers that have the fearlessness to frankly admonish its friends when they are, or appear to be, doing wrong." The Laurier government had done well, "but it is not immaculate, and in frankness it must be confessed that certain phases of its policy which have brought adverse criticism, seem to have deserved it. The Tribune has not hesitated to acknowledge upon several occasions in the past, that the government did not rise fully to its opportunities."[5] Plainly the paper was anxious to justify its growing criticism of the government on the matter of reducing expenditures, on the tariff, and on Yukon policy.

On occasion Richardson even offered Sifton some homespun philosophy. When the minister was under attack for alleged nepotism, the MP from Lisgar advised, "I presume you have been long enough in politics not to worry much over newspaper criticism. The best way is to keep right ahead & in the words of the old rhyme 'Trust in God & do the right.' A man who follows the right path need pay little attention to the slanderer. All will come right in its own good time."[6] None of Richardson's recent behaviour was calculated to reassure Sifton about the continued usefulness of the *Tribune*. It was probably about this time that he decided to acquire the *Manitoba Free Press*.

Stretching back to his college association with the *Acta Victoriana*, Sifton had had a long and nearly continuous connection with newspapers. He had become a shareholder in the *Brandon Sun* almost as soon as he reached the city and contributed to its columns for some years. While in the provincial government, he had not failed to see that the *Sun* received a hefty slice of the patronage pie, which it perhaps deserved as the strongest government organ in western Manitoba.[7] Shortly after he arrived in Ottawa, he had helped to engineer a reorganization of the *Sun* under the Western Publishing Company. This weekly paper was, of course, very important to his home constituency, and he appears to have owned as much as one-third of the capital stock, held in trust for him by the directors.[8]

To move from a minor political investment in a small weekly paper to absolute control of the largest, most influential journal in western Canada entailed some political and financial risk. The *Free Press* had been founded in 1872 by William F. Luxton and John A. Kenney and was the only newspaper to survive in Winnipeg—termed by the *Tribune* "a journalistic cemetery"—throughout the ensuing turbulent quarter-century. Luxton had early carved out a substantial constituency of support. He attacked the dual cultural institutions of Manitoba, as might have been expected of a good Ontario Grit. He supported prohibition, attacked the protective tariff and dominion lands administration, and generally reflected the views of many transplanted easterners. After 1878 the Conservatives made repeated attempts to establish a viable Tory paper which would defend protection, railway monopoly, and other policies of the Macdonald government; each was an ignominious failure. The *Free Press* had a *raison d'être* as the advocate of incipient Winnipeg metropolitanism and the voice of western frustrations; the others had almost nothing beyond their immediate political purposes.

The *Free Press* editor also liked to make much of his political independence, but it was never complete and gradually became more circumscribed.[9] The paper expanded its facilities in 1885, but its precarious financial position the following year forced Luxton to incorporate as a joint stock venture, The Manitoba Free Press Company, with an authorized capital stock of $100,000. As the major shareholder, Luxton continued as managing editor and president. Other directors included Alexander Macdonald, D.H. McMillan, W.F. Alloway, D. Archibald McNee, and D.L. McIntyre.[10] Luxton was not sufficiently astute as a politician or businessman to appreciate how vulnerable his position was becoming.

By 1888 Prime Minister Macdonald was not only disgusted with the shape of Manitoba politics, but also fed up after a decade of continuous failure to establish a Conservative organ. *The Call*, the latest such venture, was verging on collapse and Macdonald decided to ask the CPR to bail it out. President Sir George Stephen was not enthusiastic. "It is not a good thing for the C.P.R. Co. to be supposed to have anything to do with newspapers, if it can be avoided," he told the prime minister. Should it prove essential, some trusted man would have to hold the stock; "I could not, nor could any CPR man." The problem lay "in the all out certainty that the paper cant be made to pay, & that it must sooner or later 'bust.' "[11]

For the time being Macdonald was stymied. Then, desperately in need of funds, the *Free Press* accepted, on 6 September 1888, a five-year loan from Sir Donald Smith of $26,000, for which Smith received 796 shares (face value, $79,600) as collateral.[12] This suggested a new plan to Macdonald. Perhaps it could be arranged to have the *Free Press* absorb *The Call*. Luxton might thus be induced to tone down his attacks on the Conservatives and the National Policy, while continuing to flail away at Greenway, as the price for the elimination of one of his principal competitors. A few months later Sir William Van Horne, who had succeeded Stephen as president of the CPR, was persuaded to purchase *The Call* for $33,500. In February 1889 the capital stock of the *Free Press* was increased to $133,500, the additional 335 shares being turned over to Van Horne in return for *The Call*. Finally, at the beginning of 1890 the *Free Press* was loaned $40,000—probably by Smith—to buy out the *Sun,* its last competitor in Winnipeg.[13] Thus, in less than two years the *Free Press* had secured its financial survival and supremacy in the field— but it had lost its editorial independence. Luxton had sold his soul to the devil. The devil would exact his due.

# AN OVERWORKED ORGAN.

WILFRID LAURIER—I'm afraid this blaze is going to be somewhat bigger than any stream Van and Clif will be able to pump out of that old masheen.

—Toronto Telegram.

Plate 17. When the *Winnipeg Tribune* published this cartoon (12 November 1898), it was in the midst of efforts to raise a revolt among western Liberals against Sifton. Laurier had already repudiated the appeals of the dissidents. It was assumed that Sir William Van Horne and the CPR still had a voice in the Sifton-controlled *Free Press*.

Plate 18. William Ogilvie's tenure as Yukon commissioner was one of the least happy chapters in the life of the famous northern explorer and surveyor. He was an ineffective administrator, unable to cope with the tensions between the local populace and the administration at Ottawa.

BOUNDARY LINE ON CHILKOOT PASS ALASKA 1898

Plate 19. At the provisional boundary on the Chilkoot Pass in disputed territory thousands of gold seekers paused for customs inspection by the North-West Mounted Police. The hordes of prospectors posed unprecedented difficulties for the dominion government, which resulted in some of the most serious political attacks on Sifton.

Plate 20. Mechanization, including the use of steam engines, began to have a limited impact upon prairie farming in the 1890's.

Plate 21. Ceremonies with the Chipewyan Indians at Fort Smith on 17 July 1899 constituted the last phase of the negotiation of Treaty No. 8.

Plate 22. As they pulled into Winnipeg, thousands of immigrants had their first glimpses of the prairie lands to which they were being drawn in increasing numbers by the turn of the century. Sifton not only helped to stimulate the increased flow of immigrants, but also to settle them on the land with astonishingly few administrative problems.

Plate 23. "In the traditions of the sect . . . that first generation of Doukhobor women in Canada are remembered, not as builders of houses, but as breakers of land . . . women of the North Colony attached towlines to their ploughs, tied sticks at intervals to the lines, and in teams of twenty-four, two to each stick, dragged the ploughs, guided by old men, through the thick prairie sod." (G. Woodcock and I. Avakumovic, *The Doukhobors*, p. 162.)

It was not long before Luxton found that Smith and Van Horne had little compunction about exerting pressure. Unfortunately, he did not know when enough was enough. Despite Van Horne's desire for an accommodation with the Greenway government following the 1891 election, the *Free Press* editor continued to attack Greenway and Sifton. Writing early in 1893 to John Mather, an Ottawa businessman whom Van Horne had asked to supervise the paper for him and Smith, the CPR president angrily declared, "I do not think we should mince matters any longer. I begin to believe that Mr. Luxton is partially insane, and that we have no alternative but to put somebody else in charge of the concern."[14] Van Horne was convinced that Luxton's reckless course was likely to ruin the *Free Press* and endanger the money of those who had invested in it.

Accordingly, Luxton was advised that if he could raise the capital loaned and the interest upon it, Van Horne and Smith would gladly leave the paper to him. In the financial climate of 1893, however, it was impossible to raise such a sum. As soon as the five-year deadline on Sir Donald Smith's loan expired and absolute control of the company passed to him, the *Free Press* directors met and fired Luxton. They replaced him with Molyneux St. John, a CPR publicity writer and a friend of Laurier with suitable Liberal leanings. "I have no doubt," wrote Sifton with marked pleasure, that the editorial policy of the *Free Press* "will be very much more satisfactory to the Liberal party at large than it has been for the past four years."[15]

So it was for two years. St. John was released for some reason in the summer of 1895 and replaced by D.L. Beaton, an able and efficient wordsmith of no marked convictions. He followed a course that became increasingly critical of the Manitoba government as the dominion election of 1896 approached; there seems little doubt that this reflected the wishes of Sir Donald A. Smith. Following the election there was another sharp shift, first to neutrality, and then to increasing favour toward Sifton and the Laurier government.

Smith and Van Horne were reluctant newspaper proprietors. For most of the time that they had been connected with the paper, it had not been profitable. From a public relations point of view, it was a disaster. In 1893, after the ouster of Luxton, Van Horne wrote to the *Tribune* to explain his position, adding, "My small and accidental interest is now in the hands of Mr. Mather, and I may say, by way of advertisement, that it has long been for sale at less than cost." The same held true, he told a correspondent, for the interest of Sir Donald Smith.[16] But the times were no more auspicious for any would-be purchaser than they had been for Luxton. Smith and Van Horne, after all, had together put $99,500 into the venture.

The Winnipeg Conservatives were able to raise about $40,000 to start a new Tory organ, the *Nor'Wester,* in 1894 with Luxton as editor; it was a weak, money-losing proposition that eventually became the *Winnipeg Telegram.*[17] Having invested so heavily in their own paper, it was thereafter practically impossible for the Tories to consider buying the *Free Press*. Following the general election of 1896, Hugh John Macdonald scouted the possibility and was informed by Van Horne that "it certainly could not be bought for less than $75,000."[18] Such a sum was out of the question with the party treasury practically empty. That the Tories were interested at all simply reflected the dismal performance of the *Nor'Wester*.

Nor had the Liberals been interested as long as the *Tribune* was suitable. They were angered periodically at *Free Press* criticism, for it carried a good deal of weight. Premier Greenway wrote to Sifton early in 1897 threatening a break with the CPR unless the paper's policy changed. Sifton showed the premier's letter to Mather and to Van Horne; the latter promptly denied having any great influence upon the paper. It was "absurd," Van Horne told Major Walsh, to believe that he controlled it, though he admitted that on occasion his word carried weight with Mather in determining policy. "I gave up my stock in the *Free Press* long ago," he wrote, "and charged the whole thing to profit and loss simply because I did not wish to have anything to do with a newspaper."[19] The statement bordered upon downright fabrication. Technically he had assigned the stock to Mather, but there was no question as to where the real control of the paper lay.

Upon receipt of a further letter of complaint from Attorney General J.D. Cameron of Manitoba, Sifton told Mather that *Free Press* policy had caused Manitoba Liberals "to be exasperated to the last degree." The paper was regarded as "about the worst enemy we have." Neither Sifton nor his friends desired to control or influence the paper's political views. "We do not ask for its support, we only ask that it shall be conducted as a decent and reliable news paper, coming as near to telling the truth as to what is going on as news papers generally do. At the present time it is as far removed from these characteristics as can well be imagined."[20]

Probably Sifton's intentions went no further than he indicated to Mather. During the spring of 1897 the *Free Press* moderated its attitude to Greenway and was very favourable to Sifton, which was hardly surprising when it is remembered that the Crow's Nest Pass Railway arrangements were under negotiation. Sifton had even been attempting to strengthen the *Tribune*'s position. Since shortly after the involvement of Van Horne and Smith in 1889, the *Free Press* had secured a marked competitive advantage because it had exclusive access in Winnipeg to all North American telegraphic news services through the CPR telegraph and its connections. Its evening competitors blatantly copied news items from the *Free Press,* which was a morning paper. To strike at the competition, the *Free Press* began issuing an evening news bulletin, delivered free to subscribers. In the spring of 1897 Sifton attempted to reach an agreement with the *Free Press* which would result in cancellation of the evening bulletin and the sharing of the franchises with the *Tribune*.

Two factors conspired to kill the scheme. One was Greenway's revival of the Winnipeg-Duluth railway project, to which both the CPR and Sifton were opposed, but which Richardson and the *Tribune* supported. The second was Sifton's own growing disenchantment with the *Tribune*. In midsummer 1897 J.B. Somerset, business manager of the *Free Press*, arrived in Ottawa, ostensibly to discuss the proposed arrangements with the *Tribune*. Almost certainly the real subject of his talks with Sifton was the possible purchase of the *Free Press*. Somerset believed that completing any such arrangement as that contemplated with the *Tribune* would seriously weaken the future prospects of the *Free Press*. Shortly thereafter Sifton told Richardson that the Winnipeg-Duluth railway scheme "has knocked my arrangements . . . all to pieces. I had the matter practically arranged and it would have been consummated by this time were it not for the fact that this scheme came up, and for reasons which will readily lend themselves to you the people in control did not feel disposed to let go." The minister of the interior still professed a willingness to make the arrangements.[21] It was a grand deception, and Richardson was completely taken in.

Circumstantial evidence would place Sifton's interest in purchasing the *Free Press* no later than some time in July 1897. By the time he returned from his trip to the Yukon, the process for the takeover was well advanced. Even assuming a minimum of two months in which to conduct a careful investigation into the standing and prospects of the paper and keeping in mind the timing of Somerset's visit to Ottawa, the decision could not be placed any later. Sifton's explanations to Richardson sounded plausible, but merely obscured his real intention.

The unanswered questions asked ever since have been, why would the CPR officials sell the paper to Sifton and what was their *quid pro quo?* It has been speculated that it was a reward for pushing the Crow's Nest Pass agreement through or for some supposed interest that Van Horne and Smith acquired in the Yukon. The probability, however, is that Sifton's was the first viable offer that Van Horne and Smith had received. There is plenty of evidence that they had wished to sell their interest for some years, even at a considerable loss. The *Free Press* seems to have been acquired by Smith and Van Horne solely as a political obligation, and Van Horne believed that he would be farther ahead financially if his money were in a bank drawing interest. By 1897, furthermore, the paper badly required some new equipment, if not an altogether new plant, an investment in which neither Van Horne nor Smith wished to become involved. Finally, Van Horne had as high an opinion of Sifton as he did of any politician and for the time being counted him as friendly to the CPR. Quite possibly it is not necessary to look any farther than this for an explanation of the sale.

The exact amount paid by Sifton to acquire control of the paper is not known, but it would not likely have been less than the $75,000 which Van Horne had quoted to Hugh John Macdonald a year earlier. By the end of January 1898 some 1120 of the 1335 authorized shares had been transferred to Sifton's lawyer, C.A. Masten of Toronto. Van Horne also sent Sifton a complete financial statement early in January, along with a request that Somerset be continued as business manager.[22] The whole operation was heavily shrouded in secrecy, as only Van Horne and Smith, Somerset and Mather, Masten and J.A.M. Aikins, the CPR lawyer in Winnipeg, were cognizant of the real change in ownership. Great pains were taken to keep Sifton's name out of the transaction.

The purchase is the best available indicator of Sifton's comfortable financial position. He was said to hold at least $100,000 in first mortgages on western lands when he went to Ottawa,[23] and this probably was but a small part of his wealth.[24] As seen, he had also absorbed some $18,000 in connection with political protests, he had purchased a fine home in Ottawa which he lavishly furnished, and he would continue to pour large sums both into the *Free Press* and the Liberal political machine. The paper was to be a business as well as a political investment, reflecting Sifton's confidence in the future of a first-class newspaper in the expanding western metropolis.

The large investment necessary for buildings and machinery in the next few years could only be justified if the paper could maintain its competitive edge. This was supposed to be guaranteed by the exclusive telegraphic franchises. As Sifton wrote a little later, "it was the franchise that constituted the important part of the transaction, as the plant of the paper was practically worthless."[25] Before Sifton gained control of the Free Press Company, it had had a contract with Associated Press by which the latter was to give its despatches exclusively to the *Free Press* in Winnipeg and another contract with the Canadian Pacific Telegraph Company to deliver those despatches. Then the old Associated Press Company was dissolved, and a new one under the same name and manager was established; it was understood by J.B. Somerset that a new contract continuing the privileges of the Free Press Company was to be executed. Such was the state of affairs when Sifton acquired the newspaper.

Appearances were deceiving. Much to Sifton's consternation, Associated Press refused to honour the understanding with Somerset and signed a ten-year contract giving exclusive delivery rights in Canada to Canadian Pacific Telegraph. This, Sifton angrily told Van Horne, would render the *Free Press* "dependent on the good will of the Canadian Pacific Telegraph Company to deliver despatches and they can be shut off at any moment as far as can be seen."[26] A settlement became urgent by fall because during the summer the *Telegram* had begun receiving alternate news despatches via the Great North-West Telegraph Company, endangering the exclusive advantages hitherto enjoyed by the *Free Press*. In addition, the Associated Press made arrangements to provide despatches to other Winnipeg papers. Unable to reason with the press agency, Sifton continued to pressure Van Horne to enforce the *Free Press* monopoly through the Canadian Pacific Telegraph Company. By the summer of 1900 Van Horne was somewhat exasperated at Sifton's demands and retorted sharply, "We have no control whatever over the Associated Press. The fact of our agency has nothing to do with it. If instead of the C.P.R. the Great North Western Company had been made the agent of the Associated Press the situation would have been precisely the same, except that the Free Press would not have enjoyed the protection we have been able to give it without regard to any contract, a protection which it still enjoys and a protection which it would at once lose if we were now to resign the Associated Press agency."[27]

There the matter rested. Naturally other papers sought press agency despatches. Sifton was probably inclined to overestimate their value and to underestimate the other advantages that the paper had. By and large the new owner should have had little serious complaint about the general condition of the business. A thoroughly conservative financial manager, J.B. Somerset had carefully guarded the narrow margin of profitability with cautious restraint on expenditure. Upon inspecting the property Masten reported that "the concern seems to be in a profitable condition."[28] He had a generally favourable impression of Somerset's abilities and fidelity to the interests of the paper.

Yet, despite everything, Sifton was not enthusiastic. The general manager had certain qualities, undoubtedly, but he seemed to have neither drive nor vision. He did not have much appreciation of anything beyond his ledger books. "I wish you would write to Somerset," Sifton told Masten, "and tell him that the paper seems to be badly folded and not cleanly cut, and therefore has an untidy appearance; that defect ought to be remedied at once." The more he looked into the paper the less satisfied Sifton was. Writing again to Masten he said,

> I have some doubts about whether it will be advisable to make any permanent arrangement with the present Manager. I have had a hint or two that matters are not in very good shape, and certainly the appearance of the paper to my mind is very discreditable considering the facilities at his disposal. I think, therefore, the arrangement had better be a temporary one, and the Manager's attention ought to be called again and very pointedly to the fact that the appearance and get up of the paper are not at all satisfactory. I was looking at it yesterday, and it is the reverse of creditable. While the gentleman has a pretty good financial instinct I do not think he has the slightest notion of what a paper ought to look like.[29]

The most curious individual in all these negotiations was John Mather, the president of the Free Press Company. He had been a resident of Winnipeg for some years and had begun investing in western Canada in the late 1870's. His principal investments were in the Bank of Ottawa, Keewatin Lumber and Power Company, and the Lake of the Woods Milling Company, in the last of which there was probably some CPR money. He had been involved since 1889 in the CPR takeover of the *Free Press*, eventually holding Van Horne's and Smith's shares in trust and generally overseeing the business under the direction of Van Horne. By 1898 he was resident in Ottawa and willing to resign his position if it suited Sifton.[30] The new owner, however, preferred to refrain from disturbing the status quo and persuaded Mather to stay on until 1906. It suited Sifton, too, to have Mather in Ottawa, where business could be discussed regularly without arousing public interest in the minister's involvement with the paper and where correspondence could be minimized. Mather was completely discreet and self-effacing, willing to carry out Sifton's orders and offering advice only as requested.

Sound business management was important, but equally vital to the success of any paper was the editor. Good editors in Sifton's day required sound business sense as well as an ability to write copiously and reasonably intelligently on a wide range of subjects. They were the chief personnel officers, at least for editorial and reportorial staff. They had the difficult task, as party journalists, of toeing a line of policy determined more on partisan than business grounds; at the same time they were responsible for making the property prosperous, maintaining a growing readership, and not offending key personalities and interests in the community. Again, they were the political feelers of the owners and had to be intimately aware of the internal and organizational side of politics. The selection of an editor obviously would be crucial to the success of the *Manitoba Free Press*. Sifton did not hesitate long in making his choice. Arnott J. Magurn, the Ottawa correspondent of the Toronto *Globe*, whom Sifton had once described as "one of the most capable newspaper men in Canada," was designated to fill the editorial chair.[31]

Magurn had served about a decade in Ottawa for the *Globe*, and in this capacity he was well posted with all the leading Liberals and generally with dominion politics. Correspondence between Sifton and Magurn is extant from 1895, though probably their acquaintanceship antedated that time. When Sifton arrived in Ottawa he maintained a close relationship with J.S. Willison, editor of the *Globe*, and he was entirely satisfied with Magurn's work in the confidential and privileged position which he occupied as Ottawa correspondent of the leading Liberal paper in Canada.[32] It was no accident that Sifton selected Magurn to accompany him on his trip to the Yukon in 1897. In addition to requiring effective publicity, he was taking the opportunity to develop a relationship with the man whom he already had in mind to be his editor. The formal appointment was delayed until the following summer, apparently to allow Magurn to finish covering the 1898 parliamentary session. After the Yukon trip, however, while Sifton returned to Ottawa, Magurn had remained for a time in Winnipeg, familiarizing himself with the situation and writing articles for the *Free Press* in his characteristically vigorous language. Curiously no one seemed to guess the connection with Sifton, for Magurn simply wrote under the title of Ottawa correspondent of the *Free Press.*[33] Thus from November 1897 the newspaper expressed the point of view of both Sifton and the CPR on issues of the day. During the next few months the paper gradually was swung over to steady support of Sifton and extensive coverage of his speeches.

The Conservatives seem to have been surprisingly slow to smell a rat in all of this. Not until 6 April 1898 did Nicholas Flood Davin rise in the House of Commons to accuse Magurn of being "the henchman of the Minister of the Interior" as well as being Ottawa correspondent of the *Free Press.* These statements apparently came as quite a surprise to Richardson of the *Tribune.* The revelation of the connection between Magurn and the *Free Press,* he observed, "explains the authority and the character of the reports which have appeared in the Free Press recently, and in which the action of certain western members and the measures they have introduced have been persistently abused and misrepresented."[34]

Even so, Davin's remark about the connection with Sifton evidently was not credited by Richardson. When word leaked out at the same time about mysterious shifts in the stock of the *Free Press,* Richardson unleashed a vast barrage of intemperate invective at Magurn and the rival paper, but he still failed to see Sifton behind it. The *Tribune* now predicted "the complete flop of the newspaper [the *Free Press*] to lick-spittle support of the government at Ottawa, the C.P.R. thus thinking to curry more favor with the powers that be." Only a "nominal" shift of stock would take place; it would continue to be held by CPR "stool pigeons." Although its support of Sifton cooled rapidly, as late as two months after Davin's accusation, the *Tribune* still specifically exempted Sifton from being a party to the changes in the *Free Press.* Apparently Richardson found it difficult to accept the idea of so complete a change of ownership or that he had been so duped.[35]

It was arranged that Magurn should resign his position with the *Globe* and commence a three-year contract with the *Free Press* on 1 August 1898. He and his wife left Ottawa for Winnipeg on 22 July. On that date the *Tribune* attacks were sharply stepped up, but Mather and Sifton agreed that they should be ignored and that the *Free Press* should maintain a more dignified tone. "I have no doubt of your ability to conduct the warfare," Sifton observed to his explosive editor, "but I want to warn you against taking any personal notice of the editor [of the *Tribune*] or in any way mention[ing] his name. Allow nothing of the nature of a personal row to appear in the columns of the Free Press."[36]

The reasons for his policy were sound. During a time of transition in ownership and policy, and given Sifton's determination to play down public discussion of his connection with the newspaper, a middle-of-the-road position would cause the least disturbance among the paper's clientele. Sifton also had no desire to worsen the divisions which already beset the Liberals in Winnipeg. Magurn was highly emotional and capable of intemperate outbursts entirely equal to those of Richardson. Furthermore, he was not yet familiar with the western situation, and his temper could easily lead him astray. Sifton's expectations were great. The paper was to be expanded, asserting its primacy in Manitoba and the West, to become a strong party organ, the foundation stone of a widespread propaganda network, and a financial success. Could the editorial and business staff in the months and years that lay ahead fulfil his demands?

The opportunity was certainly there. Despite being flogged earnestly throughout the province by the Tory organization, the *Telegram* was steadily losing money; similar Liberal support for the *Tribune* had not markedly increased that journal's circulation in recent years. Government patronage still accounted for much of Richardson's profit margin. Shortly that would be lost, leaving the *Tribune* for some time in a precarious position. To be fair, the *Free Press* was not without virtue and could attribute some of its continued success to the negativism of the *Tribune;* and in Winnipeg at least it had a much greater circulation than either of its competitors, thereby winning substantially larger advertising revenues.

Prior to Magurn's arrival the directors, with Sifton's approval, had decided to purchase new type, which markedly improved the appearance of the paper; they had suggested expansion of the evening news bulletin into a full-fledged separate edition designed to attract advertising in the same way that had made the *Toronto Telegram* such a commercial success; and, because the *Free Press* offices were located on a side street, they decided to open a small advertising office on Main Street.[37] Immediate action was also necessary to locate new premises for the paper itself, partly because it was short of storage space for newsprint; but mostly because, as Magurn put it, "the present building is liable to be blown over on a windy night. At present under a wind, the top story rocks like a cradle, and a disaster of this kind would involve great loss of life."[38]

The most serious problem, however, was in management. Editor and business manager embodied two wholly conflicting philosophies. Magurn's ideas for aggressive promotion undoubtedly had impressed Sifton. He hoped to hire a man to produce a weekly illustrated magazine which would enhance the saleability of the paper in rural Manitoba and, not incidentally, attract rural advertisers as well as metropolitan sponsors. Somerset pooh-poohed the idea as too costly and likely to conflict with existing advertising arrangements. Magurn nevertheless did manage to produce special editions covering the Dominion Wheelmen's meetings on 3 September and a remarkably full and sympathetic treatment of the Dominion Trades and Labour Congress meetings in Winnipeg between 16 and 20 September. After these efforts, however, Somerset prevailed and such extravagances were curtailed.

Personally Somerset was pleasant enough, reported Magurn, but he was "slow." The recent success of the paper could only be attributed to good times. In Magurn's opinion, Somerset "seems to be more of a cashier or accountant, watching the outgo closely and making as good arrangements as he can in regard to business that comes in. There is, as far as I can observe, an utter absence of energy, and it is energy that moves mankind." Somerset did not make the slightest effort to advertise the paper, to the point where "even the name of the paper is not conspicuous on the building itself." To one of the editor's promotional suggestions, Somerset replied that "everybody read the Free Press and it was not necessary to advertise it."[39]

Sifton too was increasingly irritated by the "complete lack of energy and enterprise" and the "carelessness" of the management. He told Mather, "I think myself that the business management of the paper should be thoroughly overhauled with the object of infusing a little more life and energy into it. I quite agree that Somerset is a good man so far as saving money is concerned, but he has no comprehension of the expansive power of a newspaper in a growing country and he has no idea of the requirements of the situation."[40] What most angered Sifton was that "the circulation of the weekly has fallen off most disgracefully and that without any reason whatever except indolence on the part of the management." The daily circulation in the city was satisfactory, and that was where the profits were made. But political reward was to be found chiefly in the rural districts. Most farm households subscribed to at least one weekly edition of a major metropolitan paper. Most large city dailies therefore produced a weekly farmer-oriented edition, which partisan organizations pushed among their constituents. The *Telegram* and the *Tribune* had been competing very effectively for this market. The biggest problem, oddly enough, was competition from a Montreal paper, the *Family Herald and Weekly Star*, edited by John W. Dafoe, formerly employed by the *Free Press* and familiar with how to appeal to the western market. One of Sifton's friends reported that the *Family Herald* was in "mostly every household" in the country and was considered a politically effective offspring of its influential Conservative parent, the Montreal *Star*. Sifton told Mather that there was no "reason why the Montreal paper should be able to take the circulation away from a paper printed in Winnipeg." He claimed that two energetic men ought to be able to replace the *Tribune* with the *Free Press* in two thousand households within four months and implied that this would be only the beginning of his expectations for the paper in rural Manitoba.[41]

Meanwhile, Mather investigated the business aspects of the paper and reported to Sifton. Perhaps because he had long been associated with Somerset and shared his conservative financial attitude and possibly because he disliked Magurn's eruptive personality, Mather came down on the side of the business manager, concluding that Magurn was too inexperienced in business affairs. Sifton acquiesced in this judgment, and Somerset was granted a stay of execution. "There is this to be said about it," Sifton told Magurn, "the business is paying well at the present time. Some years ago it had an enterprising pushing management and it lost money; I think the other papers are exhibiting the enterprise now, and they are losing money. That is a phase of the question that required to be considered." How could the paper be safely pushed without endangering its profits? That problem occupied Sifton's attention for many months.[42]

Meanwhile, the broader network was already being formed. Since the spring, and probably earlier, Sifton had had his principal Manitoba organizer, J. Obed Smith, at work securing a favourable rural press. A verbose, nervous, even obsequious fellow, devoted to Sifton, Smith was officially employed in the Manitoba civil service, but in fact he worked full time for the provincial and national Liberal organizations. He provided a weekly letter for rural papers presenting official Liberal views. By judicious persuasion and use of patronage, a growing number of papers were induced to toe the Liberal line. They became part of an efficient propaganda network which would publish articles, slanted news items, and editorials supplied by Sifton's machine. Many of these were produced in Ottawa under the direct supervision of the minister of the interior for insertion in the Liberal press across the dominion.[43] Almost at will Sifton could call on papers across the West to take a certain line. By mid-November the Liberal organizers told him that they controlled nineteen or twenty Manitoba papers and were working on a number of others.[44] Thus, when the attacks on Sifton's Yukon administration began in earnest in 1898, he was not exactly without resources to put across his side of the case. It was but the beginning of his plans.

During the let-down following the defeat of the Yukon railway bill, J.S. Willison suggested to Sifton that a few "fighting speeches" might be in order to help the Liberals recover some lost ground. "Although I am not much of a hand to speak unless it is necessary," replied Sifton, "I, possibly on account of my Irish blood, do not mind having a hand in a row when there is one going on."[45] He would soon have a first-class "row" on his hands in Winnipeg, one resulting most immediately from his acquisition of the *Free Press*. The origins of the difficulty reached back to Sifton's differences with Joseph Martin, which had been seriously exacerbated in 1896 when Sifton was appointed to the government. Martin's friends had never been reconciled to their champion's failure to receive Laurier's favour, and a hard core of anti-Sifton sentiment remained, at least in Winnipeg, despite the revelations of Martin's flop-over to the CPR and his defection to the Pacific coast. Although Sifton had made a certain effort to patch up the party differences by electing R.W. Jameson, a friend of the Martin group, as MP for Winnipeg, there were widespread complaints that Sifton was not handing out enough patronage to the "Martin crowd" and indeed that he was ignoring Winnipeg generally. Adding to the discontent were the tariff of 1897, the attempt to impose additional educational concessions with respect to Manitoba Catholics, and Sifton's known coolness to the Winnipeg-Duluth railway which many businessmen naturally supported.

In the summer of 1897, John Wright Sifton had advised his son of "a general rebellion among the 'western' members because they have not been consulted enough." Sifton thought his father was "misled" and that the only "serious kicking" was from Winnipeg. "I think Jameson is heading a revolt there which seems to be because . . . I am trying to do my duty instead of appointing everyone to office." He especially took exception to the disloyal Liberals who sedulously circulated stories claiming nepotism, which Sifton heatedly denied. "I am going through the same process that I did when I went into the Manitoba Government," he told Isaac Campbell. "You will remember that the papers kept lying about me until the people who did not know me thought I was a cross between a wild Indian and a New York burglar." "How would you like to be in my place for a while?" he added. "Sleep peacefully old chap." To Col. McMillan he declared, "I wish some of the d—— fools who are grumbling had my job for a week—They would quit it sadder & wiser."[46]

So it continued into 1898, constant rumours of discord, but nothing concrete or organized. Perhaps time would weary the discontented. But the trouble over the Yukon policy kept the embers alive. The apparent weakening of Sifton's popular support gave the "kickers" new hope, while his consistent choice of his closest friends and allies for the juiciest plums in the Klondike fueled the fire. The greatest stimulus to the "kickers," however, was the defection to their camp of the *Tribune*.

Sifton, after all, had betrayed R.L. Richardson. When the publisher of the *Tribune* at last realized how he had been deceived, his rage knew no bounds, his desire for revenge no constraint. Richardson became a persistent and bitter enemy, while the division among Winnipeg Liberals broadened. With his organ, and with his position as MP for Lisgar, Richardson could and did give leadership to the many Grits who had reason to be dissatisfied with Sifton. In the fall of 1898 an open revolt surfaced with startling strength and energy. Sifton's tactics in confronting the rebels were a paradigm of his general approach to political organization.

During the late summer, the *Tribune* launched a full-fledged assault on the Yukon administration, delivered sermons denouncing "machine politics" and "machine newspapers," and praised independence of thought. Magurn wheeled the *Free Press* around to an enthusiastic defence of Sifton, though sometimes his vehemence led to ridiculous statements. For example, in defending Major Walsh's activities in the Yukon, the *Free Press* claimed that the commissioner "was clothed with unquestioned authority to do even illegal things."[47] "The Tribune has practically embarked as an opposition organ," declared Sifton with a full measure of self-righteousness; and he wrote a simmering letter to Richardson concerning the "lies" and misrepresentations being printed about the Yukon. In August he withdrew all his departmental patronage from the *Tribune* and intimated that the entire government shortly would observe the ban.[48]

For over two months after Magurn arrived, the two papers occupied themselves with skirmishes. Events moved towards a climax on 15 October, when the *Tribune* fired its first thundering salvos preparatory to a major assault by the dissidents on Sifton's positions. In an editorial entitled "For the Serious Consideration of Liberals," the paper undertook a full-scale treatment of the links between the minister of the interior and the Canadian Pacific Railway. Sifton's ownership of the *Free Press* raised a number of questions, because "we are precluded from the belief that the Canadian Pacific corporation handed over its newspaper property to the Minister of the Interior from consideration of unalloyed patriotism." "Nor can we suppose," continued the *Tribune*, "that the transfer was made from motives of spontaneous affection. The Canadian Pacific is, as we know from a somewhat costly experience, a pre-eminently 'business' corporation which may be relied upon to secure its quid pro quo, the 'quid' usually being in gigantic contrast with the 'quo.'" The fullest revelation of the facts was demanded to place the transaction above suspicion. Why, too, should the minister of the interior require a "personal organ"? The *Tribune* alleged that the "bizarre imbecilities" of "the Ottawa factotum" recently appointed editor were "bringing discredit and ridicule on the Liberal cause in the west." Finally, "the Liberals of the West" were going to make it "very clear that 'machine politics' and Liberalism are as incompatible as oil and water or acid and alkali."[49]

Two days later, Sifton's opponents took control of the Winnipeg Liberal Association's annual meeting on 17 October. Sifton's supporters were caught wholly by surprise. Isaac Campbell, one of his close friends, retired as president, delivering a rather neutral speech. Then, using their majority in a meeting which was packed in their interest, the dissidents voted in their own slate of officers. R.W. Jameson, the restive MP, was elected honorary president. And a number of Sifton's opponents were either retained in office or voted into other posts by the meeting. Jameson rose and expressed his pleasure at the defeat of the Yukon railway bill. He complained that his efforts to establish a commission to regulate railway rates had been foiled, so that while in the United States rates were set by a commission, in Canada they still were set by "railway bosses." He demanded greater government control of railways and denounced Van Horne and the Canadian Pacific, all apparently with general approval.

The election of E.D. Martin as president opened another great sore. Joseph Martin's supporters formed the nucleus of Sifton's opponents, and Joe Martin had been aiding the dissidents despite his removal to the West Coast. It was pointedly observed at the meeting that Ed Martin "was a chip off his brother," and the meeting subsequently voted to send a telegram of congratulation to Joe Martin, who had just been selected as attorney general of British Columbia. In accepting the presidency, Ed Martin denounced the "machine" which allegedly had been running the association. He objected to the filling of government positions in the West with "eastern men." The failure to improve the St. Andrews rapids to facilitate shipping down the Red River to Lake Winnipeg had been delayed, alleged Martin, by CPR opposition. "The west had a representative in the cabinet, and the C.P.R. had a representative in the cabinet, and these positions were filled by the same man. Whatever the west did was undone by a whisper in the cabinet."[50]

Attacking the attempt to make the *Free Press* the Liberal organ, in place of that "fearless, able, clean and manly " champion of Liberalism, the *Tribune*, Martin asked rhetorically, "Were the interests of the farmers and the C.P.R. identical?" "Never!" roared back his enthusiastic hearers. Generally, Martin considered that the Laurier cabinet was doing a good job, but its western member was, in effect, subverting the principles of Liberalism. What was needed was a return "to the standards of Liberalism raised by Geo. Brown, Hon. Alexander Mackenzie (loud applause) and others who gained the hold they had on the people because of their integrity and their adherence to principles." Joe Martin was assuredly in this great tradition, and, added Ed Martin, his election in 1893 had "put fresh blood into the veins of Liberals from Halifax to Vancouver."[51]

Sifton's supporters were stunned. Not one spoke in his defence. Nor were they subsequently encouraged to do more by the *Free Press* which, adhering to Sifton's strict orders, declined to become embroiled in a personal controversy with the *Tribune*. It carried only the briefest acknowledgement that the meeting had taken place and omitted all reference to the criticism of the minister of the interior.[52] It was a full week before the embarrassed Campbell worked up the courage to write a letter of explanation to Sifton. According to him, it had been intended that D.W. Bole, a local druggist friendly to both factions, should succeed to the presidency. Only about two hours before the meeting did word leak out that a canvass to elect Martin was under way. By then it was too late to take countervailing measures.[53]

The events were acutely embarrassing to Sifton, descending upon him at the same time that he was attempting to weather the Yukon allegations. How long could he survive when he was being attacked from within his own citadel? Sifton offered his own interpretation of the events to J.S. Willison:

There has always been a disgruntled crowd at Winnipeg, comprising a few Liberals who are not of the better class. They were very strong supporters of Joe Martin, but they have started to make a row from mere cussedness, not from admiration of Joe Martin. Richardson of the Tribune apparently has worked up a feeling amongst them. They are unfriendly to me because, to put it shortly, they are all for boodling and they do not see any chance for success so long as I am here. They put forward Ed Martin who is a narrow minded bitter fellow, because his brother did not get into the government. It appears as though the great body of Liberals paid no attention to the annual meeting of the Association and were not there in large number. Isaac Campbell was there with one or two others but apparently without any support. The other fellows took hold of the meeting and had easy control of it from the first. Notwithstanding their control, however, Martin was clever enough not to make his attack upon me before he was elected. The matter has no political significance so far as the Dominion Government is concerned. The reputable Liberals are all supporters of mine or practically all and as to the Tribune we will account for it in the due course of time.

Apart from giving the Conservatives more ammunition, Sifton claimed that the most dangerous repercussions would be for the Greenway government, against which the "kickers" were likely to turn.[54]

Sifton made it plain that E.D. Martin would always be regarded by the government as an enemy until he retracted and apologized for his statements. When he heard that the Winnipeg Liberal Association intended to endorse the *Tribune*, Sifton declared that such action would be tantamount to a declaration of opposition to the government. Compromise was no longer possible: "Any half-hearted or milk and water resolution to be passed for the purpose of harmonizing conflicting views would be to my mind infinitely worse than nothing. If there is not a majority of the Winnipeg Liberal Association that feel disposed to support the Government and to support me along with it they might as well say so and let us fight it out. . . . When war is declared it will be real war." The time had come, affirmed Sifton, when he would have to fight his own battles in Manitoba, and his friends would have to support him against the "Martin crowd." The "lying" had gone on long enough.[55]

Sifton began laying plans which he hoped would ensure his ultimate victory. To those who complained that the *Free Press* was not demonstrating any leadership, he counselled patience, explaining that it had only recently become a Liberal paper and "necessarily has to go somewhat slowly." The real reason was that Sifton was busily denying to his friends that he had any connection with the *Free Press*, and he wanted no further public exploration of the topic. But Sifton had no hesitation in asking the *Brandon Sun* to come out vigorously on the question of the party divisions. Finlay M. Young, another close friend from Killarney, Manitoba, was asked to "take in hand the newspapers along your line of railway and see that they are kept right[.] It would not do any harm for them to pitch into the Tribune a little to begin with, although too much of it would be giving the matter too great a degree of importance." The first part of the strategy was to isolate the dispute in Winnipeg as far as possible, to keep the virus from infecting Liberal organizations across the province.[56]

The next was to crush the opposition in Winnipeg. The Liberal Association held another meeting on 14 November. This time there were no errors. The Martin-Richardson faction mobilized all their supporters, but so did the Sifton side. And Sifton's supporters had an unusual advantage, if the reports of the *Tribune* are to be credited. A great deal of time was occupied early in the evening enrolling new members of the association, most of whom turned out to be local provincial and federal civil servants who were being marshalled to do their duty. Even so the kind of victory desired was not ensured, so they sat until the early hours of the morning when a number of the Martin-Richardson men had left. Then resolutions of confidence in the Laurier regime generally, and in Sifton particularly, were voted through. A satisfied Sifton, upon being advised of the result, wrote Laurier that the meeting had "passed resolutions of confidence & 'turned down' the Richardson-Martin faction by two to one. Isaac [Campbell] led the fight."[57]

Sifton must have been less pleased that on this occasion the *Free Press* utterly let down the government side. As with the meeting of 17 October the coverage was ludicrously inadequate, but this time Sifton's clear intention had been to make it a great public relations success. According to F.C. Wade, who happened to have returned from the Yukon for a few months because of ill health, the *Free Press* had only one reporter, a poor one, who was a member of the Liberal Association, and his notes of the speeches "were not even intelligible." Inadequate as such an explanation appears, no other was ever offered.[58]

There was only one way that the insurgents could have defeated Sifton, and that was by winning over the prime minister. Richardson attempted to do so shortly after the October meeting. He wrote to Laurier alleging gross corruption in the Yukon administration, enclosing a letter making many serious charges and demanding a thorough investigation. The enclosure also raised an associated issue. While in the Yukon, Sifton was supposed to have declared himself opposed to the Winnipeg-Duluth railway, because it was "against the interests of the national railway, the C.P.R." "In this respect," continued the writer, "I think that Hon. Mr. Sifton takes a wrong view of his duty as he should be above all things, distinctively the representative of Manitoba and the Manitoba farmer."[59] This was a complaint that went to the heart of the discontent. Many western Liberals believed that Sifton had sold out to eastern interests and monopolists, by definition oppressors of the farmer. He had failed to be the mouthpiece of popular western opinion. Sifton's own conviction that he represented the long-term best interests of the West simply was not yet accepted.

Laurier's reply to Richardson was immediate and threatening. Recording his admiration for Sifton's "great ability and sterling character," the prime minister demanded a retraction. He expected solid support from those who claimed to be friends of the government, and continued,

> One thing is quite plain to me at this moment: it is that there is a section of the Liberal Party in the West, who are prepared to deal with the Laurier Government as they dealt with the Greenway Government at its origin. For two years, the Greenway Government was attacked in the same manner as the Laurier Government is now attacked, not by its opponents, not by its enemies, but by its professed friends, and those friends of the Greenway Government made use of the same weapons as are now made use of against Sifton; Charges of corruption, malfeasance of office, subserviency to big corporations flew thick in the air, just as they are now flying, at this moment, against Sifton.
>
> You remember the action and fate of Luxton. Your action is just as his and your fate will be the same as well. I have always been friendly to you for a great many years past; I still want to be friendly, but I look upon your course . . . as a declaration of war against the Government, and there will [be] no alternative left to me but to treat it as such.[60]

No minister could have asked for stronger support from his leader. Rarely did Laurier write so uncompromising a letter. He had consulted Sifton, probably had gone over all the charges, and having received satisfactory explanations, he was prepared to back him to the hilt. In reply, Richardson hardened the lines of division. There was nothing to retract, he declared. His charges were substantially correct, and he believed that Laurier would soon regret his stand.[61]

Shortly after Richardson had been rejected, R.W. Jameson belatedly got around to trying to patch things up a bit with Sifton.[62] His was only the first indication of growing unease in the ranks of the bolters. Repudiated by Laurier, with little evidence of sympathetic support outside Winnipeg, they now began to have sober second thoughts. It now appeared, Sifton cheerfully told Laurier on 15 November, that "our Winnipeg bolters" were "desirous of not being cast out of the Synagogue." But the minister of the interior was not inclined to leniency. "There are certain men," he threatened, "who have proven conclusively that they are *enemies* & I will treat them accordingly." It would take time, but ultimately "the only possible method of arriving at peace and harmony" would be "to summarily eject them from the Association. They would do a thousand times less harm as members of the Conservative Association than they would as members of the Liberal Association.[63]

When Sifton got his propaganda organization into full operation, he was able to call on papers not only in Manitoba but across the West, including such dailies as the Regina *Leader* and Victoria *Times,* to attack the *Tribune* and come to his defence. More important, Magurn and Wade finally moved the *Free Press* to zealous support of its owner against the charges of the *Tribune* and dissident Liberals. At last the paper seemed ready to emerge as the real leader of western Liberalism. In a gesture which he hoped would consolidate his triumph, Sifton addressed a banquet of one thousand of his faithful followers in Winnipeg on 14 December, where a rather routine defence of the government's record was reportedly received with great enthusiasm.[64]

Sifton's strategy contained the revolt and asserted his power. It revealed him as a fighter determined to impose party discipline, not a diplomat inclined to achieve unity through compromise and consensus. It would be easier to sympathize with Sifton's victims were they demonstrable idealists devoted to certain principles; neither of the Martins nor Richardson would fit this category, and there was at least some truth in Sifton's assessment of them. Equally, however, there was some truth in their assessment of him. He would have done well to recognize the justice of some of their complaints. Despite Sifton's hopes, by no means all the sinners had repented. There were real, unresolved issues opened during the party revolt in Winnipeg. If a battle had been won, the war was far from over.

# 10

## Ebbing Popularity
## (1898–99)

Attempting to satisfy a coquettish electorate, to please diverse interests and changing tastes, to avoid giving offense to too many is a problem which perplexes all politicians. The West was as difficult to please as any part of the country. By the end of 1898 every indicator pointed to a strong economic recovery, and the region was more prosperous than it had been in years. Yet discontent over the tariff continued to fester. Railway construction was proceeding rapidly, both on the Crow's Nest Pass line and towards the Saskatchewan country. Still there were howls of protest over alleged CPR monopoly and influence and demands for greater government control. Excellent crops and high prices did not satisfy the farmers, who believed that the railway and elevator monopolies were skimming off profits properly belonging to them. At last settlers were appearing again in large numbers. Were they welcomed? Was the government praised? Quite the reverse. The allegedly inferior "quality" of the newcomers aroused the passions of Anglo-Saxon purists, giving Sifton some of his worst political headaches.

The popularity of the minister of the interior was at a low ebb, though the government itself was not as unpopular as it might have been because of the prestige of Laurier, who somehow always managed to give the impression that his distinguished and elegant personage was above ordinary politics. Sifton, by contrast, was aggressive and pugnacious. He told his friends on several occasions that he had never been used to, and did not intend to begin, being a conciliator of differences between "friends" of the Liberal party. He preferred to save his energies for battling the "enemy," revelling in vigorous verbal jousts with the Tories. In the House of Commons, when not speaking himself, he was reportedly an enthusiastic team player, sending notes to Tory MPs such as "How do you like that?" or "Take your medicine!" When he rose, he laid it on to a degree that some considered excessive. One reporter suggested that Sifton had been "too much 'on his muscle' " in flaying Sir Charles Hibbert Tupper, but allowed that "the Liberals are perfectly happy, rejoicing in the slugging administered to the two Tuppers."[1] A superb stump speaker, capable of inspiring infectious zeal among his followers on the campaign trail, Sifton's tactics were often less effective between campaigns when the binding up of wounds and delicate diplomacy were the skills most in demand.

One such case was Sifton's relationship to the prohibitionists. Temperance was one of those subjects on which the government could be found wanting by some portion of the electorate no matter what it did. The Liberals had complicated a touchy issue by their promise at the 1893 convention to hold a plebiscite on the question if returned to power. They reluctantly agreed to allow it on 29 September 1898, ostentatiously avoiding any commitment either on the principle at stake or on any subsequent course of action. And so the Canadian electors streamed to the polls to declare whether or not they favoured total prohibition. The vote was close, but 278,487 voters favoured it, approximately 14,000 more than were opposed. What was the government to do? Should it introduce a dominion-wide prohibitory law? It would be patently unenforceable. It was true that in Canada, a parliamentary democracy, a plebiscite was but an expression of opinion and did not carry the force of law. The government nevertheless had to explain why the opinion of the majority should not prevail. It argued that the majority really was not a majority: those who voted in favour of prohibition constituted "less than 22¾ per cent, or a trifle over 1/5 of the electorate."[2]

In Manitoba the problem was especially delicate for the Liberals. Provincially the prohibitionists had mostly voted Liberal in 1888 and 1892; in 1896, some votes went to the Patrons, but many remained Liberal simply because the Conservatives did not appear to be a promising alternative. Yet prohibitionists had been angered at the failure of the Greenway ministry to take any effective action following the 1892 plebiscite and again after the Judicial Committee of the Privy Council ruled in 1896 that the provinces indeed did have considerable powers to effect prohibition. In the 1898 plebiscite Manitobans voted overwhelmingly for prohibition, 12,419 to 2,978. In the constituency of Brandon the vote had been 3,696 in favour, to 507 opposed.[3] How could Greenway ignore this further evidence of the popular mood? More to the point, how could Clifford Sifton ignore it? After all, he had sponsored the resolution of 1893 praying that the dominion authorities introduce prohibition or empower the provinces to do so.

Prior to the dominion plebiscite Sifton had maintained that "I have always been clearly and emphatically an advocate of prohibition and my personal views upon the subject have increased in strength and intensity as I have had more experience of the effect of liquor upon the community."[4] Still, he made no effort to campaign personally for a prohibitionist vote or to promote the cause afterward. He claimed to have been surprised at the low turnout; surely this implied a lack of general concern. In face of this fact, it would be impossible to carry out legislation. There was no chance that such a measure could be enforced in Québec, and it was unlikely that enough support could be mustered to pass legislation in the House of Commons. Therefore it would not "be wise, prudent or statesmanlike to attempt total prohibition throughout the whole of Canada."

What, then, was the alternative? Sifton proposed to throw the ball back to the provinces and support "a prohibitory measure applicable to any Province which might see fit to adopt it." A resolution requesting such legislation was to be debated in the House, and Sifton thought he would support it. However, "I do not feel favourably disposed towards that portion of it which calls for a prohibitory enactment upon a *bare majority* of the electors voting." On the contrary, "I have always held the opinion that a majority of the qualified electors should vote favourably before it could be considered that there was any reasonable probability of public sentiment sustaining the enforcement of a prohibitory law." If they did not like that, he told the prohibitionists, they ought to recall that neither provincially nor federally had the Conservative Party done anything to advance their cause, and therefore they ought to continue in their Liberal allegiance.[5]

When the resolution came before the House, it had been amended to meet Sifton's objections, and as he promised he gave it his general support.[6] It duly passed, but led to no government legislation. It was reintroduced in 1900 while Sifton was absent in Europe and was lost. For the temperance people, this performance was not good enough. There was a marked softening of support for the Liberals in Manitoba. Indeed, when in 1899 Hugh John Macdonald and his resurgent provincial Conservative party adopted a prohibitionist plank in their platform, they kicked yet another post from under the sagging structure of Greenway Liberalism.

If the Liberals were embarrassed by the temperance question, they were positively squirming on the school question. The Manitoba Tories must have been delighted as the very issue which the Grits had so shamelessly exploited to partisan advantage now rounded on them, drove a wedge between the dominion and provincial governments, and visibly undermined that coalition of interests on which the Greenway Liberals had relied.

The failure to settle the question finally in the spring of 1897 had embittered both Greenway and Archbishop Langevin. Open feuding between the two continued. The Greenway ministry appointed a Catholic inspector, Télésphore

Rochon, but he was not approved by Langevin, who proceeded to undermine his authority. The provincial government also pressed the advisory board to adopt textbooks used in Ontario separate schools, some of which were entirely in French; yet the Archbishop remained hostile. He launched a new and extraordinarily effective offensive to reopen Catholic separate schools. "The clergy," wrote J.D. Cameron to Laurier, "are putting up a more determined fight now than at any time heretofore. Instead of there now being 35 or 36 schools reorganized under the Act as there were a short time ago there are now not fifteen possibly less. In every direction they have been disbanded and so called 'separate' schools organized in their stead. Father Cherrier states that he has 82 in operation so I am informed. Rochon is capable and energetic but if things continue in the future as they have in the recent past he will be in the position of an Inspector with nothing to inspect."[7]

Langevin could hardly have been more successful in demonstrating the will of his flock to maintain their own schools against high odds; how long they could have held out will never be known. Rome itself destroyed the foundation of his plans when it issued the papal encyclical *Affari Vos* in December. Essentially the papacy, as Merry del Val had reluctantly recommended, had come to terms with political reality in Canada. Therefore, however unjust the act of 1890, however inadequate the concessions of the Laurier-Greenway compromise, the Catholics were enjoined to accept the situation and, in effect, to work within the system to secure whatever advantages they could.[8]

Probably with deep misgivings, Langevin issued orders to his schools to accept the provincial regulations and admit Inspector Rochon. Rev. George Bryce, the Presbyterian divine who also sat on the advisory board, then met with Laurier and agreed on a list of concessions to be passed as resolutions of the board. These included extending teaching permits of Catholic teachers for two years; provision of a normal school session for Catholic teachers under the instruction of persons approved by the archbishop; certificates for bilingual (French-English and German-English) schools and examinations; French and English Catholic inspectors; agreement with the Catholics on school texts; acceptance of the four Winnipeg voluntary Catholic schools and their teachers by the Winnipeg school board; and appointment of Langevin and another Catholic to the board.[9]

To Laurier it was all very simple. The advisory board could pass the concessions, which would give him ample reason to introduce resolutions into the House of Commons to pay the Manitoba government the promised $300,000 out of the school lands fund, at $100,000 per year over three years. But with the school issue nothing had ever proven as simple as it seemed, and this was no exception. Laurier's talks with Bryce were supposed to be kept secret, but the substance of them was leaked to the Winnipeg *Tribune,* leading to widespread public debate and bringing the passage of the concessions to an abrupt halt. The provincial government meanwhile delayed its session and then postponed the introduction of its estimates in the vain hope that Laurier would rescue it from financial embarrassment. The addition of nearly one hundred Catholic schools into the system all at once would mean a great drain on the budget, complained Cameron and Greenway. Unless Laurier announced the resolutions in Ottawa, they would be forced to tell the legislature that revenues would be short by about $100,000. Then the Winnipeg school board proved truculent when asked to accept the Catholic schools, and difficulties arose over textbooks. Tempers were short when Laurier decided to tell Greenway and Cameron that passage of the agreed-upon concessions by the advisory board and willingness on the part of the provincial government to face some public criticism would "greatly facilitate matters"—that is, the introduction of the financial resolutions. The prime minister's attitude caused an "explosion" in the provincial cabinet, according to Provincial Treasurer McMillan, who told Sifton that Laurier's letter to Greenway "can only be considered as a threat, and is so regarded here." The provincial government had acted in good faith and was carrying out its part of the bargain, contended McMillan. But the Catholic minority had been unco-operative, disdaining the concessions offered, so that between the actions of the dominion government and the Catholic minority, there was much "feeling of resentment after the manner we have been played with."[10]

Neither Laurier nor Greenway had the courage or faith to act with resolution. Tarte had once described Greenway as "un peureux,"[11] an appellation richly deserved, for he seemed paralyzed by public opinion; but Laurier was equally reluctant to act with the decision which he had urged upon the Manitoba premier.

Upon receipt of McMillan's letter, Sifton rushed James Smart to Winnipeg, ostensibly on departmental business, but in fact to try to smooth the ruffled feelings of the Manitobans. Shortly Smart was able to report that the advisory board would take up the concessions again but that the government wanted it to wait until the session was over to avoid debate in the legislature. This was a case of excessive nervousness because the opposition had been studiously avoiding reference to the subject.[12] Still, once the session was over, serious discussions began again, and most of the concessions demanded by Laurier were implemented in one form or another by the end of the year, excepting an agreement with respect to Winnipeg schools.[13]

Sifton played an important role again in shaping the nature of the concessions. There were those from Québec, like the young Henri Bourassa, who believed the Laurier-Greenway compromise had been a sellout of French-Canadian interests and who pressed the prime minister to exact more concessions. "We are having a hard time with Bourassa and one or two other of the leading men from Quebec," Sifton told Cameron. He pointed out to the dominion cabinet that no more concessions were politically possible in Manitoba. French Canadians there were merely seen as another local ethnic group who were trying to secure special privileges through the influence of Québec at Ottawa. The settlement must not appear to be at the dictation of Québec, any more than that negotiated in 1896. At the same time that a French normal school was being established, care was taken to ensure that a German school operated "co-incidentally" at Gretna. Bilingual texts in German and English as well as French and English were adopted. To a recommendation that some wholly French readers be adopted. Sifton replied that he "would not suggest that anything of the kind should be done. 1st because I was unalterably opposed to it myself, and second, because I did not think it could be done. The bi-lingual system I think is all that could be asked for."[14]

When pressed, the Church was, as might have been expected, more prepared to make concessions on matters of language than on matters of faith. It was more important to secure a French-Canadian version of history and geography ("translated and expurgated"), readers with a "Catholic influence," and the expurgation of English history from the curriculum than to ensure largely French-language instruction.[15] Conversely, the willingness of the provincial authorities to make more concessions in the area of religion than that of language underlines the fact that the issue was perceived rather more in racial than in religious terms.

With negotiations moving along well in June, Laurier at last permitted the introduction of the financial resolutions. Despite some French Catholic obstruction, they shortly passed the House, but they were thrown out by the Conservative-dominated Senate. The government had argued that since education was an exclusively provincial jurisdiction, the province should control the use of the fund. The Conservatives replied that the fund was an endowment, only the interest of which should be paid to the province. Manitoba authorities seem to have accepted the defeat philosophically. The controversy seemed to be toning down; and "if matters progress as favorably as they now look and promise," wrote Cameron, "I do not see any reason why we should not renew our application for the $300,000 with better hope of success."[16]

Although the school question in Winnipeg remained unsettled, Laurier was able to say with some pleasure by January 1899 that "a satisfactory situation now exists in the rural parts of the Province." But he broke faith with Greenway and declined to reintroduce the financial resolutions, claiming that it would be done after a year or two, when the Liberals had a majority in the Senate.[17] His lack of political courage embarrassed Greenway and his colleagues. The Manitoba Conservatives publicized the concessions being made to the Catholics and the provincial government's fiscal difficulties. The only reason that the issue was not more fully exploited was apparently owing to Sir Charles Tupper, who with commendable spirit firmly rebuffed Hugh John Macdonald:

I may tell you frankly that no prospect of political gain will ever induce me
to lend myself to what I regard as the greatest misfortune that could
happen to Canada—that of arraigning race against race or religion
against religion. The cardinal principle of the platform so firmly established by your late revered father and so steadily maintained by myself
since my entrance into public life, of opposing in every way any attempt to
promote party ends at the expense of racial or sectarian discord, makes it
impossible for me to contemplate for a moment any such course.[18]

For his part, Archbishop Langevin was never reconciled to the new conditions, and the situation in Winnipeg allowed the embers of discord inter-
mittently to be fanned into flame for some years to come. In rural Manitoba,
however, there was a breathing space during which a badly disrupted educational system among French Catholics was permitted to begin a slow
recovery.

After a decade of strife and three years after Laurier acceded to power,
what had become of the principles which Sifton had defended with such
vigour? An independent separate school system no longer existed, but neither
did the pristine purity of the national school system which Sifton, when he was
attorney general of Manitoba, had said must not be compromised. By the
summer of 1899, with Sifton's help, the Manitoba government had conceded
almost every point demanded by the Dickey-Desjardins-Smith Commission
in the spring of 1896, which Sifton and Cameron had declared could never be
done without destroying the integrity of the national school system. There
were guarantees of Catholic teachers in schools of mixed denominations;
guarantees of textbooks satisfactory to the Catholics; Catholic inspectors;
Catholic representation on the advisory board, and on the board of examiners
for teachers; public assistance for a Catholic normal school; a two-year period
for Catholic teachers to meet provincial standards; and flexibility in the
application of rules regarding religious teaching, though not exemption from
those rules. In addition there were legal guarantees, limited as they were, for
the status of French in the school system, something which had never
previously existed. Finally, Sifton in 1897 had pushed the idea, which earlier
he had publicly opposed with vehemence, that the government could live with
*de facto* separate school districts both in rural Manitoba and in Winnipeg.

Not all the concessions had been embodied in provincial law as the 1896
Commission had asked, but Laurier had secured for the minority through
negotiation almost everything that was regarded by the Conservatives in 1896
as an acceptable solution. Sifton argued that he had protected the essence of
the national school system; but his principles, to put it kindly, had become a
great deal more flexible under the "sunny ways" of Laurier than when
staunchly braced against the stormy bluster of the Bowell and Tupper Conservatives. The real tragedy of the episode was the educational blow to the
very children whom Sifton had argued the national school system was to

benefit. Lost amidst the swirling tides of conflict between church and state, Protestant and Catholic, majority and minority, and Dominion and province was a decade of educational opportunity for thousands of French Catholic children whose schools were closed or rendered ineffective for lengthy periods. Equality of opportunity seemed as far as ever from realization.

Among the most enduring of western grievances were the alleged iniquities of the grain inspection system and of the elevator monopoly. On few issues was Sifton so at variance with prevailing opinion on the prairies. In 1898 and again in 1899 the government had allowed private members' bills which proposed to rectify the worst problems to die without proposing a viable alternative. By summer 1899 public opinion was being whipped up against the government with enormous success.

The elevator problem reached the West at the same time as the Canadian Pacific Railway. As the railway line spread westward across the prairie in the 1880's, CPR officials devised policies to encourage the construction of large mechanical elevators. Such elevators were costly—often $10,000 or more— but had capacities exceeding twenty-five thousand bushels and facilities for cleaning the grain. Particularly because of the short time between harvest and freeze-up on the Great Lakes and the lack of storage facilities both at the Lakehead and on western farms, speed and efficiency in handling grain were vital.

For all the advantages of a modern elevator system, so obvious to later generations, the first western settlers believed the price was excessive. They much preferred the system which had evolved in Ontario, where mechanical elevators had made little headway against traditional methods. In that province there might be several competing flat warehouses at a given shipping point, ranging in capacity from one to ten thousand bushels; or a farmer might even order up his own railway car and load it himself. The farmers believed that this ensured them the highest possible price locally or the opportunity of shipping their grain individually and bargaining for a good price at a larger centre. In the West there was little price competition. Typically at a given shipping point there would be only one or two elevators, constructed by large milling companies who would wire a daily price to their operators. The railway guarantee of monopoly encouraged the milling companies to invest large sums in elevators.

Attacks on the elevator system emerged in the Farmer's Union list of grievances in 1883 and were regularly ventilated thereafter.[19] The evils of monopoly were compounded by the fact that the farmers thought they detected a close linkage between the CPR and the milling companies.[20] Moreover, the local elevator operator often determined the grade of a farmer's wheat, so that the farmer naturally felt that he was being presented with a *fait accompli*: the price and the grade were probably too low. For years Van Horne had been an ardent defender of the elevator system,[21] and farmers' organizations had not carried sufficient impact to make themselves felt on the question at Ottawa.

In September 1897 the Winnipeg *Tribune* exposed a loose combination of grain interests which allegedly had conspired with the CPR to force down grain prices.[22] The western members of Parliament were under pressure to do something, and Rev. J.M. Douglas, the Patron-Liberal member for East Assiniboia, lost no time in introducing a bill designed to effect the desired reforms. Sifton made a private commitment to push it through the House of Commons,[23] but his resolve suddenly evaporated. After a short debate, in which he failed to participate, the Douglas bill was allowed to be buried in the Railway Committee. There the railway and grain officials forestalled legislation by successfully raising doubts about the efficacy of flat warehouses and by promising to do their best to meet individual demands for cars.[24]

Douglas introduced a more radical bill in 1899, this time with a provision for a government grain inspector. Sifton spoke generally favourably towards it, claiming that the government was in sympathy with its objectives if not with its every provision, and recommended referral to a special committee, where once again it was buried. This second failure to adopt the Douglas bill lent explosive ammunition to those who were charging that Sifton was anything but an efficient and reliable expositor and defender of western opinion.

His attitude on the issue was most fully revealed to G.D. Wilson, editor of the *Brandon Sun*.[25] The result of CPR policy in encouraging elevators and discouraging flat warehouses had left the "farming community . . . furnished with, I think, the finest system of elevators in the world in proportion to the amount of business to be done." Allowing flat warehouses would result in closing some elevators and would seriously hinder their future development. Sifton anticipated that the crop would treble in the next decade and that it would be impossible to move it without an efficient elevator system. "The proposition to encourage the construction of flat warehouses is practically on a par with the proposition to encourage ox-carts as compared with rail-roads. . . . A car can be loaded from an elevator in ten minutes, whereas it generally takes a couple of hours or from that to half a day to load from a flat warehouse." Despite all that, if there were any evidence of serious restriction of competition or defrauding of farmers, "I would be in favour of breaking down the combination by permitting the construction of flat warehouses, but as a matter of fact no such showing has been made before the Committee." The elevator people had met the charges made by Douglas and Richardson to the satisfaction of the House Committee. Sifton concluded therefore "that some of the farmers have been loaded up with the windy clap-trap and nonsense which appears in the Tribune and have got wrong notions about this question, but I do not propose to fall in line with what is the merest kind of demagogic shifting to catch votes, and upon the strength of speeches which are shown to be totally untrue, support legislation which may endanger one of the greatest interests of the country and which—in my judgment is certainly opposed to the interest of the farmer." That interest was "to have the best and largest possible number of elevators of the very best class." Sifton argued that it would be sufficient to regulate and inspect the elevators under a clearly defined set of rules and to empower inspectors to settle disputes. "If it was a case of dispute between farmers and capitalists I would be on the side of the farmers, but it is not such a dispute. It is an artificial agitation raised by three or four scamps for the purpose of making themselves popular, totally regardless of what harm they may do to the permanent development and interests of the country; and if it is necessary for me to fight these men I will fight them."

Whatever his fighting stance in private, Sifton for once preferred a more subtle way of outmanoeuvering his opponents. After all, it would not do, as Magurn pointed out, to allow the private bills to pass so that Richardson could "pose as a real Legislator."[26] If Douglas's bill passed it would give tremendous encouragement to the Patrons of Industry, whose influence was waning. Some action was required to offset western discontent, but it must be done so that the government, not Douglas or Richardson, received the credit. The situation was made to order for a royal commission, and in the fall of 1899 the government announced the appointment of the Royal Commission on the Shipment and Transportation of Grain in Manitoba and the North-West Territories.[27] Comprising the commission were Justice E.J. Senkler of St. Catharines, as chairman; three western farmer members, W.F. Sirrett, W. Lothian, and C.C. Castle; and C.N. Bell, a Winnipeg grain merchant, who served as secretary. It was anticipated that the commission would provide ample grounds for the government to take some action and, if carefully chosen, that it would come to the conclusions the government wished.

Claims one authority, "so sure was the Dominion government of what it wanted to be forced to do that it would entrust to no one but farmers the task of manning its early agricultural commissions."[28] The government wanted to *appear* to be sympathetic to the agricultural point of view, but it was careful in selecting the farmers to ensure that they were not supporters of government ownership—for which Richardson had drummed up much support—and that they were unlikely to come to conclusions which seriously conflicted with Sifton's views. Meanwhile there was much political hay to be made, Sifton told Magurn. The *Tribune* had charged that the commission would be heavily influenced by Bell, the grain merchant. The *Free Press* should make it clear that he was only "Secretary, and has no voice in coming to conclusions or framing a report, and three out of four members of the Commission are farmers from the Province of Manitoba." "*This is the first time in Canada* that an important commission on a business matter has had a majority of farmers upon it and you should roast the Tribune for *belittling* them and treating them with contempt." Columns were to be written twice a week on the issue, and J. Obed Smith was to ensure that "the substance of them" appeared in the rural press.[29]

In fact, the *Tribune* was correct. Much of the work of the commission fell to C.N. Bell, who planned its hearings, reported frequently to Sifton, and undertook a trip to Minnesota to inspect the system of elevators and grain handling adopted there in 1897.[30] Bell indeed played a role in drawing up the report and was the chief adviser in drafting the bill which was presented to Parliament during Sifton's absence in Europe in 1900.[31]

There is no question that the Manitoba Grain Act which resulted from the commission deliberations was entirely engineered by Sifton. It provided for the right of ten farmers in a locality to demand either flat warehouses or loading platforms, for the limited regulation of the grain trade and grading of grain, and for an inspector to oversee the elevators and warehouses. Both at the time and subsequently it was widely hailed "as a veritable agrarian Magna Charta."[32] But it was nothing of the kind, and the western members knew it. Douglas pointed out repeatedly that the recommendations of the commission flew in the face of the evidence which it had received from across the west: "The recommendation of the Royal Commission has the stamp of the Winnipeg grain trade upon it. It is not in the interest of the farmers, but in the interests of the trade." He demanded the right of any individual "aggrieved with the existing state of things" to "have the liberty to go with their product to the market and to put it on the market in any way they choose." The overwhelming majority of MPs, both Liberal and Conservative, nevertheless agreed with Laurier, who termed the western demands socialistic. If ever there was an issue before Parliament which divided the members on regional and ideological rather than partisan lines, this was it. Seven of the ten members who opposed the measure on division were from Manitoba and the Territories; equally important, with Sifton absent, not a single western vote was cast in its favour.[33]

The reservations of the westerners were well founded. As they had predicted, the Act did nothing in its manifold regulations to encourage the construction of flat warehouses, which declined rapidly. Contrary to Sifton's earlier statement, the commission had been forced to conclude that there had indeed been price-fixing by grain dealers, but its recommendations for dealing with the evil were ineffective. It would require a separate royal commission in 1906 to deal with the Winnipeg monopoly in the trade. Farmers were supposedly given the right to order railway cars to move their produce, but the act went no further than the railways were already going in practice. Neither the grain merchants nor the railways were pressed beyond what they were willing to do. The commission and bill were carefully and successfully managed to give maximum credit to the government shortly before the election of 1900.

Prior to leaving for Europe in March, Sifton told Sir Henri Joly de Lotbinière, minister of inland revenue, under whose jurisdiction the act would come, that "it is an absolute necessity to the success of the Liberal party in the west that a Bill should be carried through and the question dealt with at the present Session. . . . Our people in the North West are very much excited about the question and they would regard the failure of the Bill to become law, especially during my absence, as a very serious reflection upon me."[34] Shortly the deficiencies of the bill would move the farmers to organized defence of their interests. At the time, however, the Manitoba Grain Act was praised throughout the Liberal propaganda network as a great achievement for farmers' rights against the evil monopolists.

If ever a group of settlers had reason to feel isolated and neglected by government, it was those at Moose Mountain. They had settled on good land, optimistic that a promised railway would soon pass their way. But year after year it did not materialize. Year after year their crops increased, which in turn magnified their problem. In 1897, according to Sifton, they transported some 250,000 bushels of grain about forty miles to market.[35] These cold figures represented much toil. How many uncounted trips bumping over rutted prairie paths on an unsprung wagon pulled by a team of fatigued horses or oxen to carry 250,000 bushels? How many rainy days when dampness endangered the quality of the grain and how many bitterly cold days in the teeth of advancing winter?

Their case was unusual, but not unique. Hundreds, perhaps thousands, of settlers had taken up land before the great depression of the middle nineties struck, in the expectation that projected railways would soon reach their homesteads. The change of government in 1896 at first seemed unlikely to enhance their prospects despite improving economic conditions. The Liberals were committed to a policy of budgetary restraint, had long argued that the Tories had been much too lavish in funding railways, and were burdened with many members who believed that all subsidies for railways should cease forthwith and that future development should be determined by private enterprise and the free market economy. Such sentiments of course were not found in districts awaiting railways. Many Liberals nevertheless considered the subsidization of the Crow's Nest Pass Railway to be a serious deviation from true Liberalism, and accordingly the government decided to subsidize no railways during 1898.

Whatever sense the policy may have made elsewhere, it certainly did not reflect the needs of western Canada. Sifton pleaded with Laurier to make an exception and allow a seventy-mile extension of the Pipestone branch of the CPR to Moose Mountain and a twenty-mile extension of the Stonewall branch. "These two extensions are urgently required in order to prevent the respective districts from becoming depopulated," he wrote. "While we are spending this year $250,000.00 for the purpose of promoting immigration we are in serious danger of actually losing a considerable number of substantial and successful settlers from these two districts by reason of the fact that they are too far from a railway to successfully market their grain."[36]

A year later when the government resumed a limited subsidy policy, it angered many Liberals. "Why not leave railway subsidies to the provinces and return to the old Liberal policy?" demanded J.S. Willison. "I see nothing but subsidy after subsidy if the Dominion is to continue the system." In any case it would be impossible to satisfy "the excessive demands of the west." Sifton retorted sharply: "I think for the Dominion to shut down on railway subsidies at the present time would be a suicidal policy. The country has now an opportunity which it has never had before of developing itself and getting population. My own view is that twenty years ought to see at least 12,000,000 people in Canada, but if this result is to be accomplished small ideas (no offense intended) of trying to cut off expenditure on public works and railways will have to be dropped. For myself, I am altogether in favour of going ahead."[37]

"Going ahead" meant for Sifton that the government should use subsidies and guarantees to induce private capitalists to build needed roads and impose needed regulations. Railways were a natural monopoly only partially constrained by competition; and Sifton recognized the need to enforce regulations in the public interest. He believed that by extracting reasonable concessions in return for subsidies and guarantees, the government could obtain the control it needed without impairing the efficiency of private enterprise.

Those who suggested government ownership of railways because of their overwhelming importance to the everyday lives of all westerners were dismissed as socialists. The *Tribune* was one of the strongest advocates of government ownership of railways and elevators, policies which greatly appealed to rural Manitoba. The *Free Press* therefore was Sifton's chief instrument in trying to counteract the virus: "If the railways are to be owned in common, if that is the best policy, why would there not be common ownership, or state ownership, of all the agricultural implement industries? But this is Socialism, some one says. Well, that is not going to frighten the advocate of government ownership of railways." While anarchists and socialists ought not to be confused, "there is a well-grounded suspicion that the aim of both the Anarchists and the Socialists is the same; that each reaches the end by different means; one by peaceful agitation and the other by violence. Both aim at the overthrow of government." Thus, by a simple leap in logic, the *Tribune* and others who supported government ownership were socialists whose object was the overthrow of the British system of parliamentary government. It was logical, at least to Magurn and Sifton, to conclude that "public ownership of railways and other natural monopolies means public ownership of the land. If the land is the source of all wealth, how much more will it relieve the public burdens if there is common ownership of land, as well as common ownership of railways."[38] Whether the farmers were at all convinced by this form of reasoning is impossible to assess.

In his speeches Sifton emphasized the enormous costs of government construction and ownership, arguing that the system of obtaining concessions in return for guarantees or subsidies could provide almost all the same benefits at little or no cost to the taxpayer. But, in fact, it remained highly improbable that the Canadian government could have sold to central and eastern Canada the idea of government construction and ownership of the required railways in frontier areas, with the concomitant increase in taxes and debt.

The government, however, was not wholly consistent in opposing government ownership. One of the principal goals of the minister of railways and canals, A.G. Blair, a strong advocate of government ownership, had been the extension of the Intercolonial Railway from Québec to Montreal. He hoped that access to the larger market would make the government-owned line financially viable and won his colleagues' consent to purchase the Drummond County lines in 1899. Sifton had only reluctantly supported the measure, and he was despatched to Montreal to soothe CPR officials, who had lobbied hard against the policy.[39]

For some years he had been friendly to the Canadian Pacific, because he valued its support in elections and its aid in moving immigrants. He required its co-operation in building branch lines which were vital politically and would open new districts to settlement. Nevertheless, he was by no means in the pocket of the company. Both he and the CPR officials recognized that theirs was a political alliance, which either side would drop as soon as it suited their interest. The signs of friction began to be pronounced in 1898 and 1899. Sifton believed that Van Horne had not been wholly honourable when it came to transferring the *Free Press* franchise rights. He also considered that the CPR was abusing its great power. In 1899 he attacked a CPR announcement that freight rates on flour transported to the West Coast would be increased by twenty cents a barrel. "I cannot myself understand the principle upon which this change is to be made," he complained to Van Horne, "except it be that the Company considers itself entitled to charge all the traffic will stand."

> This is the kind of proceeding which makes people hostile to your company and I think justly so. Manitoba has given you your most profitable business & as soon as her millers have worked up a coast trade you are proceeding to levy an additional tax upon it. I cannot refrain from expressing the opinion that such a policy is short sighted and tyrannical. It is certainly contrary to the interests of the Wheat growing areas of the

West and I think it is equally contrary to the true interests of your Company.[40]

Also increasing friction was a simple conflict of personalities. Van Horne and Sifton were cut out of similar cloth—vigorous, forthright, expansive, energetic, devoted to growth and development—and they understood and respected one another, whatever their temporary differences. But in 1899 T.G. Shaughnessy succeeded Van Horne as president of the CPR, and he and Sifton did not get along. Shaughnessy was able and efficient, but also conservative and preoccupied with defending the CPR from encroachments on its monopoly which the Laurier government seemed all too willing to encourage.

Finally, from a purely political point of view, Sifton could not much longer afford to be suspected of being in bed with the CPR, a suspicion which had been markedly increased with his purchase of the *Free Press*. To emphasize his independence from the Canadian Pacific, he voted in 1898 in favour of the Kettle Valley line, a project which he had privately opposed and against which the CPR mounted a powerful lobby. The backers of the scheme proposed to build a line drawing ore from southeastern British Columbia to a smelter at Northport and to market via Washington State and to do so at no cost to the dominion treasury. To a British Columbia correspondent Sifton commented, "I feel that in the interests of British Columbia I ought to give a most uncompromising opposition to any scheme the result of which would be to draw business to the south rather than develop the business in British Columbia itself." Despite the fact that it would cost far more and would entail a dominion subsidy for the CPR to build into the area in question, the government should support development in Canada:

> We suffer from one end of Canada to the other from the fact that our trade is drawn off through American channels and the bulk of the business goes to the people on the other side of the line instead of to our own people, and while I do not favour anything in the way of retaliatory legislation I do favor a continued and persistent effort to stop these leaks and get the benefit of our own natural resources.

However eloquent his nationalism in private, when the vote came he supported the Kettle Valley Railway Bill, which was defeated nevertheless. He rationalized his action by declaring that "the Government would under no circumstances be justified in giving a bonus to the C.P.R. to build into the Boundary Creek District when another Railway was willing to build for nothing." Yet, he also confessed that "a considerable number of the Members voted for the Bill for the simple reason that they did not wish to be classed as voting in support of the C.P.R. although in their hearts they believed that the building of the Kettle River Valley Railway would not be conducive to

Canadian interests."[41] Sifton was certainly among them; and probably he had voted for it in full realization that a substantial majority of the House were opposed.

It would take much more than a vote against the wishes of the CPR to convince westerners of Sifton's independence. What was required was an effective and competitive alternative to the Canadian Pacific in western Canada. Neither the Canadian economy nor the business generated in the West was sufficiently advanced for the government yet to contemplate a second transcontinental line. Perhaps there was, however, justification for considering a second outlet at the Lakehead for western grain. Because of dominion spending restraints in 1897 and 1898, the initiative had to lie with Manitoba.

Premier Greenway's options were decidedly limited in 1897. Mackenzie and Mann's Lake Manitoba Railway and Canal Company had been a success as far as it went, but that was only from Gladstone northwest to the Dauphin country, a pioneer road serving as a feeder for the Canadian Pacific and Northern Pacific lines. At that stage Mackenzie and Mann had no plans for great expansion in the province, so that the only alternative was the Northern Pacific. But its lines lost money in Manitoba almost every year, some $766,000 over ten years on operating expenses alone and excluding its $300,000 annual interest obligation on its bond issue. Northern Pacific and Manitoba President James McNaught, whose management of the line has been charitably described as "bizarre," proposed to solve the difficulties by expansion within the province and construction of an outlet to Duluth. Both Van Horne and James J. Hill of the Great Northern actively opposed the project, which the CPR president dismissed with a snort as "a line to carry wheat for the Manitoba farmers for love or something less." Greenway could only justify support for the scheme if it produced another reduction in freight rates, which the debt-ridden Northern Pacific understandably could not promise. The premier abandoned his negotiations for a time early in 1898, and Van Horne cheerfully commented that "wheat will not be carried for 6 cents [per bushel] for a good while yet."[42]

In 1898 Mackenzie and Mann received provincial backing to extend their lines toward the northwest corner of Manitoba. By the end of the year they were in control of the Manitoba and South-Eastern and the Ontario and Rainy River, the two largest, though incomplete, links in what was by then a clearly defined intention to build to Port Arthur. They had reorganized themselves as the Canadian Northern Railway late in 1898, and several months later approached Sifton for dominion backing in their schemes. Sifton told Provincial Treasurer McMillan of Manitoba that "I quite approve of the proposition of a line of railway from Port Arthur, by way of Winnipeg to Prince Albert, and later on, if possible, to Edmonton, believing that the development of the Saskatchewan Valley on the one side, and the Rainy River country on the other, is of great importance to the North West." He expressed the hope that the Dominion and the province could harmonize their views and support the enterprise "upon the condition that the line is kept thoroughly independent, and kept in such a position as not to be acquired by the Canadian Pacific."[43]

Harmony was impossible. In the spring of 1899 there was a great "Northern Pacific boom" in Manitoba, with tremendous popular pressure on the government to come to some agreement with that company. President Andrew Mellon of the Northern Pacific arrived in Winnipeg during the first week of July, but negotiations foundered on Greenway's firm insistence upon a guarantee of a ten-cent rate on the Winnipeg-Duluth line.[44] The popularity of the Northern Pacific stemmed from the widespread but erroneous belief that Mackenzie and Mann were a front for the CPR. One of the principal evidences of this supposed connection was that Sifton was known to be friendly to both. It was inconceivable, apparently, that he could push competing railways. When Isaac Campbell suggested that given the tenor of western opinion, government ownership was the only viable alternative to Northern Pacific construction, Sifton exploded that the idea was "a ridiculous fad" which had no "hold whatever in Eastern Canada." "The difficulty of our Western people," he continued, "is that they do not see anyone's circumstances but their own. We will do the best we can to put the Ontario and Rainy River on a satisfactory basis, but I have not any idea that it will satisfy the demagogues." Manitobans had their ideas concerning the relations of railways altogether wrong. The CPR and NPR were "undoubtedly in a pool," quarrelling about some things, but co-operating in others. "They are only making a cat's paw of the Manitoba business to settle up their disputes about some thing else. Our people in Manitoba of course cannot understand that and look upon the Northern Pacific as a great philanthropic institution." In fact only Mackenzie and Mann were "Free from any entanglements" and "likely to be independent."[45]

The result was that Greenway and his colleagues, mesmerized by public opinion, refused to negotiate at all with Mackenzie and Mann, could not make up their minds to plunge ahead with government ownership, and had failed altogether with the Northern Pacific. Mackenzie and Mann could progress toward their goal with work mainly outside Manitoba, but all Greenway could take into his fall election campaign was his tattered banner calling bravely for a ten-cent rate. By mid-summer 1899 the question remained unanswered: did the Liberals, provincial or federal, have any coherent plans to provide a needed second outlet to the Lakehead and competition for the CPR?

First impressions are often lasting ones, and so it was with the unfortunate

Magurn of the *Free Press*. From the point of view of Winnipeg Liberals, he had begun as a miserable failure. Observed T.A. Burrows, Sifton's brother-in-law, "the present Editor of the Free Press has not displayed any journalistic ability since he came here" and was altogether "too small a man" for the task that lay before him. Isaac Campbell wrote in the same vein. E.M. Wood, a Liberal organizer, reported that "the general prevailing opinion is that Magurn does not 'fill the bill'; is not of sufficient weight, intellectually, to divert or concentrate public opinion on any given subject."[46] Sifton nevertheless steadfastly backed Magurn, who had been instructed to avoid a personal battle with the *Tribune* and *Telegram*.

If Sifton's support of Magurn was baffling to western Liberals, doubly mystifying was the paper's relationship to Sifton. It was obvious in every issue that Sifton had a controlling influence. Magurn had been told, and with astonishing innocence continued to believe, that nothing had really changed with respect to the real ownership of the paper, and he published statements to that effect to answer charges that Sifton owned or controlled it. The story given to Magurn was that while Mather was the financial power behind the paper and would oversee the business end of it, Sifton's advice regarding editorial policy was to be accepted. If Magurn disagreed with Somerset or Mather, as he often did, he would write to Sifton and ask him to use his influence with Mather. Sifton would reply that he would see what he could do. Plainly the paper had become Sifton's personal organ, but the questions "How?" and "For what consideration?" continued to puzzle Winnipeg Liberals. When they asked Sifton for explanations, he did not hesitate to deny everything:

> my own judgment [he piously told Isaac Campbell, one of his oldest and most trusted friends] is that it is an extremely injudicious thing for any man in public life to own a newspaper. I do not own the Free Press or any interest in it directly or indirectly, although I take a very considerable interest in the management of it editorially, and Magurn being personally well known to me is quite willing to adopt any reasonable suggestion I may make to him; I have, however, no financial interest whatever in the paper, it is in perfectly independent hands.[47]

Any person who cared to investigate of course would not have found Sifton's name attached to a single share of the Free Press Company stock; they remained in the name of Toronto lawyer C.A. Masten. Magurn "may sometimes listen to my advice in the conduct of the paper," he told another old friend. "Naturally, however, I do not care to interfere very often or to obtrude my advice upon him."[48]

Perhaps not. On most broad issues of national policy Sifton and Magurn understood each other well enough that regular instructions were unnecessary. They had worked together closely in Ottawa preparing stories in defence of the government. On local issues, however, Sifton finally gave in to Winnipeg Liberal opinion and asked Isaac Campbell, J.D. Cameron, and F.C. Wade to contribute articles and editorials, after which the complaints subsided. He also read the three Winnipeg dailies with minute attention to detail and frequently wrote to Magurn about particular matters which concerned him. Once he detected a new writer on the staff: "I think that his material is fairly good but a little light,—possibly it may not be the worse on that account." A little later he told Magurn that this new writer was too careless: "some of his paragraphs bear evidence of being written hastily and not revised with sufficient care." Sifton also had a sharp exchange of correspondence with T.G. Shaughnessy over what he considered to be the Conservative bias of Canadian Pacific telegraphic news services from the West Coast.[49]

One issue which had to be handled with special care, in Sifton's opinion, was the delicate matter of the Imperial relationship. Although they were not above criticizing the British, it was Sifton's conviction that Manitobans took the relationship very seriously. He once reprimanded Magurn for "two or three very flippant references to Mr. Chamberlain, the Colonial Secretary." Sifton presumed that these remarks were "from your American editor. Long residence in the North West has taught me that there is a very strong pro-British sentiment there; references of that kind to a member of the British Government cannot fail to be very unpopular. They might do in the Toronto Telegram, but I am sure you would not care to have anything in the Free Press that would be suitable only for the Toronto Telegram." The *Free Press* accordingly took a generally pro-British stance in international relations, supporting England in her growing difficulties in South Africa and advocating the idea of a Canadian monetary contribution to the Royal Navy after the example of other colonies.[50]

At the same time, loyal as she was, Canada was also a self-governing Dominion, and in Sifton's experience at Ottawa, the government had had several differences of opinion with Governor General Lord Aberdeen which suggested that the British still had a great deal to learn about the degree of independence inherent in dominion status. When Aberdeen retired in 1898, a British newspaper suggested that he would be a good model for his successor, Lord Minto. In what might have passed for a direct expression of Sifton's personal views, the *Free Press* took exception to these comments. Too often Aberdeen had exceeded his constitutional powers:

> The ministers at Ottawa should not be subjected to trouble by any idea of personal government or of personal responsibility, and a sense of moral accountability for the actions of his advisers. . . . A Governor General who takes himself too seriously in his relations with his advisers is liable to make mischief. . . . When an English newspaper proposes that Lord Minto should take his pointers in all these matters from his predecessor

and make him his model, we have too great a regard for Sir Wilfrid Laurier or any other prime minister not to enter a protest. If we are to have second or third rate men sent to Canada as the representatives of the sovereign, it is all the more necessary to discuss these things openly, so that a new incumbent of the office will be able to know some few things which his constitutional adviser could not for the sake of diplomacy, whisper in his ear.[51]

It was a blunt challenge to Minto, a discordant contrast to the welcome generally accorded the new governor general and prophetic of the lack of harmony which would exist between him and the minister of the interior.

By the beginning of 1899 Sifton's Winnipeg allies had grudgingly accepted Magurn and the *Free Press* and had begun to hope that the internal difficulties of the Winnipeg Liberal Association which had become so public would dissipate with the passage of time. There had been no truce, however, and the situation resembled a stalemate, with the government and the insurgents respectively well entrenched, taking periodic pot-shots at one another across a no-man's land, each waiting for an opportunity to destroy the other. Meanwhile the Conservatives who, however weak, were the real enemy, gleefully sat back and lobbed in a shell here and a few volleys there just to make things interesting.

Two events shook the uneasy political calm late in February. The first was the apparent suicide of R.W. Jameson, MP, on 21 February, probably as the result of some financial embarrassment. The second was Sifton's pronouncement a week later at Perth, Ontario, that the tariff was a settled and dead issue.[52] The former opened an extremely sensitive vacancy in the House of Commons, which the Liberal dissidents determined to exploit. The latter provided them with what they believed would be a sound platform on which to attack the minister of the interior and rally support in rural Manitoba. Sifton could be shown to be the representative of the businessman, not the farmer.

To some extent the dissidents were correct. Sifton had scarcely entered the cabinet when he told one of his colleagues that the government should be seen to be "desirous of meeting business men, and facilitating business wherever it is possible for them to do so." Not only had he blossomed into a moderate protectionist, but also businessmen trusted him to see that their interests were not overlooked by zealous tariff reformers.[53] He had few complaints about the Fielding tariff, believing it reflected good business judgment. The tariff, after all, had to be adjusted on the basis of the national good, not simply for the advantage of the West; in the long run this was to the westerners' advantage. The West was disappointed? Well, the West would get over it. Times were prosperous, the Tories were if anything for a higher tariff than the government had devised, and if only the Liberals in the West would leave well enough alone, the issue would vanish. "There is no possible use in talking about reducing the tariff on agricultural implements at the present time," Sifton upbraided J. Obed Smith, "and it is better to stop talking about it. It is thoroughly well understood in the Province of Ontario that the people of Manitoba and the North West Territories are the most prosperous people in Canada at the present time." "There is not the least chance of opening the subject and it would be better to do your talking on another subject."[54]

Sifton would have saved himself a good deal of trouble had he followed his own advice. Early in 1899 he delivered several speeches in which he contended that the tariff was finally settled. The Conservatives and the Liberals, he said, had fundamentally opposed views on the tariff: "protection was the basis of the Conservative policy and only an incident to the Liberal policy." The Fielding tariff "was satisfactory to the country at large." His audiences were probably unimpressed by Sifton's figures to support his contention that there was a vast gulf between Liberal and Conservative policies. Under the Tories the average tariff had been 18.28 per cent, while under the Liberals it was 16.80 per cent. However significant a reduction of almost 1.5 per cent was to the minister of finance, it did not excite the public.[55] By the time he reached Perth at the end of February he was categorical: the tariff issue was dead. The Fielding tariff was not merely the first instalment of reform, it was to all intents and purposes the end of it.

The Martin-Richardson faction promptly tried to capture the Winnipeg Liberal Association at a meeting 13 March and to pass a resolution denouncing Sifton's statements. Isaac Campbell and D.H. McMillan were ready for them and successfully fought down any resolution of censure. Meanwhile, Sifton spoke again at Stratford, attempting to clarify his stand. He did not retract an inch: "The tariff question in Canada . . . is settled. It is, I venture to say, a dead issue. There will be changes, but as an issue between parties it is dead." The dissidents did not agree, considering that Sifton's statements ran counter to historic Liberal policy. At the April meeting of the party, the question was fought out again. A letter from Sifton was read in which he claimed that his remark about the tariff had "a directly opposite meaning to that which has been attributed to it." "My argument," he asserted, "was intended to show, not that the Liberal party had abandoned tariff reform, but that the Conservative party could not, if in power, return to the principle of extreme protection." After some debate a resolution was proposed which neatly avoided condemning anyone, being passed with only one dissenting vote.[56]

Sifton was infuriated by this latest disruption. When the trouble had first begun, he had laid down the principle that Liberals ought to "stand by their leaders and defend the Government and their policy. Any other course means the destruction of the leaders and also destruction of the followers. A political party must either hang together or hang separately." Once again the self-centred antics of the Martin faction threatened the survival both of Sifton and of the Liberal party in Manitoba. A face-saving resolution for the public benefit could hardly restore unity to the party.

The Greenway government were deeply disturbed by all this, since they had an election in the offing. Col. McMillan told Sifton that "matters are not in good shape in the city or throughout the Province." Posing as a friend of the farmer and of the people generally, Richardson and the *Tribune* were having a seriously detrimental effect. His faction was furthermore determined to nominate E.D. Martin as Liberal candidate for Winnipeg. Only Isaac Campbell could hope to prevent the split by accepting the nomination, and he did not want it. With no other suitable candidate in sight, McMillan concluded that "a settlement with Richardson" was essential.

But if McMillan thought that Sifton would consider compromise, his illusions were shortly dispelled. There would be no agreement, retorted Sifton; he wanted to "fight these fellows to a finish...just as we fought Luxton and the Free Press." Yet he was forced to admit that Richardson, whom he termed a "blathering hypocritical windbag," could wreak havoc in provincial politics, and the minister therefore agreed, not to forgive his enemies, but to play down the dispute until after the provincial election. Renewed attempts by Laurier and Sifton to persuade Campbell to accept the Winnipeg nomination were unavailing, and the undaunted Martin soon announced his candidature.[57]

Once again Sifton endeavoured to explain the "very unsatisfactory" situation in Winnipeg to J.S. Willison. And once again his letter was oddly revealing:

There are about twenty fellows there who might be called party heelers on the Liberal side, who hate me ... like the devil hates holy water. There are a variety of reasons for it. I suppose I might size it up by saying that the fact that I occasionally wear a silk hat and a dress coat and do not drink whisky in the bar of a third-class hotel will give you the best comprehension of the reasons why they do not like me. I never had anything to do with them and never would. They were all great pushers of Joe Martin. Joe was their ideal of what a public man ought to be.

As he had earlier, Sifton attributed the division to disappointed would-be boodlers. Because Campbell had refused to run and Martin had announced his candidacy, the government had decided to delay the election "and let the Martin crowd have a summer's exercise," by which time it was hoped the obvious futility of their endeavours would bring them to time.[58]

Beyond these local troubles, Sifton was very optimistic about Liberal prospects, especially at the federal level. "The indications are generally that we are going to have prosperity for a few years to come." he told Campbell, "which, whether it ought to or not, no doubt helps the party in power." At the same time, his onerous duties were taking their toll. "I have a very strong disposition to get out of the government after the next election," he wrote, although "I think we are responsible for piloting the ship that far." Beyond that his course was uncertain: "Circumstances may change, but my present idea is that I would as soon spend life in a treadmill as carrying the load of work I have to do now."[59]

# 11

# Immigrants and Indians

For more than two decades near the end of the nineteenth century Canada witnessed an unprecedented exodus. Between 1880 and 1891, more than a million Canadians and immigrants, equivalent to one-fifth of the total dominion population, left to seek greater opportunity in the United States. Emigration exceeded immigration by 205,000 in the 1880's; while in the 1890's, as the trend continued, the net loss was 181,000.[1] Small wonder, then, that the Laurier government was as concerned with devising policies to retain Canadians as it was with attracting immigrants.

The story of the prairie West had been scarcely less discouraging than that of the Dominion as a whole. The population had indeed grown slowly and steadily, but the statistics hid the stories of tens of thousands of disappointments and tragic failures on prairie farms which resulted in deeply rutted trails leading southward. Some of the homesteaders were incompetent or the victims of visionaries or swindlers, but most were defeated by frost, pestilence, insufficiently advanced technology, and an economic system which made them vulnerable to the slightest shifts in the winds of fortune.

Clifford Sifton believed that one of the chief causes of western stagnation had been the stumbling and insensitive administration of dominion lands. Settlers still faced a bewildering chain of authority and restrictive regulations when trying to secure their promised free homestead. Sifton promptly moved to centralize the administration in Ottawa by abolishing the Dominion Lands Board, which had been located in Winnipeg. By this means he eliminated much duplication of effort, expedited business, and incidentally saved some $20,000 in salaries.[2] In 1898 he continued his efforts, begun the previous year, to make the regulations of the Dominion Lands Act both simpler and more flexible. Now, under certain conditions, group settlement could more easily be permitted. Clerks were empowered to take affidavits, cutting red tape in registry offices. Provisions regarding second homesteads and pre-emptions were clarified. Homesteads could be granted in separate areas not totalling more than 160 acres. In Manitoba, the Dominion and the province rationalized their respective land holdings by an exchange. Provision was made to eject squatters where necessary. Finally, so-called time sales were cancelled and made available for settlement.[3]

The problems thus rectified, however, were picayune compared with the railway land reserves. Commencing with the 25,000,000 acres granted for the construction of the main line of the Canadian Pacific Railway, some 39,725,130 acres had been committed to subsidize railway construction by 1898. But this was not the full extent of the problem. The railway contracts specified that the land must be "fairly fit for settlement," but did not require the railways to select and patent the land within any time limit. The railways were exempted from taxation on their undeveloped lands for twenty years after receiving patent; even so, they understandably were in no hurry. As a result, Sifton estimated in 1898, some 67,000,000 acres, or nearly half of arable western lands, were being withheld from settlement pending railway selection. Of some 28,561,354 acres actually earned by completed railways by 1898, only 2,093,707 had been patented.[4]

When Sifton arrived in Ottawa, he apparently thought the problem could be quickly resolved. He was rudely surprised, as were many of his impatient western supporters. In 1898 he launched a thorough investigation of the legal position and of the value and location of railway lands. Early the following year he assigned William Pearce, an able and experienced officer, to devote all his time to locating suitable lands to fulfil the requirements of the railway contracts. At the beginning of the session of Parliament in 1900, Sifton was forced to confess that eighteeen months of intensive activity had been a failure and that almost no patents had been issued to the stubborn railways. Their contracts seemed ironclad.[5]

Although a final resolution would require a new line of attack over the next few years, there was some hope of progress as irrigation techniques were being introduced into the Territories. Large areas of the arid southwestern prairies might be made arable, a matter of great interest to CPR officials whose lines ran for many miles through this relatively unsettled and unproductive region. The earliest attempt at irrigation had taken place near Calgary in 1879, but neither this nor several other small-scale projects over the succeeding decade had aroused much interest. By the early 1890's, however, William Pearce had engendered some public enthusiasm and had managed to persuade officials of the CPR and the Canadian government that large-scale irrigation could transform a substantial part of southern Alberta.[6] The Mormon settlers and others in the extreme southern portion of the district, moreover, had demonstrated that irrigation was practicable. The North-West Irrigation Act, passed in 1894, suppressed riparian rights in those rivers and streams which could be used in irrigation and vested their control in the Crown.[7] One of the evident purposes of the act was to allow the CPR to secure lands *en bloc* along its right-of-way east of Calgary. These lands would in turn become the centre of a massive irrigation project, and securing them would satisfy a substantial part of the company's outstanding land claim.

The project, however, had not been pushed forward with any despatch by the Conservative government, and consequently it was one of the first important issues confronting Sifton when he assumed office. According to a report prepared in 1896 by J.S. Dennis, chief inspector of surveys, the project could not proceed without substantial changes in both irrigation and dominion lands legislation. Lands to be reclaimed by irrigation would have to be granted on terms more liberal than those applied to normal homesteads, and permission must be granted to settle and cultivate such lands "under the colony or hamlet system," rather than by homesteading. Such lands must be granted in large sections, the grantee undertaking to colonize and develop the lands. Common control of water rights would be essential. The governor-in-council must have the discretionary authority to devise appropriate regulations for the sale and settlement of each block of land. Carried out intelligently, Dennis predicted, irrigation projects could bring 6,325,000 acres under cultivation, large tracts of arid lands contiguous to the irrigated lands could be used for grazing with a regular supply of water guaranteed, and the region would be rapidly settled.[8] Before long, the government of the North-West Territories, granted more independence in 1897, asked for control of irrigation policy, claiming that it was of merely local interest, it "rounds out our powers," and it would further discourage the cry for provincial autonomy for Alberta.[9] At a time of gloomy immigration prospects, when there was a chance to populate an otherwise unproductive area and also to help to settle the vexing land grant of the CPR, Sifton was bound to be interested. In 1898, after "a good deal of consideration," he introduced bills which gave effect to Dennis's recommendations and partially met the demands of the territorial government.[10] The administration of irrigation was centred at Regina, and Dennis, who became deputy commissioner of public works in the Territories, also acted as agent for the Department of the Interior on irrigation matters.[11]

The deputy minister of the interior wrote in 1897, "the experimental stage of irrigation in the Territories may now be said to be passed." Sifton gave enthusiastic encouragement to a number of projects, with striking results. In 1896 there were in southern Alberta some 157 ditches and canals totalling 350 miles in length and capable of irrigating 63,000 acres of arid land. By 1900 there were 200 ditches and canals totalling 525 miles in length and bringing some 669,000 acres under irrigation. The irrigation works were valued in 1900 at $550,000; but the land affected had risen in value by some $1,337,514. And, as expected, more grazing land was made available, settlers were pouring in, and more large projects were under way.[12] In 1899 Sifton and the CPR began serious talks concerning the large-scale scheme so long anticipated. The following year he had so warmed to its potential results that he enthusiastically predicted that "Calgary would reach a population figure over 100,000 within ten years of the Bow River project being started."[13] Early in the twentieth century, it was launched.

Sifton's support for irrigation reflected his general administrative tendencies. His basic goal was to people the West with a productive agrarian population. If some parts of the region, such as the southwest, were unsuited to the homestead philosophy of the Dominion Lands Act, then the theory would have to go and new approaches be adopted. He moved in this direction with much greater decisiveness and flexibility than his Conservative predecessors. At the same time, he believed that such policies could only be implemented with great powers of ministerial discretion, which he proceeded to secure both by legislation and by centralization of the administration. His goals, therefore, were much the same as those of the Conservatives; but existing policies were re-examined in terms of their effectiveness. Within two years he had eliminated the perpetual backlog of business which had characterized the department. Almost overnight it had become aggressive and businesslike, stamped with Sifton's personality.

How successful was he in retaining Canada's own population? Insofar as government policy had anything to do with the decisions of Canadians to move west instead of south, the policies enjoyed some success. Canadians registering with the immigration authorities at Winnipeg rose from less than 2,400 in 1897 to over 13,100 in 1898, nearly 11,600 in 1899, and nearly 8,500 in the first six months of 1900. With remarkable consistency Canadians continued to make one-third or more of the homestead entries throughout the period 1896–1900, despite a rapid rise in levels of immigration.[14] Canadians proved as responsive as immigrants to generally improving economic conditions, to a refurbished image of the West, and perhaps to a more efficient administration.

The government could do nothing overt to encourage the westward migration of Canadians, which made their numbers more remarkable. While many people suggested that the government should spend part of its immigration budget promoting the West in central and eastern Canada and stemming the flow southward through subsidized fares to the prairies, such ideas were politically impossible. For years rural depopulation had been a matter of great concern in the Maritimes, Québec, and Ontario. Promotion of migration from the Maritimes, A.G. Blair rather testily told Sifton, "would mean a still further depopulation of that part of the Dominion, and I know of no good reason why people should be encouraged to leave there and go to the West."[15]

Nor did Sifton countenance suggestions that the urban unemployed be aided in establishing homesteads as a means of relieving the social congestion of central Canadian cities. "Experience shows," he wrote, "that workingmen from the cities and towns are the most helpless people in the world when they are placed upon the prairie and left to shift for themselves."[16] Ironically, the government had long been forced for political reasons to maintain agents in the United States to try to repatriate those Canadians who had departed the country, a thankless and unrewarding task. With the returning prosperity, however, the southward stream of Canadians slowed dramatically, and the flow westward markedly increased. "I want to say," Sifton declared proudly to a cheering Toronto audience in 1898, "that the exodus of Canadians to the United States has been stopped," and instead "our agents are taking thousands of the best farmers in the western states today and settling them upon our western prairies."[17] The minister of the interior could be forgiven some exaggeration; his remarks pointed to the already evident success in what he had always regarded as his principal task when he came to Ottawa—the attraction of immigrants to the West.

By the end of his first year in office Sifton had entirely transformed the Immigration Branch of the Department of the Interior. His own men were in most of the important positions of authority. Placed under Deputy Minister James A. Smart was Frank Pedley, a Liberal lawyer from Toronto, who became superintendent of immigration. From a base in Ottawa he would directly oversee all aspects of the immigration service. It was decided to place a commissioner of immigration at Winnipeg to supervise the settlement work west of the Lakehead. Under his charge would be receiving immigrants at Winnipeg, caring for them in the city, and ensuring that they were properly transported to and settled upon their land. W.F. McCreary, a lawyer and former Winnipeg mayor, proved to be an excellent choice for the post.

In the lower echelons of the service, too, Sifton's organizing hand was soon in evidence. It was made clear to all agents that their positions and salary would largely depend upon the energy with which they pursued immigrants. One agent noted "that Mr. Sifton, when appointing me, indicated the desirability of 'results' in excess of those up to that date."[18] The principle of paying agents by commission for immigrants who actually settled on the land was widely extended. Only those showing unusual ability or promise were hired. Of one applicant Sifton observed, "The valuable part of his letter consists in the knowledge which it displays of the actual details of the movement of people from Iowa and Indiana into the North Western States." Such a man could "get hold of the people who are already on the move, and he also knows Manitoba thoroughly and can tell them where to go. His letter is not of the ordinary vague style which comes from a man who has no acquaintance with what he is talking about."[19] Too many applications fell into that latter category, causing Sifton to write with irritation that "the idea which some of our friends have that there is always room for another man in the immigration service is an entire mistake."[20]

Sifton believed in the hard sell. "In my judgment," he told the House of Commons, "the immigration work has to be carried on in the same manner as the sale of any commodity; just as soon as you stop advertising and missionary work the movement is going to stop."[21] The available media were exploited heavily to extol the virtues of western Canada. From a mere sixty-five thousand pieces of immigration literature produced in 1896, the volume was expanded to over one million in the first six months of 1900—an activity which incidentally was used to subsidize Liberal newspapers across the country by awarding them the printing contracts.[22] The object was to flood the rural districts of the United States, Great Britain, and Europe; accordingly the pamphlets were produced in a wide variety of languages.[23] Tours of the West for American and British journalists who agreed to write about their impressions were often arranged, and advertisements were frequently inserted in suitable newspapers in those countries. Indeed the department was entirely prepared to underwrite the production of "editorial articles" for insertion in foreign newspapers, articles—as Sifton put it—"referring to Canada and incidentally giving information about Canada of such a nature as an English paper would be willing to publish and would consider to be interesting to its readers and also incidentally *not doing any injury* to the present administration."[24]

A number of other techniques were used, among the most popular of which were testimonial pamphlets and visits from successful homesteaders directed at their former home districts and Canadian displays at regional exhibitions in Britain and the U.S.A. Both led naturally to another approach central to Sifton's ideas of successful immigration promotion: active pursuit of the individual settler. Sifton never believed that blanket advertising would do more than arouse interest, plant a seed in the minds of potential settlers, and perhaps dispel some myths and prejudices and create a favourable impression about Canada. It would not, however, by itself persuade many settlers to come. That had to be done by individual contact, by knowing where people were on the move and "talking up" Canada to the most desirable of them, by spotting an interested party at an exhibition and following up, and generally by getting out and talking to as many individuals as possible. One of his agents recalled that Sifton had told him, "When you go after a man, stick to him until you have exhausted every hope of securing him."[25]

Nowhere were these techniques put to better use than in the United States. Sifton had the wit to recognize, as the Conservatives generally had not, that the great Republic was much more than the home of many former Canadians;

it was itself a vast potential source of ideal settlers. The whole thrust of the department's efforts in the U.S. had been to repatriate former Canadians. In 1896 there were but six agents, four of them working among expatriate French Canadians, a fifth at Chicago for English-speaking people, and a sixth working among the Scandinavians.[26] Sifton promptly appointed W.J. White, formerly editor of the *Brandon Sun,* to take charge of the press campaign in the United States and then made him inspector of Canadian immigration agencies in that country. He removed the head office from Chicago to St. Paul, located many other offices, and expanded the service to eighteen full-time agents and nearly three hundred sub-agents.[27]

It was not easy to persuade Americans of the virtues of the Canadian West. Although it was at least a decade since there had been large tracts of good free homestead land in the United States, there were still substantial unsettled lands available at a price from a great variety of businessmen, railway companies, and speculators. There was fierce competition for settlers and even "raiding" of settlers' parties on trains by avid salesmen. Needless to say, American railway lines did not willingly facilitate the movement of settlers from their hinterlands to Canada. Much of the success of moving settlers into the dominion depended upon the co-operation of the CPR, which had extensive trackage in the U.S. and could provide attractive fares to the West. Sifton was forced to be constantly vigilant to see that the Canadian Pacific offered competitive freight and passenger rates, because the American lines structured their fares to draw traffic away from Canada.[28]

The crucial factor, as Sifton and his officials realized, was to start a substantial flow of Americans into Canada, for then others would follow more willingly. The programme on the whole was successful for the number of Americans entering Canada rose from less than 2,500 in 1897 to over 9,000 in 1898, nearly 12,000 in 1899, and more than 8,500 in the first six months of 1900. Homestead entries by Americans grew just as dramatically, from 164 in 1897 to 1,307 in 1900.[29] Moreover, most Canadians deemed it a desirable influx. Many of the Americans were experienced western farmers, they often came with considerable capital and goods, and they generally were considered racially compatible. The Winnipeg *Tribune,* for example, reported concerning a body of German settlers who arrived from Michigan in the late summer of 1897 that "they are a set of strong, able-bodied men, all of them possessed of more or less means, and just the kind of people who are sure to succeed in that new country. Most . . . are the head of families, and they propose to erect houses and make comfortable homes for their wives and families, who will follow them in the spring."[30]

Operations in Great Britain had somewhat more mixed results. Canada regarded itself as essentially a British nation: therefore, any Canadian government must be seen to be attracting a steady supply of British immigrants. This became vitally important as the numbers of non-British immigrants began to swell. The Laurier government, however, faced several serious obstacles. With returning prosperity, fewer "desirable" people wished to emigrate. Not a large proportion of British emigrants chose to come to Canada for, as Sifton once commented, "Owing to the persistent representation in Britain of Canada as a land of ice and snow emigration has been chiefly going to Australasia and South Africa, and it is now the endeavour of the department to counteract the effect of such literature."[31] He might have added that many more went to the United States. Of those who did come to Canada, the majority were not suited to prairie farming, although there seemed to be an unlimited supply of unskilled or semi-skilled labourers. Ireland had once supplied many agricultural settlers, but the flow of emigrants had all but dried up by the turn of the century. Similarly, there were few prospects among farm labourers of England and Scotland because they were in short supply at home and wages had risen accordingly.[32] The result was that in the years from 1897 to 1900 British immigration fluctuated very little, some ten or eleven thousand arriving each year.[33]

An additional important factor in this limited success was the inefficiency of the Canadian immigration operations in Great Britain. Traditionally, the supervision of both the British and European promotion had fallen to the Canadian high commissioner in London. The incumbent high commissioner was the septuagenarian Sir Donald Smith, created Baron Strathcona and Mount Royal in 1897. Laurier did not see fit to replace him, since his friendship could be valuable to the government. Unfortunately, this resulted in something less than full co-operation between the high commissioner's office and the Immigration Branch. Strathcona sought to retain all his prerogatives and influence and was annoyed when Sifton's officials began to write directly to immigration agents in Britain rather than routing correspondence through his office. Sifton at once made it clear that although "a general supervision of the Agents should be exercised by your office," it would be "quite impossible to make any fixed rule which would preclude me from having direct communication with an Agent when I consider it advisable."[34] This policy plainly riled several of Strathcona's officials and did nothing to facilitate the smooth transaction of business. More was involved than a centralization of control from Ottawa on the one hand versus a hide-bound tradition on the other. The London office, observed one of Sifton's agents, "regards the advent of a Liberal Government into power as a most peculiar and unfortunate event, not likely to happen again during this or the next century, and this view is reflected in the treatment accorded officials appointed since 1896."[35] So far could the Canadian and British jurisdictions work at cross-purposes that the Department of the Interior and the high commissioner's office could each appoint agents to work essentially the same territory.[36] Finally, Strathcona did not view the promotion of emigration as his first priority, and he no longer had the energy to see that it was undertaken with the desired zeal.

The remaining field for Canadian endeavour was Europe. Here the government had to tread with caution. Most European governments were hostile to emigration promotion; several prohibited it. There was, nevertheless, a vast agricultural population, especially in eastern Europe, which had scarcely been tapped but which was showing signs of joining the general exodus of millions of Europeans which had occurred in periodic waves since the end of the Napoleonic wars. Until Sifton came into office, the Canadian government had not enjoyed marked success in Europe. The Dominion had followed the practice of several other countries of paying a bonus to shipping agents who directed settlers to Canada, but this provided neither system nor incentive. The agents could collect a bonus from any one of several countries, so there was no great effort to redirect migrants headed for, say, the United States or Argentina. Nor were there many significant groups of European settlers in Canada who would serve to attract their fellow countrymen. The department determined to do everything possible to establish block settlements of various European ethnic groups, in the expectation that they would have the desired magnetic effect.

It began by making arrangements with individual shipping agents at key ports of embarkation. These agreements, usually secret, were considered by departmental officials to have been in large part responsible for the dramatic rise in continental immigrants between 1897 and 1899. Such success decided Sifton to organize the European work more efficiently. He appointed W.T.R. Preston, a former Liberal organizer of malodorous reputation in Ontario, to be inspector of agencies in Britain and Europe. It helped little that Preston evinced a monumental disdain for Lord Strathcona. Later he would create numerous problems for Sifton as well, but for the time being his ferocious energies were well occupied in rousing officials abroad.[37] By the end of 1899 Preston had been instrumental in the formation of the North Atlantic Trading Company, a clandestine organization of European shipping agents who agreed to try to divert agricultural settlers to Canada in return for an increased bonus. The Canadian government undertook to pay £500 per annum for promotional literature and to regard persons over twelve, rather than eighteen, as adults for purposes of the higher bonus. However, the government was to pay only for actual agricultural settlers, and the head of each family was to be possessed of not less than $100 upon arrival. Lord Strathcona commented that the new arrangement did not differ in principle from earlier plans, but it did ensure that the work would be carried out more systematically. Sifton was delighted because, except for the literature, the government paid only for effective results, not on the haphazard basis of the past.[38]

There was an understanding with the company that the agreement would apply to immigrants from particular countries: Russia (probably understood to include Finland), Germany, Austria, Romania, Switzerland, northern Italy, Holland, Belgium, and France.[39] The first four countries reflected the strongest sources of continental agriculturalists in the previous few years.

Northern Italy was viewed as a good source of desirable agricultural labourers. The inclusion of France was politically essential in Canada, despite a dismal record of emigration; the work in Belgium was somewhat more successful in producing French-speaking immigrants. The choice of countries also reflected the general failure of attempts to secure immigrants from Scandinavia (except for Iceland), and the common belief that immigrants from southern Europe would not make successful prairie farmers.

The clear evidence that Canada was receiving substantial numbers of good agricultural settlers from Europe should have been proof positive that Sifton's policies were successful. Surely he could reasonably expect that the rising tide of western settlement would help to offset the discontent which had arisen over the Yukon, the tariff, and the other assorted western grievances. It was not to be. Rather, the immigrants were met with an unprecedented groundswell of nativist hostility across western Canada. The newcomers may have been excellent farmers, but that did not qualify them as desirable settlers in the minds of many westerners, who believed that the dominant Anglo-Saxon Protestant society was seriously threatened. The agitation, which reached the boiling point in 1899, focused mainly on three groups: the Galicians (or Ukrainians) and the Doukhobors on the prairies and the Orientals in British Columbia.

In a sense the hostility, though deeply regrettable, was understandable. The newcomers from central and eastern Europe formed a very large proportion of actual western settlers in these years. Most immigrants to Canada did not choose to go to the West; in 1896, for example, of 16,835 immigrants, only 6,214 declared their intention to settle in Manitoba, the Territories, or British Columbia.[40] Similarly, of nearly 24,000 immigrants reaching the eastern seaports in the first half of 1900, it would appear that just over 10,000 reached Winnipeg. The rate of attrition between the ports and Winnipeg was highest among British immigrants: in the first half of 1900 some 5,141 arrived at the ports, but only 2,119 reached the Manitoba capital. Comparable figures for the Galicians and Bukowinians were 4,583 at the ports and 4,992 at Winnipeg, which suggests that some were even reaching western Canada via the United States.[41] Between 1897 and 1899 the Galicians consistently equalled or outnumbered the combined totals of British and American immigrants at Winnipeg. The worst year was 1899 when under 6,000 Britishers and Americans were overwhelmed by 6,914 Galicians and 7,400 Doukhobors.[42] It was no use for Sifton to point out that less than half the total immigrants to Canada in any year, and usually far less than half, were continental in origin. It was what was happening in Winnipeg that concerned westerners as large unassimilable pockets of assorted ethnic groups began to establish themselves piecemeal across the West. This perceived threat fuelled the demands for a racially selective, even exclusionist immigration policy.

The government was not responsive. The Liberal party had generally favoured an open-door policy since the time of Alexander Mackenzie; and Prime Minister Laurier was philosophically a laissez-faire Liberal, who, initially at least, was unhappy with and inclined to resist restrictive immigration measures. Moreover, since few Orientals or Europeans were settling among the larger population of central and eastern Canada, the question never seized the centre of the political stage as it did in the West. Most important, Clifford Sifton was a highly pragmatic politician determined to populate the West with a productive agrarian population which he would seek wherever he could find it, despite western agitation. He would employ the laissez-faire theory when it suited his purposes, though he had far fewer inhibitions about restrictive legislation than the prime minister.

Illustrative of their personal differences was the issue of Oriental immigration. Agitation reached a fever pitch in 1899 when British Columbia tried to place a $500 head tax on all Orientals. There ensued a bitter debate in the House of Commons in which western members attempted to outdo one another in denouncing the social evils attendant upon Oriental immigration. Nicholas Flood Davin described with passion the low race and character of the Chinese, revealing to the House that the Chinese women were without exception prostitutes whose practices were "indescribable." E.G. Prior, MP for Victoria, declared that "these Chinamen are a lower class of human beings than white people are" and that "they never assimilate with the white people. A woman has to descend very low before she would think of marrying a Chinaman." Sifton declared himself in sympathy with Prior's sentiments, motivated in part by his conviction that Orientals would not make successful prairie settlers and were not essential for anything else.[43] Equally important was his responsibility for the fortunes of the Liberal Party in British Columbia at the next general election; he could not afford to appear weak on this vital issue.

Laurier complicated matters by disallowing the provincial legislation of 1899, partly because of imperial considerations and partly because he opposed it in principle. Early in 1900 Sifton proposed an alternate plan, a $250 Oriental head tax under dominion legislation. He also wanted a Canadian version of the so-called "Natal Act," a measure to eliminate Oriental immigration by application of a European language test. Laurier assented only to a doubling of the Chinese capitation tax to $100 and a commission to investigate Oriental immigration. The British government informed Canada that a Natal act was indeed within the competence of the dominion Parliament, but Laurier would have none of it. He informed the House that such a measure would cause complications for British policy in Japan.[44] Failure by Ottawa to act could only cause political difficulty for Liberals in British Columbia. They were able to contend, however, that the government was not soft on Orientals and had refrained from acting only out of the highest regard for the welfare of the Empire.

No less virulent than anti-Oriental sentiment was the bitter hatred on the prairies toward central Europeans, particularly the Galicians. They came with few goods, little cash, and unpronounceable names from the unknown depths of Austria-Hungary and Russia. They were illiterate peasants, Catholics (it hardly mattered that few were Roman Catholics), drinkers, diseased, wife-beaters, criminally inclined, with no sense of democratic institutions. So ran the prejudice which began to mount, a product of fear and ignorance. A Brandon paper denounced "Hon. Mr. Sifton's grand 'round up' of European freaks and hoboes." The Galicians and Doukhobors were "a menagerie," "ignorant and vicious foreign scum." "Importing such creatures into our country," declared one irate journalist, "is about as sensible as deliberately bringing vermin into a new house." After a murder allegedly committed by a Galician, the Conservative *Winnipeg Telegram* commented, "Another horrible crime has been committed by the foreign ruffians whom Mr. Sifton is rushing into this country." The Galicians, it appeared, were barely human, "herding with cattle" and "in the habit of selling their wives."[45] Perhaps the campaign of vilification reached a climax of sorts during the provincial election campaign in Manitoba in 1899, with the Conservatives running as hard against Sifton as they were against Greenway. Hugh John Macdonald, by now leader of the Opposition, made vicious attacks on the immigrants and blatant appeals to racial and religious prejudice:

> He did not want to have a mongrel breed in this portion of Canada [Macdonald was reported to have said]. He did not want Slavs introduced among us, whether from Austria, Poland or Russia, men who are practically serfs and slaves. He wanted white men. . . . [These immigrants] do not know what free government is. They are not free men and they will simply be up for sale. . . . They will be influenced by the Church; they are Roman Catholics.[46]

Such nonsense found a ready audience, as Sifton was well aware. Some of the charges even had a small kernel of truth. The Galicians often were poverty-stricken, dirty, and diseased, but only because of the atrocious conditions they endured while migrating. They were often misled and relieved of their funds by unscrupulous agents in Europe, herded on to overcrowded vessels with poor food and little health care. Small wonder that they disembarked at Halifax and other ports in shocking condition, afflicted with lice at least, and smallpox or other contagious diseases at worst. Every case of disease in Canada that might conceivably be traceable to the immigrants was blown out of proportion by the press, forcing Sifton to be vigilant that they were properly inspected and quarantined. But such medical matters were not within his jurisdiction; they came under the minister of agriculture, who was somewhat less than seized with the urgency of adequate facilities. As a result, in 1898 the Galicians reportedly were being held in quarantine in Halifax in the most appalling circumstances, exposed to constant rain and wind and in mud from four to eighteen inches deep. They were bathed and disinfected in batches of one hundred in water ditches along the railway track while their clothes were disinfected in steam chests. Not only were the conditions humiliating, but the agents at Halifax were forced to send the Galicians on to Winnipeg before they were properly cleaned up because they were dying of exposure.[47]

People who could endure such conditions presumably could endure almost anything. That was one assumption which Sifton seemed too willing to make. He did not share the nativist fears of the continental influx. His belief was that the Doukhobors and Galicians, and the Slavic peoples generally, were peculiarly suited to tolerate the bitter winters and difficult farming of the prairies. They were peasant races, simple stock, wedded to the land, certain to set down deep roots and raise large families that would remain generation after generation to provide a return on the investment involved in attracting them. They would be much more reliable than many of the English farmers who gave up at the first difficulty or whose sons and daughters were unlikely to remain on the farm. He was right about one thing: the Galicians would endure, not because of any unique love of the land, but because they had no alternative.[48]

The department of the interior probably did less to help the Galicians than any other immigrant group. There were constant charges in the press and from opposition politicians that the government was spending great sums in subsidizing the continental immigration. In fact, prior to the formation of the North Atlantic Trading Company late in 1899, the government was only paying the standard bonus to shipping agents and supervising the immigrants from the ocean ports to their lands. Once on the land, the immigrant was expected to make it on his own. Assistance to relieve destitution was given only grudgingly, if at all, and was made a lien on the settler's property. Indeed, on occasion the department was wilfully determined not to see the most abject poverty among the Galicians.[49] Sifton opposed in principle any form of assisted settlement: "Once a man is taken hold of by the Government and treated as a ward he seems to acquire the sentiments of a pauper, and forever after will not stand on his own feet or try to help himself." Every earlier attempt had been "an absolute failure, and so far as can be learned altogether for the reason that I have mentioned."[50]

Mounting opposition to the Galicians had become so powerful by the spring of 1899 that Immigration Commissioner McCreary advised Sifton to drop the bonuses then being paid to continental shipping agents. There were nearly twenty thousand Galicians in Canada, and there was a general belief "that we have sufficient for the present, as many as we can assimilate for some years." Already the officers in Winnipeg were finding difficulty in establishing recent arrivals because of the tremendous local opposition when any new colony was announced. While the families who had arrived had between $50 and $250 each, there was some likelihood that many future immigrants might be nearly destitute. Stopping the bonus would not hamper continental immigration, in McCreary's view, because "Germans, Russians and others do not wish to be placed near these Galicians, and it would rather help immigration from other European countries to know that they were not going to be settled among Galicians." Furthermore, the number of Galicians would continue to expand steadily by natural increase and the arrival of friends and relatives of those already in Canada. Perhaps the clinching argument was the danger to the Liberals at the forthcoming provincial election.[51]

Sifton accordingly bowed to the popular will and announced the dropping of all continental bonuses, effective 1 June 1899. He had at first been inclined to resist the pressure: "We cannot take the stand that we are going to drop bringing in people and the people will either have to endorse our policy or vote against us," he told A.J. Magurn.[52] After further thought, however, he concluded that the bonuses could be dropped for the benefit of public consumption and reinstated in the *sub rosa* arrangements of the North Atlantic Trading Company a few months later. The Galicians therefore continued to arrive at a rate of over five thousand per year.[53]

To many Canadians the seventy-four hundred Doukhobors who arrived in 1899 were further proof that Sifton's policies were indiscriminate. These Russian pacifist farmers had come seeking the opportunity to pursue their communal way of life without government harrassment. They were as bent on avoiding assimilation in Canada as they had been in Russia. The government provided three settlements for them near Yorkton and Prince Albert, where at least for a while they would be preoccupied with breaking the land and establishing homes. The Doukhobors had not required special privileges, beyond a promised exemption from military service and some rather vague commitments about education. They could hold their land communally under existing regulations, provided they entered for the homesteads individually. The government agreed that the bonus usually paid to shipping agents could be placed in a fund to help finance the transportation and care of the Doukhobors until they reached their land. This left the government open to the politically damaging, though unfair, charge that it was assisting the settlement of foreigners while it would do nothing for Britishers or Canadians. Demagogues such as Hugh John Macdonald announced that it would be their policy to prevent the Doukhobors from voting until they agreed to fight for Canada when necessary, while an educational requirement ought to be made a part of the franchise act.[54] The pacifist sect even posed problems for Sifton within his own party because they were not as amenable as most immigrants to subtle suggestions that they purchase supplies from approved Liberal businessmen. "They are a cranky set of people," he told his friend, Col. McMillan, "and therefore very hard to do anything with, like most people who have too much religion."[55]

A great deal of hostility surfaced when the government's proposed locations for Doukhobor colonies were announced. One area, near Edmonton, had to be abandoned because Galician settlements had already provoked a furore and because Frank Oliver, the local MP, was intransigent. The settlements which were finally selected were well away from existing homesteads and fifteen miles from the nearest railway. Yet William Mackenzie, promoter of the Canadian Northern Railway, protested that the colony would result in slow development of the land by the Doukhobors and would discourage "our better class of settlers" from taking up the lands along the railway. At this, Sifton, who had endured a long series of complaints and protests, angrily replied, "I think if you will consider the matter for a few minutes and realize that we are putting up on your line of railway in one bunch as many people as you have in the whole Dauphin settlement you will come to the conclusion that you are very much more interested in the matter than the Government is." The Doukhobors were "extremely intelligent and capable people, and they know exactly what they are about.... I will venture to say that they will improve their portion of the country faster than any other part of it will be improved."[56]

The influx of continental immigrants was as upsetting to organized labour as it was to Anglo-Saxon homesteaders. Sifton had little instinctive sympathy for unions, although the workers seemed to have a legitimate complaint. The Alien Labour Act, which the Laurier government had passed in 1897, apparently indicated a policy of protection for Canadian labour. But such was not the intention of the government, as the labour movement was beginning to discover. The prime minister himself opposed the law in principle, as restrictive of free trade between nations; he tolerated it only as a necessary and, he hoped, temporary retaliatory measure against similar American legislation.[57] Neither he nor Sifton had any firm commitment to enforce the letter of the law, which until 1901 came under the jurisdiction of the Department of Justice. Sifton had obtained power for W.F. McCreary to enforce the law in 1897, it is true; but the power was to be used selectively to keep large bodies of contract labour, such as Italian railroad navvies, from being imported to construct the Crow's Nest Pass line. It definitely was not to be applied against intending farmers from the United States or elsewhere who might wish to earn some cash from the construction. Indeed, some immigrants had been induced to come on the promise that such work would be available to help tide them over until they were established on their farms. Immigrants from Wales, England, and eastern Europe were all employed on the project.

Despite some labour opposition and the scandal that broke over the dreadful working conditions on the Crow's Nest line, the government policy initially did not seriously arouse the labour movement. Many Galicians and Doukhobors, however, began to seek work in Winnipeg and Brandon and on some railway projects, frequently undermining local wage structures. Organized labour was immediately hostile. These were immigrants who had been encouraged with government bonuses on the assumption that they were farmers, and here they were competing for urban jobs. One exasperated union official told Sifton that "all the hundreds of thousands of dollars to aid immigration have been extorted principally out of the laboring classes in order to make the price of labor cheap, to inundate and slaughter the labor market." The government's immigration and tariff policies were "most ingeniously devised to swindle the working man for the benefit of the rich every day of the year."[58] Sensitive to the political difficulties of Winnipeg, Sifton had already tried to discourage the Doukhobors from taking work, without much success. He replied soothingly, suggesting that the unions should take a broader view of affairs: "I think you will, on consideration, be inclined to agree with me that the labouring men in particular of Winnipeg are vitally interested in the filling up of the country and the consequent growth and prosperity of the cities and towns in which they will expect to procure employment at [favourable?] rates and under conditions that will enable them to live in comfort."[59]

Such was Sifton's constant message: settling the prairies with productive farmers would mean growth and prosperity for all. Before these considerations, persons of limited vision must be swept aside. By 1899 or 1900 no one could deny that Sifton was attracting agricultural settlers to the West. At the same time, the critics had changed their emphasis from "quantity" to "quality." The editor of the *Canadian Magazine* noted, "Mr. Sifton is doing clever work, but his policy is a mistaken one. The immigrants he is securing are not so desirable as those from the British Isles. They are rude, barbarous and uncultured. We do not want slaves; we want men." "Is Canada," he demanded, "to become as rude, as uncultured, as fickle, as heterogeneous, as careless of law and order and good citizenship as the United States?"[60]

Sifton mounted a vigorous counteroffensive in the Liberal press throughout the country, spearheaded by the *Manitoba Free Press.* In 1898 the paper declared that a policy of excluding "foreigners" would preclude the full development of the country. "There is no danger of assimilation. The Anglo-Saxon is itself a conglomerate race, and every century and every generation it becomes more so. That is its strength. It has never yet failed to absorb all elements that come within its influence, and there is not the least danger that it ever will." Canada, contended the *Free Press,* was doing much better than the United States because, while American cities were "filling up with Italians, Poles, and other alien races," the "foreigners" coming to the Dominion were settling on the western lands:

In Canada if you get the immigrant on the land he becomes at once naturalized and nationalized. As the years go by the fact that he owes his prosperity and his greatly improved position to British laws and British institutions is brought forcibly home to him by reading in his patent that he received the land from the crown, and he very quickly grows to feel that he is a Canadian and a member of the British empire. Any man, no matter what his nationality, so long as he desires to earn an honest living and is willing to till the soil, is a welcome addition to this western country, and his arrival is a national blessing.[61]

Privately, Sifton believed that it would be preferable to have a five-year, rather than a three-year naturalization period.[62] But he had no doubt that the experience of forging a livelihood from the prairie soil would instil in the immigrant the virtues of the individualist ethic which Sifton thought had shaped and characterized his own ancestors: men who knew what a hard day's work was, who valued their freedom and independence. Such men would do far more than create material prosperity. Upon the moral fibre that sprang from and was toughened by their experience could be laid the foundation of national greatness.

Less likely to contribute to national growth and development, in the government's opinion, were the Indians. After years of steady decline, the Indian population began to stabilize and even showed a slight recovery. Slowly it dawned on the government that a rethinking of Indian policy was essential. The *Manitoba Free Press,* having ruminated upon the situation in 1900, concluded: "That the tendency of the Indian race within the limits of the Dominion is not in the direction of becoming extinct, may be fairly concluded from the figures presented in the annual report of the Department of Indian Affairs."[63] So the Indians were not simply going to disappear. They would have to be lived with. But that was becoming a far more onerous obligation to the taxpayer than the government had envisaged when the treaties were signed in the 1870's. The reserve system then established and the government obligations incurred had been considered necessary during a difficult transitional phase for the Indians. But it was anticipated that the Indians who survived would become self-supporting and independent. Failing that, at least their children would reach that goal. Unfortunately, the goal seemed as far away as ever. Indian children educated at great expense were still dominated by old tribal customs and traditions. Prairie Indians were not yet successful farmers by and large, nor could they compete with white labour for unskilled and semi-skilled jobs. They still depended upon annuities and government aid to deal with destitution and starvation.

Sifton fully concurred that economic independence and ultimate acculturation were the proper objectives of Indian policy.[64] As usual, his criterion for evaluating policy was its effectiveness. After he had reduced and reorganized the Indian service, various programmes came up for review. The first and most obvious target was Indian education. The government was contributing over $70,000 annually to Indian schools in Manitoba and the Territories,[65] schools which plainly were not enjoying much success. Frank Oliver, an aggressive critic of Indian expenditures, voiced perfectly the ambivalent public attitude on the subject when he told the House of Commons, "We are educating these Indians to compete industrially with our own people, which seems to me a very undesirable use of public money, or else we are not able to educate them to compete, in which case our money is thrown away."[66] Because it was such a sensitive area, Sifton ordered a complete report on education policy shortly after he entered office. It was soon apparent that departmental officials agreed with some of Oliver's sentiments. One of the hopes of the industrial school system had been that by taking the Indian children out of the tribal atmosphere, boarding them, and teaching them a trade, they would leave the schools equipped to survive in white society. The policy had been an abysmal failure. The new thought in the department, commented J.D. McLean, secretary and chief clerk, was "that no extra effort should be made to train the Indian pupils as carpenters, cabinet makers, shoemakers, tailors, &c., as there is not much likelihood for many years to come of Indians so trained being capable of earning a livelihood at such trades in competition with white people. The chief aim should be to train the Indian pupils to earn a livelihood when they return to the reserves."[67] Sifton accordingly refused to permit any expansion of the industrial school system, which was by far the most costly and specialized. He directed that the emphasis should be on boarding schools to provide a general education for as many Indian pupils as possible and that no pupils should be permitted to remain in school beyond the age of eighteen.

An increased level of education for more Indians, it was hoped, would gradually lead to self-sufficiency on the reserves. Since the reserves were now being accepted as the place where Indians would live, skills in agriculture received a heavier emphasis in the schools. On the reserves, both farm instructors and Indians were given incentives to produce for sale beyond immediate personal and family requirements. The government began to clamp down on the issuing of rations of meat and flour, determined to force the Indians to cultivate more land and farm more efficiently.[68]

At the same time, the reserve system itself was coming under attack. It had been viewed as an essential part of a transitional phase, a means by which the Indians could be protected from the worst abuses of the advancing settlement frontier, enabling them to adopt the agricultural way of life and leading to gradual acculturation. However, two decades of experience, observed a departmental official to Sifton, "does not favour the view that the system makes for the advancement of the Indians."[69] On the reserve the tribe retained its identity and exercised powerful control over its members. It shaped values and thought. Indian children returning from the schools, even after several years, shed their white education quickly. They remained alien to the aggressive, competitive, individualistic white man's world. For the time being, nevertheless, Sifton was not prepared to undertake a radical attack on the reserve system, professing to believe that departmental goals could be achieved by more rigorous and efficient application of traditional methods.

The reserves were also under attack on a second and ultimately more dangerous front. The same westerners who reasoned that fewer Indians required fewer officials concluded that fewer Indians required less land. The size of Indian reserves had been based on the number of people in the band when the treaties were signed. Most bands and tribes had diminished considerably, and few Indians appeared to be very good farmers. Consequently, large tracts of reserve land remained undeveloped, eyed hungrily by speculators, neighbouring farmers, and potential homesteaders. Why, they demanded, should not the excess land revert to whites, who would put it to better use? Some were quite prepared to suggest that Indians on good agricultural land be removed to reserves more suited to hunting and fishing, leaving such land open for efficient exploitation. Sifton himself appears to have held such views when he first went to Ottawa. He made several attempts to appropriate Indian lands by executive order. His officials and those of the Department of Justice soon explained to him that there were definite procedures which had to be followed to secure the surrender of Indian reserve lands, the most important of which was obtaining the consent of the Indian bands concerned.[70] He therefore soon found himself in the position of defending the law and turning away importuning speculators and politicians. "The law," he once told Frank Oliver, "is very specific and clear. . . . In no case in which Indians are in possession of a reserve can the same be taken from them without their consent and the money placed to the general credit of all the Indians in the country." Even where the department thought that sale of some land would benefit a band, nothing could be done if the Indians refused to co-operate.[71]

On a crisp November day in 1897, Sifton received visitors in his private car in Calgary. He was returning from his tour of the Yukon-Alaska boundary region and was preoccupied with the tensions of nationalism and competition for trade which required immediate attention. Before him stretched the inevitable parade of officials, supplicants, and sycophants who bedevilled government ministers wherever they stopped; there were endless administrative trivia, appeals of departmental decisions, seekers of patronage and government favours. Among them was a brisk military figure, Major James Walker, retired from the North-West Mounted Police, whose message immediately secured Sifton's full attention. Gold seekers travelling north from Edmonton to the Yukon had generated, through their careless disregard for the native people, a great deal of hostility among the Indians of northern Alberta and Athabasca. These Indians had not been treated with in the 1870's; now, unless some accommodation were reached with them to secure their rights, serious violence might well occur. Only twelve years after the North-West Rebellion of 1885, Walker's warnings carried chilling implications. Moreover, as he subsequently pointed out to Sifton, treating with the northern Indians was simply good policy: "They will be more easily dealt with now than they would be when their country is overrun with prospectors and valuable mines be discovered. They would then place a higher value on their rights than they would before these discoveries are made and . . . they may object to prospectors or settlers going into that country until their rights are settled."[72]

Once back in Ottawa, Sifton discovered that plans to arrange a treaty six or seven years earlier had been dropped, probably because of the cost involved and because there seemed to be no pressing need.[73] He issued orders for preparations to negotiate a treaty in the spring and summer of 1898. It would encompass the region north of Treaty 6, from Lesser Slave Lake north to Great Slave Lake and the upper Mackenzie basin, where prospectors were already staking mining claims, and from Lake Athabasca to northeast British Columbia. By mid-April, however, it was concluded that the Indians could not be notified in time to arrange to meet the treaty commissioners, and the negotiations were postponed for a year to permit adequate advertisement.[74]

A postponement was well advised in any event. The boundaries of the proposed treaty were still under active debate in the department. Sifton was soon informed as well that the negotiations would have to encompass more than the estimated twenty-seven hundred Indians in the region. Approximately seventeen hundred mixed bloods, or Métis, could not be ignored; unless their rights were recognized, noted the Indian commissioner, "it may be confidently expected" that the Métis would use their "powerful influence" over the Indians "to retard negociations for the ceding of the territory."[75] When Sifton eventually appointed the treaty commission, therefore, he decided to grant it considerable latitude in determining the precise terms of the treaty and the region to be encompassed. Hon. David Laird, Indian commissioner in Winnipeg, was to head the treaty negotiations, assisted by J.A.J. McKenna of the Department of Indian Affairs, and by J.H. Ross of the North-West Territories government. They were to be guided by the principle "that no greater obligations will, on the whole, be assumed . . . than were incurred in securing the cession of the territory covered by the treaties which were made with the Indians of the other portions of the North West." Should any of the Métis prefer to be dealt with as Indians, the commissioners were empowered to permit such arrangements at their discretion. Otherwise the Métis were to be issued money scrip or land scrip on terms no more "liberal . . . than were accorded the Halfbreeds of Manitoba and the organized territories."[76]

Further consideration led to some modification of these arrangements in 1899 shortly before the commissioners were to depart. The Indians feared that they would be placed on reserves and their hunting and fishing privileges sharply curtailed. Sifton therefore departed from earlier policy and left optional the establishment of reserves. The Indians would be entitled to land should they so desire it in future; they would be permitted to hold their land collectively in reserves or in severalty, a concession to their way of life and less structured tribal organization; and they were to be assured that the government would not force upon them substantial changes in their style of life, except in those limited areas where settlement or development might take place. Sifton further appointed a separate halfbreed commission, consisting of Major Walker and J.A. Coté of the Department of the Interior, who would deal with Métis claims concurrently and in close consultation with the treaty commissioners.[77]

The negotiation of Indian Treaty 8 in the summer of 1899 was a political success.[78] The Indians generally seemed eager to negotiate, and Canadians on the whole seemed relieved that government authority had been peacefully extended to another vast tract of the Dominion. The only criticism directed at the government occurred when the halfbreed commissioners somewhat exceeded their discretionary authority and altered the form of scrip authorized by Sifton. The Métis thus were enabled to dispose of their scrip more easily. Sifton told the House of Commons that, while it was desirable that the Métis derive as much "benefit" as possible from the negotiations, "the financial benefit to the half-breeds is not the primary object the Government had in view in making this arrangement." Rather, "the main reason for making this arrangement is to pacify and keep pacified the North-West Territories" and to avoid "having an Indian trouble on our hands, the very slightest of which would cost us two or three times the amount of scrip we issue."[79] Government policy had been determined principally by expediency and by the conventions of native policy established for more than two decades.

In the context of the times, Sifton's record as superintendent general of Indian affairs had been creditable, if conservative. With the country slowly emerging from depression and the emphasis on getting the prairies settled, it would have been impossible to undertake any radical or costly departures from past policy. Except for regular complaints about overspending, government Indian policy created no serious political controversy. Treaty 8, finally, was not the result of humanitarian or ideological concern for the Indians of the region, but a pragmatic response to a perceived need to head off a potentially violent clash between cultures.

12

# The Young Napoleon
## (1899–1900)

Liberal party fortunes had never appeared so bright as early in 1899. For the first time, Clifford Sifton observed cheerily in March, there was not a single Tory administration in the Dominion. The Liberals could ill afford complacency, however. The Conservatives had been bitterly disappointed by their failure in 1898 to dislodge the long-established Liberal government in Ontario. They were hungrily eyeing Manitoba, where a provincial contest would soon be required. "The whole Tory party of Canada," Sifton warned Provincial Treasurer McMillan, "is going to make an assault on you."[1]

The Conservatives were indeed making thorough preparations. Rodmond P. Roblin, the former Liberal who emerged as the dominant figure and most effective strategist among the Conservatives after 1896, decided to resign the leadership of the party in favour of Hugh John Macdonald. The move was cunningly calculated. Although Macdonald had inherited little of the political genius of his father, he was well known as a genial former member of Parliament and minister of the interior from Winnipeg and as a pillar of the Manitoba bar for over fifteen years. Macdonald was better placed than Roblin to take advantage of Greenway's "softening" on the school issue, to arraign federal policies on the tariff and immigration, and to attract urban support. Most important, as a longtime CPR solicitor and being connected with the establishment of the dominion party, he was well situated to bring outside financial aid and organizational support to the provincial party. The Conservatives were demonstrating unprecedented vitality, organizing throughout the province and mounting vigorous press campaigns and public meetings.

Premier Greenway dismissed the new Conservative leader with a smirk, utterly unable to believe that Macdonald would present a serious political threat.[2] How could anyone expect, after all, that a CPR solicitor would have any impact in rural Manitoba? Would anyone be seriously taken in by his sudden conversion to government ownership of railways or to temperance? Surely the Conservative press was less influential than the Liberal journals. Surely no one would be misled by Macdonald's mixing of federal and provincial issues. There was no great scandal or controversial issue in provincial politics upon which to hang the government.

It was just this lack of a great issue that made Sifton uneasy. Greenway's intention was to hold the local contest before the dominion one to try to avoid the introduction of unpopular federal policies into the provincial campaign. Sifton thought it would make more sense to follow the dominion election, expected in 1899 or early 1900, and presumably have the prestige of a newly elected Liberal government in Ottawa behind the Manitoba government.[3] There were just too many imponderables. Greenway's liaison of convenience with the CPR had broken up as the premier began to woo other railways to construct his long dreamed of Winnipeg-to-Duluth line and other competition for the larger corporation. But no new alliance had been formed, which could be crucial in a tight election. Indeed, Greenway had managed to alienate the NPR as well. The coalition which had hitherto supported the government on the school question had shaken loose and was being picked apart by the Conservatives. Greenway remained serenely oblivious. The temperance vote, furthermore, could certainly see nothing to lose in supporting a Conservative party now pledged to action. The ministry itself had little vitality; and Greenway, after repeated bouts of illness, had his eye on his reward in the pleasant pastures of the Senate.

Following the end of the legislative session in July, the premier and his colleagues showed no sign of preparing for an election, although it was generally known that Greenway intended to call it in the late fall. He made a short speaking tour early in August, during which he confessed that it was three years since he had addressed a political meeting. From mid-August to early November, however, he only appeared once, in Dauphin on behalf of T.A. Burrows, the sitting MLA.[4] J. Obed Smith, the chief Liberal organizer in Manitoba, told Sifton the local Liberals thought that any antagonism toward the party stemmed from federal policies and party divisions attributable to the minister of the interior. Apparently they had decided to wait for Sifton to come west, settle the difficulties, and head up the provincial campaign. Sifton was furious. "It is little short of madness for your people to lie down and wait until I get up there to hold meetings," he snapped. "I have been seeing reports of Hugh John Macdonald's meetings for the last two years, and busy as I have been I venture to say that I have spoken at more meetings in the last two years than all of your Ministers put together. They had better get up and get to work. There is no earthly use in waiting for me."[5] But still nothing was done.[6]

In September Sifton announced a speaking tour of Manitoba and the North-West Territories, to begin in the latter part of October.[7] It was essential to rouse the troops and put the political organization in order, even though Laurier had not determined finally whether to hold the dominion contest. However, the crisis in October over sending Canadian contingents to aid Britain in the South African War, which eventually decided the prime minister against a fall election, forced Sifton to put off his tour for a few days.[8] He seemed little troubled by the imperialistic excitement, however, perhaps underestimating its political implications, and was anxious to attend to his fence-mending in the West.

Sifton had been quietly anticipating the dominion election for some months. He asked his friend Charles Adams to supervise the revision of the electoral lists in Brandon and elsewhere. "It may also be possible that it may be necessary to expend a small amount of the root of all evil," he cautioned Adams, "in which case as you know the average rural member is likely to be in a somewhat hesitating frame of mind." Sifton had no such inhibitions. He had undertaken personally to pay the expenses of the central office of the Manitoba Liberal Association and in September forwarded $1,500 as a first payment of that obligation. He also decided to spend $250 to put the *Free Press* into one thousand homes in his constitutency from August to the end of the year. "I understand there are about three weekly Tribunes to one weekly Free Press in my constituency," he told Adams. "If we send in 1000 more of the Free Press it will even it up."[9]

Apart from these and countless other details, Sifton had to confront some serious problems. The divisions with the Martinite Liberals and the *Tribune* were festering wounds. Federal tariff and immigration policies were particularly unpopular, and on these issues and the Yukon administration the Tories plainly considered Sifton to be vulnerable. They intended to mount a campaign directed at him which would undercut the provincial Liberals. Sifton hoped that a thoroughly organized series of public meetings would create a display of "complete and aggressive unity in our party" and "discourage the enemy, both in local and Dominion matters."[10]

At Winnipeg on 24 October Sifton defended his record. He insisted that despite almost impossible conditions the government had made the Yukon "as well governed and administered as any portion of Canada." Law and order were well established, in sharp contrast to gold rush experiences elsewhere in the world. The royalty on gold production was simply "a matter of business." The gold fields were "the property of the people of Canada, and . . . the people were going to have a share of the gold taken out." After the expenses of government, police, and military forces were deducted, claimed Sifton, there was "a net surplus of $629,000 in the treasury." Immigration was no less a matter of business, particularly the Galician and Doukhobor immigrants. The Opposition contended that more was being spent on foreigners than on

Britishers. The facts, declared Sifton, were that the Doukhobors had cost $7.61 per head, Galicians $4.94 per head, and all other groups $9.23 per head, allowing for expenses of all kinds. "Businessmen of Winnipeg know that the whole future of the country depends upon the agricultural population west of Winnipeg," he added. "This city can only grow by the increase of the rural population." Finally, Sifton held that the government's railway policy had benefited the West. The Crow's Nest Pass line had opened up the British Columbia market to the prairie farmer and stimulated the development of the mineral resources of that province. At the same time, the government was supporting the expansionist plans of Mackenzie and Mann, because Sifton "considered that the greater competition [in railways] the better the results." To those who claimed that the government should build and operate the line, Sifton replied that the cost would be prohibitive. The line between Port Arthur and Winnipeg would cost $10,000,000; by contrast, the government subsidy of $1,623,000 had enabled the line to be built at much less cost to the taxpayer, while conditions in the contracts gave the government practically every advantage that would be gained by a government-owned line.[11]

Sifton subsequently carried his message around Manitoba until 7 November, when he began to tour the Territories. But any semblance of unity which he had hoped to create was shattered on 27 October, only three days after his Winnipeg address, when Joseph Martin addressed a meeting which was prominently attended by the dissident Liberals. He attacked the tariff and railway policies of the government and its machine politics. The government was not sufficiently responsive to the popular will. And the Yukon administration and Yukon railway had been unmitigated disasters. Having assailed the government and flogged Sifton, Martin still dared to write to Laurier to arrange a political deal. If the dominion government would let E.D. Martin have the vacant Winnipeg seat unopposed, Martin believed that the "kickers" and the *Tribune* would about-face and support the Greenway government. Laurier retorted that Martin's speech had been nothing less "than a declaration of war against the administration," but he did not altogether close the door. By this time, however, Martin's friends and the *Tribune* were so heavily committed against the government that they could not shift course in time to be of any use.[12]

Hard on the heels of Sifton and Martin came Sir Charles Tupper, who began a month-long Manitoba tour with a great rally in Winnipeg on 7 November. Accompanied by George E. Foster and Clarke Wallace, two of his most prominent colleagues, the old Conservative warhorse focused on Sifton and the enormities of the Yukon administration, along with the incompetence of the government's South African policy. Tupper had been planning for months, arranging for financing from sources in Montreal and Toronto. "I regard it as of the utmost importance to the party to win this election," he had written; and he threw himself heart and soul into the campaign.[13] Greenway and his ministers continued in blissful inactivity. Then, all of a sudden, on 16 November, the premier roused himself. The provincial election, he announced, would take place 7 December. At long last, and confronted by his self-imposed deadline, he commenced intensive work to rescue his government.[14]

Sifton had been trying for weeks to move Greenway and his colleagues, with no success. During his tour of the province he had arranged for the *Free Press* weekly to be sent to seventeen thousand people from late October to the end of the year. Even while he was touring the Territories, a constant stream of orders flowed from his private car. The provincial ministers must divide up the province and begin a series of meetings in each, he told J. Obed Smith. "Do not let one of the Ministers have a wink of sleep until this is done." The Conservatives were doing everything possible to attract the Orange vote. It was therefore vital, urged Sifton, to get a Liberal speaker out to deal with the Orange settlements and "arrange with him to deliver a series of lectures on an open Bible & the Protestant faith with special reference to Tuppers attitude on the Remedial Bill."[15] The Liberals should arrange for an article to be published comparing in parallel columns the opposing statements of Tupper and Macdonald, demonstrating Conservative inconsistencies:

> Tuppers statement re equal rights opposite Hugh John's statement re Galicians and franchise. Tuppers statement that Laurier was the only man in Canada who said the School question was settled opposite the statement of Hugh John's in a late speech that the School question was settled. Tupper on Government Ownership opposite the Conservative Local platform on Government Ownership of railways. Then follow with copy of what Tupper said in regard to the Remedial Bill. This should be written up with some degree of care, printed and sent to every newspaper office—should be reprinted in all our local papers and kept in. . . . I think there should be about 100,000 printed, and have bundles sent to every Member. I know what will make votes in this election and this material properly used and rubbed in is going to win the election. See that it is done at once.[16]

Earlier Sifton had helped out his brother-in-law, T.A. Burrows, whose seat in Dauphin was dangerously uncertain. The popular Conservative candidate happened to be the local Massey-Harris representative. Sifton spoke to Lyman Jones, who replied that the man concerned would either retire as Conservative candidate or resign from the company. "This is, of course, all we can do," added Jones. "I hope that he will, like a sensible fellow, decide to remain with the Company and withdraw his name from nomination." It was equally important that French-speaking Liberals should work the French constituencies; and Sifton asked Laurier to try to ensure that the influence of the church authorities was brought to bear on behalf of the Grits.[17]

"I am just beginning to get my war paint on," Sifton had written from Ottawa to a friend in Winnipeg in September, "and by the time I get there I think I will be able to appreciate an old time scrimmage. I have seen more fun at political meetings in Winnipeg than any place else I have ever been." By late November the campaign was rather more than vigorous fun. As soon as he could escape from his obligations in the Territories, Sifton responded to Greenway's pleas for assistance and rushed back to the province where Tupper appeared to be making the battle a personal fight. "We will have the hottest time that has ever been in Canada," he anxiously told Sidney Fisher.[18] The Tories were going so far as to import election workers from eastern Canada, men who "do not care a straw about the Manitoba Government, or who is in power in Manitoba, except for the fact that if Hugh John carries Manitoba they will parade him in the east of Canada as the great son of a great father and try to raise Tory enthusiasm in the Dominion fight." Even more important, Sifton was convinced that the Tories wanted to carry Manitoba so that they could "make deals with Railway Companies which, while bank-rupting the Province, would enable them to secure the support of the C.P.R. in the East." Liberals across Canada "regard this as the most important fight that we can have excepting the Dominion general election, and it will have a great effect on the Dominion General election when it is held."[19]

Writing to Laurier a few days later, Sifton was more optimistic. Tupper and Foster supposedly were losing rather than gaining votes for the provincial Tories, their "lies" were not accepted, and Sifton hoped to "beat them badly." If only the local government "had been at work for the last year instead of doing nothing," a Liberal victory would be certain.[20] By the eve of the election, however, Sifton sensed that defeat was probable.[21] He was correct; all his efforts proved unable to keep Greenway's sinking ship afloat. The Liberals won by the narrowest of pluralities in the popular vote with 23,312, to 23,172 for the Conservatives, and 601 for Independents. But in seats, where it counted, the Tories had scored an upset victory, with twenty-two seats to seventeen Liberals and one Independent.[22]

Complex as the causes of defeat were, Sifton blamed it on the "absolute indolence" of the provincial government: "They tried to crowd a year's work into three weeks and naturally failed. The only surprise is that they almost succeeded." Sifton was prepared to concede that party divisions and federal policies had been a factor, but naturally he played them down. "If the result of the election shows the Liberal party throughout Canada that they require to do something else besides stand around and swear at the Government," he told a friend, "the reverse will not be an unmixed evil."[23]

Writing more fully to Laurier, Sifton observed, "There is no question about it that the verdict of the Province was against Greenway. He had the influence of the Provincial Government, all the influence of the Dominion Government exerted in every possible way, and everything that I and my friends could do." He considered that "I have nothing to reproach myself with" and, probably unrealistically, that neither Richardson nor the *Tribune* had had any impact. More accurate was his comment that "the principal cause [of defeat] is that the Conservatives who first came over to support us on the railway monopoly question years ago, and who came to us in large numbers when we were fighting the school question, have practically all gone back to the Conservative party." Both the Northern Pacific and the CPR had turned against Greenway. "The whole Tory organization from the East was here and made the best fight it knows how to make. We have got its measure and know what it can do and how it will work." As a result, "I have learnt a good deal that will be valuable in the Dominion elections particularly in the Province of Ontario. I am very glad now that the general election was not called on. It will take a large amount of preparation to meet the kind of campaign that these fellows are going to put up against us, and it cannot be done in less than six months."[24]

It was an acutely embarrassing reverse for Sifton, whatever his rationalization. He was supposed to be the political strongman of the West, the master of Manitoba, and he had been defeated in his first serious contest. The victory rejuvenated the Tories and forced the Liberals to try to regroup. Even this proved more difficult than Sifton anticipated. First he tried to restore Liberal spirits by contesting some of the more questionably obtained Tory seats. He was unable to generate much enthusiasm among the stunned Grits. Whatever support he might have found was quickly dispelled after Greenway resigned on 6 January 1900, because the new Tory government of Hugh John Macdonald soon charged that Greenway and his ministers had misled the public on the issue of railway subsidies. It appeared that Greenway had been playing a double game, and the provincial Liberals' credibility almost disappeared.[25]

The revelations also frustrated a second scheme of the minister of the interior. He had long believed that Greenway was a liability to the Liberal cause, and the defeat appeared to provide an excellent opportunity to reward the premier with his coveted senatorship and revitalize the dispirited Liberals under a new leader. Many local Liberals, however, thought that their position in the new legislature would be untenable if Greenway were not present to answer the charges now being aired. In the end their views prevailed, and Sifton gave the two vacant senatorships to his defeated friends, Finlay F. Young, a Killarney grain dealer, and Robert Watson. Nothing could be done about reorganizing the provincial party, Sifton wrote disgustedly, because "our friends funked and insisted on Greenway remaining with them." "My view," he told J.D. Cameron, "is that you will have to re-organize with the younger element of the Party before you can hope to win an election and get back to power."[26]

Laurier's decision not to seek a dissolution meant that the Winnipeg federal by-election could be postponed no longer. "The Martin crowd" had had "a summer's exercise" as Sifton had suggested, but their enthusiasm showed no sign of diminishing. At the annual meeting of Winnipeg Liberals on 9 October, the "kickers" had dominated proceedings and replaced E.D. Martin as president with T.G. Mathers, another Martinite.[27] The dissidents believed that they had the government over a barrel and could dictate their terms of cooperation. These included a promise that E.D. Martin should have the seat unopposed by any Liberal. Their confidence did not seem misplaced. The only other announced candidate was Arthur Puttee, an unknown labour man with no apparent chance of winning. The Conservatives intended to put their strength behind Martin if a government candidate were announced. "Nothing could be more humiliating to Sifton," chortled Sir Charles Tupper, "than to be compelled to see a man elected with whom he refused to shake hands and one whom he knows to be his bitter enemy."[28]

Sifton was determined to get a "straight" Liberal to contest the seat and, whether the chances were good or not, to demonstrate that no deals would be made with the Martinite malcontents. He made every effort to persuade Isaac Campbell to accept the nomination. Campbell was one of the few Liberals with public prestige and friends in both camps. The *Free Press* was ordered to intensify its attacks on Martin. Sifton arranged for a "representative" nominating convention to select Campbell. Every effort was to be made to canvass the labouring men of the city and bring in the "outside vote." Sifton himself intended to come to Winnipeg in the week before the election to take charge of the Liberal organization.[29]

In the midst of this flurry of activity, correspondence began to pour in from the demoralized Manitobans. Key men, including J.D. Cameron, E.M. Wood, and J. Obed Smith, gloomily agreed that defeat was inevitable. Sifton might have forced Campbell's nomination, but he realized that unless the fighting spirit was there, "the battle was lost before [it is] begun." In disgust he told Campbell that he might as well withdraw.[30] Sifton called the by-election for 25 January 1900 and sourly remarked that he expected in a few days to be able to congratulate the Winnipeg Liberals on being represented by Martin. Should the Dominion Liberals put the best face on it that they could and jump on the bandwagon? Campbell and McMillan thought there was no chance of Puttee defeating Martin. But A.J. Magurn offered a different view. With no government candidate to oppose, the Conservative vote would be free to support either candidate and might well prefer Puttee, "who is a Conservative." Indeed, Sifton's organizers reported that Puttee had been actively seeking Tory support through Hugh John Macdonald. A few days later J.W. Sifton told his son that Winnipeg Liberals were in a muddle as to whom to support and that the prospects appeared fairly even.[31]

Slowly Sifton became aware that Martin might be in trouble, and he directed the *Free Press* to give more time and support to Puttee than Martin. As the election day closed in, the Martinites suddenly realized how vulnerable they were without the party machinery behind them. Withholding active support from Martin, wrote McMillan to Sifton, had shown the rebels better "than anything else that could have happened" "that their following did not amount to anything." At the last minute McMillan and Cameron threw their support to Martin, but they were too late. To the astonishment of almost everyone, Puttee squeaked through.[32] The result was no triumph for Sifton, but at the same time he was not displeased. Unable to defeat even a weak man such as Puttee, the dissidents lost much of their credibility.

West of Manitoba, Liberal prospects appeared rather brighter. Sifton had held some forty-five meetings prior to the Manitoba election campaign and reported to Laurier that "the party is in pretty good shape."[33] Given Liberal uncertainty in Ontario and Manitoba, the four Territorial and six British Columbia seats could be very important.

The Territorial seats were fairly secure for the Liberals, though Sifton was not entirely happy with them. The least troublesome seat was Saskatchewan, where T.O. Davis had been busily consolidating his controversial victory of 1896. He had provided unswerving loyalty to the government, going so far as to christen one son Clifford Sifton Davis. His only worry was Sifton's delay in settling the outstanding land claims of the mixed bloods in his district. Sifton finally announced the commission in 1899, and it toured the Territories doling out land and money scrip shortly before the 1900 election, much to the Liberals' satisfaction.[34]

In the District of Alberta, Independent Liberal Frank Oliver was well entrenched, somewhat to Sifton's annoyance. Both in the House of Commons and through the columns of his *Edmonton Bulletin,* Oliver had been one of the most persistent critics of the Yukon railway, the tariff, central European immigration, Sifton's Indian and land policies, and the handling of patronage matters. At times Sifton thought him rather more useful to the Tories than a straight Conservative would have been. J.S. Willison of the Toronto *Globe* once queried Sifton about Oliver, provoking an exasperated response:

> I am unable to advise you as to what should be done with him. Sometimes I think we ought to summarily discipline him and sometimes I think we had better give him all the rope he wants. His criticisms of my Department have been both plentiful and wonderful. I have treated them with absolute indifference and for the present they have ceased, but I have no doubt he will break out again. He is one of those men who have a little knowledge, which is a very dangerous thing. It is quite impossible to convince him permanently and my judgment is that any time that is spent on him will simply be wasted.[35]

Some of their disputes reflected their differing assumptions about politics.

Both were pragmatic, ambitious, and possessed of rather flexible principles. But Oliver was something of a populist, believing that he should mirror the ideas—and prejudices—of his constituents. Sifton was a machine politician who believed in government run on business principles; he was impatient of public opinion which differed from his idea of sound business policy, and he was prepared to override or circumvent the popular will. In Alberta, Sifton irritated Oliver by basically continuing the Tory policy which favoured the ranchers of the south, whom he viewed as capable businessmen efficiently exploiting land unsuited to homesteading. He made few concessions to the anti-rancher sentiment among the homesteaders, who in turn were Oliver's principal supporters. Sifton's views generally were those of the metropolitan centre, whether of Winnipeg or of central Canada; Oliver, by contrast, reflected the views of an isolated and frustrated urban centre on the outer fringes of the hinterland. The Alberta member's fanatical devotion to Edmonton as the gateway to the Yukon and his hatred of the National Policy tariff stemmed equally from his passionate boosterism in an ambitious frontier community. As a cabinet member, Sifton naturally had to have a broader perspective on policy, but that also made him more insistent upon unswerving loyalty from the party faithful. He was impatient with men like Oliver, who he believed played on and stirred up popular passions. He was realistic enough, however, to realize that for the foreseeable future Oliver was untouchable and would have to be supported.

In Assiniboia East J.M. Douglas, the Patron-Liberal member, was also popular and safe. Although the Patron movement had expired in 1898 in Manitoba,[36] it was by no means dead in Assiniboia, probably owing to Douglas's ability. His grain trade bills of 1898 and 1899 had only entrenched his position. The government was not unhappy, however, because on most other issues it enjoyed Douglas's support. He was given control of patronage in the constituency, despite objection from some partisan Liberals, and Sifton expected to support him in the general election.[37]

The most delicate situation in the Territories was Assiniboia West, constituency of the redoubtable Nicholas Flood Davin. He had barely escaped from the Liberals' clutches in 1896 and 1897; at the general election both the government and the local Liberals were determined that he should finally be defeated. Unfortunately, the Liberals of the constituency were far from united. One of Sifton's most active and loyal political friends was James H. Ross, a prominent Moose Jaw rancher and member of the territorial government. Through Ross, Sifton engineered the election of Walter Scott of the Regina *Leader* as Liberal representative and distributor of patronage in the constituency. Scott had performed well in defusing the agitation to unseat Davin in 1897 and was unanimously supported by the central executive of the Assiniboia West constituency organization. Sifton was pleased, commending Scott as "a very able man" who was "going to be one of the leading journalists of Canada."[38] Some of the rank and file, however, considered Scott to be nothing more than a front for Sifton and machine politics and a recent convert to active Liberalism. As a straight Liberal, furthermore, he was not acceptable to many of the Patrons who had co-operated in trying to defeat Davin in 1897. Scott appeared to them to be, as a rival newspaper argued, a "slavish supporter of the government in all its iniquity."[39] Every effort must be made to bring about a reconciliation, Sifton told Scott: "One of the difficulties in politics in the West is that matters do not run in well settled grooves which exist in the older communities. There is therefore extra need for friendliness on all hands."

The situation had so deteriorated that two rival Liberal associations had been established in Regina. During his tour of the Territories in 1899, Sifton met with the leaders of the two associations and persuaded them to call a representative convention to reconcile their differences and establish machinery for the forthcoming election. The pro-Sifton Liberals managed to outmanoeuvre their opponents, secure an endorsement of the policies of Sifton and Laurier, and approve Scott once more as distributor of patronage. Such proceedings did not heal the breach, of course, but they strengthened the pro-Sifton forces throughout the constituency and gave apparent popular endorsement to Scott.[40]

The morass of British Columbia politics mystified almost everyone east of the mountains, not least Clifford Sifton. He represented the coastal province in the cabinet, but never evinced much interest in its affairs nor succeeded in giving leadership to its Liberal partisans. Fortunately, the Conservatives were in even worse shape. In 1896 the Tories' share of the popular vote had plummeted from an astounding 71.6 per cent to 45 per cent, and they were showing no signs of increased strength.[41] The major questions as the next election approached were two: would the Liberals destroy themselves through internal squabbling, and would the increasingly independent labour vote detract more from the Liberals or the Conservatives?

Undoubtedly, one of the reasons that Laurier did not add a British Columbian to the cabinet was the failure of any strong provincial Liberal to emerge. The government hoped to provide some leadership when in 1897 it appointed William Templeman, proprietor of the *Victoria Times,* to the Senate. But Templeman had no patronage at his disposal and no personal strength among provincial Liberals. Any hope that Templeman could lead a united Liberal party was dashed when Joseph Martin precipitated himself into the British Columbia political scene in 1898. He blasted his way to the top with astonishing speed, managing even to cling tenuously to the premiership for a few months in 1900 before the turmoil of local politics swept him from office. "I am afraid the storm centre has been transferred from Manitoba to BC & your people are nearly as volatile as ours," Sifton wryly observed to G.R. Maxwell, MP for Burrard. "Has the *ozone* travelled to the coast?"[42]

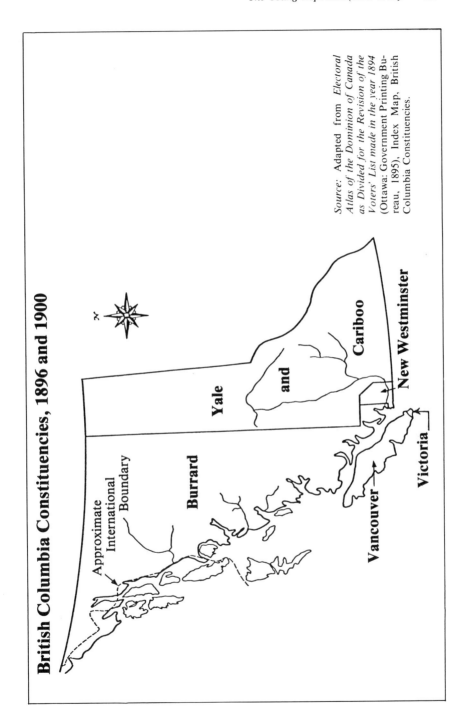

British Columbia Constituencies, 1896 and 1900

*Source:* Adapted from *Electoral Atlas of the Dominion of Canada as Divided for the Revision of the Voters' List made in the year 1894* (Ottawa: Government Printing Bureau, 1895), Index Map, British Columbia Constituencies.

Indeed it had, and while Martin was active there, it would prove impossible for the Laurier government to establish a unified and loyal Liberal party in the province. Efforts had been made to produce a local Liberal organization in 1898, but in the chaotic political infighting that succeeded the provincial elections of that year, there were almost as many varieties of Liberals as there were of Socialists. Martin was in his element. He told J.C. McLagan, publisher of the Liberal Vancouver *World,* that he had "no respect for the Ottawa Government" and "that he would ... show that in leaving him out of his Cabinet, Sir Wilfrid had committed a grievous blunder." He and his followers became known as the "Anti-Siftonites," thus carrying the quarrel even into the alien ground of coastal politics.[43] If the Liberals managed to hold their four B.C. seats, it would be despite Sifton and Martin, not because of them.

The *Manitoba Free Press* remained central to Sifton's political planning. Unhappily J.B. Somerset, the business manager, and Arnott J. Magurn, the managing editor, found it as difficult to co-operate in management as Sifton and Martin did in politics. In May 1899 the president of the Free Press Company, John Mather, having investigated the causes of the persistent squabbling, decided to back Somerset's financial restraint. Irate, Magurn appealed to Sifton. "It is really criminal," he fumed, "to have such an incompetent silly old man pottering with the business and old Mather is as bad as Somerset and believes all of Somerset's lies and fancy figuring." Probably the company's books did require an audit, admitted Sifton, but meanwhile Magurn ought to take Mather's advice and co-operate with Somerset. The business manager was sustained at the annual meeting of the company, when the directors in effect placed the editor under the judgment of the business manager in matters respecting expenditure.[44]

Magurn reacted childishly, still unaware that Sifton was the actual owner of the paper. If Somerset were to have such authority, Magurn declared, he would no longer put forth his best effort. The directive from the management went directly against his contractual understanding. Sifton retorted sharply that Magurn was being unreasonable. He agreed that there were difficulties with Somerset, "but something of the spirit of conciliation will have to be shown if any satisfactory results are to be achieved." The latter part of Magurn's letter, added Sifton, "practically amounts to the statement that you do not intend to fulfil the terms of your contract with the Company as to holding yourself to the advancement of the interests of the property."[45] At this rebuff Magurn quite forgot himself. "My dear Mr. Sifton," he replied,

I did not think you were capable of writing such an intensely stupid letter. ... Don't you think that instead of telling me whats right and whats wrong concerning a newspaper you should ask my opinion, as that of an expert?

Otherwise what am I doing here. . . . I am insisting on the ignorance of such laymen as yourself and on my own knowledge and skill. I do not think you would accept my opinion on matters of law. I do not have any great respect for your opinion as to whether a paper is best in 8[,] 12 or 16 pages. . . .

. . . [T]he main point is whether the directors have that want of confidence in my capacity and judgment [which] they are displaying, and whether after contracting that I should have "a free hand" (to use your own expression at the time) [they] wish to give the mossback business travesty [Somerset] a veto on every move necessary to manage a paper.[46]

Understandably, correspondence ceased between the two men for two months. Sifton did not want to make any hasty changes in management in face of the impending provincial election and the Winnipeg by-election. In the midst of the Manitoba provincial campaign, Sifton even gave him a vote of confidence when writing to Mather: "Magurn is editing the Daily very well now, and giving pretty good satisfaction."[47]

What Sifton did discover during the provincial campaign was a decided lack of enterprise in pushing the *Free Press* weekly. This was the province of the business manager, and Sifton promptly decided that Somerset would have to be replaced. Shortly after he returned to Ottawa, Sifton began to search for a man whose vision of the possibilities of the paper would coincide with his own. C.W. Taylor, the business manager of the Toronto *Globe,* recommended E.H. Macklin, then a bookkeeper with the Toronto paper. Macklin, reported Taylor, was "a thoroughly first-class man and you would do well to take him up. . . . He is without exception the best man I know of in the Canadian field. We have no desire to part with him. At the same time his going to the west will be [a] considerable advance and it may be sometime before we can give him promotion here." It was a strong recommendation, which Sifton accepted, appointing Macklin business manager of the Free Press Company in a letter of 8 March 1900.[48]

Macklin assumed his new duties in April 1900 and was an instant breath of fresh air. He was directed to begin by doing everything possible to promote the weekly edition. Because many rural families subscribed to an eastern as well as a local weekly, it was common for eastern and western papers to enter into "clubbing" arrangements to maximize circulation and minimize costs. The subscriber was offered the two at a lower total subscription price. To make the most of Liberal influence, Sifton hoped to make a clubbing arrangement with the weekly *Globe.* Macklin was directed to co-operate with Liberal organizers in each electoral division in promoting circulation.

By the summer of 1900 Macklin's promotional campaign was in full swing.

New subscribers were offered the weekly *Free Press* to the end of the year for fifty cents. Each would also receive a patriotic painting of General Botha surrendering his Boer troops to the Canadian Mounted Infantry in South Africa. Macklin sent a personal letter to some twenty-five hundred former subscribers, offering the premiums for renewing their subscriptions. Those who failed to respond to this enticement received a more elaborate letter pointing out the features of the *Free Press:* the cartoons of Sam Hunter ("his pictures alone are worth the price of the subscription"), news, features, and mechanical improvements in the premises. Macklin's approach was a complete reversal of that of Somerset, who believed that it was sufficient to send cold threats of cancellation unless subscriptions were renewed. Advertisements for Macklin's offers were being carried in eighty-five papers in Manitoba, the Territories, and British Columbia; and the paper paid local agents on a commission basis for new subscriptions. Letters were sent to postmasters across the West, asking them to promote the *Free Press* among their customers.

Macklin set out after new advertising revenues just as aggressively. He posted a special agent in Toronto to secure advertising there. A letter was sent to prospective advertisers enthusiastically praising the potential of the West, particularly Manitoba, and suggesting that the *Free Press* was the best medium to reach the consumers of the region. "It seems to me," declared Macklin in his circular, "that a journal like the Manitoba Free Press, controlling the telegraphic news franchises, with a circulation double the combined circulation of all the Manitoba dailies, a paper that circulates and is eagerly looked for by the people of Manitoba, Alberta, Saskatchewan, Assiniboia West, Assiniboia East, North-Western Ontario, the rich Gold Field District, and British Columbia; that finds its way into every nook and corner of the vast West, the threshold of which it takes the Eastern paper by fast express 2½ days to reach—it seems to me that this is a desirable paper for Eastern Commercial men to use." The new immigrants in the rapidly expanding West needed enormous quantities of goods. "Winnipeg is the Gateway to this Great West," asserted Macklin, "the distributing point, and the Free Press is the medium by which the people of the West may be reached."[49]

E.H. Macklin quickly showed that he was the ideal business manager for the *Free Press,* and both Sifton and Mather were well pleased. In spite of debts incurred in 1899 for a new Meikle press and new premises, as well as the costs of the promotional campaign, the concern was almost breaking even by late summer 1900. "It looks to me as if the Institution has turned the corner and will be all right shortly," Mather wrote. "The debts owing the Coy if paid will put it on velvet." Macklin was given a free hand in his plans and expenditure and amply justified the confidence reposed in him. The property, concluded Mather, was in excellent shape "and keeps increasing in value and influence."[50]

The average daily circulation of the *Free Press* during the week 8–14 July, Macklin told Sifton, was 14,421. The weekly had 4,800 regular subscribers, and 2,600 on three-month subscriptions. A semi-weekly edition had 1,100 subscribers. In August the advertising revenue had increased by $1,419 over the same month in 1899; in October the increase was $2,175, or about 50 per cent greater than in 1899. Sifton replied that he was "very much gratified" at this news, but he wanted even more done to push the circulation of the weekly which he was "very anxious" to see grow.[51] Macklin agreed that the weekly was in difficulty, despite some twenty-five to forty-five new subscriptions per day. The clubbing arrangement with the *Globe* had not worked out, partly because it was found that both papers were associated in the public mind with the CPR. The greatest problem, however, was still the extraordinary appeal of the *Family Herald and Weekly Star.* Some weekly papers which clubbed with the *Free Press* found it essential to club with the Montreal paper as well. "We cannot, of course, expect to compete on equal terms with the Star nor hope to secure as many subscribers as that journal," Macklin told Sifton. "Professedly a Farmer's Weekly, publishing little political news but much matter of interest to the Farmer's wife, sons and daughters, it finds a lodgment almost everywhere. Politics does not bar its entrance." Limited as the paper's editorial and political commentary was, "every editor of Reform papers to whom I have spoken, every Reformer with whom I have talked, seems to attribute to the Star a capacity for injuring, almost diabolical." "The Star is today proving every week," concluded Macklin, "that the political influence a journal wields is in inverse ratio to the amount of political matter it publishes."[52] Sifton concurred with Macklin's assessment. He thought, however, that the explanation of the *Star's* success was fairly simple:

The Government is not injured by the opposition papers' editorials, nor is the Government much helped by the friendly newspapers' editorials, although they are all right up to a certain point, and are necessary. What actually injures the Government is some carefully concocted piece of alleged news which is prepared for the purpose of informing the readers of the papers that the Government has done something very offensive to the reader, it is not given as an attack upon the Government, it is simply given as an item of news. The simple-minded farmer swallows it, and a great many people who are not farmers and who ought to know better. I am quite convinced, however, that the damage is done by the news columns and not by the editorial columns. In the circulation of the Weekly Free Press we will derive much more benefit from a skillful handling of semi-political news than from the editorial articles.[53]

Sifton's letter was a fascinating reflection of a view that he had long been putting into practice. He constantly analysed the news stories in the Liberal and opposition press for their political impact and systematically prepared carefully slanted news items for insertion in the Liberal journals. They were often eagerly adopted by hard-pressed small-town editors who were short of interesting news for their weeklies and who could almost always use the patronage that accompanied a decision to join the government camp. W.H. Hunt, publisher of two "independent" Liberal papers at Rat Portage, Ontario, for example, asked Sifton for increased patronage, adding cheerfully that he regularly published the " 'editorials' turned out with neatness and despatch from 'Sifton's Editorial Factory' in Ottawa." They were, of course, published as news items, not as editorials.[54]

Government patronage was essential to maintain the newspaper network that Sifton was attempting to build. It was a form of partisan subsidy blatantly used by any party in power, and it not infrequently was the difference between life and death for small rural papers and even for some larger city dailies. Patronage included the publication of official notices and advertisements. Even more valuable were over-priced government printing contracts, prominent among which was the flood of literature required for Sifton's immigration promotion. At election time, Liberal journals were subsidized with contracts to print ballots, electoral lists, and government propaganda. While Sifton was in office in Ottawa, the *Free Press* never wanted for such business, and most of the weeklies did well besides. On occasion a local newspaper might not succumb. At Melita, an important centre in the southern part of Sifton's constituency, for example, the local editor and publisher refused to co-operate. Sifton therefore decided to put $300 of his own money into founding a competitive paper, the Melita *Western Progress* and, with the help of patronage and vigorous promotion, to try to "crowd out" the established journal. Elsewhere the Liberals stifled a struggling socialist paper by pressuring its advertisers and by bringing on a costly lawsuit.[55]

The *Free Press* remained the vital centre of Sifton's constant campaign to sell the policies of the Laurier government. From the Winnipeg paper, it was understood, the editors of the smaller journals would borrow freely, with or without acknowledgement. The *Free Press,* therefore, gave extensive publicity to the activities of the Department of the Interior, the Yukon administration, the immigrants who were arriving each day or week, and so forth. It could support positions for which Sifton personally had little enthusiasm but which were important for partisan reasons. He never much warmed to Canada's South African adventures, for example, but his paper was unhesitatingly pro-British, as it had to be in a city where a pro-Boer speaker was once pelted with rotten eggs by a large, insistently "patriotic" crowd.[56] Similarly, the paper gave sympathetic coverage to William Lyon Mackenzie King's report on sweating practices and approval to proposals to ban such conditions in government contracts.[57] The crucial labour vote in the city must be carefully courted. Attempts to appeal to the farming community were reflected in the articles of E. Cora Hind, then secretary of the Manitoba Dairy Association and just beginning what would prove to be a long and influential career in agricultural journalism.[58]

The worst enemy of the government in Manitoba was the *Tribune*. It made its attacks from within the Liberal camp, from a stance of supposed pristine adherence to historic Liberal doctrines. The problem, as the *Tribune* saw it, was not with Liberalism, but with the deviants, unprincipled crooks, and machine politicians who were corrupting it and whom the prime minister, despite good intentions, had allowed into his camp until he himself was tainted. The greatest villain, naturally, was Clifford Sifton. Richardson and the *Tribune* portrayed themselves as the conscience of the party, the voice of the people. The *Tribune* became the most vigorous advocate of policies popular in the countryside: free trade, government-owned railways and elevators, purity in politics. It was not coincidental that Richardson's espousal of such policies had become much more enthusiastic since he began to represent a rural riding. Richardson was pushing the *Tribune* weekly as hard in his constituency and throughout rural Manitoba as Sifton was promoting the weekly *Free Press*. Little wonder that the average Liberal voter was confused.

From Sifton's point of view, Richardson's unprincipled demagoguery and lack of consistency should have been evident to all. Instead, the farmers were being aroused and excited by Richardson's foolish, ill-considered agitation. Sifton believed that there was no solid ground for agrarian complaint; the farmers were merely the victims of professional trouble-makers. Such activity could be undermined with skilful and thorough attention. The *Tribune* was making much capital out of the situation, he told Magurn, and "you are not counteracting it. These Farmer's Institute meetings at which everyone who is discontented abuses the Government when fully reported as they are in the Tribune and sent throughout the country do a very great deal of harm." No half-hearted effort would do: "You have to get down into the same place where the other people are and fight or they will cut the ground away from under your feet." He also ordered J. Obed Smith to aid in countering the meetings by seeing that the local press took them up in the right way and by endeavouring to ensure a pro-government speaker and a favourable majority in the audience at each meeting. If done properly, he confidently predicted, such careful manipulation would soon bring the troublesome meetings to an end.[59]

Sifton's confidence was misplaced, as Smith hastened to point out. It was very much more difficult to control the meetings than the minister imagined. The sense of agrarian grievance was well entrenched, and the farmers were particularly worked up over the issue of government ownership of railways; even Sifton's friends among farmers were being seduced by the panacea of public ownership.[60] Sifton recognized that the *Free Press* was still identified in the public mind with the CPR and therefore was not well placed to mount a campaign against government ownership. He directed Magurn to feed articles to the rural press through Smith; then the *Free Press* could quote widely from the country papers to prove that the *Tribune's* position was not widely accepted in rural Manitoba.[61] Before long, however, Sifton would discover that the "simple-minded farmer" was no longer easily manipulated.

By any normal standard Clifford Sifton had been endowed with a robust physique. His relentless drive and energy were legendary. He was said to be able to work all night after a hard day and, after a few hours' sleep, to greet his staff as the office opened in the morning completely refreshed. His attention to administrative and political detail seemed unflagging, the range of his concerns almost unlimited. Inexorably the tensions began to take their toll. He had been exhausted by the summer of 1897 and claimed to recognize that he would have to be more careful. The weight of the Yukon administration on top of his other duties, however, aggravated his tendency to insomnia, headaches, and high blood pressure. In the summer of 1898, shortly after leaving for his holiday at Lake of the Woods, he apparently had a short but serious collapse that necessitated a rest of several weeks.[62] By the end of 1899, he was once again in a state of near-exhaustion.

Adding to his concern was perpetual worry about his gradually worsening deafness, and he determined to seek treatment abroad. When Laurier decided to hold another session of Parliament in 1900 before calling an election, Sifton quickly arranged to miss most of it and travel to Europe in search of relief. He left Ottawa about 10 March, sailed from New York, spent a few days in London, and then travelled to Vienna. There he stayed in the Hotel Bristol, "the best house in Vienna but pretty expensive," while receiving treatment from a Dr. Politzer, an aurist who "is the most eminent man in his profession." Early in April, Politzer went to Paris, where Sifton was treated for another two weeks. "I am having a delightful rest," he told Laurier, "which I find I needed very much."[63] In Paris he met Israel Tarte, who told Laurier that Sifton thought there was some improvement. "Je regrette de dire," added the minister of public works, "que je ne trouve pas de changement chez lui. Il va de soi que je ne lui tiens pas ce langage."[64] Sifton quite understandably was anxious to believe that the treatments had been successful. When he returned to Canada early in the summer, he optimistically told J.S. Willison, "I got back very considerably benefitted as to my hearing and relieved from the nightmare which has been hanging over me for fear that I might become totally deaf. My hearing is improved and I think the disease is checked." The disease was not cured, however, and a few months later Sifton conceded that "the benefit [from the treatment] is not very great."[65]

The effects of the deafness carried over into his family life. In 1900 the five boys ranged from three to fourteen years of age, all lively and demanding. But they did not have an easy relationship with their father, although he was concerned about their welfare and education.[66] Sifton was inclined to play the role of the Victorian man of affairs, content to leave his household and family under the management of his wife and servants. His aloofness nevertheless probably owed more to his deafness than to the customs of the day. Often he simply could not enter into the daily banter with and chatter of small children. Like so many others, the boys found that a simple question shouted into the earphone could produce a lengthy disquisition in reply. Though he was intimidating, he was proud of his sons and proved an exacting parent who hoped that they would share his abstemious, driving character.[67]

Clifford and Arma Sifton were soon renowned in Ottawa society for the dinners and balls which they held at their comfortable Metcalfe Street residence or, on occasion, at the Russell Hotel. One such ball even provoked some lighthearted comments in the House of Commons as the members reflected on the terpsichorean skills of the minister of the interior. The Siftons also were active in Ottawa horse-racing circles. The personal break with Brandon and the West was almost complete. Sifton's financial investments remained chiefly western, of course; apart from the *Free Press* and smaller newspapers, his money was still mainly in western lands, both in the town of Brandon and in various rural properties in Manitoba and the Territories.[68] Other business investments appear at this stage of his life, to have been limited.[69]

After 1896 the Liberal government had skilfully used the advantages of power, associated with returning prosperity, to consolidate its position. Apart from the necessary re-election of those appointed to the cabinet after June 1896, the government had taken thirty-two by-elections to three for the Conservatives and one each for the McCarthyites and Labour. By September 1900 the government had a majority of fourteen seats in the key province of Ontario, whereas in 1896 they had obtained the same number of seats as the Tories.[70] A degree of complacency had set in by 1899, but it was rudely shattered by the unexpected Liberal reverse in Manitoba and the adverse reaction throughout English Canada to the government's half-hearted participation in the South African conflict. Another imponderable for Laurier and his colleagues was the potential effect of the growing alienation of the Canadian Pacific Railway. The CPR was angered by the government's decision in 1898–99 to acquire the Drummond County lines in Québec to allow the Intercolonial Railway direct access to Montreal. It was further enraged by Sifton's encouragement of the Canadian Northern and other lines which would provide competition in the West. Israel Tarte had been counting heavily on CPR support for his Québec organization and was frantic at the prospect of the railway's opposition. His expressions of concern may have been the decisive factor in Laurier's postponement of the election in 1899. In 1900 the Liberals even brought Lord Strathcona from London to try to reason with T.G. Shaughnessy, the CPR president.[71]

Clifford Sifton was keenly aware of the situation. Even when he was in London in the early spring, he detected a "very pronounced" rumour "that Shaughnessy is intriguing against the Govt."[72] He had already tasted the bitter fruits of CPR opposition during the provincial election in Manitoba. During 1900 he was exercised because Shaughnessy persistently refused to co-operate in building a branch line in Sifton's constituency, a project which Sifton's organizers assured him would be worth two hundred votes. The relationship between the two men became increasingly frigid. Writing to Sifton late in September 1900, James Sutherland, chief Liberal organizer in Ontario, gloomily observed, "If the [CPR] President is not actively against us, it is because he thinks the Government is almost sure to be sustained. At present, he is certainly not with us, and I am satisfied he is against you. You will have to be on the look-out, to find out how much."[73]

The warning was unnecessary. Sifton had been preparing the Liberal campaign for months. His careful planning, his mastery of strategy and tactics, had earned him the sobriquet "the young Napoleon" from opposition spokesmen. Upon his shoulders had fallen much of the responsibility for the political organization in English Canada. He had been instrumental in developing and expanding a central information office for the party at Ottawa.[74] He worked to extend the Liberal newspaper network in Ontario as well as the West. He was a frequent speaker on political platforms across Ontario, was a close student of its politics, and assiduous in his support for Liberal organization in that province. His work was necessarily behind the scenes, trying to keep business support in line, organizing party finances, helping out in the fighting of by-elections or the details of effective constituency organization. As the date of the general election drew near, however, he naturally had to leave Ontario and the central office in the charge of Sutherland and devote his energies to the western campaign.[75]

The only way to deal with British Columbia, Sifton had concluded, was to delegate the responsibility to Senator Templeman. He had told Templeman that he would accept the latter's advice "*absolutely,*" and generally he did so. Templeman reported directly to Sifton, who confined himself mainly to doling out literature, funds, and patronage as requested. All the BC constituencies were well endowed with money: Sifton told a complaining Templeman that he had more for his ridings than any of the other western constituencies, and more than twice the allotment per constituency in the East.[76] Still, it never seemed enough. The regular party funds were supplemented by the granting of liquor permits for the Yukon. Those granted permits were willing to contribute $1 per gallon to the Liberal coffers. Thus, when W.A. Galliher, the Liberal candidate in Yale-Cariboo, declared that it would require $15,000 to keep the riding Liberal, he was informed that it was impossible to provide such a sum; but it was possible to grant a permit for 5,000 gallons, for which Galliher had been promised $5,000, to supplement regular party funds. Sifton had refrained from allowing permits for many months prior to the election, and the object became clear during the campaign as speculators greedily lined up for the opportunity to slake the gold miners' thirst. At one point Templeman wired Sifton in a manner vaguely reminiscent of Sir John A. Macdonald's celebrated desperate appeal of 1872: "Province must have 40,000 [gallons]." Sifton assisted in many other ways. In particular, he arranged to delay the Yale-Cariboo vote for a week after the general election. He was informed that the restive labour vote combined with CPR intrigues made a Liberal victory very uncertain, and he determined to campaign there personally with the prestige of a re-elected ministry behind him.[77]

In the North-West Territories, Sifton also delegated most of the responsibility for organization, in this case to J.H. Ross. The most serious problem was Assiniboia West, where it was expected only a great effort could elect Walter Scott over Davin. The sitting Tory was an experienced, wily campaigner and infighter, a brilliant orator, who could count on the active support of the CPR and the local Roman Catholic archbishop and exploit the unhealed divisions among Liberals. "We are extremely anxious to win West Assiniboia, and will do anything possible to assist," Sifton advised Scott early in the summer. "If you should come to Ottawa as the man who had relieved the House of Commons of Davin you may rely upon it that the undying gratitude of a great many people would be yours." "Whatever else you do or do not do," Sir Richard Cartwright adjured Sifton, "bring us back Davin's scalp."[78] Scott was generously endowed with party funds, the Patron vote was assiduously cultivated, and Frank Oliver was brought in to stiffen up dissident Liberals. Sifton himself spent a good deal of time in the constituency reviewing the details of the campaign and engaging in public debate with Davin at Regina, Swift Current, and Medicine Hat.[79]

Both J.M. Douglas in Assiniboia East and T.O. Davis in Saskatchewan were likely to be re-elected without trouble. So was Frank Oliver in Alberta. And that was a bitter pill for Sifton to swallow, because Oliver was so strong that the Liberals had no choice but to support him. Oliver had managed to alienate both the ethnic vote and the railways, and it would take some effort to get them into line. "All these matters require to be got into shape," wrote Sifton. "If we are going to support Oliver we do not want to have him beaten." Oliver seemed less than grateful. His paper, the *Edmonton Bulletin,* soon predicted that not two government supporters west of Lake Superior would be elected. "You had better have a talk with Oliver," Sifton angrily told his brother, "and tell him that is not a good way to rouse the enthusiasm of the Grits in his riding. Ask him to be sensible for the next three months even if he has to be otherwise afterwards."[80]

The Liberals' most serious problems were in Manitoba. There Sifton faced a Conservative party revitalized in wake of Hugh John Macdonald's election victory, the opposition of the CPR and the Northern Pacific, and the determination of the federal Tories to strike a crippling if not fatal blow at the minister of the interior and his Manitoba stronghold. Sifton knew that every device would be used to secure his personal defeat in Brandon; he realized that only his re-election by a substantial majority could vindicate his record and disarm his critics. His strategy was to ensure that Brandon was impregnable and only then to concern himself directly with other constituencies. From the Tory point of view this was not an unmixed blessing. If Sifton was kept occupied in fortifying his own position, he would be less able to give his valued assistance to other Liberal candidates.

Brandon had always been carefully tended by Sifton, and he had complacently begun preparation for his re-election early in 1899. The Liberal defeat of that year severely shook his confidence, however, and a new, intensively detailed organization was rapidly established. On 2 March 1900 Sifton met with more than twenty organizers from all parts of his constituency to review details and stimulate enthusiasm. Even while he was in Europe that spring, Sifton kept closely in touch with the progress in his constituency and throughout the province. Upon his return the organization was galvanized into frantic action as a flood of orders began to flow from his ministerial desk.[81]

It was going to be "the hottest contest that there has been in Canada for many long years," he wrote. "It is the open boast of the Conservative party that they are going to defeat me in Brandon and knowing the fact that the constituency has been of a somewhat Conservative complexion, if we are to win our friends will have to spare no effort." His organization's calculations of the political sympathies of the electors bore him out. A.P. Collier, his private secretary, reported that outside of Brandon City there were 3,472 Liberal voters, 3,379 Conservative voters, 778 "Liberal Doubtful," and 852 "Conservative Doubtful." It was hoped that a large proportion of the doubtful vote would go for Sifton. There were also eligible 526 Liberal and 497 Conservative voters who lived outside the constituency. Finally, it was expected that Brandon city would give Sifton a majority of between 100 and 200. Everything "is in first class shape," reported Collier. "The organization will be as perfect as it was in the McCarthy election."[82]

No stone was left unturned. Special workers were brought in to cultivate the labour vote, the Icelandic vote, the French vote, and the Patron vote. English voters were blanketed with every "loyal" statement made by Laurier to counter Conservative charges that the prime minister was being led by anti-imperialists such as Tarte and Henri Bourassa. It was expected that twenty-five hundred voters in rural districts would be receiving the weekly *Free Press,* while over one thousand in Brandon City were receiving the daily, or nearly one per family. To pacify the temperance vote, Magurn was instructed to have the paper show a more friendly attitude to prohibition. And a special supplement of the *Free Press* on the elevator question was run off in ten thousand copies for distribution in rural Brandon and throughout southern Manitoba.[83]

All these preparations were being made without any idea of who the Tories were going to field against Sifton. Early in September it was announced that Hugh John Macdonald would resign the premiership in favour of Rodmond Roblin and stand against the minister of the interior. On the surface, Sifton reacted in a jocular vein. Macdonald he snorted, would not "have any snap and he will get all that is coming to him. Of course he has a very popular nose, and if we can only manage to put that out of joint we will be allright. He is also an accomplished liar which is a great gift during election time, but we have one or two that can come near him in that respect."[84] Under it all, however, Sifton knew that Macdonald would be a dangerous opponent.[85]

Macdonald shamelessly exploited the nativist sentiment in the overwhelmingly British constituency. The fact that his government had passed a limited prohibition measure appealed to the temperance vote, although some prohibitionists were wavering because its constitutional validity was in question and the Liberals were implying that Macdonald had known all along that the act was beyond the powers of the province. Sifton, ironically, had the novel experience of enjoying the support of the hotelmen of the constituency, who were said to be "sore" at Macdonald's legislation. The Conservatives, in turn, were particularly angered at a whispering campaign mounted by the Grits exploiting the fact that Macdonald's personal habits were far from abstemious; indeed the Tories had been keeping careful watch during the campaign to see that Macdonald was kept free from "liquid temptation."[86] Probably because they had an early start at organization, the Liberals thought they had an edge in the campaign until the beginning of October. Then Macdonald, desperate for an issue to undermine Sifton, announced in a Brandon speech that he would support free agricultural implements. Hugh John's statement "is going to hurt us like the deuce," Sifton wrote anxiously. At once the Liberal press attempted to counter Macdonald by demonstrating that he had completely reversed his previous record on the tariff and added that Macdonald could never persuade his Tory colleagues of Ontario and Quebec to carry out such a policy.[87]

What Sifton most desired was the opportunity to debate publicly with Macdonald. But the wily Tory organizers knew that their man was no match on the platform for the minister of the interior. They waited until Sifton announced his schedule of public meetings and promptly arranged for Macdonald to visit the same places a few days later. An offer by Sifton to rearrange his schedule was not accepted. The Tories knew that it would require an abler gladiator than Macdonald to destroy Sifton in public combat. They believed that they had such a speaker in Sir Charles Hibbert Tupper; it was anticipated that his pugnacious manner and detailed knowledge of the Yukon charges would deal a crippling blow to Sifton's campaign. Sifton was delighted. For weeks the Tories had been avoiding combat, scurrying about with "lies" about the Yukon and corruption. Now they would be flushed out. A joint debate was quickly arranged for Brandon on 13 October.

From Souris, Carberry, McGregor, and points all over the constituency people flocked into Brandon by train or by wagon or on foot, expectant of a classic verbal joust. When Sifton and his father arrived at 8:15 P.M., the four thousand people jamming the local rink burst into spontaneous cheering. Yet it was a Tory gathering to which Sifton had offered to come, and by all appearances he had walked into the lions' den. To the left of the chairman were seats for Sifton, his father, and three Liberal officials. To the right was Tupper. In the rear the remainder of the stage was occupied with serried ranks of western Tory officials; curiously absent was Hugh John Macdonald. The plan of the meeting was for Tupper and Sifton to speak in turn, each for an hour and a half, followed by a half hour for Tupper's rubuttal.

"This administration has inaugurated a carnival of crime," declared Tupper, and he went on to reiterate many of the charges he had made in the House of Commons. Not only had Sifton been "grossly negligent" in his administration, not only had he arranged the Ogilvie Commission to whitewash his record, but his defence of his administration in the House of Commons "was a screaming, howling farce." Most damning of all, Sifton had allegedly played favourites and broken the law in giving his former law partner in Brandon, A.E. Philp, a liquor permit for the Yukon. Throughout the speech, however, Tupper refrained from directly implicating Sifton in most of the alleged crimes and admitted that he had only secondhand knowledge of the situation.

Sifton rose and pointed out that Tupper had been somewhat less forthright than he had been in a recent speech in Calgary. "It is said," he added with a smile, "that the presence of an opponent has a tempering effect. Sir Hibbert Tupper said I was the man he was after. He has been after me a long time and is not catching up very fast." Once again Sifton argued that there were no specific charges apart from those which he had already answered in the House. The Tories, he alleged, had employed men "for the purpose of getting hold of disappointed miners who had lost all their money and often that of their friends as well and have got them to make all sorts of statements without evidence or proof and these have been circulated by the Conservative press." Tupper had claimed that Major Walsh had once been drunk in the Yukon. Sifton denied the charge, but it gave him an opening for an effective thrust: "I agree that a man who gets drunk has no right to occupy an official position (Cheers). If I got drunk I would not be fit for the position of minister of the interior or member for Brandon. I suppose I might say the same thing about

Sir Hibbert Tupper and Hugh John Macdonald. (Tremendous cheering.)"

Sir Hibbert had reiterated charges made in Brandon in 1899 by his father, Sir Charles Tupper, that Sifton had been an active partner in Philp's obtaining a liquor permit. Sifton then had promptly denounced Tupper's statement as a lie, and Philp had sued Sir Charles for libel. Only a few days before the Tupper-Sifton debate, Sir Charles Tupper had consented to an unconditional withdrawal of the charge and an apology. Even Sir Charles Hibbert had not known of the settlement, and as Sifton triumphantly read the correspondence to the astonished crowd, the Tory champion must have glumly realized that he had walked straight into a devastating ambush. "Those of you who were here last year and heard Sir Charles Tupper upon the platform and heard him make that charge ... will realize the depth of the humiliation of that gentleman in signing a complete, absolute recantation"; and, added Sifton, if Sir Hibbert cared to "place some of his statements in a categorical form in the same way he will have the pleasure of signing a document like this, or paying damages."[88] Sifton's defiant challenge was received with deafening cheers, and Sir Hibbert's rebuttal never got off the ground. The *Free Press* reported that Liberal organizers were delightedly claiming that the meeting had gained one hundred votes for the government side, and they may have been right. Certainly it was a blow from which Macdonald's campaign never recovered.

It was unremitting attention to detail, however, that would be the decisive factor. It had been a bad crop year, and the tariff question, the CPR monopoly, the elevator issue, and many other problems had left the Liberal rank and file distinctly restive. The party organizers knew that nothing could so reconcile many voters to Sifton and the government as five minutes' conversation with the minister himself. Lists of the discontented were carefully compiled along with their reported grievances, and Sifton spent many long hours on dusty roads, in farmyards, and in numerous little towns reassuring his constituents. As the time of the election drew near, he sent personal letters to all the outside voters requesting their support.[89]

Not only was Sifton unable to devote much time to other constituencies, but the continuing divisions among Manitoba Liberals took their toll. In Winnipeg it remained impossible to run a "straight" Liberal. E.D. Martin still had hopes that the government would yield and back him as the Liberal candidate. Sifton concluded that the best strategy would be to place the party machinery behind A.W. Puttee and deal a death blow to the Martin forces. In two more ridings, Marquette and Provencher, the sitting Tory members, W.J. Roche and A.A.C. LaRivière, were well entrenched, and Sifton devoted comparatively little attention to them. Two other ridings were uncertain. In Selkirk the sitting Liberal MP, J.A. Macdonell, was so weak that the party dumped him and nominated Immigration Commissioner W.F. McCreary comparatively late. McCreary was able, but he had to establish himself in the riding practically from scratch. In Macdonald riding J.G. Rutherford had not proven to be a particularly able member and seemed unable to do his political homework; he faced a wily, experienced Tory machine politician in Nathaniel Boyd, whom Sifton had unseated in 1897 for corrupt practices.

The constituency which most concerned Sifton, however, was Lisgar, represented by R.L. Richardson. The minister of the interior harboured a passionate hatred for the renegade Liberal and was determined to do everything possible to secure Richardson's defeat. It would be a strenuous battle. Richardson's posture as a true defender of the farmer and western interests was very popular. His newspaper too was a formidable weapon. When Sifton ordered that the weekly *Free Press* be sent to five or six hundred carefully selected names in the constituency, J.O. Smith, the local organizer, reported that supplanting the *Tribune* was exceedingly difficult because Richardson "*wont allow a man to drop his paper.*" Finally, and perhaps most importantly, the Tories again decided that their best strategy would be to humiliate Sifton by backing his enemy. In return for the *Tribune*'s support of Tories elsewhere, the Conservative machinery in the riding would be placed behind Richardson, an offer that was gladly accepted by the sometime champion of political purity.[90]

Sifton personally selected the Liberal nominee, Valentine Winkler, a farmer and Liberal MLA, and arranged for his "spontaneous" nomination by riding Liberals. He hoped that Winkler would sweep the Mennonite vote and appeal to the French vote and that with the aid of Greenway, some Orange support, and the backing of the "grain men" in the constituency, the Liberal nominee would have a good chance.[91] The *Free Press* hammered at the "Triple Alliance" of Roblin, Rogers and Richardson and underscored the conversion of the incumbent member to the methods of machine politics. Richardson, Sifton told his supporters, was "the most useless and dishonest humbug in the House." The "Triple Alliance" retaliated with such emotionally charged slogans as "Arch Rebel Riel's Son Rewarded by Sifton"[92] and "Vote for Richardson, the Independent Candidate, and crush Sifton, Tarte and disloyalty."[93]

It had been a long, bitter struggle. The election of 7 November 1900 gave the Laurier ministry a convincing victory, with decisive majorities in the Maritimes and Quebec. Ontario, however, went heavily against the government, giving a majority of eighteen seats to the Tories. Taken as a whole, the West reflected the national mood. The government took four of the six British Columbia seats; the Tories, as in 1896, took only the dual constituency of Victoria. The Liberals also swept the Territories. But Manitoba was once again a maze of contradictions. The Conservatives took three seats: Marquette, Macdonald, and Provencher. The Liberals took two: Brandon, where Sifton's majority was 669; and Selkirk, where McCreary squeaked through by one vote. The two Independents, Puttee and Richardson, won their respective ridings. In the five ridings where there were straight Liberal-Conservative contests the vote was almost evenly divided, with 14,764 for government candidates to 14,716 for the opposition.[94]

The Tories were bitter at the result in Brandon. T.M. Daly told Sir Charles Tupper that despite Macdonald's "splendid fight" and organization, the Liberals' "Klondike Gold was too much for us—they resorted to every known device and the peelers were everywhere. Sifton's majority is the best evidence of the awful debauch—he is welcome to his victory—the result in the other constituencies of Manitoba is the true index to the opinion of the people generally."[95] By contrast, on balance the Liberals were not unhappy with the Manitoba result. The Tories had recently won the province; the local Grits were depressed and in partial disarray; and the skills of able men such as Roblin, Rogers, and Boyd and the whole machinery of the provincial government had been much in evidence. Davin was defeated in the Territories. In Winnipeg the sound trouncing administered to Martin by Puttee and the Liberal machine amounted to a government victory and completed the destruction of the Martinites, allowing the rebuilding of the Grit party in that city. Lisgar was disappointing, but Winkler had done quite well against the combined Conservative and dissident Liberal forces and, in Sifton's opinion, had given heart to the supporters of the government there. He expected that Richardson's triumph would be short-lived. Meanwhile, all things considered, ten Liberal seats to five Conservatives and two Independents was a most satisfactory result for the West as a whole.

Custom decreed that the victors must celebrate their triumph at an interminable series of banquets for the party faithful. For several weeks Sifton was on tour again; but now he encountered happy crowds, festively decorated halls, tables laden with the fashionable multiple-course meals, programmes of "patriotic" recitations and songs, toasts to the venerable Queen, Lord Minto, the prime minister, the victorious Sifton, and on down to the local party officials, all topped off with another round of speeches. It was recognized that Sifton had confirmed his position as a politician of national stature. "If Sifton was the young Napoleon," wrote J.W. Dafoe, "this was his Austerlitz."[96] His victory was so understood by his party, and at a great banquet for him in Toronto both Laurier and Tarte paid tribute to their western colleague. The minister of public works, undoubtedly well primed and certainly with unaccustomed warmth, declared that "without flattery, there are very, very few as able, straight, energetic, strong, politically and mentally, as Mr. Sifton. It is among men of that kind that Québec has made up her mind to throw in her lot."[97]

Many Québeckers would have been astonished that such an interpretation could be placed upon their votes. Yet the recognition accorded the minister of the interior was genuine enough. He had come far since his first electoral success twelve years earlier and had grown dramatically since his first halting speeches in his father's campaign in 1882. His aggressive style had helped to create an effective national Liberal organization and to integrate the West into that organization. Without his constant attention to party machinery after 1896, the government would probably have fared even more badly than it did in Ontario and the West in light of imperialist disgust with Laurier's South African policy. Sifton privately admitted that his personal feuds with Richardson and Martin had injured the party in two seats, but this, in his opinion, was a small price to pay for establishing a responsive, flexible party machine. The creation of such machinery was, in turn, justified as essential to reconcile the West to the government's policies of national development.[98]

As he spoke at the various banquets, Sifton's message was one of optimism about Canada's future, especially that of the West. The election had seemingly vindicated his record; but he preferred not to dwell on the past. The task of the government was not to rest on its laurels or to retrench, but to build up the country. The core of this future development, he predicted at Brandon, would be a second transcontinental railway to open the Saskatchewan River valley to the Rockies and on to the coast. The same spirit marked his peroration in Winnipeg on 12 November.[99] He admitted that there were those who desired reduced expenditures and an end to railway bonuses. But, he declared,

> So far as I am concerned and so long as I have a voice in the advising of the government in regard to these matters I shall never advise them in accordance with any such policy. I believe that the five or six million people of Canada have had bestowed on them the greatest national heritage ever bestowed on a people. We have many rich and varied resources. Wherever you find it, the question of development is a question of transportation, the question of making these resources available to the toiler and brought to the market in such a way as to be profitable to the producer. These things cannot be done without the expenditure of large sums of money and the question is not the amount of the expenditure, but whether the expenditure is producing the desired result. I point you to the construction of the Crow's Nest Pass railway. Is there a man in his senses who would say put that money back into the treasury and wipe out the railway, wipe out the towns along the line, wipe out the mines and wipe out the trade of that country[?] There is not a man in Canada, outside of a lunatic asylum, who would make such a suggestion. My last word to you to-night is that so long as I am a member of the government I shall be for a policy of progress and a policy of development.

Buoyed by his victory, Clifford Sifton was no longer thinking of quitting the government. His critics had been silenced for the time being. Now he looked forward to a period of consolidation and reorganization. The *Free Press* was in need of stronger leadership. There remained enemies among Manitoba Liberals who had to be eliminated so that Sifton's brand of "Laurier Liberalism" could be more firmly established. The Yukon required an administrative overhaul and encouragement of more systematic and businesslike development. But Sifton would never be content merely with carrying on in established patterns. Except for the railway land problem, the difficulties that had confronted him in the Department of the Interior in 1896 were substantially resolved. Sifton always thrived on a challenge, and there was, by his definition, one major challenge remaining for the government, now that the immigration and tariff issues had been taken in hand: the establishment of an efficient, competitive, all-Canadian transportation system. He had outlined his new interests in his post-election speeches; it remained to be seen whether the prime minister would allow his ambitious western lieutenant the wider scope for his talents and influence on policy that he plainly desired. Equally important, it remained to be seen how long the differing visions of the nature of Canada and the role of government held by Laurier and Sifton could be accommodated within the same cabinet.

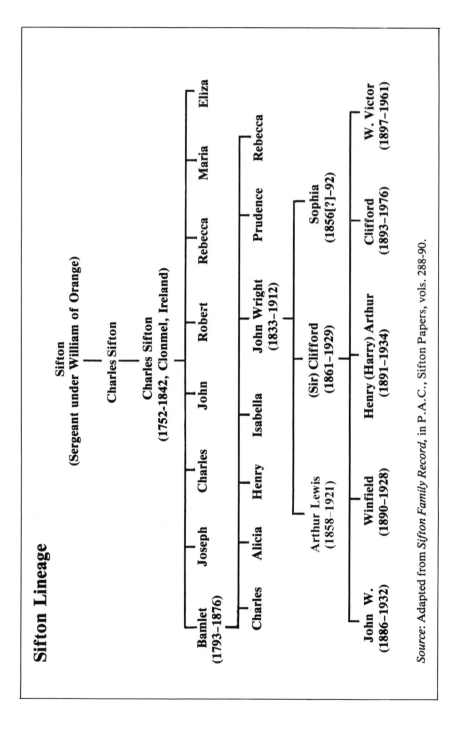

**Sifton Lineage**

**Sifton**
(Sergeant under William of Orange)

**Charles Sifton**

**Charles Sifton**
(1752-1842, Clonmel, Ireland)

**Bamlet** (1793–1876)

Joseph    Charles    John    Robert    Rebecca    Maria    Eliza

Charles    Alicia    Henry    Isabella    **John Wright** (1833–1912)    Prudence    Rebecca

Arthur Lewis (1858–1921)    **(Sir) Clifford** (1861–1929)    Sophia (1856[?]–92)

**John W.** (1886–1932)    **Winfield** (1890–1928)    **Henry (Harry) Arthur** (1891–1934)    **Clifford** (1893–1976)    **W. Victor** (1897–1961)

*Source:* Adapted from *Sifton Family Record,* in P.A.C., Sifton Papers, vols. 288-90.

# Note on Sources

This study is based principally on the large collection of Sir Clifford Sifton Papers deposited in the Public Archives of Canada. When Col. Clifford Sifton decided to send his father's papers to the Public Archives, he entrusted the task of sorting them and extracting personal and business papers to F.W. Gibson, a task which Professor Gibson undertook with remarkable fidelity to the family's wishes. The result was a collection practically devoid of family and business correspondence, with almost nothing to betray, for example, Sifton's life-long passion for horses. The papers are nonetheless remarkably complete for Sifton's political career, the great bulk of them concentrated on the period 1896–1905. In part it was this peculiar distribution of the papers which necessitated division of the biography at 1900.

More recently, in 1977 and 1978, Mr. Michael Sifton contributed another eighteen volumes of papers which will allow a limited insight into Sifton's business interests after 1900, and a few personal matters in the 1920's. Only a few letters on the Yukon administration fall into the period covered by the present volume. Historians nevertheless will be grateful for so substantial a contribution to the records of the period. It should be added that there is a small collection of Sifton materials at the Manitoba Provincial Archives, mostly comprising papers from Sifton's Manitoba career.

Other important collections include the Thomas Greenway Papers in the Manitoba Provincial Archives and the Sir Wilfrid Laurier Papers, Sir Mackenzie Bowell Papers, Sir John A. Macdonald Papers, Lord Minto Papers, Royal Canadian Mounted Police Records, Sir Charles Tupper Papers, Sir William Van Horne Papers, and Sir John S. Willison Papers at the Public Archives of Canada.

John W. Dafoe, *Clifford Sifton in Relation to His Times* (Toronto: Macmillan, 1931) is the only substantial biography to date. Dafoe was able to make use of the Sifton Papers, a task which few have attempted since, and as a close friend and confidant of Sifton, he naturally drew a very sympathetic portrait which omitted or glossed over some difficulties and failed altogether to deal with Sifton's acquisition and use of the *Manitoba Free Press*. It remains, however, an unusually sophisticated and accurate biography of its type.

Since Dafoe's book appeared, there have been a great many excellent and useful studies of the Macdonald and Laurier eras. This book has drawn heavily upon them, and the most important ones are acknowledged in the footnotes. A more detailed bibliography of primary and secondary sources may be found in my dissertation, "The Political Career of Clifford Sifton, 1896–1905" (University of Toronto, 1973, pp. 940–61).

# Abbreviations

| | |
|---|---|
| AASB | Archives de l'Archevêché de St. Boniface |
| *CHR* | *Canadian Historical Review* |
| CPR | Canadian Pacific Railway |
| *CJEPS* | *Canadian Journal of Economics and Political Science* |
| *CSP* | Canada, Parliament, *Sessional Papers* |
| *DCB* | *Dictionary of Canadian Biography* |
| *Debates* | Canada, Parliament, *House of Commons Debates* |
| DIA | Department of Indian Affairs |
| *JCS* | *Journal of Canadian Studies* |
| *MFP* | *Manitoba Free Press* |
| *MSP* | *Manitoba Sessional Papers* |
| PAC | Public Archives of Canada |
| PAM | Public Archives of Manitoba |
| PANS | Public Archives of Nova Scotia |
| PAO | Public Archives of Ontario |
| PAS | Public Archives of Saskatchewan |
| RCMP | Royal Canadian Mounted Police |

# Notes

## NOTES TO THE PROLOGUE

1. Edward Allen Talbot, *Five Years' Residence in the Canadas* (London: Longman, 1824), p. 4.
2. F. Landon and O. Miller, *Up the Proof Line: The Story of a Rural Community* (London, Ont.: D.B. Weldon, 1955), p. 80.
3. Talbot, *Five Years' Residence,* pp. 17–27.

4. Ibid., p. 83; Landon and Miller, *Up the Proof Line,* p. 13.
5. Talbot, *Five Years' Residence,* p. 61.
6. Ibid., p. 105.
7. See *Sifton Family Record* (privately printed for the Sifton family, 1955; copy in PAC, Sir Clifford Sifton Papers, vols. 288–90).

## NOTES TO CHAPTER ONE

1. John W. Dafoe, *Clifford Sifton in Relation to His Times* (Toronto: Macmillan, 1931), pp. 7–8.
2. *MFP,* 20 September 1912, obituary of John Wright Sifton; George Maclean Rose, *A Cyclopaedia of Canadian Biography* (Toronto: Rose Publishing, 1888), 2:46; *Canadian Parliamentary Companion and Annual Register, 1879,* pp. 369–70.
3. Rose, *Cyclopaedia;* Jean Turnbull Elford, *History of Lambton County,* 2d. ed. (Sarnia: Lambton County Historical Society, 1969); Victor E. Lauriston, *Lambton's Hundred Years 1849–1949* (Sarnia: Haines Frontier Printing Co., [1949]), pp. 157–87; *Mitchell and Company's Canada Classified Directory for 1865–66* (Toronto: Mitchell & Co., [1865]), p. 355. See also Edward Phelps, "Foundations of the Canadian Oil Industry, 1850–1866," in *Profiles of a Province: Studies in the History of Ontario,* ed. E.G. Firth (Toronto: Ontario Historical Society, 1967), pp. 156–65.
4. Interview with Col. Clifford Sifton, Toronto, 18 December 1968.
5. The Canada Southern Railway, built between 1870 and 1874, ran from Fort Erie to Amherstburg. It was never financially successful and in the 1880's came under the control of the Michigan

Central Railway (PAO, "Historical Sketch of Canada Southern Railway Company," [1946]).
6. *MFP,* 20 September 1912; *City of London and County of Middlesex Gazetteer and Directory 1874–75* (London: Irwin & Co., 1874), p. 176.
7. C.B. Sissons, *A History of Victoria University* (Toronto: University of Toronto Press, 1952), p. 154.
8. PAC, Sir Clifford Sifton Papers, vol. 237, p. 927, Sifton to Archibald Dwight, 23 July 1900; vol. 287a, newspaper clippings, *Lethbridge Herald,* 17 April 1929.
9. *CSP,* 1875, no. 7; 1876, nos. 6, 82; 1877, no. 6. Sifton also obtained contract no. 23, 4 October 1875, to supply 56,000 railway sleepers.
10. *MFP,* 9 November 1874.
11. The family arrived in November 1875; *MFP,* 5 November 1875.
12. D.J. Hall, "'The Spirit of Confederation': Ralph Heintzman, Professor Creighton, and the bicultural compact theory," *JCS* 9 (November 1974): 29–30, 37–38. On French-English tensions in 1875, see *MFP,* 29 April, 3 and 5 May 1875.
13. *MFP,* 15, 27, and 29 July 1875; 27 May 1876. On Sifton's endeavours to impose prohibition on his workers, see *Report of the Royal Commission on the Liquor*

*Traffic in Canada,* in *CSP,* 1895, no. 21, pp. 199–200.

14. *MFP,* 23 October 1876.
15. Ibid., 13 October 1876; 12 May 1877.
16. Ibid., 4 January and 7 February 1878.
17. Ibid., 20 March and 21 September 1877; 12 March 1879; Rose, *Cyclopaedia.*
18. *MFP,* 29 January 1879.
19. Ibid., 14 and 20 August, 1877; PAM, James Colcleugh Papers, Colcleugh to Mr. and Mrs. George Colcleugh (parents), 23 September 1877.
20. Ryerson Prize for First in Scripture History (1877); Sailsbury Prize in Logic (1878); McClure Bursary, First in Moral Philosophy and Christianity (1879); First Class Honours and Gold Medal (1880) (*Calendar of the University of Victoria College, Cobourg, 1877–1881* [Toronto: Methodist Book Room, 1877–1881]; Nathanael Burwash, *The History of Victoria College* [Toronto: Victoria College Press, 1927], p. 256; Sissons, *History of Victoria University,* p. 153).
21. Victoria University Archives, *Acta Victoriana* 1, no. 6 (March 1879): 10; no. 7 (April 1879): 9; ibid. 2, no. 2 (November 1879): 10; Burwash, *History of Victoria College,* pp. 239–40; Sissons, *History of Victoria University,* pp. 146, 151–52, 329.
22. Victoria University Archives, *Prospectus, Acta Victoriana* (May 1878); *Acta Victoriana* (1878–1880), passim.; Sissons, *History of Victoria University,* pp. 152–53.
23. *MFP,* 17 January 1878; 2 May 1879. Molesworth was the son of T.N. Molesworth (1824–1879), an Irish immigrant who became a surveyor and civil engineer in Canada West (*DCB* 10, pp. 516–17).
24. *MFP,* 18 and 27 August 1879.
25. Ibid., 31 July 1879.
26. Ibid., 9 March 1878.
27. Ibid., 23 and 31 August 1878; PAM, Colcleugh Papers, Diary, 21 and 27 August, 30 August–16 September 1878.
28. *MFP,* 5, 9, and 13 September 1878.
29. Ibid., 19 September and 19 November 1878; PAM, Colcleugh Papers, Diary, 17 September 1878; James Colcleugh to George Colcleugh (father), 5 October 1878.

30. *MFP,* 3 March and 16 October 1878. See also R.O. MacFarlane, "Manitoba Politics and Parties after Confederation," Canadian Historical Association, *Annual Report* (1940): 50–51; Gerald Friesen, "Homeland to Hinterland: Political Transition in Manitoba, 1870 to 1879," Canadian Historical Association, *Historical Papers, Saskatoon 1979,* pp. 33–47.
31. *MFP,* 18 and 19 December 1878; PAM, Colcleugh Papers, Diary, 1 November–18 December 1878.
32. *MFP,* 29 May 1879. The provincial subsidy then stood at $90,000.
33. Ibid., 30 May–4 June 1879; MacFarlane, "Manitoba Politics and Parties," pp. 51–52; Friesen, "Homeland to Hinterland," pp. 40–46.
34. *MFP,* 5 June 1879.
35. Ibid., 17 and 18 December 1879; PAM, Colcleugh Papers, Colcleugh to "Willie," [December 1879].
36. *MFP,* 16 August 1878.
37. *Journals of the House of Commons of Canada,* 17, 1879, Appendix No. 2, "First Report of the Select Standing Committee on Public Accounts in Reference to Expenditure on the Canadian Pacific Railway between Fort William and Red River," pp. iii–iv, xv, 9.
38. *MFP,* 22 May 1879.
39. Ibid., 18 September 1880.
40. *Report of the Canadian Pacific Railway Royal Commission,* 3 vols. (Ottawa: S. Stephenson & Co., 1882).
41. Ibid., 3: 124–27; appendix, pp. 497–99; and see 1:89–121; 264–74, 324–27 (evidence of J.W. Sifton); pp. 595–605 (evidence of John L. Connors).
42. Ibid., 3:218–27, 495–96.
43. *The Inter-Ocean* (Selkirk), 25 July and 29 August 1879; 13 February 1880.
44. *MFP,* 17 June, 13 October, 27 November 1879; 6 January, 26 and 28 February, 6 March 1880; Ruth Elizabeth Spence, *Prohibition in Canada* (Toronto: Ontario Branch of the Dominion Alliance, 1919), pp. 122–38.
45. *MFP,* 6 March 1880; 20 April 1881.
46. John H. Thompson, "The Prohibition Question in Manitoba 1892–1928" (M.A. thesis, University of Manitoba, 1969), p. 8.

## NOTES TO CHAPTER TWO

1. Pierre Berton, *The Last Spike* (Toronto: McClelland and Stewart, 1971), pp. 23-32.
2. *Brandon Sun,* 7 July 1882.
3. Norman Ernest Wright, "An Historical Survey of Southwestern Manitoba to 1899" (M.A. thesis, University of Manitoba, 1949), pp. 192-94; J.A.D. Stuart, *The Prairie W.A.S.P.: A History of the Rural Municipality of Oakland, Manitoba* (Winnipeg: Prairie Publishing, 1969).
4. Gerald A. Friesen, "Studies in the Development of Western Canadian Regional Consciousness 1870-1925" (Ph.D. diss., University of Toronto, 1974).
5. *MFP,* 6 November 1882; *Brandon Sun,* 9 and 30 November 1882; Dale and Lee Gibson, *Substantial Justice: Law and Lawyers in Manitoba 1670-1970* (Winnipeg: Peguis, 1972), pp. 127-29.
6. *MFP,* 29 November 1881; 28 September 1882; *Brandon Sun,* 9 March, 6, 13, and 20 April, 7 and 13 July, 5 October, 16 November 1882.
7. *MFP,* 31 May 1882; James A. Jackson, "The Disallowance of Manitoba Railway Legislation in the 1880's: Railway Policy as a Factor in the Relations of Manitoba with the Dominion, 1878-1888" (M.A. thesis, University of Manitoba, 1945), pp. 8-9.
8. *MFP,* 6 May 1882; *Brandon Sun,* 16 November 1882.
9. *MFP,* 23 October 1882.
10. *Brandon Sun,* 20 April and 21 September 1882.
11. The first issue of the *Brandon Daily Mail* appeared 19 December 1882.
12. *Brandon Sun,* 9 November 1882.
13. Ibid., 23 November and 21 December 1882.
14. Ibid., 15 June 1882.
15. *Brandon Mail,* 20 December 1882; *Brandon Sun,* 11 January 1883.
16. *Brandon Mail,* 21 December 1882; *Brandon Sun,* 28 December 1882.
17. PAC, Sir John A. Macdonald Papers, vol. 390, pp. 185635-40, T.M. Daly to Macdonald, 21 January 1883.
18. Larry John Fisk, "Controversy on the Prairies: Issues in the General Provincial Elections of Manitoba 1870-1969" (Ph.D. diss., University of Alberta, 1975), p. 105; John L. Holmes, "Factors Affecting Politics in Manitoba: A Study of the Provincial Elections 1870-99" (M.A. thesis, University of Manitoba, 1936).
19. *Brandon Sun,* 25 January 1883.
20. J.W. Dafoe, *Clifford Sifton,* p. 10; W.E. Sterner, "Sir Clifford as a Young Campaigner," Toronto *Saturday Night,* 27 April 1929.
21. *MFP,* 18 April 1929.
22. *Brandon Mail,* 21 August 1884; PAC, Sifton Papers, vol. 181, p. 146304, memorandum by C. Sifton, February 1907; A.H.D. Ross, *Ottawa Past and Present* (Ottawa: Thorburn and Abbott, 1927), pp. 54-55.
23. *MFP,* 25 July 1929; PAC, Sifton Papers, vol. 287a, clipping, Toronto *Star,* 18 April 1929, interview with Victor Sifton.
24. *Brandon Sun,* 26 April 1883.
25. Martin Kavanagh, *The Assiniboine Basin* (Winnipeg: Public Press, 1946), pp. 229-30.
26. *Brandon Mail,* 31 January 1889.
27. *Brandon Sun,* 14 June 1883.
28. *MFP,* 17 September 1881.
29. Ibid., 2 August and 1 September 1882.
30. Ibid., 20 May 1882.
31. Ibid., 14 June 1882.
32. Ibid., 18 May and 14 September 1882.
33. Ibid.; William Howard Brooks, "Methodism in the Canadian West in the Nineteenth Century" (Ph.D. diss., University of Manitoba, 1972), p. 306; J. Warren Caldwell, "The Unification of Methodism in Canada 1865-1884," *The Bulletin* 19 (1967) (United Church of Canada, Committee on Archives): 3-61.
34. *Brandon Sun,* 26 April 1883; 24 May 1884.
35. Brian Robert McCutcheon, "The Economic and Social Structure of Political Agrarianism in Manitoba: 1870-1900" (Ph.D. diss., University of British Columbia, 1974), pp. 97-107.
36. Ibid., p. 111; *Brandon Blade,* 8, 22, and 29 November 1883.
37. McCutcheon, "Economic and Social Structure of Political Agrarianism," pp. 140-46.
38. *Brandon Sun,* 8 November and 6 December 1883.
39. T.D. Regehr, *The Canadian Northern Railway: Pioneer Road of the Northern*

*Prairies 1895–1918* (Toronto: Macmillan, 1976), p. 7.

40. McCutcheon, "Economic and Social Structure of Political Agrarianism" pp. 146, 181–86; *Brandon Sun*, 24 April and 5 June 1884.

41. McCutcheon, "Economic and Social Structure of Political Agrarianism," pp. 187–99; *Brandon Sun*, 12 June and 3 July 1884.

42. *Brandon Sun*, 26 February 1885.

43. Ibid., 17 July 1884; 5 March 1885; *MFP*, 17 July 1884. For an account of the proceedings more sympathetic to Burgess, see *Brandon Mail*, 17 and 24 July 1884.

44. *Brandon Sun*, 12 March 1885; *MFP*, 12 February 1885, 25 July 1929.

45. *MFP*, 2 April 1885; E.V. Jackson, "The Organization of the Canadian Liberal Party, 1867–1896, with Particular Reference to Ontario" (M.A. thesis, University of Toronto, 1962), p. 55.

46. *MFP*, 1 April 1885; McCutcheon, "Economic and Social Structure of Political Agrarianism," p. 229.

47. *Brandon Sun*, 10 June 1886.

48. McCutcheon, "Economic and Social Structure of Political Agrarianism," pp. 221–25; Joseph A. Hilts, "The Political Career of Thomas Greenway" (Ph.D. diss., University of Manitoba, 1974), pp. 82–91; and see below, ch. 9.

49. Dafoe, *Clifford Sifton*, pp. 16–17; *Brandon Sun*, 28 January 1886.

50. Fisk, "Controversy on the Prairies," pp. 116–18; *Brandon Sun*, 6 January 1887; *MFP*, 4, 5, and 13 November 1886; J.R. Miller, "The Impact of the Jesuits' Estates Act on Canadian Politics, 1888–1891" (Ph.D. diss., University of Toronto, 1972), p. 263. The *Brandon Mail*, by now no friend of Norquay, also had attacked the French language and educational privileges (see *Mail*, 28 January 1886; and Fisk, "Controversy on the Prairies," p. 117).

51. *Brandon Sun*, 8 July 1886.

52. Ibid., 25 November 1886.

53. Ibid., 15 July, 5 and 26 August 1886.

54. Ibid., 2 September, 4 and 18 November, 2 and 9 December 1886. Daly was in fact correct that votes had been brought in from Winnipeg. Clifford Sifton himself had been busy rounding up people in Winnipeg who owned property in Brandon and therefore were legally entitled to vote; one contemporary believed that as many as fifty such votes had been brought in by the Siftons. Daly, of course, had been implying that the procedure was improper, if not illegal, which explains Sifton's heated response (see PAM, Alexander Reid Papers, Reid to his father, 3–14 November 1881; University of Manitoba, Elizabeth Dafoe Library, J.W. Dafoe Papers, Philip McKenzie to Dafoe, 3 February 1932).

55. Fisk, "Controversy on the Prairies," p. 119.

56. *Brandon Sun*, 3 and 31 March, 19 May, 23 June 1887; 5 September 1889; PAM, Colcleugh Papers, Colcleugh to George Colcleugh (father), 8 October 1887.

57. Regehr, *Canadian National Railway*, pp. 7–14; Hilts, "Thomas Greenway," ch. 3. Van Horne later claimed that the CPR had been as anxious as westerners to be rid of the monopoly clause and that all the agitation enabled the dominion government to provide concessions to relieve the fears of European investors in the CPR (PAC, CPR Records, Van Horne letterbook 56, pp. 122–25, Van Horne to Dr. G.R. Parkin, 8 February 1899).

58. *Brandon Sun*, 10 and 24 May 1888.

59. Ibid., 31 May 1888.

60. Ibid., 12 July 1888; Dafoe, *Clifford Sifton*, pp. 3–6, 15–16; Fisk, "Controversy on the Prairies," pp. 124–34; Holmes, "Factors Affecting Politics in Manitoba," pp. 16–17.

## NOTES TO CHAPTER THREE

1. Hilts, "Thomas Greenway."

2. PAC, Macdonald Papers, pp. 225482–87, T.M. Daly to Macdonald, 24 January 1888.

3. Grant MacEwan, *The Battle for the Bay* (Saskatoon: Western Producer Books, 1975), p. 70; T.D. Regehr, "The National Policy and Manitoba Railway Legislation 1879–1888" (M.A. thesis, Carleton University, 1963), pp. 169–70; Hilts, "Thomas Greenway," pp. 107–9, 113–14.

4. Regehr, "National Policy," p. 172; Re-

gehr, *Canadian Northern Railway*, pp. 15–17; Hilts, "Thomas Greenway," pp. 141ff.

5. Hilts, "Thomas Greenway," pp. 143–44; Dafoe, *Clifford Sifton*, pp. 16–22.

6. *Brandon Sun*, 30 August 1888; *MFP*, 29 August 1888.

7. PAM, Thomas Greenway Papers, p. 1037, Sifton to Greenway, 6 September 1888.

8. *Brandon Sun*, 30 August 1888; Dafoe, *Clifford Sifton*, p. 23.

9. Regehr, *Canadian Northern Railway*, pp. 18–20; PAM, Greenway Papers, p. 1192, Sifton to Greenway, 31 October 1888.

10. *MFP*, 15 November 1888, 20 February 1889. See also W. Kaye Lamb, *History of the Canadian Pacific Railway* (New York: Macmillan, 1977), pp. 155–64.

11. *Brandon Sun*, 9 January 1884. Five months earlier the *Sun* had printed the comment: "Half-breed politicians are a peculiar product of Manitoba! Louis Riel defied the Dominion and was bribed by Sir John to get out of the way. Mr. Norquay, for acting as the dirty catspaw of the Bleus, will be bribed by-and-bye with a Dominion appointment. Louis Riel sank beneath contempt, and so will Norquay" (9 August 1883).

12. *MFP*, 2 March 1889.

13. Miller, "Jesuits' Estates Act," p. 167.

14. Ibid., p. 162; *MFP*, 25 February 1889; *Brandon Sun*, 14 and 28 March, 2 May 1889.

15. *MFP*, 21 and 26 November 1888; *Brandon Sun*, 14 March 1889.

16. Miller, "Jesuits' Estates Act," pp. 263–70.

17. *Brandon Sun*, 21 March, 2, 16, and 30 May 1889.

18. Ibid., 13 October 1887; *Census of Manitoba, 1885–86* (Ottawa: Maclean, Roger & Co., 1887), pp. 7, 14–15, 22–23.

19. Hilts, "Thomas Greenway," p. 201.

20. Miller, "Jesuits' Estates Act," pp. 272–73.

21. *Brandon Sun*, 11 and 18 July 1889.

22. *Brandon Mail*, 11 and 18 July 1889.

23. *Brandon Sun*, 8 August 1889.

24. *MFP*, 5 and 7 August 1889; J.R. Miller, "D'Alton McCarthy, Equal Rights, and the Origins of the Manitoba School Question," *CHR* 54 (1973): 369–92.

25. *MFP*, 7 August 1889.

26. Ibid., 10 and 12 August 1889; PAM, Greenway Papers, p. 2111, Martin to Greenway, 6 and 9 August 1889.

27. PAC, Sifton Papers, vol. 191, p. 152907, clipping of *Vancouver Daily News-Advertiser*, 28 February 1909, reporting a speech by Martin in Vancouver of 26 February 1909.

28. The resignation of Prendergast resulted in Sifton's name being considered for the first time for a cabinet post. Greenway wanted to have either Sifton or Isaac Campbell, then a member for Winnipeg, but Martin reportedly scotched the idea. Either man would have been a strong rival within the cabinet. As a result, the premier selected a close personal friend, though a weak politician, Daniel McLean, member for Virden. McLean was the second change in Greenway's cabinet, for Lyman Jones had retired in the spring to pursue a lucrative business career in Ontario. He had been succeeded as provincial treasurer on 7 May by Daniel Hunter McMillan, a forty-three-year-old Winnipeg financier and former militia officer. McMillan was a capable administrator, though not a strong political figure outside Winnipeg (see PAC, Macdonald Papers, vol. 264, pp. 120185–87, J.C. Schultz to Macdonald, 9 September 1889).

29. Ibid., pp. 120196–99, Schultz to Macdonald, 9 December 1889.

30. Ibid., letterbooks, vol. 26, pt. 2, pp. 373–76, Macdonald to Schultz, 8 January 1890.

31. Ibid.

32. *MFP*, 29 January and 4 February 1890.

33. Ibid., 12 February 1890. In *Attorney-General of Manitoba vs. Georges Forest* the Supreme Court of Canada unanimously found on 13 December 1979 that the language law was ultra vires of the provincial legislature.

34. Ibid., 20 and 25 February 1890; W.L. Morton, *Manitoba: A History* (Toronto: University of Toronto Press, 1957), p. 248.

35. John Higham, *Strangers in the Land: Patterns of American Nativism 1860–1925* (New York: Atheneum, 1963), pp. 59–60.

36. Miller, "Jesuits' Estates Act," ch. 7.

37. *Brandon Sun*, 20 March 1890; *MFP*, 10 and 11 March 1890; *Winnipeg Daily Tribune*, 10 and 11 March, 8 April 1890.

38. *Winnipeg Daily Tribune*, 29 March 1890; *Brandon Sun*, 17 April 1890. The legislature elected in 1888 included nineteen

farmers, six lawyers, five merchants, four grain buyers, an agricultural implement manufacturer, a surveyor, an insurance agent and a banker. In religious affiliation, eighteen were Presbyterian, seven Catholic, seven Anglican, four Methodist, and two Baptist. Eighteen of the thirty-eight members had never sat in the legislature before, and two more only since January 1888 (*Brandon Sun,* 19 and 26 July 1888).

39. PAC, Macdonald Papers, vol. 264, pp. 120237–42, Schultz to Macdonald, 31 March and 9 April 1890.
40. *Brandon Sun,* 5 September, 3 October, 14 November 1889; 27 February and 6 March 1890; *Brandon Mail,* 8 and 22 January, 12 February, 19 March 1891.
41. *Brandon Mail,* 19 February and 26 March 1891; *Brandon Sun,* 30 April and 4 June 1891.
42. PAC, Macdonald Papers, letterbooks, vol. 27, pt. 2, Macdonald to T.M. Daly, 20 December 1890.
43. *Tribune,* 10 and 12 February 1891; *Brandon Sun,* 12 February 1891.
44. PAM, Greenway Papers, p. 3274, Joseph Tees to Greenway, 4 February 1891; PAC, Macdonald Papers, vol. 494, pp. 247676–77, R. Rogers to [H.H.] Smith, 5 February 1891.
45. *Tribune,* 12, 25, and 27 February, 7 and 9 March 1891; *Brandon Mail,* 26 February 1891; *CSP,* 1891, no. 27a, pp. 282–84.
46. *Manitoba Gazette* 20 (1891): 228, 240; PAM, Greenway Papers, pp. 3669, 3676, 3630, Sifton to Greenway, 22 and 26 April, 9 May 1891; letterbooks, Greenway to Sifton, 29 April 1891. On earlier provincial cabinet changes see above, n. 28.
47. PAM, Greenway Papers, p. 3626, W.C. White to Greenway, 2 May 1891; *Brandon Mail,* 7, 21, and 28 May, 4 June, 16

July 1891; *Tribune,* 1 June 1891.
48. *Brandon Sun,* 6 August 1891; PAM, Greenway Papers, p. 3791, Sifton to Greenway, 5 July 1891.
49. PAM, Greenway Papers, p. 3817, Sifton to Greenway, 12 July 1891. This was borne out by Cliffe's bitter post-election complaint that obviously many who had pledged themselves to him during the campaign had not actually voted for him (*Brandon Mail,* 13 August 1891).
50. PAM, Greenway Papers, pp. 3791, 3836, 3843, 3889, Sifton to Greenway, 5, 23, and 29 July, 3 August 1891; p. 3829, J.M. Walsh to Greenway, 15 July 1891.
51. Ibid., pp. 3817, 3843, 3889, Sifton to Greenway, 12 and 23 July, 3 August 1891.
52. *Brandon Mail,* 31 January 1889; 25 June, 6, 13, and 27 August 1891; *Tribune,* 18 and 20 August 1891. "Money, money everywhere," piously exclaimed J.N. Kirchhoffer, John Sifton's opponent of 1886. "No concealment, No attempt at it. The constituency is thoroughly debauched and demoralized. There are scores nay hundreds of cases we already know, any of wh. wd. void the election, & they are coming in daily—$25 a vote was paid in many instances which is high in this country, but will fetch most of them. I don't suppose there is any use in a protest as the General Election is so near. Except to expose the corruption, but for that purpose it really ought to be gone into."

"I tell you what. If they have anything like the sums expended here for use at the General Election, and flash it out in the same way, they will knock the stuffin out of a good many of our side" (PAM, C. Acton Burrows Papers, p. 53, Kirchhoffer to Burrows, 11 August 1891).

## NOTES TO CHAPTER FOUR

1. P.E. Crunican, "The Manitoba School Question and Canadian Federal Politics, 1890–1896: A Study in Church-State Relations" (Ph.D. diss., University of Toronto, 1968), p. 47.
2. *Manitoba Reports* 7 (1891): 329 (judgment of Chief Justice Taylor, 2 February 1891).
3. PAC, Sir John Thompson Papers, vol.

125, p. 14974, Blake to Messrs. Ewart and Brophy, 26 March 1891.
4. PAC, Sifton Papers, vol. 269, pp. 5–6, Sifton to Martin, 19 June 1891.
5. Supreme Court of Canada, *Reports* 19 (1891): 374–425. After the Supreme Court decision, Edward Blake reversed himself and again offered his services to the minority in preparing the case for the

Judicial Committee of the Privy Council (AASB, J.S. Ewart files, Edward Blake to Ewart, 28 October 1891). For some reason still unclear, Blake was not retained.

6. This move had been anticipated two years earlier by the *Free Press. (MFP,* 2 August 1889).

7. PAC, Sifton Papers, vol. 269, pp. 81–82, Sifton to Martin, 18 December 1891; *Manitoba Reports* 8 (1892): 3ff., *Logan vs. the City of Winnipeg.* The most detailed examination of the Logan case is W.T. Shaw, "The Role of John S. Ewart in the Manitoba School Question" (M.A. thesis, University of Manitoba, 1959), pp. 205–25.

8. *Winnipeg Daily Tribune,* 11 April 1892; *Statutes of Manitoba,* 55 Vict., c. 13; John L. Holmes, "Factors Affecting Politics in Manitoba," pp. 86–88, 91–96. 97–98; Hilts, "Thomas Greenway." pp. 225–26. Roblin, a former Liberal, had broken with the government over its railway policy.

9. *Tribune,* 16 March and 8 April 1892.

10. *MFP,* 11, 12, and 13 April 1892.

11. Ibid., 11 and 23 March, 9, 11–13 April 1892.

12. PAC, CPR Records, Van Horne letterbook 36, pp. 125–26, Van Horne to C.H. MacIntosh, M.P., 21 November 1890.

13. Ibid., letterbook 28, p. 173–76, Van Horne to Sir George Stephen, 9 November 1888; letterbook 30, p. 252, Van Horne to W. Whyte, 29 May 1889; letterbook 30, pp. 462–63. Van Horne to R. Baker, 7 June 1889; letterbook 32, p. 893, Van Horne to J.A. Codd, 11 November 1889; letterbook 31, p. 161, Agreement with Manitoba and North Western Railway, 7 August 1889; letterbook 32, pp. 392–95, Van Horne to W. Whyte, 5 February 1890; letterbook 38, pp. 628–29, Van Horne to W. Whyte, 2 October 1891; Hilts, "Thomas Greenway," p. 156.

14. Hilts, "Thomas Greenway," pp. 161–62; PAC, CPR Records, Van Horne letterbook 36, p. 621, Van Horne to Walsh, 27 January 1891; letterbook 37, pp. 40–43, Van Horne to Greenway, 20 March 1891.

15. PAC, CPR Records, Van Horne letterbook 37, pp. 874–85, Van Horne to R.P. Roblin, 18 June 1891; Hilts, "Thomas Greenway," pp. 162-67.

16. Hilts, "Thomas Greenway," pp. 168–69;

PAC, CPR Records, Van Horne letterbook 39, p. 774, Van Horne to Greenway, 1 February 1892; letterbook 40, pp. 361–62, Van Horne to Walsh, 8 April 1892.

17. PAM, Greenway Papers, p. 4917, Sifton to Col. D.H. McMillan, 26 May 1892; p. 4664, Sifton to Greenway, 29 May 1892; *Tribune,* 21 and 26 May 1892. The changes may have been partly in response to feeling that Brandon was overrepresented in the cabinet; see PAM, J.J. Moncrieff Papers, R.H. Myers to Moncrieff, 16 May 1892.

18. *Tribune,* 28 February, 1 March, 22 April 1892.

19. Ibid., 6 May, 14 June, 6 July 1892; *Brandon Sun,* 21 July 1892.

20. Holmes, "Factors Affecting Politics in Manitoba," pp. 18–19, 91–96; Fisk, "Controversy on the Prairies," pp. 142–49.

21. *MFP,* 21 April, 22, 23, and 25 July 1892. At least one Liberal contended that the corruption was all on the Tory side in his constituency (see PAM, Moncrieff Papers, R.H. Myers to Moncrieff, 27 July 1892).

22. PAC, CPR Records, Van Horne letterbook 41, pp. 268–69, Van Horne to J.M. Walsh, 31 July 1892; pp. 284–85, Van Horne to W. Whyte, 31 July 1892; pp. 448–49, Van Horne to Walsh, 12 August 1892; p. 550, Van Horne to Walsh, 20 August 1892; Hilts, "Thomas Greenway," pp. 168–69.

23. Dafoe, *Clifford Sifton,* p. 61; *Tribune,* 30 July 1892.

24. R.A. Olmsted, ed., *Decisions of the Judicial Committee of the Privy Council relating to the British North America Act, 1867 and the Canadian Constitution 1867–1954* (Ottawa: Queen's Printer, 1954), 1:272–86. For a sharp criticism of the decision, see Lovell C. Clark, "A History of the Conservative Administrations, 1891 to 1896" (Ph.D. diss., University of Toronto, 1968), pp. 258–67.

25. *Tribune,* 30 July and 27 August 1892. Thompson, the Roman Catholic minister of justice, became prime minister in November 1892.

26. PAM, Greenway Papers, p. 6800, Clifford Sifton to Greenway, 6 July 1894.

27. 52 Vict., c. 15.

28. R.E. Spence, *Prohibition in Canada* (Toronto: Dominion Alliance, 1919), pp.

150–58.

29. *CSP*, 1894, no. 21, *Royal Commission on the Liquor Traffic, Minutes of Evidence,* vol. 3, *Provinces of Manitoba, North-West Territories and British Columbia,* p. 98 and passim.

30. *MFP*, 12 February 1889.

31. Ibid., 20 and 21 March 1890; *Tribune*, 20 March 1890.

32. This was confirmed only partially by the Judicial Committee of the Privy Council in 1896; see Olmsted, *Decisions of the Judicial Committee,* pp. 343–66; and below, note 40.

33. *Tribune,* 13 April 1892.

34. *Brandon Sun,* 30 June 1892.

35. Spence, *Prohibition in Canada,* pp. 169–75. Prohibitionists objected that equal time was given the enemies of prohibition.

36. Ibid., p. 262: *CSP*, 1895, no. 21, *Report of the Royal Commission on the Liquor Traffic in Canada,* p. 173.

37. *Tribune,* 22 and 23 February 1893.

38. Ibid., 24 February 1893.

39. Ibid., 22, 23, and 24 February, 2 March 1893; *MFP*, 2 March 1893; *Brandon Sun,* 9 March 1893; PAC, Sifton Papers, vol. 269, pp. 583–85, Sifton to J.K. McLennan, 11 February 1893; Dafoe, *Clifford Sifton,* pp. 52–56. Sifton noted pointedly in his annual report that "the Government expenditure upon the enforcement of the 'Liquor License Act' steadily increases as the municipalities of the Province appear to do less and less every year towards the carrying out said Act. The City of Winnipeg, which is the strongest municipality in the Province does absolutely nothing beyond receiving a large sum accruing from their liquor license fees. Many of the provisions of the Act show clearly that it was intended that it should be locally enforced but these provisions have practically become a dead letter" (*MSP*, 1893, no. 9, p. 178).

40. *Tribune,* 16 November 1894; *Brandon Sun,* 1 August 1895; Spence, *Prohibition in Canada,* p. 219; Olmsted, *Decisions of the Judicial Committee,* pp. 343–66; *CSP*, 1895, no. 21, *Royal Commission on the Liquor Traffic,* pp. 502–3. The substance of the Judicial Committee decision was to uphold the primacy of the Canada Temperance Act, 1886; but the provinces could pass their own local option legislation which could be adop-

ted in districts which had not elected to adopt the dominion legislation. Provinces thus were found to have power to prohibit the sale of liquor and to prohibit its manufacture when it could be shown to be a purely provincial concern, but not to prohibit its importation.

41. *Tribune,* 16 and 20 November 1894; PAC, Sifton Papers, vol. 1, 55–56, Margaret W. Bayne to Sifton; vol. 2, pp. 388–90, R. Paterson to Sifton, 26 November 1894; vol. 2, pp. 500–508, Rev. W.A. Vrooman to Sifton, 29 September, 4 and 21 October, 5 and 8 November 1894; Spence, *Prohibition in Canada,* pp. 146–47; Thompson, "The Prohibition Question in Manitoba," pp. 39–45.

42. Spence, *Prohibition in Canada,* pp. 146–47.

43. *Western Law Times* 5, no. 3 (1894): 26–27; Manitoba Legislative Assembly, *Journals,* 1894, p. 112.

44. All appointments are listed in the annual reports of the provincial secretary in *MSP*; and see Dale Gibson and Lee Gibson, *Substantial Justice,* pp. 176–77.

45. Gibson and Gibson, *Substantial Justice,* p. 180; W.E. Perdue, "Fusion of Law and Equity in Manitoba," *Canadian Law Times* 2 (1882): 428–31.

46. *Tribune,* 31 January and 3 March 1894; *Western Law Times* 5, no. 1 (1894): 4–9; no. 2, p. 13; no. 9, pp. 111–12.

47. *Western Law Times* 6, no. 7, (1895): 63–65, "The New Code of Procedure."

48. Gibson and Gibson, *Substantial Justice,* p. 180; and see Dafoe, *Clifford Sifton,* pp. 56–57.

49. *MSP*, 1893, no. 9, p. 171.

50. Ibid., 1894, no. 10, p. 230; 1895, no. 16, p. 281; 1896, no. 23, p. 285.

51. *Tribune,* 3 March 1893; 7 April 1892.

52. PAC, Sifton Papers, vol. 269, pp. 935–37, Sifton to J.H. Housser, 23 January 1894.

53. Ibid., pp. 341–42, Sifton to L.M. Jones, 19 August 1892; p. 345, Sifton to T.J. McBride, 19 August 1892.

54. *Tribune,* 9 February 1893 and 31 January 1894; *MFP*, 9 February 1893; Dafoe, *Clifford Sifton,* pp. 59–60.

55. PAC, Sifton Papers, vol. 1, pp. 91–92, Cameron to Sifton, 3 April 1894.

56. Ibid., vol. 269, pp. 549–51, Sifton to W.B. Underhill, 26 January 1893; pp. 935–37, Sifton to J.H. Housser, 23 January 1894; vol. 270, pp. 48–50, Sifton to H.D.

Cameron, 10 April 1894; pp. 493–95, Sifton to Senator J.N. Kirchhoffer, 13 May 1895.

57. PAM, Greenway Papers, p. 6983, Sifton to Greenway, September 1894.

58. McCutcheon, "Economic and Social Structure of Political Agrarianism," pp. 278ff., 297–301, 331–33.

59. Ibid., pp. 321–26; *Tribune,* 17–19 January 1894.

60. McCutcheon, "Economic and Social Structure of Political Agrarianism," pp. 318, 327.

61. PAC, Sifton Papers, vol. 269, pp. 974–76, Sifton to Roderick McKay, 17 February 1894.

62. Ibid., vol. 270, pp. 164–66, Sifton to W.B. Underhill, 24 August 1894; McCutcheon, "Economic and Social Structure of Political Agrarianism," pp. 328–29.

63. McCutcheon, "Economic and Social Structure of Political Agrarianism," p. 328.

64. Jackson, "Organization of the Canadian Liberal Party," pp. 154–55.

65. PAC, Sifton Papers, vol. 269, pp. 558–61, Sifton to Laurier, 2 February 1893.

66. Ibid., pp. 451–52, Sifton to Laurier, 3 December 1892.

67. *Official Report of the Liberal Convention . . . Ottawa, Tuesday, June 20th, and Wednesday, June 21st, 1893* (Toronto, 1893), pp. 22–23, 107–8, 158; John W. Lederle, "The Liberal Convention of 1893," *CJEPS* 16 (1940): 42–52.

68. PAC, Sifton Papers, vol. 269, pp. 829–30, Sifton to Laurier, 29 November 1893; Sir Wilfrid Laurier Papers, vol. 7, pp. 2664–65, 2672–73, 2666–67, Isaac Campbell to Laurier, 8, 11, and 21 November 1893; pp. 2670–71, L.G. Power to Laurier, 11 November 1893; 6 December 1893; *Tribune,* 23 and 24 November 1893; K.M. McLaughlin, "Race, Religion and Politics: The Election of 1896 in Canada" (Ph.D. diss., University of Toronto, 1974), p. 30.

69. *Tribune,* 9 October 1894; *Brandon Sun,* 11 October 1894.

70. *MSP,* 1892, no. 7, pp. 13–15; *MFP,* 22 April 1892; *Brandon Sun,* May–September 1894. In October 1892, J.W. Sifton became acting chief clerk, and in 1893 chief clerk, of the Department of Public Works in addition to his other duties (see PAM, Letterbooks of Inspector of Public Institutions and Buildings, and of the Chief Clerk, Department of Public Works, 1891–1900).

71. *Tribune,* 23 January and 9 May 1892.

72. Keith Wilson, "The Development of Education in Manitoba" (Ph.D. diss., Michigan State University, 1967), pp. 104, 150.

73. *MSP,* 1897, no. 18, passim.

74. PAC, Sifton Papers, vol. 269, pp. 914–16, Sifton to Rev. C.H. Mason, 16 January 1894.

75. PAM, Clifford Sifton Papers, draft speech to Canadian Club, Regina, 1927, p. 12; *Tribune,* 28 February 1894.

76. W.L. Morton, *One University: A History of the University of Manitoba* (Toronto: McClelland and Stewart, 1957), p. 57; *Tribune,* 28 February 1894 and 19 February 1895; *MSP,* 1897, no. 18, p. 279.

77. *MFP,* 23 February and 10 March 1893; *Tribune,* 23 February and 10 March 1893; Morton, *One University,* pp. 46–47.

78. Morton, *One University,* pp. 47–51; *Tribune,* 23 February 1893; 9 February 1894; 7 March 1896; *MFP,* 23 February 1893.

79. *Tribune,* 30 November 1892; Shaw, "Ewart," pp. 282–83; PAC, Sifton Papers, vol. 269, pp. 436–37, Sifton to J.S. Willison, 30 November 1892; AASB, Ewart files, J.S. Ewart to Sifton, 26 November 1892, and reply, 27 November 1892.

80. PAC, Sifton Papers, vol. 269, p. 419, Sifton to George G. Mills, 11 November 1892; and see J.T. Saywell, ed., *The Canadian Journal of Lady Aberdeen 1893–1898* (Toronto: Champlain Society, 1960), xxxvi–xxxvii.

81. Shaw, "Ewart," pp. 293–300.

82. Ibid., pp. 299, 322–23; R.E. Clague, "The Political Aspects of the Manitoba School Question, 1890–1896" (M.A. thesis, University of Manitoba, 1939), p. 191; *Tribune,* 2, 3, and 14 October 1893. The province had sent F.C. Wade to acknowledge receipt of the case, but Wade was under specific instructions not to argue it.

83. *Tribune,* 14 October 1893; and see 16 March 1893.

84. *Report of the Department of Education, Manitoba, for the Year 1894* (Winnipeg, 1895), p. 47.

85. PAM, J.C. Schultz Papers, copy of

report; McLaughlin, "Race, Religion and Politics," p. 26; PAC, Thompson Papers, vol. 172, p. 21544, J.C. Schultz to Thompson, 7 January 1893 [erroneously dated 1892].

86. PAM, Schultz Papers, memoranda of Schultz and Taché, undated [1893]. By contrast, however, schools in the Icelandic settlements were taught almost entirely in English (see *Report of the Department of Education, Manitoba, for the Year 1894,* p. 30).

87. PAC, Sifton Papers, vol. 2, pp. 440–41, F. Schultz to Sifton, 11 January 1894.

88. PAC, Thompson Papers, vol. 172, p. 21544, vol. 175, p. 21975, vol. 194, p. 24334, vol. 197, p. 24685, J.C. Schultz to Thompson, 7 January, 8 February, 28 December 1893, 19 January 1894.

89. *Tribune,* 8 February 1894.

90. Ibid., 13 February 1894; PAC, Sifton Papers, vol. 2, p. 442, F. Schultz to Sifton, 15 February 1894; Clague, "Political Aspects of the Manitoba School Question," p. 191.

91. *Tribune,* 13 February 1894; PAC, Thompson Papers, vol. 266, pp. 496–97, Thompson to J.C. Schultz, 17 February 1894. On this episode, see Clark, "History of Conservative Administrations," pp. 298–302.

92. PAC, Thompson Papers, Taché to J.C. Schultz, 16 February 1894 (copy); vol. 201, p. 25132, Schultz to Thompson, 21 February 1894.

93. *Report of the Department of Education, Manitoba, for the Year 1894,* pp. 42–47. The figures supplied are sloppy and inconsistent; also, under the term "French schools" are included at least one district of Scots Catholics and six described as "Mixed."

94. AASB, Bourret à Taché, le 6 août 1892; Bourret à Langevin, le 7 septembre 1895; Dufresne à Taché, le 2 avril 1894. I am grateful to M. Lionel Dorge for bringing these letters to my attention.

95. PAC, Thompson Papers, Schultz to Thompson, 21 February 1894; Sifton Papers, vol. 2, pp. 535–41, A.L. Young to Sifton, 12 December 1894. Young noted that the strongest continuing resistance to national schools was to be found "in the parishes of St. Norbert. Ste. Agathe, St. Jean Baptiste, Lorette, Ste. Anne and La Broquerie."

96. AASB, Clifford Sifton to N. Bawlf, 2 August 1894; and see pp. 7479–81, Mr. N. Bawlf's Statement re the School taxation, 9 January 1897.

97. *MSP,* 1896, no. 31, p. 313.

98. PAC, Sifton Papers, vol. 1, pp. 279–81, Laurier to Sifton, 3 December 1894; Laurier Papers, vol. 8, p. 3415, Sifton to Laurier, 8 December 1894.

99. PAC, Sifton Papers, vol. 270, pp. 320–21, Sifton to Laurier, 4 January 1895; *Tribune,* 2 and 4 January 1895. The appellant after whom the case was named was Gerald Brophy, a law partner of J.S. Ewart.

100. Olmsted, *Decisions of the Judicial Committee,* pp. 316–43.

101. *MFP,* 30 January 1895.

102. *Tribune,* 28 February 1895; *MFP,* 28 February 1895.

## NOTES TO CHAPTER FIVE

1. Crunican, "The Manitoba School Question," p. 6.

2. There has been a continuing debate on the subject. See D.G. Creighton, "John A. Macdonald, Confederation, and the Canadian West," in *Minorities, Schools, and Politics,* ed. R. Craig Brown (Toronto: University of Toronto Press, 1969), pp. 1–9; D.G. Creighton, "Confederation: The Use and Abuse of History," *JCS* 1, no. 1 (1966): 3–11; W.L. Morton, "Confederation, 1870–1896: The end of the Macdonaldian constitution and the return to duality," *JCS* 1, no. 1 (1966): 11–24; Ralph Heintzman, "The Spirit of Confederation: Professor Creighton, Biculturalism and the Use of History," *CHR* 52 (1971): 245–75; Hall, " 'The Spirit of Confederation,' " pp. 24–43.

3. *Winnipeg Daily Tribune,* 12 January 1892.

4. Ibid., 28 February 1895.

5. K.M. McLaughlin, "Race, Religion and Politics," pp. 15–16. For an excellent discussion of the dilemma faced by Catholics between the demands of, and loyalty to, the larger community on the one hand and the imperatives of loyalty

to their faith, on the other, see Neil G. McCluskey, S.J., *Catholic Viewpoint on Education* (Garden City: Hanover House, 1959), ch. 2, "The Price of Pluralism."

6. McCluskey, *Catholic Viewpoint*, pp. 70–71. For a penetrating consideration of these issues from a Catholic perspective, see his chapter 3, "The Evolution of the Secular School."

7. Paul Crunican, *Priests and Politicians: Manitoba Schools and the Election of 1896* (Toronto: University of Toronto Press, 1974), pp. 183–84. Catholic authorities by no means considered their position in Ontario to be satisfactory (see Franklin A. Walker, *Catholic Education and Politics in Ontario* [Toronto: Nelson, (1964)], ch. 1).

8. J.S. Ewart, *The Manitoba School Question. A Reply to Mr. Wade* (Winnipeg, Manitoba Free Press Co., 1895), p. 7.

9. Wilson, "The Development of Education in Manitoba," p. 130; McCluskey, *Catholic Viewpoint,* passim.; George P. Grant, *Philosophy in the Mass Age,* rev. ed. (Toronto: Copp Clark, 1966), pp. 83–86.

10. For a discussion of some of these issues, see D.A. Schmeiser, *Civil Liberties in Canada* (London: Oxford University Press, 1964), p. 125, and passim.

11. See Crunican, *Priests and Politicians,* passim.

12. Hilts, "Thomas Greenway," p. 233; *Tribune,* 26 February 1895; *CSP,* 1895, no. 20, pp. 15–17.

13. *CSP,* 1895, no. 20, p. 73; *Tribune,* 19 February and 6 March 1895. McCarthy's figures were correct (see *Census of Canada 1890–91,* 1:10, 226).

14. PAC, Sifton Papers, vol. 270, pp. 432–34, Sifton to McCarthy, 11 March 1895.

15. PAC, Sir Mackenzie Bowell Papers, vol. 77, pp. 91–93, Bowell to Schultz, 7 March 1895.

16. See H.B. Neatby, *Laurier and a Liberal Quebec* (Toronto: McClelland and Stewart, 1973), p. 63; Crunican, "The Manitoba School Question," pp. 118–19.

17. *CSP,* 1895, no. 20, p. 189.

18. *Tribune,* 23 and 28 March 1895; PAC, Sir John S. Willison Papers, vol. 12, pp. 3906–7, 3912–14, J.D. Cameron to Willison, 4 March and 5 April 1895.

19. PAC, Sifton Papers, vol. 270, pp. 432–34, Sifton to McCarthy, 11 March 1895; pp. 400–402, Sifton to Laurier, 2 March 1895.

20. E.J. Noble, "D'Alton McCarthy and the Election of 1896" (M.A. thesis, University of Guelph, 1969), ch. 7; PAC, Laurier Papers, vol. 9, 3746–47, Alexander Smith to Laurier, 3 April 1895; PAM, Greenway Papers, p. 7585, Sifton to Greenway, 7 April 1895.

21. University of Manitoba, Dafoe Papers, R.G. MacBeth to Dafoe, 31 March 1932.

22. Toronto *Globe,* 15–25 April 1895. The census gave the French–Canadian population of Manitoba in 1891 as 11,102; *Census of Canada 1890–91,* 1:119.

23. Toronto *Globe,* 15 April 1895.

24. AASB, Ewart file, Langevin to Ewart, 19 May 1895.

25. *Tribune,* 10 June 1895; Saywell, *Canadian Journal of Lady Aberdeen,* pp. xlix–lcl.

26. *Tribune,* 18–20 June 1895; *MFP,* 18 and 19 June 1895; *CSP,* 1895, no. 20, pp. 350–54.

27. AASB, Ewart file, Ewart to T.M. Daly, 6 February 1895; Ewart to C.H. Tupper, and to J.A. Ouimet, 23 June 1895; Langevin to Ewart, and reply, 24 June 1895.

28. *CSP,* 1896, no. 39, pp. 1–3; AASB, Ewart file, Langevin to Ewart, 5 July 1895. Langevin lost no time in letting it be known that he regarded the draft bill as "the extreme limit of compromise," and that the Church could not accept anything less (see ibid., Langevin to Ewart, 5 August 1895).

29. PAC, Sifton papers, vol. 270, pp. 541–42, Sifton to McCarthy, 12 July 1895.

30. F.C. Wade, *The Manitoba School Question* (Winnipeg: Manitoba Institute for the Deaf and Dumb, 1895). Sifton himself wrote a short piece on the school question for the *Review of Reviews,* which was published in the *Tribune,* 7 October 1895. It added nothing to the debate (12 October 1895, pp. 452–53).

31. J.S. Ewart, *The Manitoba School Question.* Ewart failed to appreciate that much of the effectiveness of Sifton's and Wade's approach to the subject was their appearance of offering reasoned, dispassionate arguments. Too frequently Ewart tried to reply with sharp wit and ridicule, sometimes missing the point altogether. In particular he responded to

Wade's statistics on crime and illiteracy by taking refuge in the argument that statistics can be used to prove anything, without explaining how Wade's particular use of statistics could be questioned.

32. *Tribune,* 16 December 1895; Hilts, "Thomas Greenway," p. 238.

33. *CSP,* 1896, no. 39, pp. 3–7.

34. *Tribune,* 23 and 30 December 1895.

35. PAC, Sifton Papers, vol. 200, pp. 158727–6, Sifton to J.W. Dafoe, 17 November 1913.

36. *Tribune,* 2 and 3 January 1896.

37. Ibid.; and *Globe,* 6 and 16 January 1896.

38. Brian R. McCutcheon, "The Patrons of Industry in Manitoba, 1890–1898," in *Historical Essays on the Prairie Provinces,* ed. Donald Swainson (Toronto: McClelland and Stewart, 1970), pp. 159–63; Wright, "An Historical Survey of Southwestern Manitoba," pp. 176–79; PAC, Sifton Papers, vol. 270, pp. 640–41, Sifton to D. McNaught, 3 October 1895.

39. PAC, Sifton Papers, vol. 270, p. 755, Sifton to W.A. Matheson, 23 December 1895.

40. The independents were James Fisher (Russell) and James E.P. Prendergast (St. Boniface); the Patrons were W.F. Sirrett (Beautiful Plains) and W. Crosby (Dennis). R.P. Roblin, the Conservative leader, was elected for Woodlands. The percentage vote was Liberal, 46.5; Conservative, 38.9; Patron, 9.1; Independent, 5.6. With nearly one-quarter of the constituencies returning Liberals by acclamation, however, it would be misleading to read too much into these figures. (Fisk, "Controversy on the Prairies," p. 167; Holmes, "Factors Affecting Politics in Manitoba," pp. 101–9; McCutcheon, "Economic and Social Structure of Political Agrarianism in Manitoba," p. 341).

41. *MFP,* 17 January 1896; *Tribune,* 17 January 1896.

42. "When the campaign opened," wrote Sifton, "it seemed utterly hopeless to try to oppose [the Patrons ] but I think it may be regarded as certain that they will never be able to show the same strength again" (PAC, Sifton Papers, vol. 270, p. 802, Sifton to G. Sylvester, 18 January 1896; p. 810, Sifton to G.A. Hall, 23 January 1896).

43. Jackson, "The Disallowance of Manito-

ba Railway Legislation," pp. 130–31.

44. PAC, CPR Records, Van Horne letterbook 41, p. 845, Van Horne to Walsh, 15 October 1892; and see letterbook 43, pp. 335–36, Van Horne to H. Abbott, 23 March 1893.

45. Ibid., letterbook 47, pp. 401–2, Van Horne to H.J. Macdonald and J.S. Tupper, 8 September 1894; letterbook 48, pp. 481–82, Van Horne to William Hone, 9 March 1895.

46. Ibid., letterbook 44, pp. 12–14, Van Horne to T.M. Daly, 17 June 1893.

47. *Tribune,* 2 January 1896.

48. Hilts, "Thomas Greenway," pp. 295ff.; Regehr, *Canadian Northern Railway,* p. 27. Van Horne believed the Manitoba and South Eastern would be a waste of money, as the country through which it would run was so poor that it would never cover its working expenses (see PAC, CPR Records, Van Horne letterbook 40, p. 750, Van Horne to A.F. Eden, 22 May 1892).

49. PAC, CPR Records, Van Horne letterbook 50, p. 174, Van Horne to T.M. Daly, 5 November 1895; p. 161, Van Horne to Sifton, 4 November 1895; p. 149, Van Horne to C.C. Castle, 26 October 1895.

50. Ibid., letterbook 43, pp. 312–13, 393, Van Horne to Walsh, 22 and 31 March 1893; letterbook 44, pp. 336–38, Van Horne to W.A. Elin, 19 July 1893.

51. Regehr, *Canadian Northern Railway,* pp. 27–28, 39–42; and Regehr, "Canadian Northern Railway: Agent of National Growth, 1896–1914" (Ph.D. thesis, University of Alberta, 1967) pp. 12–13.

52. PAM, Manitoba, Railway Commissioner, Mortgages, Leases, Agreements between the Railway Commissioner of the Province of Manitoba and the Canadian Northern Railway Company Lines, 1896–1916, Indenture dated 1 August 1896, between the Lake Manitoba Railway and Canal Company and the Government of Manitoba—Mortgage to secure bonds of Lake Manitoba Railway and Canal Company; Regehr, *Canadian Northern Railway,* p. 42.

53. *Tribune,* 29 February 1896; PAC, Sifton Papers, vol. 270, pp. 918–21, Sifton to Walter Barwick, 3 March 1896.

54. Canada, House of Commons, *Bills,* 1896, Bill 58; *Debates,* 1896, cols. 1512–13 (11 February 1896).

55. AASB, Langevin letterbook, Langevin to Father Lacombe, 14 March 1896.
56. PAC, Sifton Papers, vol. 6, pp. 3344-45, Laurier to Sifton, 28 January 1896.
57. Saywell, *Canadian Journal of Lady Aberdeen,* pp. lxvi, 318, 323, 324; *Tribune,* 17-21 February 1896; PAC, Sifton Papers, vol. 270, p. 907, Sifton to Smith, 25 February 1896.
58. *Tribune,* 27 February 1896.
59. PAC, Willison Papers, vol. 25, pp. 9008-10, Edgar to Willison, 27 February 1896.
60. Ibid., p. 3922, Cameron to Willison, 21 March 1896.
61. Hilts, "Thomas Greenway", pp. 248-49.
62. PAM, Sifton Papers, McCarthy to Sifton, 24 March 1896.
63. PAC, Sifton Papers, pp. 2224-25, J.D. Edgar to Sifton, 21 March 1896; University of Manitoba, Dafoe Papers, copies of two undated, unsigned memoranda [March 1896]; Dafoe, *Clifford Sifton,* pp. 88-90. The memoranda may have been written by James Sutherland (see PAC, Sifton Papers, vol. 270, p. 965, Sifton to Sutherland, 2 April 1896).
64. *CSP,* 1896, no. 39C, pp. 1-2; PAC, A.R. Dickey Papers, telegram to Mackenzie Bowell, [n.d.].
65. AASB, Memorandum of Negotiations at Winnipeg, by J.S. Ewart, n.d. [April 1896]; PAC, Sir Charles Fitzpatrick Papers, vol. 1, J.E.P. Prendergast to Fitzpatrick, 24 December 1896.
66. *Tribune,* 28 March 1896.
67. *CSP,* 1896, no. 39C, pp. 2-6.
68. Ibid., pp. 7-11; *Tribune,* 25 March-4 April 1896; *MFP,* 25 March-7 April 1896; and see PAC, Sifton Papers, vol. 4, pp. 1875-77, Dickey to Sifton, 21 June 1896.
69. PAC, Sifton Papers, vol. 270, pp. 962-64, Sifton to McCarthy, 2 April 1896; p. 965, Sifton to James Sutherland, 2 April 1896.
70. Ibid., vol. 7, pp. 3880-84, McCarthy to Sifton, 4 April 1896.
71. See the discussion in Saywell, *Canadian Journal of Lady Aberdeen,* pp. lxviii-lxx.
72. McLaughlin, "Race, Religion and Politics," pp. 272-77, 373-78, 345-46, 401.
73. PAC, Laurier Papers, vol. 8, pp. 3370-71, Alexander Smith to Laurier, 24 November 1894; pp. 3399-402, Joseph Martin to Laurier, 2 December 1894;

Sifton Papers, vol. 270, pp. 410-11, Sifton to Alexander Smith, 4 March 1895.
74. McLaughlin, "Race, Religion and Politics," pp. 347-55, 408-9; Noble, "D'Alton McCarthy," pp. 121-26; Paul D. Stevens, "Laurier and the Liberal Party in Ontario 1887-1911" (Ph.D. diss., University of Toronto, 1966), pp. 129-30.
75. PAC, Sifton Papers, vol. 270, pp. 990-92, Sifton to McCarthy, 11 April 1896.
76. Ibid.
77. Ibid., vol. 7, pp. 3888-91, 3892, 3893, McCarthy to Sifton, 16, 17, and 29 April 1896.
78. Ibid., vol. 270, pp. 968-69, Sifton to Thomas Dickey, 3 April 1896.
79. *MFP,* 8 April 1896.
80. PAM, Greenway Papers, letterbook, Greenway to Major Walsh, 7 May 1896.
81. PAC, Willison Papers, pp. 3923-24, 3925, J.D. Cameron to Willison, 28 May and 2 June 1896; p. 20303-4, 20306-7, Joseph Martin to Willison, 30 May and 10 June 1896; *Brandon Sun,* 7, 14, and 21 May 1896; *MFP,* 15, 18, and 19 May 1896.
82. *MFP,* 26 May 1896.
83. E.G. Cooke, "The Federal Election of 1896 in Manitoba" (M.A. thesis, University of Manitoba, 1943), pp. 63-64; Dafoe, *Clifford Sifton,* p. 95; Noble, "D'Alton McCarthy," p. 132; *Brandon Sun,* 4 June 1896.
84. *Brandon Sun,* 28 May 1896.
85. *MFP,* 20 June 1896.
86. McLaughlin, "Race, Religion and Politics," pp. 328, 345ff., 409. The popular vote was Conservative, 46.1 per cent; Liberal, 45.1 per cent. It should be added that most of the independent vote went to Patrons and McCarthyites and was therefore opposed to dominion remedial legislation.
87. Cooke, "Federal Election of 1896," p. 204.
88. Ibid., pp. 208-9; and see PAC, Laurier Papers, vol. 11, p. 4412-15, A.F. Martin à Laurier, le 24 juin 1896.
89. *Tribune,* 23-25 June 1896; PAC, Willison Papers, p. 20306, J. Martin to Willison, 10 June 1896; pp. 3926-27, J.D. Cameron to Willison, 24 June 1896; pp. 1732-35, A.B. Bethune to Willison, 30 May 1896.
90. PAC, CPR Records, Van Horne letter-

book 51, p. 652, Van Horne to Jaffray, 15 July 1896; pp. 396–98, 650–51, Van Horne to Joseph Martin, 28 May and 15 July 1896; pp. 414–15, Van Horne to Major Walsh, 30 May 1896; Willison Papers, vol. 91, pp. 3349–50, Van Horne to Willison, 1 December 1898.

91. PAC, CPR Records, Van Horne letterbook 51, p. 383, Van Horne to Sir Charles Tupper, 25 May 1896; W. Vaughan, *The Life and Work of Sir William Van Horne* (New York: Century, 1920), pp. 249–50. It is possible that elsewhere the CPR helped certain Liberal candidates (see PAC, Willison Papers, vol. 25, pp. 9008–10, J.D. Edgar to Willison, 25 January 1896; and Van Horne letterbook 50, p. 958, Van Horne to T.R. Parker, 23 March 1896).

92. PAC, CPR Records, Van Horne letterbook 51, p. 548, Van Horne to J.D. Edgar, 29 June 1896; letterbook 52, p. 39, Van Horne to Major Walsh, 23 September 1896.

93. Dafoe, *Clifford Sifton,* p. 96.

94. PAC, Willison Papers, pp. 20308–9, Martin to Willison, 25 June 1896.

95. PAC, Laurier Papers, pp. 4717–18, 5863–66, 5867–68, 6367–69, Martin to Laurier, 26 June, 28 July, 17 August 1896; pp. 4687–88, W.E. Perdue to Laurier, 25 June 1896; p. 5978, A.H. Sc[-?-], Victoria, to Laurier, 3 August 1896; pp. 5998–6000, Archer Martin to Laurier, 4 August 1896; pp. 6013–15, Smith Curtis to Laurier, 5 August 1896; pp. 6031–35, petition of meeting of over one hundred Winnipeg Liberals to support Martin, 3 August 1896 (see *Tribune,* 4 August 1896); pp. 6204–6, J.A. Smart to Laurier, 11 August 1896; pp. 6370–71, K. McKenzie to Laurier, 11 August 1896 (pledging support of Patrons in Portage-la-Prairie area); A.M. Campbell to Laurier, 20 August 1896; pp. 7001–7, further Winnipeg Committee resolution, 11 September 1896.

96. Ibid., Myers to Laurier, 26 June 1896; p. 6037, J.A. Macdonell to Laurier, 4 July 1896; pp. 5637–40, F.C. Wade to Laurier, 14 July 1896; pp. 7432–34, J.G. Rutherford to Laurier, 23 September 1896.

97. As reported in *Brandon Sun,* 6 August 1896.

98. PAC, Laurier Papers, vol. 15, pp. 5855–58, Martin to Laurier, 27 July 1896.

99. PAM, Greenway Papers, p. 9168, Sifton to Greenway, 5 August 1896; letterbook, Greenway to Sifton, 10 August 1896.

100. Ibid., p. 9091, Sifton to Greenway, 14 August 1896; PAC, Laurier Papers, vol. 18, pp. 6624–27, Willison to Sifton, 17 August 1896 (forwarded to Laurier); O.D. Skelton, *Life and Letters of Sir Wilfrid Laurier* (New York: Century, 1921), 2:13–14; Stevens, "Laurier and the Liberal Party in Ontario," p. 158.

101. PAC, Laurier Papers, vol. 18, pp. 6584–86, 6622–23, Sifton to Laurier, 26 and 28 August 1896; vol. 19, pp. 6869–73, Sifton to Laurier, 1 September 1896; Sifton Papers, vol. 6, pp. 3349–50, Laurier to Sifton, September 1896.

102. PAC, Laurier Papers, vol. 20, pp. 7107–8, 7149–50, Ross to Laurier, 16 and 17 September 1896; pp. 7176–79, R. Watson to Laurier, 18 September 1896; vol. 19, pp. 7042–43, H.M. Howell to Laurier, 14 September 1896; *Tribune,* 12 September 1896. See also Martin's Vancouver speech of 26 February 1909, in which he termed his exclusion from the cabinet "a gross breach of contract" on the part of the federal Liberals (PAC, Sifton Papers, vol. 191, p. 152907, clipping of *Vancouver Daily News-Advertiser,* 28 February 1909).

103. PAC, Laurier Papers, vol. 18, pp. 6584–86, Sifton to Laurier, 26 August 1896; Sifton Papers, vol. 6, pp. 3349–50, Laurier to Sifton, September 1896; *Brandon Sun,* 3 September 1896; *Tribune,* 9 September 1896; *MFP,* 28 September 1896.

104. *Tribune,* 2 October 1896.

105. PAC, Laurier Papers, vol. 21, pp. 7537–38, Robert Jaffray to Laurier, 27 September 1896. The exact nature of the arrangement only became public at a later date.

106. Ibid., vol. 24, pp. 8232–34, J.G. Rutherford to Laurier, 24 October 1896; PAC, Sifton Papers, vol. 271, pp. 16–17, Sifton to Laurier, 18 September 1896.

107. Laurier L. LaPierre, "Politics, Race and Religion in French Canada: Joseph Israel Tarte" (Ph.D. diss., University of Toronto, 1962), pp. 310–21; PAC, Laurier Papers, vol. 25, pp. 8611, 8612, Tarte to Laurier, 30 October 1896; vol. 24, p. 8402, T.G. Shaughnessy to Laurier, 31 October 1896.

108. AASB, Langevin "Post-Scriptum"

[1896], (memorandum by Langevin covering his exclusion from the settlement, 1896). In a draft letter of 4 November 1896, Langevin wrote,

Il me semble qu'il nous faut absolument:

1/ Un certain contrôle des écoles
2/ Des districts scolaires partout, à Winnipeg et ailleurs
3/ Des instituteurs et institutrices *formés par nous.*
4/ Un inspecteur catholique
5/ Des livres de lecture et d'histoire catholique anglais et français, et la liberté de l'enseignement religieuse.
6/ Le droit à nos taxes scolaires et aux subsides publics et l'exemption de taxes pour les écoles autres que les nôtres.

Avec cela, nous concéderons l'inspection du Gouvernement, le con-

trôle de l'argent et des brevets par le gouvernement.

109. *CSP,* 1897, no. 35; PAC, Hon. R.W. Scott Papers, vol. 2, pp. 8893–95, copy of Order-in-Council No. 5560-G.
110. *Brandon Sun,* 18 November 1896.
111. *Tribune,* 23 November 1896; LaPierre, "Politics, Race and Religion," p. 316.
112. *Tribune,* 23 November 1896; *Northwest Review* (Winnipeg), 25 November 1896.
113. See esp. AASB, J.E.P. Prendergast à Langevin, le 3 décembre 1896; PAC, Laurier Papers, J.D. Edgar to Laurier, 7 December 1896, and copy, Edgar to archbishop of Toronto, 5 December 1896.
114. PAC, Willison Papers, pp. 3928–30, Cameron to Willison, 25 November 1896.
115. *MFP,* 24 November 1896.
116. *Canada Gazette,* 21 November 1896.

## NOTES TO CHAPTER SIX

1. PAC, Sifton Papers, vol. 249, pp. 748–49, Sifton to Hon. Chas. Fitzpatrick, 18 December 1902.
2. *Tribune,* 21 August, 23 and 27 October, 26 November 1896; *MFP,* 26 November and 14 December 1896.
3. Herbert Douglas Kemp, "The Department of the Interior in the West 1873–1883: An Examination of Some Hitherto Neglected Aspects of the Work of the Outside Service" (M.A. thesis, University of Manitoba, 1950), pp. 1–11; Lewis H. Thomas, *The Struggle for Responsible Government in the North-West Territories 1870–97* (Toronto: University of Toronto Press, 1956), pp. 60–61. The department was established by 36 Vict., c. 4, which came into effect 1 July 1873.
4. *Tribune,* 9, 12, and 16 December 1896; *MFP,* 2 and 14 December 1896.
5. Wilfrid Eggleston, *The Queen's Choice: A Story of Canada's Capital* (Ottawa: Queen's Printer, 1961), p. 153.
6. Dafoe, *Clifford Sifton,* p. 108, n. 1, citing O.D. Skelton.
7. Ibid., p. 107.
8. PAC, Sifton Papers, vol. 218, p. 927, Sifton to C.B. Heyd, MP, 30 March 1897; vol. 222, pp. 437–38, Sifton to I. Campbell, 18 August 1897.
9. Born in Brockville, Ontario, in 1858,

Smart had been in Brandon since 1881 (see H.J. Morgan, *Canadian Men and Women of the Time,* 2d. ed. [Toronto: William Briggs, 1912], p. 1031).
10. *Tribune,* 10 December 1896; PAC, Laurier Papers, vol. 28, pp. 9349–53, Mrs. M.B. Burgess to Lady Aberdeen, 20 December 1896.
11. *Tribune,* 9 February 1897; PAC, Joseph Pope Papers, vol. 43, Diary, 18, 26, and 27 February, 1 March, 1 April 1897; *Canada Gazette,* 10 April 1897.
12. PAC, Sifton Papers, vol. 31, p. 20641, Ross to Sifton, 5 March 1897.
13. Ibid., vol. 214, pp. 746–49, Sifton to Oliver, 29 December 1896; vol. 218, pp. 669–70, Sifton to Capt. F.W. Gautier, 23 March 1897; pp. 688–89, Sifton to Mark Fortune, 24 March 1897; Dafoe, *Clifford Sifton,* p. 109; *Tribune,* 18 March 1897.
14. *Tribune,* 12 April 1897. Liberal estimates of the saving in 1897 were about $1.5 million.
15. Canada, House of Commons, *Debates,* 1897, col. 1677, 1693, 4 May 1897; 1898, cols. 4559–60, 4 April 1898; *CSP,* 1897, no. 47, "Opinion of the Minister of Justice with Respect to Salary Increases."
16. See Morris Zaslow, *Reading the Rocks: The Story of the Geological Survey of Canada 1842-1972* (Toronto: Mac-

millan, 1975), esp. pp. 199, 202–3; *Debates,* 1898, cols. 4559–60, 29 April 1898; Don. W. Thomson, *Men and Meridians: The History of Surveying and Mapping in Canada,* vol. 2, *1867–1917* (Ottawa: Queen's Printer, 1967), ch. 18.

17. *Tribune,* 12 December 1896; see D.J. Hall, "Clifford Sifton and Canadian Indian Administration 1896–1905," *Prairie Forum* 2 (1977): 127–51.

18. PAC, Sifton Papers, vol. 19, pp. 12029–40, A.E. Forget to Sifton, 20 January 1897; Department of Indian Affairs (DIA) Records, vol. 3635, file 6567, Frank Pedley to Sifton, 24 March 1904.

19. DIA Records, vol. 3984, file 168921, James A. Smart, Return to the House of Commons concerning dismissals, June 1896 to April 1898; vol. 3635, file 6567, D.C. Scott to the deputy superintendent-general, 3 March 1904, pp. 17–18; file 3877, file 91839-1; PAC, Sifton Papers, vol. 278, file 12; vol. 279, file 13; vol. 280, file 18576-7.

20. PAC, Sifton Papers, vol. 220, pp. 777–78, Sifton to J.G. Rutherford, MP, 4 June 1897.

21. Ibid., vol. 214, p. 554, Sifton to Smart, 25 December 1896; also p. 476, Sifton to C.S. Hyman, 23 December 1896.

22. Ibid., vol. 214, pp. 692–94, Sifton to Smart, 28 December 1896; pp. 710–11, Sifton to E.F. Stephenson, 28 December 1896; pp. 867, 874, Sifton to A.M. Burgess, 30 December 1896; pp. 470–72, Sifton to F. Oliver, 23 December 1896.

23. *Debates,* 1897, cols. 2798, 3723, 25 May and 10 June 1897; cols. 2798–2900, 4118, 25 May and 15 June 1897 (Dominion Lands Act Amendment, 60–61 Vict., c. 29); *Tribune,* 18 March 1897.

24. PAC, Sifton Papers, vol. 217, pp. 404–5, Sifton to John A. Ross, 19 February 1897.

25. Ibid., vol. 218, pp. 643–44, Sifton to Oliver, 23 March 1897.

26. See Chester Martin, *"Dominion Lands" Policy,* ed. L.H. Thomas (Toronto: McClelland and Stewart, 1973), passim.; R.C. Brown, "For the Purposes of the Dominion: Background Paper on the History of Federal Public Lands Policy to 1930," in *Canadian Public Land Use in Perspective,* ed. J.C. Nelson, R.C. Scace, and R. Kouri (Ottawa: Social Science Research Council, 1974), pp. 5–15.

27. *Brandon Sun,* 22 October 1896; *Tribune,* 23 and 27 October 1896.

28. PAC, CPR Records, Van Horne letterbook 52, pp. 772–74, Van Horne to Sifton, 9 February 1897.

29. Ibid., letterbook 42, pp. 31–33, Van Horne to Hugh John Macdonald, 13 November 1892. In 1889 Van Horne had written optimistically, "The cheap lands in the United States are practically exhausted, and our turn is coming now" (ibid., letterbook 29, pp. 116–17, Van Horne to A.M. Fraser, 11 February 1889). Canadians expressed the same vain hope year after year.

30. Ibid., letterbook 41, p. 891, Van Horne to Daly, 24 October 1892; letterbook 45, p. 7, Van Horne to William Whyte, 9 November 1893; PAC, Acton Burrows Papers, Van Horne to Burrows, 21 December 1892.

31. PAC, Willison Papers, vol. 91, pp. 33828–29, Van Horne to Willison, 25 September 1896; CPR Records, Van Horne letterbook 52, p. 62, Van Horne to J. Heber Haslam, 16 January 1897.

32. *Tribune,* 29 February 1896; *MFP,* 29 February 1896.

33. *Debates,* 1897, col. 2801–4, 25 May 1897; PAC, Sifton Papers, vol. 218, p. 615, Sifton to W. Preston, 20 March 1897.

34. *MFP,* 17 November 1898; and see D.J. Hall, "Clifford Sifton: Immigration and Settlement Policy, 1896–1905," in *The Settlement of the West,* ed. H. Palmer (Calgary: University of Calgary, 1977), pp. 60–85.

35. *Tribune,* 2 August 1897, citing *Belleville Sun.*

36. PAC, Laurier Papers, vol. 15, pp. 5743–45, 5820–21, Sifton to Laurier, 17 July 1896, and reply, 24 July 1896.

37. *Tribune,* 7 and 15 January 1897; PAC, Willison Papers, vol. 11, pp. 3923–24, Cameron to Willison, 22 December 1896; Sifton Papers, vol. 217, pp. 513–14, Sifton to David Mills, 22 February 1897; House of Commons, *Journals,* 1898, app. 28, and 1899, app. 1, pp. v–vi, xiv–xv, xvii–xxiv, 1–60, 91–209.

38. *Tribune,* 12 January 1897; PAC, Sifton Papers, vol. 216, pp. 61–62, Sifton to Watson, 14 January 1897.

39. *Tribune,* 26 February and 2 March 1897.

40. PAC, Sifton Papers, vol. 214, pp. 927–28, Sifton to H.M. Howell, January 1897.

41. Ibid., vol. 22, p. 13765, H.M. Howell to Sifton, 20 February 1897; Laurier Papers, pp. 12926-27, Charles Fitzpatrick to Laurier, 13 March 1897.

42. D.H. Bocking, "Premier Walter Scott: A Study of His Rise to Political Power" (M.A. thesis, University of Saskatchewan, 1959); C.B. Koester, "The Parliamentary Career of Nicholas Flood Davin, 1887-1900" (M.A. thesis, University of Saskatchewan, 1964); Thomas, *Struggle for Responsible Government,* pp. 251-52; George Richardson, "The Conservative Party in the Provisional District of Alberta 1887-1905" (M.A. thesis, University of Alberta, 1977).

43. PAC, Willison Papers, Cameron to Willison, 28 May 1896; D.J. Hall, "T.O. Davis and Federal Politics in Saskatchewan, 1896," *Saskatchewan History* 30 (1977): 56-57.

44. PAC, Sifton Papers, vol. 27, pp. 17427-30, McPhail to Sifton, 20 January 1897; vol. 31, pp. 20626-27, J.H. Ross to Sifton, 26 January 1897.

45. PAC, Laurier Papers, vol. 15, pp. 5743-55, Sifton to Laurier, 17 July 1896; Sifton Papers, vol. 17, pp. 10643-44, 10651-54, Davis to Sifton, 28 and 29 January 1897; vol. 27, pp. 17422-23, McPhail to Sifton, 16 March 1897; D.J. Hall, "T.O. Davis and Federal Politics," p. 61.

46. PAC, Sifton Papers, vol. 6, p. 3361, Laurier to Sifton, 1 December 1896; Laurier Papers, vol. 24, p. 8293, Sifton to Laurier, 2 December 1896.

47. PAC, Sifton Papers, vol. 9, pp. 5037-41, Ross to Sifton, 22 December 1896; vol. 31, pp. 20611-16, 20629-31, Ross to Sifton, 9 January 1897; Bocking, "Premier Walter Scott," pp. 31-33.

48. PAC, Sifton Papers, vol. 221, pp. 913-18, Sifton to Scott, 1 August 1897; vol. 31, pp. 20662-66, 20673-75, 20680-85, Ross to Sifton, 4, 7, and 25 June 1897; vol. 222, pp. 528-29, Sifton to Isaac Campbell, 21 August 1897.

49. Ibid., pp. 523-24, Sifton to H.M. Howell, 21 August 1897; and references in note 37, above.

50. Thomas, *Struggle for Responsible Government,* p. 259.

51. Ibid., pp. 260-61.

52. PAC, Willison Papers, vol. 78, pp. 29023-25, Tarte to Willison, 9 November 1896; AASB, J.N. Ritchot, Saint-Norbert, à Mgr. Langevin, le 29 décembre 1896; Paul Benoît, Etat des écoles de Notre Dame de Lourdes et des missions dépendantes, le 8 décembre 1896; L. Favreau, OMI, Mission St. Lazare, à Langevin, le 8 décembre 1896; J.M. Jolys, St. Pierre, à Langevin, le 21 décembre 1896.

53. AASB, Langevin à M. Giroux, le 15 juin 1896; *Northwest Review* 17 (February 1897); *Tribune,* 15, 20, and 22 February 1897.

54. Stevens, "Laurier and the Liberal Party in Ontario," pp. 162-69.

55. Hilts, "Thomas Greenway," p. 266.

56. Ibid., p. 264.

57. PAC, Sifton Papers, vol. 219, pp. 322-24, Sifton to Rutherford, 10 April 1897.

58. Hilts, "Thomas Greenway," pp. 278-79; PAC, Sifton Papers, vol. 220, pp. 383-84, Sifton to J.D. Cameron, 22 May 1897; R.W. Scott Papers, vol. 2, p. 932, "Resolutions Proposed to be Adopted by the Department of Education, Manitoba."

59. PAM, Greenway Papers, p. 9487, Laurier to Greenway, 28 May 1897.

60. Ibid.; Hilts, "Thomas Greenway," pp. 278-95.

61. PAC, Sifton Papers, vol. 220, pp. 654-55, Sifton to Laurier, 1 June 1897; Laurier Papers, vol. 48, pp. 15378-81, del Val à Laurier, le 30 mai 1897.

62. PAM, Greenway Papers, p. 10513, Sifton to Greenway, and reply, 16 June 1897.

63. Hilts, "Thomas Greenway," p. 286; PAC, Sifton Papers, vol. 221, pp. 357-59, Sifton to Col. McMillan, 10 July 1897; R.W. Scott Papers, pp. 54-55, Scott to Sir Oliver Mowat, 5 July 1897; Laurier Papers, vol. 49, pp. 15692-94, 15803-10, Scott to Laurier, 12 and 20 July 1897; pp. 15696-99, C. Fitzpatrick to Laurier, 12 July 1897.

64. PAC, Sifton Papers, vol. 218, pp. 244-46, Sifton to James Fleming, 13 March 1897.

65. R.C. Brown, *Canada's National Policy, 1883-1900: A Study in Canadian-American Relations* (Princeton: Princeton University Press, 1964), pp. 262-80; Bruce Fergusson, *Hon. W.S. Fielding,* I, *The Mantle of Howe* (Windsor, N.S.; Lancelot Press, 1970), pp. 171-213.

66. PAC, CPR Records, Van Horne letter-

book 50, p. 968, Van Horne to T.R. Parker, 23 March 1896; letterbook 51, pp. 632–33, Van Horne to Thomas Reynolds, 11 July 1896; Sifton Papers, vol. 45, pp. 30165–68, Jones to Sifton, 11 August 1898.

67. Professor V.C. Fowke, in *Canadian Agricultural Policy: The Historical Pattern* (Toronto: University of Toronto Press, 1947), p. 262, quotes what appears to have been an exceptional statement by Sifton—if, indeed, it is accurate—at Deloraine during the dominion campaign of 1896: "Free coal oil, free clothing, and free implements you shall have if the Liberal Party are returned to power."

68. For example, *MFP*, 28 October 1896.

69. PAC, Sifton Papers, vol. 218, pp. 244–46, Sifton to James Fleming, 13 March 1897; the letter is cited more fully in Dafoe, *Clifford Sifton*, pp. 115–16.

70. PAC, Willison Papers, vol. 109, pp. 17794–95, Laurier to Willison, 28 June 1896; Laurier Papers, vol. 33, pp. 10854–56, Laurier to Charlton, 18 January 1897.

71. Cited in R.T.G. Clippingdale, "J.S. Willison, Political Journalist: from Liberalism to Independence, 1881–1905" (Ph.D. diss., University of Toronto, 1970), p. 412.

72. PAC, Sifton Papers, vol. 216, pp. 533–34, Sifton to John Williams, 27 January 1897; Brown, *Canada's National Policy*, pp. 270–71; Fergusson, *W.S. Fielding*, pp. 179–82; Edward Porritt, *Sixty Years of Protection in Canada 1846–1907, Where Industry Leans on the Politician* (London: Macmillan, 1908), pp. 381ff.

73. PAC, Sifton Papers, vol. 271, pp. 102–3, Sifton to James Fisher, 13 November 1896; vol. 5, pp. 2284–85, Fisher to Sifton, 20 November 1896; vol. 216, p. 553, Sifton to D.C. Barker, 27 January 1897; vol. 217, pp. 336–38, Sifton to Col. McMillan, 18 February 1897.

74. Ibid., vol. 2, pp. 643–44, Richardson to Sifton, 25 February 1895 [*sic;* should read 1897]; *Tribune,* 27 and 28 January 1897.

75. PAC, Sifton Papers, vol. 31, pp. 20443–44, Richardson to Sifton, 13 March 1897.

76. PAC, Laurier Papers, vol. 41, pp. 13361–64, Francis T. Frost to Laurier, 23 March 1897; Sifton Papers, vol. 218, pp.

265–66, Sifton to Richardson, 16 March 1897.

77. *Tribune,* 24 and 27 April 1897; Brown, *Canada's National Policy,* pp. 275–78; PANS, W.S. Fielding Papers, vol. 505, folder 11, p. 744, Sifton to Fielding, 7 May 1897.

78. PAC, Sifton Papers, vol. 220, pp. 652–53, Sifton to William Cairns, 21 May 1897; vol. 219, pp. 322–24, Sifton to J.G. Rutherford, 10 April 1897.

79. *Tribune,* 5 July 1897; PAC, Sifton Papers, vol. 220, pp. 946–47, Sifton to I. Campbell, 16 June 1897; vol. 222, pp. 283–84, Sifton to R.L. Richardson, 12 August 1897; vol. 21, pp. 12951–53, Greenway to Sifton, 2 August 1897.

80. W.J. Easterbrook and H.G.J. Aitken, *Canadian Economic History* (Toronto: Macmillan, 1956), p. 504.

81. PAC, Laurier Papers, vol. 44, pp. 14271–73, Sifton to Laurier, 19 April 1897.

82. *Tribune,* 27 October 1896.

83. PAC, CPR Records, Van Horne letterbook 33, pp. 435–37, Van Horne to Col. Baker, 11 February 1890; letterbook 36, pp. 526–28, Van Horne to Col. Baker, 7 January 1891; letterbook 40, p. 165, Van Horne to Hon. John Haggart, 18 March 1892; W. Kaye Lamb, *History of the Canadian Pacific Railway* (New York: Macmillan, 1977), pp. 195–201; H.A. Innis, *Settlement and the Mining Frontier* (Toronto: Macmillan, 1936), ch. 5.

84. PAC, CPR Records, Van Horne letterbook 47, pp. 919–20, Van Horne to R.L. Gault, 14 November 1894; letterbook 50, pp. 703–5, Van Horne to J.H. Turner, 7 February 1896; pp. 821–23, Van Horne to E. Dewdney, 28 February 1896.

85. It is possible that Israel Tarte was also among those favoured.

86. PAC, Willison Papers, vol. 91, pp. 33810–12, Van Horne to Willison, 11 April 1896.

87. See Clippingdale, "J.S. Willison, Political Journalist," pp. 356–79. Unbeknownst to Willison, two of the major shareholders in the *Globe,* G.A. Cox and Robert Jaffray, themselves were interested in coal development in the Crow's Nest Pass region. Jaffray had urged Willison on in his support of a railway; when his personal interest later became public it was acutely embarrassing for all concerned.

88. PAC, CPR Records, Van Horne letterbook 51, p. 97, Van Horne to T.C. Irving, 10 September 1896; letterbook 52, pp. 327–30, 338ff, Van Horne to A.G. Blair, 14 November 1896; Laurier Papers, vol. 19, pp. 6990–91, T.G. Shaughnessy to Laurier, 12 September 1896.

89. PAC, Sifton Papers, vol. 4, pp. 1998–99, G.G. Dunstan to Laurier, 22 October 1896; Laurier Papers, vol. 38, p. 12401, John Shields to Laurier, 23 February 1897; pp. 12516–17, D.J. O'Donoghue to Laurier, 26 February 1897. A good sampling of public sentiment is summarized in Clippingdale, "J.S. Willison, Political Journalist," pp. 356–79.

90. PAC, CPR Records, Van Horne letterbook 52, pp. 116–19, 287–89, Van Horne to Edgar, 2 October and 6 November 1896; p. 152, Van Horne to Jaffray, 6 October 1896.

91. Ibid., pp. 643–47, Van Horne to Col. Baker, 21 January 1897; pp. 837–38, Van Horne to Sir D.A. Smith, 16 February 1897.

92. PAC, Laurier Papers, vol. 33, pp. 11019–20, Tarte à Laurier, le 15 janvier 1897.

93. PAC, CPR Records, Van Horne letterbook 52, pp. 832–36, Van Horne to Sir D.A. Smith, 16 February 1897.

94. Ibid.; and letterbook 53, pp. 1–6, 70–71, Van Horne to W.J. White, 17 and 26 March 1897; pp. 64–67, 214–17, Van Horne to J.J. Young, 26 March and 23 April 1897; *Tribune,* 19 February 1897.

95. PAC, CPR Records, Van Horne letterbook 53, pp. 22–23, Van Horne to Sifton, 19 March 1897.

96. PAC, Laurier Papers, vol. 43, pp. 14029–32, Sifton to Laurier, 19 April 1897. It was undoubtedly this interview which Sifton had in mind shortly before he died when he recalled that Van Horne and Shaughnessy had told him the CPR "was on the verge of bankruptcy" (Dafoe, *Clifford Sifton,* p. 146, n.1). There is a good deal of evidence to suggest that the CPR officials had been misleading; also that Sifton's memory was not wholly accurate (see Lamb, *Canadian Pacific Railway,* p. 210).

97. PAC, Sifton Papers, vol. 218, pp. 491–92, Sifton to F.C. Arthur, 19 March 1897; Laurier Papers, vol. 23, pp. 8013, 8014–20, P. Ryan to Laurier, 27 February 1897, and reply, 3 March 1897.

98. PAC, CPR Records, Van Horne letterbook 52, pp. 832–36, Van Horne to Sir D.A. Smith, 16 February 1897; Sifton Papers, vol. 11, pp. 6708–18, 6721–22, J.H. Ashdown to Sifton, 2 and 13 March 1897; vol. 218, pp. 427–28, Sifton to Ashdown, 17 March 1897.

99. PAC, CPR Records, Van Horne letterbook 52, pp. 812–15, Van Horne to Sifton, 13 February 1897; pp. 287–89, Van Horne to J.D. Edgar, 6 November 1896.

100. References as in note 99, above; PAC, Laurier Papers, vol. 43, pp. 14029–32, Sifton to Laurier, 19 April 1897.

101. Ibid., Sifton to Laurier, 19 April 1897.

102. 60–61 Vict., c. 5, assented to 29 June 1897. The actual subsidy paid of $3.4 million constituted just over one-third of the cost of the railway; the CPR financed the remainder (see Lamb, *Canadian Pacific Railway,* p. 210).

103. PAC, CPR Records, Van Horne letterbook 53, Van Horne to Smith, 3 June 1897.

104. Lamb, *Canadian Pacific Railway,* p. 210; Theodore H. Harris, *The Economic Aspects of the Crowsnest Pass Rates Agreement,* McGill University Economic Studies, no. 13 (Toronto: Macmillan, 1930), pp. 8–9; A.W. Currie, "Freight Rates on Grain in Western Canada," *CHR* 21 (1940): 43–44.

105. Lamb, *Canadian Pacific Railway,* pp. 209–10; Dafoe, *Clifford Sifton,* pp. 145–48; Currie, "Freight Rates on Grain," pp. 44–46.

106. PAC, CPR Records, Van Horne letterbook 51, pp. 690–98, Van Horne to J.D. Clarke, 17 July 1896.

107. PAC, Sifton Papers, vol. 221, pp. 352–55, Sifton to McMillan, 10 July 1897; Laurier Papers, vol. 32, pp. 10251–52, undated, unsigned memorandum [spring 1897].

108. PAC, Sifton Papers, vol. 221, pp. 147–48, Sifton to Smart, 2 July 1897; pp. 303–4, Sifton to W.F. McCreary, 7 July 1897.

109. Ibid., vol. 35, pp. 2332–34, Van Horne to Sifton, 14 July 1897; vol. 221, pp. 627–29, Sifton to McCreary, 23 July 1897.

110. D.H. Avery, "Canadian Immigration Policy and the Alien Question, 1896–1919: The Anglo-Canadian Perspective" (Ph.D. diss., University of Western Ontario, 1973), pp. 25n.47, 200–201,

209–10; *CSP*, 1898, no. 90A; PAC, Sifton Papers, vol. 59, pp. 19006–8, R.W. Jameson to Sifton, 24 December 1897.

111. *MFP*, 17 November 1898, reporting Toronto speech of 15 November.

112. Sterner, "Sir Clifford as a Young Campaigner"; PAC, Sifton Papers, vol. 217, p. 9, Sifton to A.T. Wood, 9 February 1897; vol. 220, pp. 946–47, Sifton to I. Campbell, 16 June 1897.

## NOTES TO CHAPTER SEVEN

1. Cited in "The Administration of the Yukon. Law and Order Prevail," pamphlet, n.p., n.d. [Liberal election pamphlet, 1900], p. 5. Copy in PAC, Laurier Papers, vol. 75, pp. 23235–48.

2. Innis, *Settlement and the Mining Frontier*, pp. 178–79; D.R. Morrison, *The Politics of the Yukon Territory, 1898–1909* (Toronto: University of Toronto Press, 1968), pp. 7–10; PAC, Z.T. Wood Papers, p. 1; Charles Constantine Papers, vol. 3, order-in-council 1201, 26 May 1894; RCMP Records, vol. 135, file 222, memorandum, F. White, 10 May 1895.

3. PAC, RCMP Records, vol. 119, file 160, Ogilvie to E. Deville, 8 January 1896; G.M. Dawson to A.M. Burgess, 9 April 1896; F. White to Burgess, 14 April 1896.

4. *CSP*, 1897, no. 13, pt. 2, pp. 48–54; no. 15, app. DD, pp. 232–39; PAC, Laurier Papers, vol. 26, pp. 8981–83, "Summary of Report of Inspector Constantine," 20 November 1896; Constantine Papers, vol. 4, pp. 212–35, Constantine to officer commanding, Regina, 20 November 1896; William Ogilvie, *Information Respecting the Yukon District from the Reports of William Ogilvie . . . and from Other Sources* (Ottawa: Department of the Interior, 1897).

5. PAC, Laurier Papers, vol. 791A, pp. 224427–30, F. White, memorandum, 3 February 1897.

6. PAC, RCMP Records, vol. 136, file 270, White to Sifton, 1 April 1897; vol. 137, file 360, memorandum, F. White, 18 May 1897, approved by "W.L."

7. Ibid., vol. 136, file 139, J.A. Smart to Constantine, 3 May 1897; *CSP*, 1898, no. 13, p. 8; no. 13, pt. 2, p. 9.

8. PAC, Sifton Papers, vol. 28, pp. 18065–66, Sifton to Mowat, 19 April 1897; vol. 221, pp. 465–66, Sifton to Mowat, 15 July 1897.

9. Order-in-council 1189, 21 May 1897, replacing an order-in-council of 9

November 1889, *Canada Gazette* 30 (1897): 2488–90.

10. PAC, Sifton Papers, vol. 221, pp. 644–45, Sifton to J.F. Lister, MP, 23 July 1897.

11. *Winnipeg Daily Tribune*, 19 and 30 July 1897; PAC, Scott Papers, vol. 2, pp. 634–38, Scott to Laurier, 20 July 1897. By "residents in Canada," Scott apparently meant British subjects and landed immigrants.

12. *Tribune*, 22 July 1897; PAC, Sifton Papers, vol. 14, pp. 9176–77, R.J. Cartwright to Sifton, 27 July 1897; Pierre Berton, *Klondike: The Life and Death of the Last Great Gold Rush* (Toronto: McClelland and Stewart, 1958), p. 122.

13. PAC, RCMP Records, vol. 138, file 389, memorandum from Privy Council, 14 June 1897; vol. 140, file 351, memo, F. White for Sifton, 5 August 1897; R.C. Macleod, *The NWMP and Law Enforcement 1873–1905* (Toronto: University of Toronto Press, 1976), pp. 57–58, 60.

14. PAC, Scott Papers, vol. 2, pp. 634–38, Scott to Laurier, 20 July 1897; vol. 4, pp. 1638–40, Scott to Laurier, 23 July 1897; *Tribune*, 23 July 1897.

15. Order-in-council 2326, 29 July 1897, *Canada Gazette* 30 (1897): 303; "Regulations for Placer Mining along the Yukon River and Its Tributaries, N.W.T.," copy in PAC, RCMP Records, vol. 140, file 461.

16. PAC, Sifton Papers, vol. 221, p. 732, Sifton to W.H. Collins, 28 July 1897; cf. *Tribune*, 30 July 1897, calling for government ownership "to protect this great national heritage."

17. PAC, Sifton Papers, vol. 221, pp. 927–29, Sifton to Fawcett, 31 July 1897.

18. *Tribune*, 4 August 1897.

19. PAC, Sifton Papers, vol. 35, p. 22964, excerpt from letter in *Victoria Times*, 19 August 1897.

20. Ibid., vol. 221, pp. 946–47, Sifton to R.L. Richardson, 31 July 1897; pp. 989–91,

Sifton to H. Bostock, 3 August 1897.
21. Ibid., vol. 222, p. 267, Sifton to Richardson, 12 August 1897; pp. 242–43, Sifton to F. Oliver, 11 August 1897.
22. Ibid.
23. Ibid., vol. 221, pp. 989–91, Sifton to H. Bostock, 3 August 1897.
24. Ibid., pp. 925–26, Sifton to J.G. Rutherford, 31 July 1897; pp. 946–47, Sifton to R.L. Richardson, 31 July 1897.
25. Ibid., vol. 222, Sifton to Isaac Campbell, 21 August and 14 September 1897; *Tribune,* 17 August 1897.
26. *CSP,* 1898, no. 38-38C, PAC, RCMP Records, vol. 140, file 477; vol. 172, file 466; Macleod, *The NWMP and Law Enforcement,* pp. 30–32, 81. Walsh became a superintendent of the NWMP with precedence over other Police officers in the Yukon. From the time of his arrival in the Yukon the Police there were to communicate directly with Ottawa, rather than through Regina as they had done hitherto.
27. PAC, Sifton Papers, vol. 266, p. 51, Sifton to Justice McQuire [*sic*], 3 August 1897; vol. 222, pp. 474–75, Sifton to McQuire[*sic*], 19 August 1897; Morrison, *Politics of the Yukon,* p. 10; *Tribune,* 17 August 1897. By order-in-council of 17 August 1897 the Yukon was made a separate judicial district of the North-West Territories.
28. Even the Liberal Winnipeg *Tribune* was revolted at Wade's appointment. Wade's positions, it suggested, required "a judicial mind and manner, personal dignity and courtesy, and a scrupulous sense of honor. It is of course possible that Mr. Wade may possess all or most of these characteristics in a dormant or potential form, but his career as a partisan pusher and lobbyist, which is about the only capacity in which he is known to the public, has not been calculated to bring such qualities to a high state of development" (*Tribune,* 23 and 24 August 1897; *MFP,* 12 June 1896).
29. *Tribune,* 21 August and 27 September 1897; *Globe,* 25 September, 2 and 23 October 1897; Dafoe, *Clifford Sifton,* pp. 156–57. An account of the journey by Major Walsh is in *CSP,* 1898, no. 38C. Maxim guns also were transported to emphasize police authority.
30. *Globe,* 26 and 29 October, 2, 3, 4, 12, and 13 November 1897.
31. PAC, Sifton Papers, vol. 222, p. 70, Sifton to C.A. Masten, 5 August 1897.
32. PAC, Constantine Papers, vol. 3, "Report on trip to Yukon in 1894."
33. PAC, Scott Papers, vol. 4, pp. 1638–40, Scott to Laurier, 23 July 1897.
34. PAC, Pope Papers, vol. 56, file 22, Cartwright to Scott, 28 July 1897; Scott to Aberdeen, 5 August 1897; British reply, 11 August 1897; notice of president's consent, 14 September 1897.
35. PAC, Sifton Papers, vol. 221, pp. 790–92, Sifton to Blair, 28 July 1897; vol. 12, pp. 7535–36, 7539–42, Blair to Sifton, 24 July and 2 August 1897.
36. Sir Charles's approval may not have been disinterested. He was a director in a British-financed firm, The New Gold Fields Company, which had bought out the Klondike Mining, Trading and Transportation Company, which in turn had tentative plans to build a railway between Portland Canal and Teslin Lake (*Globe,* 13 November 1897; PAC, Sir Charles Tupper papers, vol. 11, pp. 5942–43, Tupper to Charles Hibbert Tupper, 15 August 1897).
37. *Globe,* 5 November 1897.
38. PAC, Sifton Papers, vol. 28, pp. 18306–7, Mulock to Sifton, 11 November 1897; *Globe,* 2 December 1897.
39. H.J. Morgan, *Canadian Men and Women of the Time,* p. 865; Don W. Thomson, *Men and Meridians,* vol. 2, *1867 to 1917* (Ottawa: Queen's Printer, 1967), pp. 147–61; Dafoe, *Clifford Sifton,* p. 180, n. 2; William Ogilvie, *Early Days on the Yukon & the Story of Its Gold Finds* (Ottawa: Thorburn & Abbott, 1913).
40. *Globe,* 10 November 1897; PAC, Constantine Papers, vol. 4, pp. 352–55, Constantine to Archibald, 9 November 1897. In his official report, Ogilvie's estimates of the wealth of the Yukon were even further expanded. On actual Yukon gold production, see Innis, *Settlement and the Mining Frontier,* p. 219, Table II and note. It is extremely doubtful that the Eldorado and Bonanza claims, even by liberal estimates, ever yielded $70 million in gold to placer miners.
41. *Globe,* 4 November 1897.
42. PAC, CPR Records, Van Horne letter-book 54, p. 420, Van Horne to T. Reynolds, 20 December 1897; pp.

399–401, Van Horne to H.M. Kersey, 17 December 1897.

43. PAC, Sifton Papers, vol. 37, p. 24311, report to Z.T. Wood, 8 December 1897; vol. 50, pp. 34326–28, A. Bowen Perry to F. White, 7 January 1898; N. Penlington, *Canada and Imperialism, 1896–1899* (Toronto: University of Toronto Press, 1965), p. 84.

44. PAC, Sifton Papers, vol. 223, pp. 954–55, Sifton to E. Goff Penny, 20 December 1897; pp. 966–67, Sifton to D.H. McKinnon, 22 December 1897.

45. Ibid., vol. 266, pp. 216–17, Sifton to Turner, 18 December 1897; PAC, Constantine Papers, vol. 4, pp. 293–96, Constantine to Commissioner [Walsh], 24 September 1897; vol. 3, petition, Committee of Yukon Chamber of Mining & Commerce, 29 October 1897, and reply, 1 November 1897.

46. PAC, Sifton Papers, vol. 11, pp. 6510–11, Alger to Sifton, 22 December 1897; vol. 266, p. 224, Sifton to Alger, 23 December 1897; vol. 224, pp. 212–16, Sifton to W. Templeman, 5 January 1898.

47. PAC, Sifton Papers, Sifton to W. Templeman, 5 January 1898.

48. An extensive file on the expedition is in PAC, RCMP Records, vol. 146, file 89; and see Sifton Papers, vol. 224, p. 416, Sifton to G.J. Meiklejohn, assistant secretary for war, Washington, 12 January 1898; vol. 266, pp. 273, 305, Sifton to Meiklejohn, 15 and 24 January 1898; vol. 49, pp. 33073–84, correspondence Meiklejohn to Sifton, January–February 1898; Laurier Papers, vol. 750, pp. 214955–56, Aberdeen to Joseph Chamberlain, 1 February 1898; Penlington, *Canada and Imperialism,* p. 86.

49. PAC, Sifton Papers, vol. 52, pp. 35969–77, "Regulations Governing the Entry and Transportation of Merchandise Destined for the Klondyke Region and North West Territory of British Columbia, *via* the United States Sub-Ports of Juneau, Dyea and Skagway, or Other Customs Ports in Alaska," Treasury Department, Office of the Secretary, Washington, D.C., 2 February 1898; *MFP,* 13 January 1898.

50. PAC, Sifton Papers, vol. 266, p. 243, Sifton to Howell, 5 January 1898; vol. 44, pp. 29784–85, 29786, 29787, Howell to

Sifton, 5, 12, and 20 January 1898.

51. Ibid., vol. 45, pp. 30276–77, J. Irving and F.C. Davidge to Sifton, 27 January 1898; pp. 28083–85, 28086–89, F. Elworthy to Sifton, 22 and 25 January 1898.

52. Ibid., vol. 224, pp. 715–17, Sifton to Edward Gurney, 27 January 1898; vol. 266, p. 317, Sifton to Prior, 27 January 1898; vol. 224, pp. 751–53, Sifton to Gage, 27 January 1898; and see pp. 695–98, Sifton to Senator William Templeman, 26 January 1898; Dafoe, *Clifford Sifton,* pp. 160–62; Brown, *Canada's National Policy 1883–1900,* pp. 301–2.

53. PAC, Sifton Papers, vol. 224, pp. 715–17, Sifton to Edward Gurney, 27 January 1898; and see note 49 above.

54. PAC, CPR Records, Van Horne letterbook 54, pp. 399–401, Van Horne to H.M. Kersey, 17 December 1897.

55. *CSP,* 1897, no. 13, pp. xxiii–xxiv; 1898, no. 13, p. 9; no. 13, pt. 2, pp. 99–140; 1899, no. 66a; PAC, Laurier Papers, vol. 37, pp. 12153–54, W.A. Foster (The Boston & Alaska Gold Mining Co.) to Laurier, 17 February 1897; vol. 791A, pp. 224427–30, F.W. White to Laurier, 3 February 1897; Sifton Papers, vol. 12, p. 7171, Alexander Begg to Sifton, 20 February 1897; vol. 222, p. 44, Sifton to T.H. Macpherson, 5 August 1897; Dafoe, *Clifford Sifton,* p. 160. The idea of using this as an all-Canadian route was mentioned as early as 1873; it had been scientifically explored by G.M. Dawson in 1887, though not with a view to constructing a railway (see Innis, *Settlement and the Mining Frontier,* p. 196).

56. In the spring session of Parliament three companies had received charters to build into the Yukon: The Yukon Mining and Transportation Company (Foreign), 60–61 Vict., c. 91; The British Yukon Mining, Trading and Transportation Company, 60–61 Vict., c. 89; and The Hudson's Bay and Yukon Railway and Navigation Company, 60–61 Vict. c. 46. The first was empowered to build a narrow-gauge line from Taku Inlet to Teslin Lake; the second to build a line from Lynn Canal via the White Pass to Selkirk; the third from Chesterfield Inlet to Great Slave Lake, via the Mackenzie River to the Porcupine or Yukon River.

57. *Edmonton Bulletin,* 5 August 1897 and August–October 1897, passim; PAC,

Sifton Papers, vol. 29, pp. 19099-100, F. Oliver to Sifton, 18 August 1897; RCMP Records, vol. 140, file 479. Some government members believed that the Stikine route ultimately would be extended to Edmonton (University of Western Ontario [UWO] Library, David Mills Papers, letterbook 1897-98, Mills to W.E. Sanford, 15 January 1898).

58. PAC, Sifton Papers, vol. 23, pp. 14582-84, W.F. King to Sifton, 29 November 1897; vol. 266, p. 287, Sifton to F. Elworthy, 20 January 1898.

59. A.W. MacIntosh, "The Career of Sir Charles Tupper in Canada, 1864-1900" (Ph.D. thesis, University of Toronto, 1960), pp. 503-4; *Tribune*, 28 December 1897.

60. The group included H. Maitland Kersey, a financier; Montreal lawyer J.N. Greenshields, a friend of A.G. Blair; Dr. W.S. Webb, a railway magnate; George Gooderham of Gooderham and Worts, president of the Bank of Toronto and of the Manufacturers' Life Insurance Company; and a "Mr. Allison," possibly James W. Allison, a New Brunswick manufacturer (PAC, Laurier Papers, vol. 63, pp. 20060-61, Kersey to Laurier, 23 January 1898).

61. PAC, Sifton Papers, vol. 224, pp. 364-65, Sifton to Van Horne, 11 January 1898; CPR Records, Van Horne letterbook 54, pp. 588-89, Van Horne to N. Kingsmill, 24 January 1898; pp. 523-25, Van Horne to D. Braeman, 8 January 1898.

62. UWO Library, Mills Papers, Mills to W.E. Sanford, 15 January 1898.

63. *Debates,* 1898, cols. 186-212, 8 February 1898; Brown, *Canada's National Policy,* pp. 307-8; *Globe,* 27 January 1898.

64. PAC, CPR Records, Van Horne letterbook 54, pp. 666-68, Van Horne to F. Elworthy, 4 February 1898; p. 615, Van Horne to Scott, 27 January 1898; Brown, *Canada's National Policy,* p. 307, n. 28.

65. PAC, Sifton Papers, vol. 224, pp. 755-57, Sifton to Walsh, 26 January 1898; Dafoe, *Clifford Sifton,* p. 163.

66. *Tribune,* 28 January 1898; *Globe,* 29 January 1898; MacIntosh, "The Career of Sir Charles Tupper," p. 504.

67. PAC, NWMP Records, vol. 146, file 78, Z.T. Wood to F.W. White, 25 December 1897; vol. 145, file 70, Sifton to White, 25 January 1898, and correspondence,

December 1897–January 1898.

68. PAC, Lord Aberdeen Papers, vol. 1, pp. 214-15, memorandum from Sifton for Aberdeen to transmit to Chamberlain, 28 January 1898; Laurier Papers, vol. 750, pp. 214952-54, Aberdeen to Chamberlain, 29 January 1898; Sifton Papers, vol. 226, pp. 238-42, Sifton to Walsh, 1 April 1898; Penlington, *Canada and Imperialism,* pp. 84-85; Brown, *Canada's National Policy,* pp. 321-22.

69. *Debates,* 1898, cols. 407-8, 11 February 1898; Penlington, *Canada and Imperialism,* pp. 84-85.

70. Penlington, *Canada and Imperialism,* pp. 87-88. Canada had to seek American permission for this expedition because it was a military rather than a commercial venture. The permission was readily granted.

71. Ibid., pp. 86-87; Brown, *Canada's National Policy,* pp. 315-22; PAC, Sifton Papers, vol. 226, pp. 273-79, Sifton to Walsh, 4 April 1898.

72. Regehr, *Canadian Northern Railway,* pp. 66-69; Brown, *Canada's National Policy,* pp. 307-8; H. Borden, ed., *Robert Laird Borden: His Memoirs,* I (Toronto: Macmillan, 1938), pp. 54-55. Tupper's speech reversing his support is in *Debates,* 1898, cols. 538-71, 15 February 1898; and see cols. 1678-1712, 10 March 1898.

73. *Debates,* cols. 571-91, 621-70, 15 and 16 February 1898; Dafoe, *Clifford Sifton,* pp. 169-70.

74. *Debates,* col. 1265, 4 March 1898.

75. Penlington, *Canada and Imperialism,* p. 92; Brown, *Canada's National Policy,* pp. 303-4, 309-10; PAC, Sifton Papers, vol. 52, pp. 35952-70, T.G. Shaughnessy to Sifton, 10 February 1898.

76. PAC, Laurier Papers, vol. 68, pp. 21321-33, 21348-49, Farrer to R. Boudreau, 8, 9, and 10 March 1898.

77. Ibid., vol. 69, Van Horne to Sifton, 18 March 1898 (forwarded to Laurier); vol. 750, pp. 214960-63, memorandum [1 April 1898], Chamberlain to Aberdeen, and reply of Canadian government of 10 April; Brown, *Canada's National Policy,* p. 304, n. 25; Penlington, *Canada and Imperialism,* p. 93. Prior to the parliamentary session, Sir Charles Tupper himself had taken this view. He stated in an interview in the Toronto *Mail and Empire* that "he did not anticipate any

trouble with the United States in transferring cargoes from the ocean boats to the river boats at Wrangel" (cited in "The Administration of the Yukon," pp. 12–13).

78. Brown, *Canada's National Policy*, p. 304; and see Ernest Gruening, *The State of Alaska* (New York: Random House, 1968), pp. 105–7.

79. PAC, Pope Papers, diary, 30 March 1898; *Globe*, 2 February 1898; PAC, CPR Records, Van Horne letterbook 54, pp. 726–27, 729, Van Horne to Sir Frank Smith, 15 February 1898; pp. 745–47, Van Horne to Sir Charles Tupper, 17 February 1898; pp. 958–63, Van Horne to Senators Carling, Wood, Sanford, Gowan, Temple, and Allan, 22 March 1898. Van Horne earlier had told Lord Strathcona that he had "reached an understanding with [Mackenzie] which will protect the interests of the C.P.R." (ibid., pp. 592–93, 25 January 1898). Just what these "interests" were is uncertain, but Van Horne certainly exerted himself unusually hard in lobbying for Sifton's bill.

80. PAC, Laurier Papers, vol. 750, pp. 214960–63; and vol. 71, pp. 22068–70, Farrer to Boudreau, 26 March 1898.

81. PAC, Sifton Papers, vol. 226, p. 508, Sifton to G.R. Pattullo, 14 April 1898.

82. *Globe*, 27 July 1899; and PAC, Laurier Papers, vol. 72, p. 22378, Laurier to S.H. Janes, 8 April 1898.

83. PAC, RCMP Records, vol. 174, file 576; M. Zaslow, *The Opening of the Canadian North, 1870–1914* (Toronto: McClelland and Stewart, 1971), p. 105; Innis, *Settlement and the Mining Frontier*, ch. 2.

84. Norbert MacDonald, "Seattle, Vancouver and the Klondike," *CHR* 49 (1968): 244–45.

85. PAC, Sifton Papers, vol. 224, pp. 63–64, 304, Sifton to Smart, 27 December 1897, 8 January 1898; order-in-council 126, 18 January 1898, *Canada Gazette* 31 (1898): 1742–46.

86. PAC, Sifton Papers, vol. 226, pp. 273–79, Sifton to Walsh, 4 April 1898; vol. 54, pp. 37538–50, F.C. Wade to Sifton, 10 April 1898.

87. Ibid., vol. 221, pp. 930–31, Sifton to Henry J. Dexter, 31 July 1897.

88. Order-in-council 125, 18 January 1898, *Canada Gazette* 31 (1898): 1684. The first concession, the so-called "Anderson Concession" on Hunker Creek, was issued to Robert Anderson of Vancouver, on behalf of a group of prominent British investors which included the Commercial Bank of Scotland (see PAC, Sifton Papers, vol. 48, pp. 32490–96, J.C. McLagan to Sifton, 4 May 1898; Lewis Green, *The Gold Hustlers* (Anchorage: Alaska Northwest Publishing Co., 1977), pp. 17–19.

89. On the background of the liquor traffic in the Yukon, see PAC, RCMP Records, vol. 135, file 222, passim.

90. 61 Vict., c. 6, "An Act to provide for the Government of the Yukon District"; *Debates*, 1898, col. 6729, 2 June 1898.

91. PAC, Sifton Papers, vol. 225, pp. 376–77, Sifton to Haultain, 28 February 1898; and reply, vol. 44, pp. 29706–8, 9 March 1898.

92. Ibid., vol. 51, pp. 35026–38, J.H. Ross to Sifton, 10 and 11 June 1898, and encl.; pp. 35083–89, T.G. Rothwell to Sifton, 18 August 1898, and encl.; order-in-council 64, 18 January 1898, *Canada Gazette* 31 (1898): 1740; C.C. Lingard, *Territorial Government in Canada* (Toronto: University of Toronto Press, 1946), pp. 23–24, 60–61.

93. PAC, Sifton Papers, vol. 226, pp. 273–79, Sifton to Walsh, 4 April 1898; vol. 54, pp. 37510–17, F.C. Wade to Sifton, 30 March 1898; RCMP Records, vol. 152, file 299, Commissioner Herchmer to F. White, 26 January 1898; *Debates*, 1898, cols. 582–84, 15 February 1898.

94. PAC, Laurier Papers, vol. 82, pp. 25342–45, Willison to Laurier, 25 July 1898.

## NOTES TO CHAPTER EIGHT

1. PAC, Willison Papers, vol. 74, pp. 27378–80, Sifton to Willison, 1 July 1898.

2. Russell A. Bankson, *The Klondike Nugget* (Caldwell, ID: Caxton Printers, 1935), pp. 108–9.

3. Ibid., pp. 121–23.

4. PAC, Willison Papers, vol. 74, pp. 27378–80; and Sifton Papers, vol. 227, p. 795, Sifton to A.J. Magurn, 2 July 1898.
5. PAC, Sifton Papers, vol. 53, pp. 36978–79, Templeman to Sifton, 4 August 1898; reply, vol. 228, pp. 207–9, 10 August 1898.
6. Ibid., vol. 46, pp. 30761–63, 30768–70, Laurier to Sifton, 12 August 1898; p. 30764, Sifton to Laurier, 12 August 1898; PAC, Laurier Papers, vol. 84, pp. 25772–75, Sifton to Laurier, 14 August 1898.
7. PAC, Sifton Papers, vol. 228, pp. 698–702, Sifton to Ogilvie, 10 September [should read October] 1898.
8. Ibid., vol. 227, pp. 779–80, Sifton to Steele, 2 July 1898; p. 878, Sifton to Smart, 8 July 1898; vol. 228, pp. 362–64, 471–72, 606–9, 703–4, 677–78, 694–95, Sifton to Ogilvie, 25 August, 23 September, 4, 5, 6, and 10 October 1898; PAC, Laurier Papers, vol. 86, pp. 26709–11, Ogilvie to Laurier, 24 September 1898.
9. *Times,* 28 September 1898.
10. PAC, Sifton Papers, vol. 228, pp. 694–95, 696–97, Sifton to Ogilvie, 10 October 1898; David R. Morrison, *The Politics of the Yukon Territory,* pp. 14–15. The miners' charges, Ogilvie's commission, and associated documents appear in *CSP,* 1899, no. 87.
11. PAC, Sifton Papers, vol. 228, pp. 696–97, 698–702, Sifton to Ogilvie, 10 October 1898.
12. Ibid., vol. 229, pp. 79–83, 401–3, 404–10, Sifton to Ogilvie, 31 October and 21 November 1898.
13. The *Report* and approximately 300 pages of evidence are to be found in *CSP,* 1899, nos. 87–87c. See also Morrison, *The Politics of the Yukon Territory,* p. 15; PAC, Sifton Papers, vol. 59, pp. 41598–606, O.H. Clark to Sifton, 8 March 1899; *MFP,* 31 May, 17 June, 4 July 1899.
14. See, for example, two sober assessments by Ogilvie and S.B. Steele: PAC, Laurier Papers, vol. 94, pp. 28567–72, Ogilvie to Laurier, 4 December 1898; vol. 102, pp. 30685–90, Steele to H. Harwood, MP, 22 February 1899. Dozens of similar letters could be cited.
15. PAC, Sifton Papers, vol. 230, pp. 894–931, Sifton to Ogilvie, 15 February 1899; Laurier Papers, vol. 92, pp. 28102–4, Sifton to Laurier, 15 November

1898.
16. PAC, Laurier Papers, vol. 94, pp. 28567–72, Ogilvie to Laurier, 4 December 1898.
17. PAC, Sifton Papers, vol. 228, pp. 788–89, Sifton to Willison, 18 October 1898.
18. Ibid., vol. 276, correspondence respecting the Joint High Commission, 1898–99, pp. 4, 5, Sir Julian Pauncefote to the Marquess of Salisbury, 27 and 31 May 1898.
19. On the issue of mining rights, see ibid., vol. 227, pp. 576–78, Sifton to G.M. Dawson, 18 June 1898.
20. PAC, Laurier Papers, vol. 34, p. 11257, Sifton to Laurier, 21 January 1897; Norman Penlington, *The Alaska Boundary Dispute: A Critical Reappraisal* (Toronto: McGraw-Hill Ryerson, 1972), pp. 37–39.
21. PAC, Laurier Papers, vol. 87, pp. 26951–53, Sifton to Laurier, 3 October 1898.
22. PAC, Sifton Papers, vol. 276, correspondence re. Joint High Commission, 1898–99, pp. 124–32; vol. 64, pp. 46652–58, Laurier to Sifton, 18 January 1899; Brown, *Canada's National Policy,* p. 382.
23. PAC, Laurier Papers, vol. 98, pp. 29917–24, Mills to Laurier, 25 January 1899; vol. 99, pp. 30199–200, Scott to Laurier, 2 February 1899; Scott Papers, vol. 4, pp. 20–21, Scott to Davies, 25 January 1899; pp. 22–27, Davies to Scott, 30 January 1899; Sifton Papers, vol. 60, pp. 42543–45, 42539–41, Davies to Sifton, 23 and 28 January 1899; vol. 230, pp. 469–72, Sifton to Davies, 25 January 1899; vol. 64, pp. 46671–75, Laurier to Sifton, 28 January 1899.
24. PAC, Sifton Papers, vol. 41, pp. 27545–46, Davies to Sifton, 14 November 1898; vol. 279, pp. 361–62, Sifton to Davies, 18 November 1898; and see R.R. Hett, "John Charlton, Liberal Politician and Free Trade Advocate" (Ph.D. diss., University of Rochester, 1969), pp. 398–413.
25. PAC, Sifton Papers, vol. 46, pp. 30833–39, Laurier to Sifton, 22 November 1898; Laurier Papers, vol. 93, pp. 28444–47, Sifton to Laurier, 29 November 1898; Brown *Canada's National Policy,* p. 370.
26. PAC, Sifton Papers, vol. 93, pp.

28444–47, Sifton to Laurier, 29 November 1898; Brown, *Canada's National Policy,* pp. 357–60.

27. PAC, Laurier Papers, vol. 93, pp. 28444–47, Sifton to Laurier, 29 November 1898.

28. PAC, Sifton Papers, vol. 230, pp. 494–97, Sifton to Laurier, 29 January 1899.

29. PAC, Laurier Papers, vol. 100, pp. 30222–25, Sir John Anderson to Laurier, 3 February 1899; Pope Papers, vol. 48, Joint High Commission diary entry, 4 February 1899; *MFP,* 4 February 1899; Brown, *Canada's National Policy,* pp. 384–85; Penlington, *Canada and Imperialism,* pp. 127–29.

30. PAC, Sifton Papers, vol. 230, pp. 826–27, Sifton to Laurier, 14 February 1899; vol. 231, p. 11, Sifton to Willison, 25 February 1899.

31. Ibid., vol. 230, pp. 894–931, Sifton to Ogilvie, 15 February 1899. Emphasis as in original.

32. PAC, Lord Minto Papers, letterbooks, vol. 1, pp. 79–83, Minto to J. Chamberlain, 15 April 1899; *Debates,* 1899, cols. 701–801, 30 March 1899 (Sir Charles Hibbert Tupper); cols. 804–85, 4 April

1899 (Sifton); cols. 1553–98, 14 April 1899 (Sir Charles Tupper).

33. PAC, Sifton Papers, vol. 231, pp. 703–6, Sifton to D.H. McMillan, 30 March 1899, and P.S. of 31 March 1899.

34. Ibid., vol. 64, pp. 46720–21, Laurier to Sifton, 5 April 1899.

35. *Debates,* 1899, col. 1014, 6 April 1899.

36. Ibid., cols. 1597–98, 14 April 1899. Emphasis added.

37. PAC, Sifton Papers, vol. 232, p. 41, Sifton to J.W. Fitzgerald, 21 April 1899.

38. *Debates,* 1899, cols. 3150–3227, 16 May 1899. "Tupper made 'another fool' of himself yesterday," remarked Sifton to Willison, abruptly dismissing the whole affair (PAC, Sifton Papers, vol. 232, pp. 558–61, Sifton to Willison, 16 May 1899).

39. *Debates,* 1899, cols. 5945–6046, 27 June 1899; cols. 6053–91, 28 June 1899.

40. Ibid., cols. 6124–65, 29 June 1899.

41. PAC, Tupper Papers, vol. 18, pp. 9514–15, Tupper to A.R. Dickey, 8 April 1899.

42. "Editorial Comment," *The Canadian Magazine* 13, no. 4 (1899): 386, PAC, Minto Papers, vol. 25, pp. 1–12, Minto to Queen Victoria, 14 May 1899.

## NOTES TO CHAPTER NINE

1. PAC, CPR Records, Van Horne letterbook 37, p. 776, Van Horne to Richardson, 8 June 1891.

2. See, for example, PAC, Sifton Papers, vol. 269, pp. 488–89, Sifton to J.S. Coleman.

3. Ibid., vol. 271, p. 1, Sifton to J.D. Cameron, 14 September 1896.

4. Ibid., vol. 31, pp. 20439–40, Richardson to Sifton, 1 March 1897.

5. *Winnipeg Daily Tribune,* 4 August 1897.

6. PAC, Sifton Papers, vol. 31, pp. 20483–84, Richardson to Sifton, 16 August 1897.

7. Ibid., vol. 1, pp. 46–52, E.A. Bailey to Sifton, 2 May 1894.

8. The tortuously complex story of the reorganization is best followed in the extensive correspondence of W.J. White, G.D. Wilson, J.W. Fleming, A.C. Fraser, and J.A. Smart, from January to March 1897, in PAC, Sifton Papers.

9. *MFP,* 26 June 1875, 11, 12, and 19 June 1879; Berton, *The Last Spike,* p. 40.

10. *Winnipeg Free Press,* 30 November 1972.

11. PAC, Macdonald Papers, vol. 271, pp. 123815–17, Stephen to Macdonald, 28 January 1888.

12. PAC, Lord Strathcona Papers, vol. 12, copy of agreement.

13. Undated, untitled memoranda in Free Press Library, Winnipeg; *Tribune,* 23 and 25 September, 4 and 10 October 1893. Luxton also tried to forestall the establishment of the *Tribune* by offering Richardson an appointment as Ottawa correspondent of the *Free Press* and a permanent post after the parliamentary session (PAM, Moncrieff Papers, file 2, Luxton to Richardson, 7 and 8 January 1890).

14. PAC, CPR Records, Van Horne letterbook 42, p. 518, Van Horne to John Mather, 10 January 1893; Macdonald Papers, vol. 288, pp. 133240, 133270–76, Van Horne to Macdonald, 3 and 28 February 1891.

15. PAC, Sifton Papers, vol. 269, p. 776,

Sifton to T.P. Gorman, 30 September 1893.

16. *Tribune,* 10 October 1893; PAC, CPR Records, Van Horne letterbook 45, Van Horne to W. Whyte, 10 November 1893.

17. *Tribune,* 28 and 29 September 1893.

18. PAC, CPR Records, Van Horne letterbook 51, p. 832, Van Horne to Mather, 10 August 1896; and see p. 161, Van Horne to Sir Charles Tupper, 21 April 1896.

19. Ibid., letterbook 52, pp. 710–11, Van Horne to Walsh, 29 January 1897; PAM, Greenway Papers, pp. 9963, 9725, Sifton to Greenway, 25 January and 3 February 1897; PAC, Sifton Papers, vol. 21, pp. 12926–27, Greenway to Sifton, 19 January 1897.

20. PAC, Sifton Papers, vol. 216, pp. 635–36, Sifton to Mather, 28 January 1897.

21. Ibid., vol. 31, file "Richardson, R.L. 1897," passim; vol. 221, pp. 946–47, vol. 222, pp. 283–84, Sifton to Richardson, 31 July and 12 August 1897.

22. PAC, Sifton Papers, vol. 47, p. 31522, Masten to Sifton, 29 January 1898; vol. 224, pp. 364–65, Sifton to Van Horne, 11 January 1898.

23. Interview with Col. Clifford Sifton, Toronto, 18 December 1968.

24. It is impossible, on the basis of presently available documents, to provide any accurate picture of Sifton's wealth at this stage of his career.

25. PAC, Sifton Papers, vol. 238, pp. 60–62, Sifton to Van Horne, 26 July 1900.

26. Ibid., vol. 225, p. 849, Sifton to Van Horne, 21 March 1898; pp. 931–32, Sifton to Masten, 23 March 1898.

27. Ibid., vol. 47, pp. 31539–44, Masten to Sifton, 9 May 1898; vol. 227, pp. 127, 840, 857, vol. 228, p. 597, Sifton to Masten, 16 May, 6 June, 8 July, 3 October 1898; vol. 47, pp. 31565–66, Masten to Mather, 26 July 1898; pp. 31635–36, Somerset to Mather, 29 July 1898; pp. 31628–31, Mather to Sifton, 3 August 1898; vol. 228, p. 211, Sifton to Mather, 10 August 1898; vol. 90, pp. 70713–16, Van Horne to Sifton, 15 August 1900. The nature of the "protection" afforded by the CPR was not indicated.

28. Ibid., vol. 47, pp. 31565–66, Masten to Mather, 26 July 1898. For a contrasting view of the profitability of the *Free Press,*

see *Tribune,* 18 February 1899, p. 3 (letter from W.F. Luxton).

29. PAC, Sifton Papers, vol. 226, p. 891, Sifton to Masten, 4 May 1898; vol. 47, pp. 31539–44, 31612–15, Masten to Sifton, 9 May 1898, and n.d. [May 1898?]; vol. 227, p. 127, Sifton to Masten, 16 May 1898.

30. See Ramsay Cook, *The Politics of John W. Dafoe and the Free Press* (Toronto: University of Toronto Press, 1963), p. 15, n. 15; PAC, Sifton Papers, vol. 47, p. 31627, Mather to Sifton, 1 April 1898.

31. PAC, Sifton Papers, vol. 222, pp. 930–31, Sifton to J.C. McLagan, 14 September 1897.

32. John A. Cooper, "The Editors of the Leading Canadian Dailies," *The Canadian Magazine* 12, no. 4 (February 1899): 349–50; PAC, Sifton Papers, vol. 270, pp. 627–28, Sifton to Magurn, 19 September 1895; Willison Papers, vol. 54, pp. 20129–30, Magurn to F.A. Acland, 22 September 1897.

33. PAC, Sifton Papers, vol. 24, p. 15909, Magurn to Sifton, 23 November 1897; *MFP,* 10 November 1897; *Tribune,* 7 April 1898.

34. Ibid. The reference is to private members' bills introduced by J.M. Douglas and Richardson to deal with western grievances concerning the transportation of grain and the elevator monopoly; both bills had been strongly opposed by the *Free Press* and by the CPR. See below, ch. 10.

35. *Tribune,* 10 and 12 April, 6, 7, and 11 June, 22 July 1898; PAC, Sifton Papers, vol. 52, pp. 35489–90, Masten to Sifton, n.d. [May 1898?] and encl.

36. PAC, Sifton Papers, vol. 47, pp. 31628–31, Mather to Sifton, 3 August 1898; vol. 228, pp. 215–16, Sifton to Magurn, 10 August 1898.

37. Ibid., vol. 47, pp. 31553–59, Masten to Sifton, 29 June 1898, and encl.

38. Ibid., vol. 46, pp. 31368–75, memorandum by Magurn, 1 September 1898.

39. Ibid.

40. Ibid., vol. 228, pp. 540–42, Sifton to Mather, 6 September 1898.

41. Ibid., vol. 229, p. 383, vol. 230, pp. 394–95, Sifton to Mather, 19 November 1898 and 21 January 1899; vol. 555, pp. 38056–57, 38059–60, E.M. Wood to Sifton, 7 and 11 November 1898; Murray Donnelly, *Dafoe of the Free Press*

(Toronto: Macmillan, 1968), pp. 33–34.

42. PAC, Sifton Papers, vol. 47, pp. 31637–40, Mather to Sifton, 20 September 1898; vol. 228, pp. 860–61, Sifton to Magurn, 17 October 1898.

43. Ibid., vol. 53, pp. 36202–3, 36294, 36335–36, J. Obed Smith to Sifton, 30 May, 1 June, 5 December 1898; vol. 226, pp. 77–78, Sifton to Willison, 26 March 1898; pp. 688–89, J.A.J. McKenna to Walter Scott, 22 April 1898.

44. Ibid., vol. 54, pp. 37896–99, W.J. White to Sifton, 19 November 1898. White formerly had been editor of the *Brandon Sun,* and although he was officially Canadian immigration agent at St. Paul, his long experience was being put to good use in helping Smith perfect the rural newspaper organization. Manitoba papers mentioned at various times in 1898 as more or less under Liberal influence included German, Icelandic, and Scandinavian papers issued in Winnipeg; the French paper *L'Echo; the Dauphin Pioneer Press,* Neepawa *Herald,* Souris *Plaindealer,* Crystal City *Siftings,* Boissevain *Globe,* Holland *Observer,* Morden *Chronicle,* McGregor *Herald, Carberry News,* Virden *Advance, Neepawa Press, Manitoba Liberal* (Portage la Prairie), Stonewall *Argus,* Crystal City *Courier, Deloraine Times,* and papers in Carman and Selkirk, as well as the *Brandon Sun* and *Manitoba Free Press.*

45. PAC, Sifton Papers, vol. 226, p. 994, Sifton to Willison, 10 May 1898.

46. Ibid., vol. 222, pp. 380–81, 437–38, 518, Sifton to Campbell, 17, 18, and 20 August 1897; pp. 520–21, Sifton to McMillan, 21 August 1897; pp. 966–71, memorandum, Sifton to J.C. McLagan, 14 September 1897.

47. *Tribune,* 20 August and 6 September 1898; *MFP,* 19 September 1898.

48. PAC, Sifton Papers, vol. 228, pp. 215–16, Sifton to Magurn, 10 August 1898; pp. 217–18, Sifton to Richardson, 10 August 1898; p. 289, Sifton to Smart, 20 August 1898.

49. On this episode, see A.R. McCormack, "Arthur Puttee and the Liberal Party: 1899–1904," *CHR* 51 (1970): 144–46.

50. The inference that Sifton was opposed to the project because of CPR influence was entirely unfounded. The Sifton Papers abound with evidence of his repeated but unavailing efforts to persuade Public Works Minister Israel Tarte to undertake the work.

51. *Tribune,* 18 October 1898.

52. *MFP,* 18 October 1898.

53. PAC, Sifton Papers, vol. 40, pp. 26667–71, Campbell to Sifton, 24 October 1898.

54. Ibid., vol. 228, pp. 961–62, Sifton to Willison, 24 October 1898.

55. Ibid., pp. 985–90, Sifton to J.D. Cameron, 26 October 1898; vol. 229, pp. 60–61, Sifton to G.D. Wilson, 31 October 1898; pp. 128–30, Sifton to Campbell, 7 November 1898; pp. 19–20, Sifton to J.O. Smith, 29 October 1898.

56. Ibid., pp. 60–61, Sifton to Wilson, 31 October 1898; pp. 133–34, Sifton to Young, 7 November 1898.

57. PAC, Laurier Papers, vol. 92, p. 28102, Sifton to Laurier, 15 November 1898; *Tribune,* 15, 16, 18, 25, and 29 November 1898; *MFP,* 15 and 18 November 1898.

58. A detailed analysis of the meeting was nevertheless supplied by Wade in several letters to Sifton (PAC, Sifton Papers, vol. 54, pp. 37568–607). Wade, who had written a great deal for the Liberal press in earlier years, tried to rectify the damage in a series of columns in the *Free Press,* beginning 18 November 1898. It is just possible that the paper had few Liberals in good standing on its staff. As late as the summer of 1898, Sifton had asked Magurn to keep on one J.J. Conklin who was not "very clever," but was "one of the few Liberals who has been allowed to remain under the present management" (ibid., vol. 227, p. 727, Sifton to Magurn, 29 June 1898; and see vol. 3, p. 1561, Conklin to Sifton, 23 November 1896).

59. PAC, Laurier Papers, vol. 89, pp. 27332–42, Richardson to Laurier, and encl., 21 October 1898.

60. Ibid., pp. 27349–53, Laurier to Richardson, 25 October 1898.

61. Ibid., vol. 90, pp. 27705–11, Richardson to Laurier, 2 November 1898; and see PAC, Sifton Papers, vol. 229, pp. 367–68, Sifton to Dr. Aubrey Husband, 18 November 1898.

62. PAC, Sifton Papers, vol. 45, pp. 30044–57, Jameson to Sifton, 7 November 1898.

63. PAC, Laurier Papers, vol. 92, pp. 28102–4, Sifton to Laurier, 15 November 1898; Sifton Papers, vol. 229, pp. 194–95,

Sifton to Campbell, 9 November 1898; pp. 365–66, Sifton to A.E. Richards, 19

November 1898.
64. *MFP,* 15, 19, and 20 December 1898.

## NOTES TO CHAPTER TEN

1. Toronto *Star,* 18 April 1929; PAC, Willison Papers, vol. 49, pp. 18594–97, John Lewis to Willison, 7 April 1899.
2. *CSP,* 1899, no. 20, "Report on the Prohibition Plebiscite," p. viii.
3. Ibid., pp. 277, 312; John H. Thompson, "The Prohibition Question in Manitoba," pp. 24, 110.
4. PAC, Sifton Papers, vol. 228, pp. 376–77, Sifton to Rev. MacBeth, 28 August 1898.
5. Ibid., vol. 231, pp. 910–11, Sifton to Geo. H. Healey, 12 April 1899; vol. 232, pp. 912–17, Sifton to John M. Fee, 2 June 1899.
6. *Debates,* 1899, cols. 8782, 8879–83, 28 July 1899.
7. PAC, Laurier Papers, vol. 57, pp. 18141–42, Cameron to Laurier, 20 November 1897.
8. Paul D. Stevens, "Laurier and the Liberal Party in Ontario 1887–1911" (Ph.D. diss., University of Toronto, 1966), pp. 173–76; Neatby, *Laurier and a Liberal Quebec,* pp. 89–91. Inspector Rochon indicated that the French Catholic separate schools were in deplorable condition owing to the poverty of the people, and were unlikely to survive very long on their own (PAC, Laurier Papers, vol. 60, pp. 19305–16, Rochon to R.W. Scott, n.d. [1898?]).
9. PAC, Laurier Papers, vol. 69, pp. 21648–54, S.A.D. Bertrand à Laurier, le 16 mars 1898.
10. Ibid., vol. 68, pp. 21319–20, Laurier to Cameron, 7 March 1898; PAM, Greenway Papers, p. 11563, Laurier to Greenway, 7 March 1898; PAC, Sifton Papers, vol. 48, pp. 32619–20, McMillan to Sifton, 16 March 1898.
11. PAC, Laurier Papers, vol. 49, pp. 15730–33, Tarte à Laurier, le 16 juillet 1897.
12. Ibid., vol. 72, pp. 22313–21, Smart to Sifton, 5 April 1898; vol. 71, pp. 22138–39, Bryce to Laurier, 30 March 1898.
13. Hilts, "Thomas Greenway," pp. 292–93.
14. PAC, Sifton Papers, vol. 227, pp. 178–79, Sifton to Cameron, 19 May

1898; vol. 42, pp. 28102–4, J.S. Ewart to Sifton, 27 May 1898; Laurier Papers, vol. 74, p. 22885, Cameron to Laurier, 29 April 1898; vol. 76, pp. 23731–34, confidential memorandum, Bryce to Sifton, 1 June 1898; W.T. Shaw, "The Role of John S. Ewart," p. 445.
15. PAC, Laurier Papers, vol. 76, p. 23731–34, Bryce to Sifton, 1 June 1898.
16. Ibid., vol. 80, pp. 24665–67, Cameron to Laurier, 30 June 1898.
17. PAC, Sifton Papers, vol. 64, pp. 46631–34, Laurier to Rev. G. Bryce, 3 January 1899 (copy); Laurier Papers, vol. 126, pp. 37760–62, Laurier to Greenway, 2 October 1899.
18. PAC, Tupper Papers, vol. 12, pp. 6042–43, Tupper to Macdonald, 4 February 1899.
19. See, for example, *Brandon Sun,* 14 and 17 January, 31 July 1884.
20. See A. Ernest Epp, "The Lake of the Woods Milling Company: An Early Western Industry," in H.C. Klassen, ed., *The Canadian West* (Calgary: Comprint Publishing Company for the University of Calgary, 1977), pp. 147–62.
21. PAC, CPR Records, Van Horne letterbook 40, pp. 751–52, Van Horne to William Whyte, 2 May 1892; letterbook 41, pp. 912–14, Van Horne to Luxton, 28 November 1892; letterbook 49, pp. 859–63, 921–22, Van Horne to Charles Braithwaite, 3 and 14 September 1895.
22. *Tribune,* 14 September 1897.
23. PAC, Sifton Papers, vol. 226, pp. 199–200, Sifton to A. McBride, 30 March 1898.
24. Ibid., vol. 229, pp. 45–46, Sifton to D. Mills, 31 October 1898; pp. 996–97, Sifton to J.P. Galbraith, 3 January 1899; *Tribune,* 29 April and 3 May 1898.
25. PAC, Sifton Papers, vol. 233, pp. 513–19, Sifton to Wilson, 13 July 1899.
26. Ibid., vol. 65, pp. 47301–4, Magurn to Sifton, 22 April 1899.
27. *CSP,* 1900, no. 81.
28. V.C. Fowke, "Royal Commissions and Canadian Agricultural Policy," *CJEPS* 14 (1948): 168–75.
29. PAC, Sifton Papers, vol. 234, pp. 737–

38, Sifton to Magurn, 9 October 1899.

30. Ibid., vol. 76, pp. 57204–14, Bell to Sifton, 14 January 1900; a pamphlet in the Sifton Papers (vol. 87, pp. 67422–55) entitled "The Warehouse and Grain Laws of the State of Minnesota, Including Laws Passed at the Thirtieth Session of the Legislature, 1897" shows clearly how the American law was adapted, with heavy editorial hand, to the Canadian situation.

31. Ibid., vol. 236, pp. 781–83, Sifton to Sir Henri Joly de Lotbinière, 7 March 1900. To be fair, it should be observed that the death of Justice Senkler shortly before Sifton's intended departure for Europe greatly complicated the completion of the report. Justice A.E. Richards of Manitoba was rushed in to replace Senkler and oversee its completion (ibid., vol. 87, pp. 67408–19, 67470–72, Richards to Sifton, 23 and 24 February 1900. These letters embody the preliminary draft report and recommended bill).

32. 63–64 Vict., c. 39; H.S. Patton, *Grain Growers' Cooperation in Western Canada* (Cambridge: Harvard University Press, 1928), p. 30.

33. *Debates,* 1900, cols. 5757–805 (21 May 1900); cols. 6258–308 (30 May 1900). Messrs. Davis, LaRivière, and MacDonnell were also absent for the vote.

34. Patton, *Grain Growers' Cooperation,* pp. 27–28, 30, n. 2; PAC, Sifton Papers, vol. 236, pp. 781–83, Sifton to Sir Henri Joly, 7 March 1900.

35. PAC, Sifton Papers, vol. 226, pp. 86–87, Sifton to Laurier, 26 March 1898.

36. Ibid.

37. Ibid., vol. 74, pp. 55730–32, Willison to Sifton, 14 May 1899; and reply, vol. 232, pp. 558–61, 16 May 1899; and see vol. 237, pp. 680–81, Sifton to T.A. Burrows, 4 July 1900.

38. *MFP,* 4 and 11 April, 10 August 1899.

39. PAC, Sifton Papers, vol. 233, pp. 324–27, Sifton to Isaac Campbell, 4 July 1899; vol. 57, pp. 39944–49, Blair to Shaughnessy, 1 September 1899 (copy); vol. 234, pp. 192–94, Sifton to Laurier, 9 September 1899; vol. 73, pp. 54315–16, Tarte to Sifton, 12 July 1899.

40. Ibid., vol. 230, pp. 946–49, Sifton to Van Horne, 17 February 1899. Van Horne replied that the CPR had granted a "temporary" reduction in rates in 1897 and was simply restoring them to earlier levels (PAC, CPR Records, Van Horne letterbook 56, Van Horne to Sifton, 20 February 1899).

41. PAC, Sifton Papers, vol. 224, pp. 217–19, Sifton to E.V. Bodwell, 5 January 1898; vol. 226, pp. 703–6, Sifton to Willison, 21 April 1898. Sifton subsequently told Magurn "to eliminate every reference to the question of the Kettle River Valley Railway whether direct or indirect" from the *Free Press* because "the knowing people in the West . . . would immediately seize upon anything . . . backing up the C.P. view as being an indication that the paper was being used by the C.P.R. and was a C.P.R. organ" (ibid., vol. 229, pp. 329–30, Sifton to Magurn, 18 November 1898). For Van Horne's views, see his blistering letter to the *Globe,* in PAC, CPR Records, Van Horne letterbook 54, pp. 921–26, 19 March 1898.

42. PAC, CPR Records, Van Horne letterbook 54, pp. 13, 219, 768, Van Horne to J.J. Hill, 25 September and 16 November 1897, 20 February 1898; p. 567, Van Horne to Gen. S. Thomas, 20 January 1898; Regehr, *Canadian Northern Railway,* pp. 56–62, 72, 85–86; Hilts, "Thomas Greenway," pp. 295–97.

43. PAC, Sifton Papers, vol. 233, pp. 191–92, Sifton to McMillan, 22 June 1899.

44. Ten cents per hundred weight, or six cents per bushel (see Hilts, "Thomas Greenway," pp. 313–14).

45. PAC, Sifton Papers, vol. 233, pp. 324–27, Sifton to Campbell, 4 July 1899; Regehr, *Canadian Northern Railway,* p. 87.

46. PAC, Sifton Papers, vol. 39, pp. 26104–5, Burrows to Sifton, 15 October 1898; vol. 40, pp. 2667–71, Campbell to Sifton, 24 October 1898; vol. 55, pp. 38056–57, Wood to Sifton, 7 November 1898.

47. Ibid., vol. 229, pp. 194–95, Sifton to Campbell, 9 November 1898; and see pp. 278–79, Sifton to W.T. Rutherford, 14 November 1898.

48. Ibid., pp. 367–68, Sifton to Dr. H. Aubrey Husband, 18 November 1898.

49. Ibid., vol. 229, pp. 278–79, Sifton to J.G. Rutherford, 14 November 1898; pp. 392–94, Sifton to Cameron, 21 November 1898; p. 390, Sifton to Campbell, 19 November 1898; vol. 54, pp. 37568, 37588–89, Wade to Sifton, 8 and 18

November 1898; vol. 228, pp. 616, 729, Sifton to Magurn, 4 and 10 October 1898; pp. 632–33, 690–91, Sifton to Shaughnessy, 4 and 8 October 1898; vol. 52, pp. 36020–29, Shaughnessy to Sifton, 6 and 24 October 1898, and encl.; vol. 49, pp. 33566–68, W.C. Nichol to Sifton, 12 October 1898.

50. Ibid., vol. 228, pp. 860–61, Sifton to Magurn, 17 October 1898; *MFP,* 9 November 1898.
51. *MFP,* 22 August 1898.
52. Ibid., 22 February 1899; *Tribune,* 1–15 March 1899.
53. PAC, Sifton Papers, vol. 214, pp. 352–53, Sifton to W. Paterson, 8 December 1896; vol. 43, pp. 28675–78, F.T. Frost to Sifton, 29 January 1898; vol. 45, pp. 30160–61, 30165–67, L.M. Jones to Sifton, 9 July and 11 August 1898; vol. 228, p. 158, Sifton to Jones, 1 August 1898.

54. Ibid., vol. 230, p. 839, Sifton to Smith, 14 February 1899.
55. *MFP,* 28 January 1899, reporting speech at Waterloo, 27 January.
56. Ibid., 14, 15, 17, and 30 March, 11 April 1899; PAC, Sifton Papers, vol. 67, pp. 48637–39, D.W. McKerchar to Sifton, 14 March 1899; D.H. McMillan to Sifton, 28 March 1899.
57. PAC, Sifton Papers, vol. 222, pp. 545–48, Sifton to J.G. Rutherford, 23 August 1897; vol. 231, pp. 209–13, 490–93, Sifton to McMillan, 4 and 21 March 1899; vol. 67, pp. 48819–21, McMillan to Sifton, 18 March 1899; and see A.R. McCormack, "Arthur Puttee," pp. 146–47.
58. PAC, Sifton Papers, vol. 232, pp. 429–31, Sifton to Willison, 10 May 1899.
59. Ibid., vol. 231, pp. 273–74, 796–99, Sifton to Campbell, 6 March and 7 April 1899.

## NOTES TO CHAPTER ELEVEN

1. J.B. Brebner, *North Atlantic Triangle* (New York: Columbia University Press, 1945), p. 224; M.C. Urquhart and K.A.H. Buckley, eds., *Historical Statistics of Canada* (Toronto: Macmillan, 1965), p. 22, series A–221.
2. Dafoe, *Clifford Sifton,* pp. 133–34; *CSP,* 1898, no. 13, p. 2.
3. *Debates,* 1898, cols. 4679–81, 3 May 1898; cols. 5937–43, 23 May 1898 (61–62 Vict., c. 31). Time sales were lands near Winnipeg and Brandon acquired on credit by speculators during the land boom of 1879–81. On their disposition, see *CSP,* 1899, no. 13, pp. xxv–xxvi; and *Debates,* 1900, cols. 9546–52, 9 July 1900.
4. *MFP,* 7 January 1899; *Debates,* 1898, cols. 668–69, 16 February 1898.
5. PAC, Sifton Papers, vol. 226, p. 397, Sifton to F. Oliver, 8 April 1898; p. 434, Sifton to H. Bostock, 1 March 1898; *Debates,* 1900, cols. 619–24, 19 February 1900; *CSP,* 1900, no. 13, pt. 1, p. 25; 1901, no. 25, pt. 1, p. 22.
6. E. Alyn Mitchner, "William Pearce: Father of Alberta Irrigation" (M.A. thesis, University of Alberta, 1966), chapters 2 and 3; N.F. Dreisziger, "The Canadian-American Irrigation Frontier

Revisited: The International Origins of Irrigation in Southern Alberta, 1885–1909," Canadian Historical Association, *Historical Papers* (1975): 211–29.
7. Dreisziger, "Canadian-American Irrigation," p. 216.
8. *CSP,* 1897, no. 13, pt. 3, pp. 40–44.
9. PAC, Sifton Papers, vol. 31, pp. 20715–16, J.H. Ross to Sifton, 17 December 1897.
10. *Debates,* 1898, cols. 4679–81, 3 May 1898 (61–62 Vict. c. 31); cols. 5662–63, 17 May 1898 (61–62 Vict. c. 35); cols. 5937–43, 23 May 1898.
11. Ibid., cols. 6123–24, 26 May 1898; cols. 7788–91, 11 June 1898; *CSP,* 1899, no. 13, p. xxiv.
12. Ibid., 1897, no. 13, p. xxvii; 1898, no. 13, p. 20; 1901, no. 25, p. xxvi.
13. Mitchner, "William Pearce," pp. 95–102.
14. *CSP,* 1897, no. 13, p. xi; 1899, no. 13, p. v; 1901, no. 25, p. xi, and pt. 2, pp. 110–11.
15. PAC, Sifton Papers, vol. 12, p. 7533, A.G. Blair to Sifton, 10 July 1897.
16. Ibid., vol. 240, pp. 200–201, Sifton to Caleb P. Simpson, 24 December 1900.
17. *MFP,* 17 November 1898, reporting Toronto speech of 15 November.
18. PAC, Willison Papers, vol. 35, pp.

12780–82, William Griffith to Willison, 29 June 1898.

19. PAC, Sifton Papers, vol. 229, pp. 2–3, Sifton to Smart, 29 October 1898.

20. Ibid., vol. 234, pp. 546–47, Sifton to Hon. Wm. Hardy, 2 October 1899.

21. *Debates,* 1899, cols. 8654–55, 27 July 1899.

22. *CSP,* 1897, no. 13, pt. 4, p. 3; 1901, no. 25, pt. 2, pp. 3–4.

23. See Hall, "Clifford Sifton: Immigration and Settlement Policy," pp. 69, 71.

24. PAC, Sifton Papers, vol. 238, pp. 393–94, Sifton to J.S. Willison, 14 August 1900 (Sifton's emphasis).

25. Ibid., vol. 48, pp. 32418–19, M.V. McInnes to Sifton, 17 June 1898.

26. *CSP,* 1897, no. 13, pt. 4, pp. 47–63.

27. Ibid., 1901, no. 25, pt. 2, pp. 162–88; PAC, Sifton Papers, vol. 218, p. 615, Sifton to W. Preston, 20 March 1897; House of Commons, *Journals* 34 (1899) App. no. 3: 281, 284. The sub-agents were paid solely by commission. For a detailed examination, see H.M. Troper, *Only Farmers Need Apply: Official Canadian Government Encouragement of Immigration from the United States 1896–1911* (Toronto: Griffin House, 1972).

28. PAC, Sifton Papers, vol. 224, pp. 665–68, Sifton to T.G. Shaughnessy, 24 January 1898; vol. 66, pp. 48451–52, M.V. McInnes to Sifton, 25 February 1899; vol. 231, pp. 93–94, Sifton to Van Horne, 27 February 1899; vol. 73, pp. 54765–66, Van Horne to Sifton, 8 March 1899; vol. 231, pp. 469–71, Sifton to Van Horne, 20 March 1899; vol. 71, pp. 52985, 52987, Shaughnessy to Sifton, 25 March 1899.

29. Troper, *Only Farmers Need Apply,* p. 148; *CSP,* 1899, no. 13, p. v; 1901, no. 25, p. xi.

30. *Winnipeg Tribune,* 13 September 1897.

31. Ibid., 25 June 1897.

32. PAC, Sifton Papers, vol. 41, pp. 27253–57, C.R. Devlin to Sifton, 31 October 1898; vol. 232, p. 119, Sifton to James Sutherland, 24 April 1899; *CSP,* 1897, no. 13, pt. 4, pp. 6–7.

33. *CSP,* 1899, no. 13, pt. 2, p. 107; 1900, no. 13, pt. 2, p. 5; 1901, no. 25, pt. 2, p. 4.

34. PAC, Sifton Papers, vol. 221, pp. 683–85, Sifton to Smith, 26 July 1897.

35. PAC, Willison Papers, vol. 35, pp. 12780–82, W. Griffith to Willison, 29 June 1898.

36. PAC, Sifton Papers, vol. 41, pp. 27253–57, C.R. Devlin to Sifton, 31 October 1898.

37. *CSP,* 1900, no. 13, pt. 2, pp. 12–19; 1901, no. 25, pt. 2, pp. 19–26; *Debates,* 1899, cols. 8569–618, 26 July 1899. See Preston, *The Life and Times of Lord Strathcona* (London: Eveleigh Nash, 1914); PAC, Laurier Papers, vol. 81, pp. 25155–59, A.S. Hardy to Laurier, 20 July 1898; and reply, 23 July 1898.

38. PAC, Laurier Papers, vol. 130, pp. 38961–75, Strathcona to Sifton, 15 November 1899, and encl. (copies). For further references, see Hall, "Clifford Sifton: Immigration and Settlement Policy," pp. 71–72, 246–47, n. 64.

39. PAC, Laurier Papers, vol. 130, pp. 38961–75, W. Preston to F. Pedley, 30 November 1899; University of Toronto Library, James Mavor Papers, Mavor to Sifton, Report No. 2, January 1900.

40. *CSP,* 1897, no. 13, p. x.

41. Ibid., 1901, no. 25, p. ix; pt. 2, pp. 4, 114.

42. Ibid., pp. 110–11.

43. *Debates,* 1899, cols. 4323–39, 5 June 1899; cols. 6828–68, 6879–903, 7 July 1899.

44. Ibid., 1900, cols. 7406–12 (Chinese Immigration Restriction Act, 63–64 Vict. c. 32); PAC, Sifton Papers, vol. 236, pp. 641–43, Sifton to Laurier, 23 February 1900; M.F. Timlin, "Canada's Immigration Policy, 1896–1910," *CJEPS* 26 (1960): 519–20; Avery, "Canadian Immigration Policy," ch. 2.

45. *MFP,* 15 October 1898, 21 January and 4 April 1899; PAC, Sifton Papers, vol. 67, pp. 48898–901, D.H. McMillan to Sifton, 7 July 1899, and encl.; vol. 65, pp. 47321–22, A.J. Magurn to Sifton, 20 May 1899.

46. Cited in *MFP,* 31 July 1899.

47. PAC, Sifton Papers, vol. 41, p. 28369, S. Fisher to Sifton, 28 May 1898; vol. 50, pp. 33982–84, 33986–87, copies of letters to Hon. S. Fisher, August 1898; Laurier Papers, vol. 81, pp. 25084–85, Sifton to Laurier, 16 July 1898; vol. 83, p. 25538, W.S. Fielding to Laurier, 3 August 1898; and see Myrna Kostash, *All of Baba's Children* (Edmonton: Hurtig, 1977), ch. 1.

48. Kostash, *All of Baba's Children,* passim.

49. Macleod, *The North-West Mounted Police,* pp. 150–52; V.J. Kaye, *Early Ukrainian Settlement in Canada 1895–*

*1900: Dr. Josef Oleskow's Role in the Settlement of the Canadian Northwest* (Toronto: University of Toronto Press, 1964), pp. 225-31, 322-46; M.H. Marunchak, *The Ukrainian Canadians: A History* (Winnipeg: Ukrainian Free Academy of Sciences, 1970), pp. 71-72.

50. PAC, Sifton Papers, vol. 230, pp. 787-89, 859-60, Sifton to W.W. Buchanan, 11 and 15 February 1899.

51. Ibid., vol. 66, pp. 48222-26, McCreary to Sifton, 20 April 1899.

52. Ibid., vol. 232, p. 557, Sifton to Magurn, 16 May 1899.

53. Ibid., vol. 232, p. 163, memo, Sifton to Smart, 26 April 1899; vol. 56, pp. 38615-17, memo, 17 June 1899; *Debates,* 1899, cols. 6851-56, 7 July 1899; *CSP,* 1902, no. 25, pt. 2, pp. 110-13, "Ruthenians."

54. *MFP,* 31 July 1899; U of T Library, Mavor Papers, Mavor to Sifton, Report No. 2, January 1900; and memorandum upon Doukhobor Affairs, 15 April 1907; PAC, Sifton Papers, vol. 56, memo, 17 June 1899; G. Woodcock and I. Avakumovic, *The Doukhobors* (Toronto: Oxford, 1968), ch. 6.

55. PAC, Sifton Papers, vol. 231, p. 845, Sifton to McMillan, 10 April 1899.

56. Woodcock and Avakumovic, *The Doukhobors,* p. 135; PAC, Sifton Papers, vol. 65, pp. 47112-13, Mackenzie to Sifton, 6 January 1899; vol. 230, pp. 123-26, Sifton to Mackenzie, 9 January 1899.

57. See Hall, "Clifford Sifton: Immigration and Settlement Policy," pp. 75, 82.

58. PAC, Sifton Papers, vol. 66, pp. 49297-98, J.T. Mortimer to Sifton, 22 June 1899; vol. 67, pp. 49300-302, Mortimer to Sifton, 6 August 1899; and see Woodcock and Avakumovic, *The Doukhobors,* p. 145.

59. PAC, Sifton Papers, vol. 233, pp. 427-29, Sifton to Mortimer, 10 July 1899; vol. 231, p. 60, Sifton to Smart, 27 February 1899.

60. *The Canadian Magazine* 12, no. 5 (1899): 467-68; 13, no. 1 (1899): 89; no. 2 (1899): 186-88.

61. *MFP,* 8 July 1898; 13 May 1899.

62. PAC, Sifton Papers, vol. 230, pp. 86-88, Sifton to D. Mills, 6 January 1899.

63. *MFP,* 9 April 1900.

64. Hall, "Clifford Sifton and Canadian Indian Administration," pp. 127-51.

65. PAC, DIA Records, vol. 1121, pp. 689-91, J.A. Smart to Rev. A.J. Vining, 30

May 1898.

66. *Debates,* 1897, col. 4076, 14 June 1897.

67. PAC, DIA Records, vol. 1121, McLean to A.E. Forget, 8 March 1898; vol. 1120, pp. 692-99, memorandum, 20 July 1897.

68. Hall, "Clifford Sifton and Canadian Indian Administration," pp. 138, 141.

69. PAC, DIA Records, vol. 3848, file 75235-1, J.A.J. McKenna to Sifton, 17 April 1898.

70. I am indebted for these remarks to conversations with Dr. John Tobias of Red Deer College and Messrs. K.J. Tyler and R.A. Wright of Tyler and Wright Research Associates, Ottawa, all of whom have been engaged in research for the Federation of Saskatchewan Indians.

71. PAC, Sifton Papers, vol. 264, pp. 87-88, Sifton to Oliver, 5 August 1897; and see p. 99, Sifton to James W. Bettes, 7 August 1897.

72. PAC, DIA Records, file 75236-1, Walker to Sifton, 30 November 1897.

73. Ibid., file 75236-1, passim. See also René Fumoleau, *As Long As This Land Shall Last: A History of Treaty 8 and Treaty 11, 1870-1939* (Toronto: McClelland and Stewart, 1975), pp. 39-43.

74. PAC, DIA Records, file 75236-1, A.E. Forget to J.A.J. McKenna, 16 April 1898; and reply, 19 April 1898.

75. Ibid., Forget to Secretary, DIA, 25 April 1898; D.J. Hall, "The Half-Breed Claims Commission," *Alberta History* 25, no. 2 (1977): 3.

76. PC 1703, 27 June 1898; PC 330, 2 March 1899 (copies in PAC, DIA Records, file 75236-1).

77. Ibid., Sifton to Laird, McKenna, and Ross, 12 May 1899; Fumoleau, *History of Treaty 8 and Treaty 11,* pp. 61-62.

78. There were, of course, subsequent differences over alleged verbal promises and the actual text of the treaty; see Fumoleau, *History of Treaty 8 and Treaty 11,* pp. 69-100; and Richard Daniel, "Spirit and Terms of Treaty 8," in *Spirit and Terms of Treaties 6, 7 & 8— Alberta Indian Perspectives,* ed. Richard Price, draft ms., Indian Association of Alberta [1977]. I am grateful to Professor John Foster, Department of History, University of Alberta, for permitting me to consult a copy of this latter work.

79. *Debates,* 1899, col. 7513, 14 July 1899; and see Hall, "The Half-Breed Claims Commission," pp. 5-6.

## NOTES TO CHAPTER TWELVE

1. *MFP,* 11 March 1899; PAC, Sifton Papers, vol. 230, pp. 627–32, Sifton to McMillan, [8] February 1899.
2. Hilts, "Thomas Greenway," pp. 316–24. On Macdonald, see Henry James Guest, "Reluctant Politician: A Biography of Sir Hugh John Macdonald" (M.A. thesis, University of Manitoba, 1973).
3. Hilts, "Thomas Greenway," pp. 316–24; PAC, Sifton Papers, vol. 234, pp. 428–30, Sifton to Isaac Campbell, 20 September 1899.
4. Hilts, "Thomas Greenway," pp. 316, 320.
5. PAC, Sifton Papers, vol. 233, pp. 703–4, Sifton to Smith, 1 August 1899; and pp. 670–71, Sifton to R. Watson, 1 August 1899.
6. Ibid., vol. 74, p. 55879, Wood to Sifton, 18 September 1899; and see vol. 57, pp. 40477–80, T.A. Burrows to Sifton, 15 and 24 September 1899.
7. Ibid., vol. 234, pp. 462–64, 710–14, Sifton to I. Campbell, 22 September and 8 October 1899.
8. On the cabinet crisis, see C.P. Stacey, *Canada and the Age of Conflict, 1, 1867–1921* (Toronto: Macmillan, 1977), pp. 60–65. Late in November Laurier was still uncertain whether to have "an early dissolution" (PAC, Sifton Papers, vol. 64, pp. 46790–800, Laurier to Sifton, 23 November 1899).
9. PAC, Sifton Papers, vol. 232, pp. 50–52, Sifton to I. Campbell, 21 April 1899; pp. 273–74, Sifton to Adams, 2 May 1899; vol. 234, p. 196, Sifton to Smith, 9 September 1899; vol. 233, pp. 667–68, Sifton to Adams, 1 August 1899.
10. Ibid., vol. 234, pp. 710–14, Sifton to I. Campbell, 8 October 1899.
11. *MFP,* 25 October 1899.
12. Ibid., 28 October. 1899; PAC, Laurier Papers, vol. 129, pp. 38628–38, J. Martin to Laurier, 3 November 1899, and reply, 10 November 1899; J. Martin to Laurier, 15 and 28 November 1899, encl. E.D. Martin to J. Martin, 22 November 1899.
13. PAC, Tupper Papers, vol. 19, p. 9853, Tupper to G.E. Drummond, 15 June 1899; p. 9871, Tupper to H.J. Macdonald, 17 June 1899; p. 9928, Tupper to H. Graham, 4 July 1899; p. 9947, Tupper to Macdonald, 5 July 1899.
14. Hilts, "Thomas Greenway," pp. 320–22.
15. PAC, Sifton Papers, vol. 235, pp. 174–75, Sifton to J.O. Smith, 13 November 1899; vol. 65, pp. 47545–47, J. Mather to Sifton, 8 November 1899.
16. Ibid., vol. 235, pp. 176–77, Sifton to Smith, 13 November 1899.
17. Ibid., vol. 63, p. 45811, 45813, Jones to Sifton, 18 and 25 September 1899; vol. 234, pp. 710–14, Sifton to Campbell, 8 October 1899; PAC, Laurier Papers, vol. 130, pp. 38833–34, Greenway to Laurier, 11 November 1899, and reply, 14 November 1899; vol. 131, p. 39240, Sifton to Laurier, 20 November 1899.
18. PAC, Sifton Papers, vol. 234, pp. 462–64, Sifton to I. Campbell, 22 September 1899; vol. 235, p. 211, Sifton to Fisher, 21 November 1899; p. 235, Sifton to A. Nicol, 23 November 1899; PAC, Laurier Papers, vol. 131, p. 39240, Sifton to Laurier, 20 November 1899.
19. PAC, Sifton Papers, vol. 235, pp. 226–27, Sifton to C.E. Hall, 23 November 1899.
20. PAC, Laurier Papers, vol. 132, pp. 39342–43, Sifton to Laurier, 28 November 1899.
21. University of Manitoba, Dafoe Papers, J.O. Smith to Dafoe, 22 February 1932.
22. The independent later supported the Tory government. See Hilts, "Thomas Greenway," p. 327; L.J. Fiske, "Controversy on the Prairies," pp. 170–83; W.L. Clark, "Politics in Brandon City, 1899–1949" (Ph.D. diss., University of Alberta, 1976), pp. 20–30; D.J. Hall, "The Political Career of Clifford Sifton 1896–1905" (Ph.D. diss., University of Toronto, 1973), pp. 489–500.
23. PAC, Willison Papers, vol. 74, pp. 27421–26, Sifton to Willison, 28 December 1899; Sifton Papers, vol. 235, pp. 375–76, Sifton to D.C. Fraser, 22 December 1899; pp. 356–58, Sifton to R.D. Foley, 22 December 1899.
24. PAC, Laurier Papers, vol. 133, pp. 39737–40, Sifton to Laurier, 10 December 1899. Greenway's recent biographer is inclined to lay the blame for defeat at Sifton's door; see Hilts, "Thomas Greenway," pp. 328–32.
25. *MFP,* 8 January 1900.
26. PAC, Sifton Papers, vol. 85, pp. 65321–23, McMillan to Sifton, 20

January 1900; vol. 236, p. 77, Sifton to Watson, 22 January 1900; pp. 99–100, Sifton to McMillan, 22 January 1900; vol. 80, pp. 61437–45, telegrams between Sifton and Greenway, 25–28 January 1900; vol. 77, Campbell to Sifton, 27 January 1900; vol. 236, p. 230, Sifton to Cameron, 30 January 1900; pp. 787–88, Sifton to W.W. Cory, 2 February 1900; Hilts, "Thomas Greenway," pp. 332–40.

27. *MFP*, 10 October 1899.

28. McCormack, "Arthur Puttee," pp. 141–49; PAC, Laurier Papers, vol. 134, pp. 39946–49, J. Martin to Laurier, 19 December 1899, and reply, 26 December 1899; Tupper Papers, vol. 19, p. 10324, Tupper to C.H. Tupper, 17 January 1900.

29. PAC, Sifton Papers, vol. 235, pp. 514–16, 537, Sifton to McMillan, 29 December 1899 and 1 January 1900.

30. Ibid., vol. 58, pp. 41113–14, Cameron to Sifton, 27 December 1899; vol. 72, p. 53750, Smith to Sifton, 30 December 1899; vol. 235, pp. 543–44, Sifton to McMillan, 2 January 1900; pp. 576–77, Sifton to Campbell, p. 578, Sifton to Cameron, pp. 579–80, Sifton to Mc-Millan, p. 584, A.P. Collier to Smith, pp. 586–87, Sifton to Smith, 3 January 1900.

31. Ibid., vol. 83, pp. 64068–82, Magurn to Sifton, 13 January 1900; vol. 78, pp. 59135–37, W.W. Cory to Sifton, 14 January 1900; vol. 89, pp. 68933–36, J.W. Sifton to Sifton, 18 January 1900.

32. Ibid., vol. 236, pp. 27, 94–96, Sifton to Magurn, 20 and 23 January 1900; p. 89, Sifton to J.W. Sifton, 23 January 1900; vol. 85, pp. 65325–26, 65330, McMillan to Sifton, 23 and 25 January 1900; McCormack, "Arthur Puttee," pp. 150–52; Hall, "Political Career of Clifford Sifton," pp. 500–505.

33. PAC, Laurier Papers, vol. 132, pp. 39342–43, Sifton to Laurier, 28 November 1899.

34. PAC, Sifton Papers, vol. 41, pp. 27618–19, Davis to Sifton, 7 August 1898; vol. 60, p. 42637, Davis to Sifton, 16 January 1899; Hall, "The Half-Breed Claims Commission," pp. 4, 6–7.

35. PAC, Sifton Papers, vol. 224, p. 276, Sifton to Willison, 7 January 1898.

36. McCutcheon, "Economic and Social Structure of Political Agrarianism in Manitoba," pp. 348–51. In 1898 the Manitoba Patrons renamed their organization the Independent Industrial Association, calling for a co-operative society, government ownership of railways and grain elevators, and political reforms including referendum and recall. It had no political impact during the prosperity of the late 1890's.

37. PAC, Laurier Papers, vol. 53, pp. 17144–47, G.H.V. Bulyea to Laurier, 15 October 1897; Gilbert Johnson, "James Moffat Douglas," *Saskatchewan History* 7 (1954): 48–49.

38. PAC, Sifton Papers, vol. 51, pp. 34999–5000, Ross to Sifton, 24 January 1898; vol. 229, pp. 788–90, Sifton to A.L. Sifton, 16 December 1898.

39. Cited in D.H. Bocking, "Premier Walter Scott," p. 45.

40. PAS, Walter Scott Papers, 201–2, 205, 207, 209, 210, Sifton to Scott, 10 and 20 October 1898, 10 January 1899, 30 and 31 October 1899; pp. 33–34, Sifton to R.W. McKinnell, 30 October 1899; Bocking, "Premier Walter Scott," pp. 45–46.

41. J.M. Beck, *Pendulum of Power: Canada's Federal Elections* (Scarborough: Prentice-Hall, 1968), pp. 71, 86.

42. PAC, Sifton Papers, vol. 224, p. 193, Sifton to Maxwell, 3 January 1898.

43. Ibid., vol. 48, pp. 32516–18, 32553–59, 32561, McLagan to Sifton, 30 September, 26 and 30 November 1898.

44. Ibid., vol. 65, pp. 47330–37, Magurn to Sifton, 3 June 1899; reply, vol. 232, pp. 945–46, 6 June 1899; reply, vol. 65, 47343–49, 9 June 1899.

45. Ibid., pp. 47362–64, Magurn to Sifton, 5 July 1899; vol. 233, pp. 504–6, Sifton to Magurn, 13 July 1899.

46. Ibid., vol. 65, pp. 47366–71, Magurn to Sifton, 19 July 1899.

47. PAC, Sifton Papers, vol. 235, pp. 172–73, Sifton to Mather, 13 November 1899.

48. Ibid., vol. 90, p. 70243, Taylor to Sifton, 10 February 1900; vol. 236, p. 809, Sifton to E.H. Maklin, 8 March 1900; Cook, *The Politics of John W. Dafoe*, p. 15; Donnelly, *Dafoe of the Free Press*, pp. 39, 40. Somerset was retired with three months' salary as severance pay and an unofficial payment of a year's salary to encourage his continued silence concerning the real financial control of the newspaper (PAC, Sifton Papers, vol. 239, p. 125, Sifton to Mather, 15 Septem-

ber 1900; vol. 95, pp. 75123–24, I. Campbell to Sifton, 2 July 1901). He died 9 March 1901, aged sixty-eight.

49. PAC, Sifton Papers, vol. 83, pp. 63818–36, Macklin to Sifton, 6 July 1900, and encl.

50. Ibid., vol. 84, pp. 64250–51, Mather to Sifton, 6 September 1900; vol. 65, pp. 47545–47, Mather to Sifton, 8 November 1899; vol. 84, pp. 64253–56, Mather to Sifton, 11 October 1900; *MFP,* 27 September and 6 October 1900.

51. PAC, Sifton Papers, vol. 83, p. 63857, Macklin to Sifton, 16 July 1900; p. 63880, Macklin to Mather, 18 September 1900 (copy); p. 64164, Magurn to Macklin, 9 October 1900, with subsequent written comment by Macklin; vol. 237, p. 881, Sifton to Macklin, 20 July 1900.

52. Ibid., vol. 83, pp. 63861–62, Macklin to Sifton, 24 July 1900; vol. 78, pp. 59234–36, W.W. Cory to A.P. Collier, 16 May 1900.

53. Ibid., vol. 238, pp. 35–36, Sifton to Macklin, 27 July 1900.

54. Ibid., vol. 81, pp. 61913–14, Hunt to Sifton, 21 June 1900.

55. Ibid., vol. 53, pp. 36335–36, J.O. Smith to Sifton, 5 December 1898; vol. 229, p. 991, Sifton to Smith, 3 January 1899; vol. 72, pp. 53485–86, Smith to A.P. Collier, 25 March 1899; p. 53488, Smith to Sifton, 27 March 1899; vol. 230, p. 655, Sifton to Smith, 7 February 1899.

56. *MFP,* 25 January and 7 February 1900.

57. Ibid., 10 October 1898 and 19 July 1900. See R.M. Dawson, *William Lyon Mackenzie King,* 1, *1874–1923* (Toronto: University of Toronto Press, 1958), pp. 65–70.

58. *MFP,* 9 January 1899. Hind's articles began to appear in the latter part of 1898.

59. PAC, Sifton Papers, vol. 231, pp. 354–55, Sifton to Magurn, 14 March 1899; pp. 541–42, Sifton to Smith, 22 March 1899.

60. Ibid., vol. 72, pp. 53488–91, Smith to Sifton, 27 March 1899.

61. Ibid., vol. 231, p. 498, Sifton to Magurn, 21 March 1899.

62. Ibid., vol. 41, pp. 27505–6, L.H. Davies to Sifton, 5 August 1898.

63. PAC, Laurier Papers, vol. 149, pp. 44160–63, Sifton to Laurier, 31 March 1900; Sifton Papers, vol. 236, pp. 639–40, Sifton to Prof. E. Haanel, 23 February 1900; vol. 240, pp. 93–94, Sifton to R.C. Murgatroyd, 19 December 1900.

64. PAC, Laurier Papers, vol. 151, Tarte à Laurier, le 15 avril 1900.

65. PAC, Sifton Papers, vol. 237, p. 674, Sifton to Willison, 4 July 1900; pp. 680–81, Sifton to T.A. Burrows, 4 July 1900; vol. 240, pp. 93–94, Sifton to R.C. Murgatroyd, 19 December 1900.

66. He even had a special French-language tutor for them; ibid., vol. 237, p. 736, Sifton to M. Ami, 11 July 1900.

67. Interview with Mr. Clifford Sifton, Toronto, 18 December 1968; interview with Mr. R.S. Malone, Toronto, June 1977.

68. *Debates,* 1898, col. 3176 (6 April 1898); PAC, Sifton Papers, vol. 224, pp. 245–46, Sifton to W.H. Hellyar, 6 January 1898; vol. 226, p. 496, J.A.J. McKenna to P.E. Duncan, April 1898; vol. 224, p. 29, Sifton to J.D. Hunt, 24 December 1897; vol. 225, pp. 392–93, Sifton to W.H. Hellyar, 28 February 1898.

69. In May 1898 he resigned as a director of the Manitoba Trust Company, for unspecified reasons (PAC, Sifton Papers, vol. 227, p. 126, Sifton to T. Robinson, 16 May 1898). Very few papers relating to Sifton's personal finances survive, at least in archival collections.

70. *MFP,* 25 September 1900; PAC, Laurier Papers, vol. 122, pp. 36773–75, Laurier to W. Mulock, n.d. [c. 1 September 1899].

71. PAC, Sifton Papers, vol. 89, pp. 69845–49, J. Sutherland to Sifton, 29 September 1900.

72. PAC, Laurier Papers, vol. 149, pp. 44160–63, Sifton to Laurier, 31 March 1900.

73. PAC, Sifton Papers, vol. 89, pp. 69845–49, J. Sutherland to Sifton, 29 September 1900; vol. 236, p. 590, Sifton to Shaughnessy, 21 February 1900; vol. 88, pp. 68740–41, Shaughnessy to Sifton, 1 August 1900; vol. 238, p. 287, Sifton to A.L. Sifton, 10 August 1900; vol. 78, p. 59229, W.W. Cory to A.P. Collier, 24 April 1900.

74. Each constituency, for example, was expected to supply the central office with a voters' list on which the political affiliation of each voter was marked: Liberal, Conservative, or doubtful for either party. This was for the purpose of

distributing literature (see PAS, Scott Papers, 211, Alex. Smith to Scott, 2 September 1899; *Debates,* 1899, cols. 379ff., 24 March 1899; 1898, col. 3044, 4 April 1898).

75. PAC, Laurier Papers, vol. 33, pp. 10876–77, Sutherland to Sifton, 12 January 1897; Willison Papers, vol. 74, pp. 274929–31, Sifton to Willison, 29 July 1900; Sifton Papers, vol. 238, pp. 290–92, Sifton to Laurier, 10 August 1900; Sifton to Cartwright, 11 August 1900.

76. PAC, Sifton Papers, vol. 239, p. 11, Sifton to Smart, 2 September 1900; p. 233, A.P. Collier to Smart, 19 September 1900; p. 412, Sifton to Templeman, 8 October 1900.

77. Ibid., vol. 80, pp. 61267–69, Galliher to Sutherland, 8 September 1900; p. 61276, Galliher to Sifton, 1 October 1900; vol. 90, file "Templeman, W. 1900," passim, esp. p. 70410, Templeman to Sifton, 20 October 1900; vol. 239, pp. 708, 709, Sifton to Wm. Mackenzie and L.M. Jones, 1 October 1900; vol. 75, pp. 56458–60, James Bannerman to Sifton, 20 October 1900.

78. Ibid., vol. 88, pp. 67651–57, Ross to Sifton, 21 August 1900; vol. 238, pp. 577–78, Sifton to Ross, 24 August 1900; pp. 201–2, Sifton to Scott, 6 August 1900; vol. 77, p. 58587, Cartwright to Sifton, 11 October 1900; PAS, Scott Papers, p. 446, Sifton to Scott, 9 July 1900.

79. PAC, Sifton Papers, vol. 239, p. 148, Sifton to Oliver, 15 September 1900; p. 558, A.P. Collier to Smart, 29 October 1900; p. 137, Sifton to Magurn, 15 September 1900; *MFP,* 8, 10, 12, and 17 September 1900; C.B. Koester, "Nicholas Flood Davin," pp. 258–61.

80. PAC, Sifton Papers, vol. 238, pp. 368–69, Sifton to A.L. Sifton, 14 August 1900; pp. 512–13, same, 22 August 1900; vol. 239, p. 40, same, 4 September 1900; p. 148, Sifton to Oliver, 15 September 1900.

81. Ibid., vol. 236, pp. 562–63, Sifton to A. Chisholm, 21 February 1900; vol. 81, p. 61975, Robert Hall to Sifton, 23 February 1900.

82. Ibid., vol. 238, pp. 166–69, Sifton to R. Hall, 6 August 1900; pp. 174–76, Sifton to Cory, 6 August 1900; pp. 271–72, Collier to Adams, 9 August 1900; vol. 78, pp. 58959–62, 58949–52, Collier to

Sifton, 19 and 21 August 1900.

83. Ibid., vol. 237, pp. 793–94, Sifton to Magurn, 19 July 1900; p. 795, Sifton to Smith, 19 July 1900; vol. 79, pp. 60646–47, E. Farrer to Sifton, 28 July 1900; vol. 238, p. 634, Sifton to Magurn, 29 August 1900; p. 535, Sifton to Smith, 22 August 1900; pp. 174–76, Sifton to Cory, 6 August 1900; p. 226, Collier to F. Schultz, 8 August 1900; p. 345, Sifton to Cory, 14 August 1900; pp. 316–17, Sifton to Hellyar, 11 August 1900; p. 346, Sifton to W.W. McMillan, 14 August 1900; p. 413, Sifton to Magurn, 16 August 1900; vol. 239, p. 84, Sifton to M. Millar, 14 September 1900; p. 164, Sifton to W.F. Sirrett, 16 September 1900; p. 718, Sifton to W.C. Caldwell, 1 October 1900.

84. Ibid., vol. 239, loose copy between pp. 769–70, Sifton to John Bain, 7 September 1900.

85. Ibid., pp. 699–700, Sifton to Alex. Smith, 7 September 1900. There is evidence in the Sifton Papers that the Conservative organization was very similar to Sifton's (see ibid., vol. 75, pp. 56277–79, R. Adamson to Sifton, 17 September 1900; vol. 81, p. 61696, Liberal–Conservative Association circular letter of 28 September 1900).

86. Ibid., vol. 78, pp. 58959–62, Collier to Sifton, 19 August 1900; PAC, Tupper Papers, vol. 12, pp. 6360–61, T.M. Daly to Tupper, 23 November 1900. The Tories themselves were masters of the whispering campaign and circulated many rumours about the opulence of Sifton's life in Ottawa and the depths of his corruption.

87. PAC, Sifton Papers, vol. 239, p. 358, Sifton to L.M. Jones, 5 October 1900; *MFP,* 6 October 1900.

88. *MFP,* 15 October 1900; and see Dafoe, *Clifford Sifton,* pp. 206–10; E.M. Macdonald, *Recollections, Political and Personal* (Toronto: Ryerson, 1938), p. 34.

89. PAC, Sifton Papers, vol. 78, pp. 59238–39, Cory to Collier, 25 May 1900; pp. 59282–84, Cory to Sifton, 2 July 1900; vol. 81, Sifton to George Hudson, 18 October 1900.

90. Ibid., vol. 76, pp 57791–800, T.A. Burrows to Sifton, 24 June 1900; vol. 237, pp. 932–33, Sifton to Smith, 23 July 1900, and reply, vol. 89, p. 69386, 23 July 1900.

91. Ibid., pp. 956–57, Sifton to Greenway, 23 July 1900; pp. 932–33, Sifton to Smith, 23 July 1900; vol. 89, pp. 69393–95, Smith to Sifton, 26 July 1900; vol. 238, pp. 261–62, Sifton to Smith, 8 August 1900; pp. 318–21, Sifton to Winkler, 11 August 1900; *MFP*, 3, 10, and 11 August 1900.

92. Jean Riel, son of Louis Riel, was said to have been granted 240 acres of land near St. Boniface during the sittings of the Scrip Commission in 1900.

93. *MFP*, 13, 27, and 29 September, 2 October, 1 and 5 November 1900; PAC, Sifton Papers, vol. 239, p. 129, Sifton to Magurn, 15 September 1900; vol. 88, p. 68398, copy of one of Richardson's campaign posters.

94. *CSP*, 1901, no. 36; Beck, *Pendulum of Power*, p. 96; PAC, Laurier Papers, vol. 176a, p. 50301n, J.H. Ross to Laurier, 8 November 1900; *MFP*, 4 December 1900. For more detail on this election, see Clark, "Politics in Brandon City," pp. 31–43; Hall, "The Political Career of Clifford Sifton," pp. 517–44.

95. A.W. MacIntosh, "Sir Charles Tupper," p. 567; PAC, Tupper Papers, vol. 12, pp. 6360–61, Daly to Tupper, 23 November 1900.

96. Dafoe, *Clifford Sifton*, p. 210.

97. *MFP*, 12 December 1900.

98. See John English, *The Decline of Politics: The Conservatives and the Party System 1901–20* (Toronto: University of Toronto Press, 1977), ch. 1, "Politics and Corruption," for a fascinating and perceptive discussion.

99. *MFP*, 18 November and 1 December 1900.

# Index

Ste. Agathe, Manitoba, 84, 318n95
St. Andrew's Rapids, 225, 336n50
Ste. Anne, Manitoba, 318n95
St. Boniface, Manitoba, 42, 346n92
St. Boniface, Manitoba (provincial constituency), 141, 320n40
St. Catharines, Ontario, 239
St. Clair Oil Company, 6
St. Clement's, Manitoba (provincial constituency), 13
St. François-Xavier by-election, 1888, 41, 46
St. Jean Baptiste, Manitoba, 318n95
St. John, Molyneux, 213
St. Michael's, Alaska, 169, 178
St. Norbert, Manitoba, 318n95
St. Paul, Minnesota, 9, 89, 259, 336n44
St. Paul, Minneapolis and Manitoba Railway, 29, 36
St. Petersburg, Treaty of, 169, 183, 199, 203
San Francisco, 159, 173
Saskatchewan, District of (NWT), 136-38, 282
Saskatchewan River, 302
Scandinavia, immigration from, 259, 262
Schultz, Frank, 83
Schultz, Dr. John Christian, 12, 45, 82-84, 93
Scott, Senator R.W., 170, 180, 200, 328n11
Scott, Walter, 138-39, 283-84, 295
Seattle, Washington, 159, 173
Selkirk, Manitoba, 8, 10, 12; (federal constituency), 50, 139, 299-300, 336n44
Senate (Canada), 185-86, 235, 275
Senate (United States), 185-86
Senkler, Justice E.J., 239, 338n31
Separate schools. *See* Catholic schools
Shaughnessy, Thomas G., 119, 151-53, 244, 248, 294, 327n96
Shaw, Flora, 196
*Siftings* (Crystal City), 336n44
Sifton, Arthur Lewis (brother), birth, 6; education, 7-11; recreation, 12; and prohibition, 12, 16-17, 163; and 1878 federal election, 13; law practice of, 16, 19, 23, 24; moves to Brandon, 17; marries, 19; moves to Prince Albert, 24; and Farmers' Union, 26; and politics in Saskatchewan, 138
Sifton, Bamlet (grandfather), 2
Sifton, Charles (great-grandfather) (1752-1842), 5
Sifton, Charles (great-uncle), 2
Sifton, Clifford (1861-1929), 318n95; family background of, 2-6; beliefs of, 3; birth, 6; education of, 7, 11; deafness of, 7-8, 157, 160, 292-93; family and social life of, 12, 23, 31, 48-49, 76, 124, 157-58, 193, 292-93; and prohibition, 12, 16, 63-67,

231-32, 297-98, 316n39; and 1878 federal election, 13; legal career of, 16, 19, 22-24, 157; and 1881 Brandon by-election, 312n54; moves to Brandon, 17, 19; interest in political career, 19; and 1883 Manitoba election, 20-22, 302; marries, 23; religious beliefs of, 23; financial status of, 23-24, 216, 335n24; and *Brandon Sun*, 24, 41, 211; and Farmers' Union, 26-27; general views of, on railway policy and freight rates, 26, 73, 102-3, 241-46; and A.M. Burgess, 27, 125-26; and Brandon Reform Association, 28; and 1885 Manitoba Liberal convention, 28; and anti-Winnipeg sentiment, 30; and 1886 Manitoba election, 30-31; and 1888 Manitoba election, 33; relations with Greenway, 34, 36, 71, 143-44; defends Greenway railway policy, 37-38; oratorical powers of, 37, 95; conflict of, with J. Martin, 38, 44, 74-75, 85, 110, 116-19, 135, 222-29, 249-51, 284-96, 302; and development of Greenway's school policy, 41, 44, 47-48; on elimination of official status of French language, 46; character of, 48, 53, 117, 229, 292-93; first considered for cabinet post, 313n28; refuses cabinet post, 48-49; and 1891 federal election, 50; as attorney general, 50-51, 53, 67-69; and 1891 Brandon North by-election, 51; and 1892 Manitoba election, 54, 56-61; and Barrett and Logan cases, 54-56, 60-61; and 1892 redistribution, 56; and Election Act amendments, 57-58; and CPR, 59, 259, 294; as friend of J.M. Walsh, 59, 167; and party organization in Manitoba, 59, 71, 74-75; and cabinet changes, 1892, 59-60; returned in 1892 election, 61; and social reform, 69; and reforms to protect farmers' rights, 69-70; and Patrons of Industry, 71-73, 100-101, 320n42; and liaison with federal Liberals, 73; views of, on <u>tariff, 73, 144-50, 249-50,</u> 326n67; and 1893 Winnipeg by-election, 74; speaks with Laurier at Brandon, 75-76; and provincial educational policy, 77-79; rejects federal interference in educational policy, 80-81; and school question, 80-87, 90-101, 104-9, 236; rejects compact theory, 88; acting premier, 1895, 93; suggests strategy to Laurier, 94; and Haldimand by-election, 94-96; sees Laurier in Montreal, 98; and 1896 Manitoba election, 99-101; seen as prospective minister of the interior, 100, 110-11; and 1896 federal election, 110-

f 1    3 5-20

11 -
11  F B
      fresh